THE ART OF UNCERTAINTY

The Victorian novel developed unique forms of reasoning under uncertainty – of thinking, judging, and acting in the face of partial knowledge and unclear outcome. George Eliot, Wilkie Collins, William Thackeray, Thomas Hardy, and later Joseph Conrad drew on science, mathematics, philosophy, and the law to articulate a phenomenology of uncertainty against emergent models of prediction and decision-making. In imaginative explorations of unsure reasoning, hesitant judgment, and makeshift action, these novelists cultivated distinctive responses to uncertainty as intellectual concern and cultural disposition, participating in the knowledge work of an era shaped by numerical approaches to the future. Reading for uncertainty yields a rich account of the dynamics of thinking and acting, a fresh understanding of realism as a genre of the probable, and a vision of literary-critical judgment as provisional and open-ended. Daniel Williams spotlights the value of literary art in a present marked by models and technologies of prediction.

DANIEL WILLIAMS is Assistant Professor of Literature at Bard College. He was previously a Junior Fellow at the Harvard Society of Fellows. His research focuses on British and South African literature, scientific and intellectual history, and the environmental humanities. He is coeditor of a special issue of *Poetics Today* on "Logic and Literary Form" (2020), and a section editor for *Literature Compass*.

Nineteenth-century literature and culture have proved a rich field for interdisciplinary studies. Since 1994, books in this series have tracked the intersections and tensions between Victorian literature and the visual arts, politics, gender and sexuality, race, social organisation, economic life, technical innovations, scientific thought – in short, culture in its broadest sense. Many of our books are now classics in a field which since the series' inception has seen powerful engagements with Marxism, feminism, visual studies, post-colonialism, critical race studies, new historicism, new formalism, transnationalism, queer studies, human rights and liberalism, disability studies and global studies. Theoretical challenges and historiographical shifts continue to unsettle scholarship on the nineteenth century in productive ways. New work on the body and the senses, the environment and climate, race and the decolonisation of literary studies, biopolitics and materiality, the animal and the human, the local and the global, politics and form, queerness and gender identities, and intersectional theory is re-animating the field. This series aims to accommodate and promote the most interesting work being undertaken on the frontiers of nineteenth-century literary studies, connecting the field with the urgent critical questions that are being asked today. We seek to publish work from a diverse range of authors, and stand for anti-racism, anti-colonialism and against discrimination in all forms.

A complete list of titles published will be found at the end of the book.

THE ART OF UNCERTAINTY

Probable Realism and the Victorian Novel

DANIEL WILLIAMS

Bard College, New York

CAMBRIDGE
UNIVERSITY PRESS

CAMBRIDGE
UNIVERSITY PRESS

Shaftesbury Road, Cambridge CB2 8EA, United Kingdom

One Liberty Plaza, 20th Floor, New York, NY 10006, USA

477 Williamstown Road, Port Melbourne, VIC 3207, Australia

314–321, 3rd Floor, Plot 3, Splendor Forum, Jasola District Centre, New Delhi – 110025, India

103 Penang Road, #05-06/07, Visioncrest Commercial, Singapore 238467

Cambridge University Press is part of Cambridge University Press & Assessment, a department of the University of Cambridge.

We share the University's mission to contribute to society through the pursuit of education, learning and research at the highest international levels of excellence.

www.cambridge.org
Information on this title: www.cambridge.org/9781009436113

DOI: 10.1017/9781009436120

First published 2024

A catalogue record for this publication is available from the British Library

Library of Congress Cataloging-in-Publication Data
NAMES: Williams, Daniel, 1983– author.
TITLE: The art of uncertainty : probable realism and the victorian novel / Daniel Williams, Bard College, New York.
DESCRIPTION: Cambridge ; New York : Cambridge University Press, 2023. | Series: Cambridge studies in nineteenth-century literature and culture | Includes bibliographical references and index.
IDENTIFIERS: LCCN 2023038830 (print) | LCCN 2023038831 (ebook) | ISBN 9781009436113 (hardback) | ISBN 9781009436137 (paperback) | ISBN 9781009436120 (epub)
SUBJECTS: LCSH: English fiction–19th century–History and criticism. | Uncertainty in literature. | Realism in literature.
CLASSIFICATION: LCC PR878.U46 W55 2023 (print) | LCC PR878.U46 (ebook) | DDC 823/.8093553–DC23/eng/20230928
LC record available at https://lccn.loc.gov/2023038830
LC ebook record available at https://lccn.loc.gov/2023038831

ISBN 978-1-009-43611-3 Hardback

Those that held that all things are governed by fortune had not erred, had they not persisted there.

—Thomas Browne, *Religio Medici*

Contents

Illustrations

Acknowledgments

I've been thinking about (and often under) uncertainty for ages, and could not have brought this book to fruition without the continual help of colleagues, friends, and family. I'm truly grateful to my advisers at Harvard for their innumerable suggestions and unflagging support. Elaine Scarry's serene encouragement and lucid advice have carried me through several uncertain moments. Philip J. Fisher has been an inspiring model of acuity and originality for over two decades. Leah Price's bracing wisdom and buoyant wit have lifted my work on many occasions. For their conversation and counsel in one Cambridge and then the other, I also thank Daniel Albright, James Engell, Deidre Lynch, Derek Miller, Adrian Poole, and Helen Vendler.

The dissertation that aired these ideas could not have been completed without my peers. I'm indebted to Jake Risinger, Alison Chapman, Maggie Doherty, and especially Kathryn Roberts, who read drafts aplenty and helped me in countless ways. I'm also obliged to those who heard me out across the project's inchoate stages, among them Urmi Banerjee, Shane Bobrycki, Maggie Gram, Jacob Sider Jost, Adam Kelly, David Nee, Matthew Ocheltree, Margaret Rennix, Adam Scheffler, Matthew Sussman, Stephen Tardif, and David Weimer. The early and enduring generosity of Elaine Auyoung, Heather Brink-Roby, and Anna Henchman was a source of intellectual sustenance. Earlier still, the caring friendship of Lee Holt kept me on track.

My friends at the Harvard Society of Fellows renewed my energy by their own inspiring example and camaraderie. For unnumbered conversations, usually far too late at night, and the company of thinking and writing in shared spaces, I thank Alexander Bevilacqua, Michaela Bronstein, Idan Dershowitz, Stephanie Dick, Rowan Dorin, Marta Figlerowicz, Len Gutkin, Daniel Hochbaum, Kevin Holden, Abhishek Kaicker, Marika Knowles, Naomi Levine, Jed Lewinsohn, Andrew Ollett, Matthew Spellberg, and Hannah Walser.

Audiences at Brown, Stanford, and Columbia gave me much to think about; for their kindness on these occasions, I want to thank Amanda Anderson and Alex Woloch. In the wider field, many colleagues were enthusiastic interlocutors, readers, and advocates: Jeffrey Blevins, Henry Cowles, Melissa Ganz, Adam Grener, Nathan Hensley, Margaret Kolb, Anna Kornbluh, David Kurnick, Elizabeth Carolyn Miller, Benjamin Morgan, Yi-Ping Ong, John Plotz, Jesse Rosenthal, Simon Stern, Michael Tondre, Johanna Winant, and Dora Zhang. My sincere appreciation to Kate Flint and Clare Pettitt for believing in this book, and to Bethany Thomas and her team at Cambridge University Press for their care and efficiency in bringing it to print.

My colleagues at Bard have welcomed me into a lively community, intellectual and otherwise. I'm especially appreciative to Cole Heinowitz and Alys Moody, who offered invaluable feedback on the manuscript, and to those whose dynamism has revived me as a teacher and scholar: Deirdre d'Albertis, Robert Cioffi, Lauren Curtis, Adhaar Desai, Marisa Libbon, Dinaw Mengestu, Matthew Mutter, Karen Sullivan, Éric Trudel, and (always last, never least) Marina van Zuylen.

Those closest to me have accommodated my particular brand of uncertainty the longest. My parents made possible this life made of words. My brother helped sustain me with his limitless cheer. Nicole Bass has been a cherished source of support. Jonathan Friedlander and Carla Heelan made a home around this book. It is my singular fortune to share a life with Kathryn Tabb, who makes every day a wonder, and now with Raphael, a new sun in the world.

*

Parts of the Introduction appeared in earlier form in "Introduction: Logic and Literary Form," *Poetics Today* 41, no. 1 (2020): 1–36, coauthored with Jeffrey Blevins. Parts of the Introduction, Chapter 4, and the Coda appeared previously in "Slow Fire: Serial Thinking and Hardy's Genres of Induction," *Genre* 50, no. 1 (2017): 19–38. In both instances I am grateful to Duke University Press for permission to reprint.

Introduction
The Bounds of Uncertainty

Will the sun rise tomorrow? In Thomas Hardy's first novel *Desperate Remedies* (1871), a young man and woman meet by accident and are struck by "one of those unaccountable sensations which carry home to the heart ... by something stronger than mathematical proof, the conviction, 'A tie has begun to unite us.'" They part, leaving one of the budding pair with "a hopeless sense of loss akin to that which Adam is said by logicians to have felt when he first saw the sun set, and thought, in his inexperience, that it would return no more."[1] Hardy alludes to a common enough experience: the rhythms of dawn and dusk, love and loss – *nihil novum sub sole*. There may be nothing new under the sun, but its diurnal course still marks out the fundamental rhythm of uncertainty, a constant yet capricious pulse. Every dawn we confront the day's possible events. Each dusk we reflect on its eventual outcomes. We rehearse routines, mull decisions, inhale anxieties, and reckon with uncertain outcomes both normal and novel. No wonder that the simple fact of the sun's rising and setting has given us a canonical image for reasoning in the face of imperfect knowledge, a touchstone for a modern revolution in how we think, judge, and act under uncertainty in which literature played an intriguing part.

Will the sun rise tomorrow? If this question has shadowed us since our mythical first day, from the eighteenth century forward many addressed it with fresh energy, contemplating how judgments are made on the basis of repeated events and applied to unexpected situations. Among sources familiar to Hardy, I might instance the theologian Joseph Butler's defense of analogical reasoning ("there is no Man can make a Question but that the Sun will rise to morrow").[2] Or the philosopher David Hume's skeptical reflection about causal assumptions ("*That the sun will not rise tomorrow* is no less intelligible a proposition, and implies no more contradiction, than the affirmation *that it will rise*").[3] Or the mathematician Pierre-Simon Laplace's framing of the problem as a game of chance, the odds against cast in terms of all previous sunrises (1,826,214 to 1 in a world a few thousand years old).[4] From Butler's *Analogy of Religion* (1736) to George Campbell's *Philosophy of Rhetoric* (1776), Hume's *Enquiry Concerning Human Understanding* (1748) to John Stuart Mill's *System of Logic* (1843), and Laplace's *Essai philosophique sur les probabilités* (1814) to George Boole's *Investigation of the Laws of Thought* (1854) and John Venn's *The Logic of Chance* (1866), different thinkers have circled around the sun's rising to hone technical models for reasoning about ordinary puzzles of uncertainty.[5]

Hardy borrowed the solar conceit from a logic primer, *The Art of Reasoning* (1853) by the schoolmaster Samuel Neil, who in turn lifted it from Samuel Taylor Coleridge:

> suppose Adam watching the Sun sinking under the horizon for the first time; he is seized with gloom and terror, relieved with scarce a ray of hope of ever seeing the glorious light again. The next evening when it declines, his hopes are stronger, but mixed with fear; and even at the end of 1000 years, all that a man can feel, is hope and an expectation so strong as to preclude anxiety.[6]

Whether the sun will rise and what fortunes it will bring were weighty questions for Hardy, living in an age when scientific and secular reasoning eclipsed faith – when the Sun, so to say, replaced God. We can distinguish two poles of uncertainty here, which I see as generative for Hardy's aesthetics and for nineteenth-century realism more broadly. One is affective, tactile, inchoate – its currency "unaccountable sensations" and vague affects: "gloom," "terror," "anxiety," the whimsical "ray of hope." The other mode is systematic, numerical, predictive – its medium countable series of events and logical conundrums. The argument of this book lives in the space between these poles. I use the shared claims of novelists and "logicians" (that is, all manner of scientific and philosophical writers) to their exposition, and reveal how a unique form of reasoning under uncertainty emerged in the nineteenth-century novel.

The Art of Uncertainty explores how novels in nineteenth-century Britain represented modes of thinking, judging, and acting in the face of partial knowledge and unclear outcome. I argue that novelists in the Victorian realist tradition – George Eliot, Wilkie Collins, William Thackeray, and Thomas Hardy – articulated a phenomenology of uncertainty against emergent models of calculation, prediction, and decision-making. Drawing on ideas in science, mathematics, philosophy, and the law while also cultivating their own distinctive responses to uncertainty as intellectual concern and cultural disposition, these novelists strove to bridge different orders of experience: affective and rational, felt and known. In so doing, they both contributed to and critiqued nonliterary models by emphasizing aspects of uncertainty as a subjective experience: hesitations that almost entirely usurp action (Eliot), legal judgments that evade finality and proof (Collins), speculations that run against the grain of fact (Thackeray), and modes of iterative and aggregative thinking that we use in everyday inference (Hardy). Yet while the novels in this book attend to uncertainty's subjective expressions, they also keep an eye on its objective dictates. They examine bodily effects and emotional tonalities of judging and acting without certain knowledge, even as they draw on predictive concepts from probability and statistics. They represent states of mind and problems of action that do not admit of easy resolution, even as they allude to technical accounts of deliberation, volition, and action in psychology. They entertain counterfactuals within a conventionally realist space of representation, shadowing narrative paths with alternate possibilities and nonbinary outcomes, even as they engage with the factual conviction and closure offered by historical tomes and legal treatises. The phenomenology of uncertainty can be traced in depictions of characters, in thematic topoi (gambling and other types of forecasting), in aesthetic and formal effects, and in the putative experience of readers and critics. It is across a range of such devices that I locate uncertainty's literary articulation. The art of uncertainty, I argue, constitutes a key motif for understanding the knowledge work of the realist novel in an era profoundly shaped by numbers and numerical approaches to the future. Reading by the light of uncertainty yields a revised understanding of realism as a genre invested in provisionality and emergence – what I will term *probable realism* – and a corresponding vision of critical judgment as hesitant, processual, and inherently open to correction.

As the "incomprehensible certainty" of faith, to use Gerard Manley Hopkins's terms, gave ground to the "interesting uncertainty" of secular life, nineteenth-century fields confronted, and attempted to model, everyday experiences of unclarity, indecision, and doubt.[7] From the intellectual progeny of mathematics, logic, psychology, rhetoric, and the law, among others, we have inherited a complex and multifaceted understanding of uncertainty, irreducible to any one account of how we reckon with numbers, reason from evidence, consult our intuitions, or translate a willed decision into bodily action. Drawing on scholarship in the history of science and philosophy, this book investigates how connected trends in the cultural perception of uncertainty – and developments in its conceptual, rhetorical, and legal expression – gave novelists different perspectives on these ideas. Following Britain's inaugural census in 1801, the explosion of statistical data and methods posed fresh challenges for the novelistic representation of persons, given the determinist repercussions of viewing individual actions in terms of aggregate patterns. By the century's end, novels navigated uneasily between particulars and aggregates, fictional beings and numerical abstractions, even as the regular configurations of statistics usurped the causal laws of Enlightenment science and led to an "erosion of determinism."[8] How characters and readers might be shown to infer, judge, and decide was inflected by the revival and renewed theorization of scientific method (in debates between Mill and William Whewell about the nature of induction, and in wider articulations of the hypothetico-deductive method), alongside the expansion of comparative and analogical methods (in fields such as philology, history, anthropology, and religion).[9] The uptake of associationist models of mind into an increasingly embodied psychology (in the work of Alexander Bain, William Carpenter, Henry Maudsley, and George Henry Lewes) added chance-driven materiality to narrative depictions of volition, deliberation, and action, bridging iterations experienced in the world and insights evolved in the mind. Finally, approaches to the concept of probability – numerical and epistemic, legal and rhetorical – at once recorded and resisted the shift to a statistical age. Narrative and generic senses of the probable were fundamentally reshaped. I trace links among these areas of inquiry, addressed in the sections below, to define a matrix of intellectual contexts encompassing the novels I examine. I aim to flesh out the surprising involvement of novelists with discourses predicated on certainty, exactitude, and abstraction (logic, mathematics), and with discourses that navigated incertitude, vagueness, and case-based particularity (rhetoric, law). I highlight scientific and philosophical figures known to my authors – including Mill, the polymath whose *System of Logic* Eliot read; and Venn, the logician after whom Hardy named a character – to underscore how the interchange between novels and other disciplines of uncertainty was often startlingly direct.[10]

Alongside contextual materials, I believe it is crucial to draw on instructive approaches to uncertainty in recent science, philosophy, and legal theory, especially because such conceptual models – including rubrics like "judgment under uncertainty" and "bounded rationality" – often trace their intellectual genealogy to the same Victorian thinkers I examine.[11] (To describe hesitation in Chapter 1, for example, I rely on nineteenth-century psychological understandings of volition and its pathologies, and on later behavioral-economic accounts of decision-making as a splintering of the self into intertemporal bargaining agents.) This methodological overlap of past and present echoes the diffuse pluralism of nineteenth-century intellectual life. Where work on literature and science has typically linked texts to one area of contemporaneous knowledge production, I join recent studies in addressing how Victorian literature refracted a range of scientific materials in various and uneven ways. I see the novel as a space of vernacular intellectual history, a clearinghouse where ideas old and new were tested and adapted, assimilated or rejected. The novelists I study were sometimes alert to new developments in uncertainty, as reported in books and periodical essays, and sometimes revived concepts from earlier intellectual eras. They often relied on both. In the other direction, novelistic intuitions about uncertainty anticipate later conceptual frameworks, with which they can be seen to engage in mutually illuminating dialogue.

The Art of Uncertainty is thus informed by a cross-pollination of historical and contemporary materials. I aim to describe how nineteenth-century novels deepened approaches to scientific knowledge and social concern with a focus on what uncertainty looks and feels like as a durably subjective phenomenon. Each chapter emphasizes a different facet of the novelistic phenomenology of uncertainty: Eliot's "indecision theory," as I call it, is characterized by twin stances of psychophysiological hesitation and reflective comparison; Collins's "unproven verdicts" eschew familiar legal binaries to probe what a "not proven" outcome might afford law, morality, and ordinary judgment; Thackeray's "counterfactual imagination" characterizes a literary career that balances prospect against retrospect, energetic speculation against dejected reminiscence, finding solace in the "might have beens"; and Hardy's "approximations" explore intuitive approaches to thinking and predicting by means of long-run serial patterns and short-range composites of mental images. These multifaceted explorations delineate a key cultural space for thinking through the difficulties of judgment where doubt is ineradicably present and where objective numbers do not clarify (and may confuse) the picture. Literary uncertainty's rich and distinctive characteristics persist even when detached from the matrix of contexts and concepts informing its representations. Both in their respective moments and now, novels help us gain perspective on problems that stubbornly edge the clearing of certain or demonstrable knowledge. The bounds of uncertainty are hazy. Its diffuse terrain extends to that nebulous area beyond what Joseph Conrad, one of the heirs to this tradition of uncertain thinking, calls the "face of facts."[12]

If the Victorian novel's fascination with other approaches to uncertainty shapes its narrative patterns and aesthetic experiments, those formal expressions conversely disclose aspects of such phenomena that we in the humanities too often surrender to explanation by other disciplines. While the following chapters invoke wide intellectual and cultural resources to read ordinary instances of uncertainty, they also evince the capacity of literary form – especially novel form – to model phenomena typically claimed by more exacting disciplines. Studying past enterprises in science, philosophy, and the law whose permeable venues stand in contrast to present disciplinary silos, I understand the literary as an indispensable form of inquiry that joins aesthetic and affective concerns to rational frameworks. The literary can bridge diverse domains of knowledge, discover overlooked facets of different disciplines, and ask what we can find beyond the purview of knowledge as such. Nineteenth-century novels traced the lines along which both expert and demotic knowledge about uncertainty became culturally vital, mediating these problems for their audiences. Such novels furnish exemplars and surprising paths through present dilemmas that bear uncanny similarities to their Victorian antecedents. My book's driving energy is a conviction that literature's distinctive modes of thought and imagination matter more than ever in a world given over, more intensely each day, to the "imperialism of probabilities" via new technologies of numerical prediction and risk management.[13]

The Art of Uncertainty joins abstract contexts and concrete estimations – large scales and little, the sun's rising and all the curious, muddling behavior under the sun. For some time, I thought about these phenomena under the sign of a term that underwrites many of the book's concerns: the English word *hap*. "Hap" titles a shockingly gloomy poem by Hardy – "why unblooms the best hope ever sown?" – about the pathos of living in a world after faith: secular, scientific, deterministic, apparently without meaning.[14] But it is also a long-standing marker of the uncertain and adventitious, as in the phrase "the hap of things" from Raphaell Holinshed's *Chronicles* (1587 edition).[15] The word's cognates mark out the basic structure of events (what *happens*), trace the occurrences drifting through human plots in accidental fashion (by *happenstance*), constitute the most basic grammatical tag for imperfect knowledge (*perhaps*), and denote that elusive antagonist of uncertain judgments and fraught decisions (*happiness*).[16] In exploring how to think and act in the hap of things, the writing I study in this book drew on, and often exceeded, models of inquiry at the forefront of science and allied fields. It found creative ways to address the experience of uncertainty in a century regularly punctuated by large-scale crises, both practical (financial panics, political agitation, industrial accidents, imperial wars large and small) and intellectual (religious unbelief, scientific naturalism and materialism, evolutionary theory).

Yet this writing's overriding concern, I argue, was with small-scale strategies that ordinarily guide us "in the absence of clear and certain knowledge," in that "State of Mediocrity and Probationership" John Locke named the "twilight ... of *Probability*."[17] Blending approaches to uncertainty and probability – as numerical concept, epistemic conundrum, legal tool, and literary protocol – novels reached for noncalculative ways of thinking and acting, glimpsing arrangements where human agents might not so exactly be counted or called to account.

***

My opening example looked at a novelist's appropriation of a logical trope. I turn now to a logician's critique of a novel, and begin to establish the reciprocal interchange among literature and a range of other discourses. In the early nineteenth century Richard Whately, author of the influential treatises *Elements of Logic* (1826) and *Elements of Rhetoric* (1828), mocked the coincidences that accrue in Henry Fielding's *Tom Jones* (1749). He complained that "several of the events, taken singly, are much against the chances of probability; but the combination of the whole in a connected series, is next to impossible."[18] Whately deemed the plot "incalculably improbable" – worse than a romance, "since one might just as reasonably calculate on the intervention of a fairy, as on the train of lucky chances which combine first to involve Tom Jones in his difficulties, and afterwards to extricate him."[19] Invoking a graded series of events, which seem improbable in combination, Whately uses the modern concept of mathematical probability to consider a difficulty with probability in a rhetorical or Aristotelian sense: what is plausible or credible, the likeness (*eikos*) that bears likelihood.[20] Whately's formulation raises several questions. How would considering the "chances of probability" help us evaluate fictional worlds already set in place by the text on the page? How can numerical prediction, that is, elude the "already written nature of narrative time"?[21] What, in a literary context, would "incalculably" mean? Why does Whately draw a distinction between "unnatural" fictions (with "some assignable reason against the events taking place as described") and "improbable" ones (with "no reason to be assigned why things should not take place as represented, except that the overbalance of chances is against it")?[22] Is there a shift in literary probability implied by his invoking a concept more precise than Aristotelian probability (that is, "not what occurs invariably but only for the most part")?[23]

In the century preceding the publication of *Tom Jones*, coextensive with early developments in the novel form, the idea of probability acquired its mathematical cast. According to Ian Hacking's influential account, the modern concept of probability emerged at first in letters between the philosopher Blaise Pascal and the mathematician Pierre Fermat concerning how to divide the stakes of a truncated game of chance. It was further developed in the work of seventeenth-century thinkers like Christiaan Huygens, Jacob Bernoulli, and the authors of the epistemological treatise known as the *Port-Royal Logic* (1662), Antoine Arnauld and Pierre Nicole, and eighteenth- and nineteenth-century mathematicians including Abraham De Moivre, Thomas Bayes, and Laplace. Historically emerging from what we might think of as frivolous cultural practices (gambling) and commercial instruments (insurance), probability captured attention in a variety of fields: philosophy, mathematics, jurisprudence, political economy, theology. In the early nineteenth century, a range of mathematical innovations by Siméon-Denis Poisson and Adolphe Quetelet, alongside the wider availability of accurate numbers about large populations, gave shape to a new framework of probability adapted to statistical information.[24] Models of probabilistic thinking and statistical inference became crucial in science and statecraft in the nineteenth century and beyond, building the foundations of what has become a complex branch of mathematics, with applications that have defined our heuristic outlooks.

Scholars in the history of science have documented these developments in mathematical probability and statistical theory, and my work is indebted to their accounts.[25] A key conceptual innovation undergirds the continued importance of this material for literary history. For Hacking, modern probability emerged in the seventeenth and eighteenth centuries as a Janus-faced concept, divided between an *aleatory* definition, "concerning itself with stochastic laws of chance processes," and an *epistemic* one, "dedicated to assessing reasonable degrees of belief in propositions quite devoid of statistical background."[26] This dual concept of probability required an understanding of evidence that was importantly distinct from earlier forms of knowledge by appeal to testimony, authority, or logical demonstration. Hacking calls it inductive or "internal evidence," the "evidence of things" that "points beyond itself in a non-deductive way."[27] In his account, advances in the mathematics of probability – and in applications that reciprocally contributed to its rise – set the stage for the modern, probabilistic notion of inference under conditions of uncertainty. They also set the stage for its skeptical regress in the problem of induction, which evaluates whether we can use an enumerated sequence of single events (like the sun's rising) to predict future events. Inaugurated for posterity by Hume's *Treatise of Human Nature* (1739–40), this problem could not have been formulated without the concept of evidence furnished by modern probability.[28] A measure of the distance between these developments and traditional logic might be seen in Hacking's ingenious analysis of Pascal's wager on God's existence. Framing the wager as an inaugural exercise in decision theory – a matter of mathematical expectation rather than syllogistic reasoning – Hacking argues that Pascal "showed how aleatory arithmetic could be part of a general 'art of conjecturing'" and "made it possible to understand that the structure of reasoning about games of chance can be transferred to inference that is not founded on any chance set-up."[29] As probability came to mean not an appeal to authoritative sources but an adjudication of numerical evidence, Hacking observes, readers and interpreters became the new authorities or "owner[s] of probability."[30]

As readers and writers, Whately and Fielding fit neatly into this lineage. Fielding is the foremost novelist of the eighteenth century to engage with probability in its modern form, "tak[ing] probable judgment as his theme and creat[ing] in his fiction structures which, to be interpreted correctly, demand an exercise of that same judgment," even as his embedded discourse on the "probable" and the "marvellous" in *Tom Jones* looks back to traditional categories.[31] Whately likewise hews to the dual form of probability in dividing fictional likelihood into epistemic ("unnatural") and aleatory ("improbable") categories even as his judgments preserve an Aristotelian flavor.[32] Witness to literature's place in "a world becoming numerical and measured in every corner of its being," Whately lived at a time when the relationship between individual judgment and aggregate measurement was constantly under negotiation.[33] An Aristotelian at the University of Oxford, later the Archbishop of Dublin and active in the Dublin Statistical Society, he embodies the tensions of an emergent numerical age, where logic could be, to use his terms, both a "Science" and an "Art" of reasoning.[34] Whately's agitated critique of Fielding shows that literature and literary criticism lay claim to the incalculable only against the background of complex and uneven shifts in calculative rationality, which allowed all readers to become probabilists, armed with tools to predict outcomes in numerical terms.

These conceptual horizons are neither arid backgrounds in a rational reconstruction of scientific progress nor superseded historical curiosities. They remain rich resources that can illuminate how uncertain thinking was understood at earlier moments in scientific, philosophical, rhetorical, and legal fields. They can also supplement our own models of judgment under uncertainty with more supple depictions of felt experience than available to current experimental, mathematical, or computational methods. At various scales, the techniques of probability have shaped uncertain reasoning since the nineteenth century. Cultural studies of statistics and its applications – in fields like political economy, public health, and weather forecasting – have described the macroscale importance of probabilistic reasoning. At issue here is a key epistemological assumption of what Mary Poovey labels the "modern fact," namely, "that systematic knowledge must draw on but also be superior to noninterpretive data collected about observed particulars."[35] Such accounts inspect uncertainty at the level of aggregate and population, the level most pertinent to the understanding, organization, and bureaucratic management of our modern "risk society."[36] By contrast, microscale accounts in cognitive science, psychology, and behavioral economics have assessed how probabilistic reasoning functions (and fails) in ordinary behavior. On a conscious level we tend to be irrational actors and poor decision theorists, even if our subconscious mental operations (according to a provocative theory gaining ground in cognitive neuroscience) can be explained probabilistically in terms of Bayesian inference, "predictive processing," and error minimization, down to the neuronal level.[37] At both scales, macro and micro, uncertainty might be shown to influence the contextual imagination of writers or the cognitive inference of readers.[38] While keeping these scalar extremes in mind, *The Art of Uncertainty* emphasizes the intermediate scale of the individual subject – where, in the words of the Victorian intellectual Mark Pattison, "everything is uncertainty" – as central for understanding how nineteenth-century novelists characterized uncertain thinking.[39] In exploring a phenomenology of uncertainty, I focus not on what other critics have called "the affective life of the average man," or "what it feels like to be a statistic," but on modes of affective and formal response anchored in individuals and set against calculative rationality.[40] I emphasize routine instances of uncertainty that underpin (or intersect with) more delimited forms and theories of decision-making in the period, including the deliberative procedures of "liberal cognition," the consumer "preferences" of neoclassical economics, and the wagers of financial speculation.[41]

How do we balance felt instincts against rational information in scenarios of judgment, decision, and action? How much weight should we give to experience in making inferences? How should we apportion credit to others' beliefs and trust our own? In the wake of modern probability, individuals and groups can with appreciable success think and act under conditions of imperfect knowledge, make conclusive inferences despite evidence that is various and partial, predict relatively certain outcomes despite significant odds, and correct intuitive capacities so they are less prone to unconscious biases, specious heuristics, or malign stereotypes. We can use tools built on the logic and mathematics of chance to minimize harmful outcomes by modeling risks – calculating providence, assessing its price. We can inspect our "life chances" – generalized expectations for how our lives will turn out, mediated by statistics and the sundry reference classes we fall into – and attempt to control such chances out of bounds entirely.[42] But such ways of thinking and acting in the world are inescapably edged by uncertainty. Surrounding the arena of more-or-less certain prediction hovers a penumbra of haze and hesitation, of shaky inferences, unclear evidence, and intermediary states on the way to judgment. Definite actions or outcomes are shadowed by paths not taken. Hazards avoided are still ghosted by the measure of their possibility. As Whately notes, "in numberless transactions of ordinary life … we are obliged practically to make up our minds at once to take one course or another, even where there are no sufficient grounds for a full conviction of the understanding."[43] In William James's punchier formulation later in the century, "for most of our emergencies there is no insurance-company at hand, and fractional solutions are impossible. Seldom can we *act* fractionally."[44] We may have instruments to aid us, heuristics to steer our predictions, institutions to administer our uncertainty. But what has been called uncertainty's "cunning" – its tendency to ramify and reemerge despite attempts to manage it – continues to plague us.[45] At some deep and abiding level we still "live in the flicker" (Conrad), we "live in the cloud" (John Ruskin).[46] We enthuse about calculative tools and forget moral and affective norms that cannot admit of any numerical character but still confound prediction. We evaluate risks to purchase what a Victorian commentator called "compulsory providence" (insurance) and find that persistent forms of luck – moral, legal, and social – make shipwreck of such assurances.[47]

The long-form literary narratives in this book provide a natural space for evaluating the complex tenor and tone of uncertainty. It may seem paradoxical to claim that novels prompt us to suspend the anxieties of real life only to court uncertainties in a fictional world. But dwelling in uncertainty via the novel form, I believe, allows us to appreciate that form's expansive cognitive capacities: its immersive modeling of thought, judgment, and decision; its ample occasions for juxtaposing prospect and retrospect from a succession of shifting vantages; its ways of affording time to sit with fictional uncertainty alongside the fret of factual life. In keeping with recent redescriptions of the nineteenth-century novel as an "open form" (Isobel Armstrong), "a process rather than a structure" (Nicholas Dames), and a site of "radical ontological flexibility" (Elaine Freedgood), I treat it as a porous intellectual space where our ordinary equipment for thinking, judging, and acting under uncertainty can be assayed and refined.[48] Unlike the scientific materials I draw on, and unlike Victorian genres of writing about risk that raised anxieties only to dispel them, these novels brood at length on a phenomenological spectrum akin to John Keats's "*Negative Capability*," that state of "being in uncertainties, Mysteries, doubts without any irritable reaching after fact & reason."[49]

My readings perform a balancing act, paying close attention to the formal and narrative textures of this "being in uncertainties" while also reaching after, and drawing on, histories of "fact & reason." Tracking motifs of uncertainty in thematic, characterological, and narrative terms, I link them to wider discourses in philosophical and scientific history, whether as direct connections or ambient resonances. A richer and more reciprocal account of literature's place in the scientific and philosophical history of uncertainty is possible if we attend to its absorption of ideas from what Raymond Williams calls "dominant," "residual," and "emergent" cultural strata. Key here is the "residual," that which "has been effectively formed in the past, but . . . is still active in the cultural process, not only and often not at all as an element of the past, but as an effective element of the present."[50] The interplay among these levels allows us to see how, in limning the contours of uncertainty, novelists juxtaposed earlier concepts (even those outdated by the nineteenth century) with more recent developments. Eliot cited Aristotle's account of probability even as she drew on the work of Mill.[51] Hardy appealed to folk notions of fate, chance, and luck while alluding to modern probabilists such as Venn. Beyond noticing the "recrudescence of mathematical ideas in areas of culture that are not disciplinarily mathematical," we should be alert to the residues that do cultural work despite, or even on account of, their obsolescence as scientific knowledge, both in the nineteenth century and now.[52] Like Eliot and Hardy, we make use of newfangled technologies and outmoded tools – including the novel, which as a way of navigating uncertainty remains, I contend, "an effective element of the present."

The book's chapters fall into two parts that explore novelistic uncertainty in terms of individual judgment and aggregate pattern. Part I, "Provisional Judgments," dwells in particular on the thought processes of individual characters in single novels, and draws connections between their uncertain judgments and those of literary critics. While continuing the emphasis on characters, Part II, "Probable Realisms," attends to narrative structures and patterns across broader oeuvres, and reflects on ideas of genre. Together they aim to showcase a multifaceted approach to literary judgment under uncertainty, responsive to its scalar range and canvassing its critical operation between claims about individual texts and appraisals of generic expectations.

I begin with George Eliot, since she tackles uncertainty in both judgment and action. Abundant moments of indecision and delay shape her last novel, *Daniel Deronda* (1876), which opens on a question, dramatizes one character's incapacity to decide on her marriage even after it has taken effect, and ponders another character's lack of knowledge about his cultural background. The novel treats uncertainty as a recursive movement between interior and exterior, potentiality and activity. Drawing on intellectual trends in mid-century comparative method and physiological psychology, especially the latter's portrait of embodied willing and pathologies of volition, Chapter 1 shows how Eliot explores action's convoluted antecedents. I use these contexts to read the novel's twin stances of practical experience and intellectual reflection: *hesitation*, the bewildering experience of having a "will which is and yet is not yet," and its rational cousin, *comparison*, "our precious guide."[53] Formal fluctuations and portrayals of mental caprice would seem at cross-purposes with Eliot's narrative control and moral coherence. Yet in discovering a "kinship" between certainty and doubt, I argue, she reinvigorates her novelistic ethics and recasts sympathy as guaranteed by "closer comparison between the knowledge which we call rational & the experience which we call emotional."[54] Her characters set store by irresolute stances of hesitation and comparison, and predictive affects like trust and hope.

Chapter 2 extends the account of hesitation and indecision into a more specific domain: the law. The nineteenth century is often seen as solidifying modern law's idealization of number, rule, and definition, setting in motion the quantification trend later denounced as "trial by mathematics" or "actuarial justice."[55] Yet Wilkie Collins thwarts this trend by adopting an essentially antinumerical example as the basis for a literary experiment, in the form of the bizarre third verdict of Scots law: "not proven." The verdict, which falls between "guilty" and "not guilty" and acts as an acquittal that nonetheless imputes a lack of evidence for conviction, guides the plot of his detective novel *The Law and the Lady* (1875). Revealing Collins's sources in trial reports and treatises of Scots law, I show how uncertainty inflects both judicial reasoning and models of reading. The hesitant verdict of "not proven" – disparaged for its erosion of the presumption of innocence but defended for its clemency – undercuts the truth claims of binary judgment at law. It throws into relief the moral psychology of suspicion swirling both inside and outside the court, subverts normative categories, and allows for more flexible visions of social judgment. Leaving his novel under the sign of "not proven," Collins makes visible a countertrend to certainty and closure in legal institutions and Victorian novels about the law. I briefly discuss other examples of novels also promoting types of inference and models of critical judgment that value the tentative, hesitant, and processual – what I call *reading without proving* – as a way to evade the calculative pressures of nineteenth-century law and life.

Following these accounts of uncertain judgment, Chapter 3 widens the frame to questions of genre. As literary realism shed earlier providential paradigms, William Thackeray inaugurated a startling interest in alternatives to reality as essential for novels that would be true to life. These "queer speculations" saturate his writing: a child that might have lived, an accident that could have been avoided, a war that would have ended otherwise if only.... Thackeray's counterfactual imagination matures from occasional stories of the 1840s, through *Vanity Fair* (1847–48), the *Roundabout Papers* (1860–63), and *Lovel the Widower* (1860). His conditionals run the gamut from frenzied anticipation to paralyzing regret, developing from wild wagers and total reversals of fortune in the early sketches to a late style where memory, narrative, and writing itself are marked by virtuality. I examine the range of uncertain experience in Thackeray's oeuvre in relation to historical writing of the eighteenth and nineteenth centuries, which often relied on suppositional thought experiments, alongside accounts of counterfactual reasoning in recent psychology and literary criticism. Probing the emotional and tonal modulations of uncertainty, Thackeray's writing widens the space of novelistic realism to include the nonmimetic, hypothetical, improbable, and open-ended – or what he terms the "might-have-beens."

Chapter 4 continues the generic attention to uncertainty by considering two contrasting models for predictive thinking and representation in Thomas Hardy. I read Hardy's depiction of repetitive phenomena in *The Return of the Native* (1878) as evoking one renovated account of logico-mathematical probability in the period, Venn's influential empirical theory about how we judge from series of instances. In the novel's palpably antiquated rural setting – where characters intuit more than they see, gamble by the light of glowworms, and infer human plots from long-run traces in the material world – the abstractions of Victorian logic acquire concrete form. By contrast, in Hardy's town novel *The Mayor of Casterbridge* (1886), serial iterations are compressed into images. Hardy designs literary equivalents of Francis Galton's "composite photographs," used to model statistical data as well as mental processes. Characters in the novel think in overlays, detecting a parent's face playing over that of a child, designing a future self by laying transparencies over the present, and imagining human plots as grids from overhead. Tracking the influence of *serial* and *composite* representation in Hardy's "approximative" theory of fiction, I demonstrate how he uses these tropes as an implicit riposte to critics and advocates for a novelistic realism tolerant of repetition, coincidence, and improbability.

Having specified a distinctive character to uncertainty in nineteenth-century literature and culture, the Coda sketches how this tradition changes in modernist writing. Uncertainty remains of vital interest to writers such as Henry James, D. H. Lawrence, James Joyce, Virginia Woolf, and E. M. Forster. Yet a more self-conscious embrace of chance, contingency, and randomness, alongside a more thoroughgoing skepticism, disengages this writing from the earlier literature's concerns. The idea of uncertainty acquires different and more precise senses in the early twentieth century: it is reconceptualized as radical indeterminacy in physics, and takes its place as the unquantifiable contrast class to calculable risk in economics. These further valences of uncertainty both intensify cultural interest in the topic and disarticulate its nineteenth-century framework. In a reading of Joseph Conrad's novel *Chance* (1914), I argue that his emphasis on the value of momentary judgments, on knowledge as mercurial and provisional, and on the role of accident in literary plots all reprise Victorian tactics, albeit in modernist guise.

There are several things to mention about my procedures of selection and organization. First, many of the works I examine shared an uneven reception, and were labeled formally defective and narratively unbalanced by Victorian critics. "I never read a story with less current," remarks a character in Henry James's review of *Daniel Deronda*. "A Novel without a Character" was suggested as a subtitle for *The Law and the Lady*.[56] Several critics thought *Vanity Fair* at once too protracted and too partial, "rather a succession of connected scenes and characters than a well-constructed story,"[57] and *Lovel the Widower* elicited confusion. Never one to receive unblemished reviews, Hardy was called a novelist with "a keen eye for the picturesque without having learnt to draw": critics disliked *The Return of the Native*'s plot ("intensely artificial"), setting ("a world of which we seem to be absolutely ignorant"), names ("unreal and unlifelike"), and chronology (hampered by "a vague uncertainty").[58] I suggest we take these views seriously less on the merits than as signs of a readerly uncertainty that calls out for explanation. Juxtaposing marginal and mainstream texts will, I hope, prove mutually illuminating.

Second, because these chapters treat interrelated elements of uncertain thinking and overlap in many ways, I have opted against simple chronology. Indeed, I intend each chapter's analysis to deepen the phenomenology of uncertainty described in the others. The assessment of hesitation as a physiological experience in Eliot adds texture to my description of hesitant legal inference in Collins, and her appeals to comparison as a device of sympathetic imagination might inform Hardy's descriptions of serial phenomena. The account of counterfactual and hypothetical thinking in Thackeray inflects my account of indecision and alternative paths in Eliot, legal uncertainty in Collins, and composites in Hardy. And my discussion of probable realism in Hardy finds analogues in the generic and representational complexities that Thackeray, Eliot, and Collins (among others) add to realism in its modulation by uncertainty.

Finally, it may be startling to encounter a novelist like Collins, typically associated with sensation and detective fiction, in company with those more firmly entrenched in the realist canon. Yet as I discuss throughout Part II, to assess genres for their engagement with the discourse of uncertainty – rather than for formal or functional qualities – means treating generic dynamism and the nineteenth-century "phenomenon of genre-mixing" in fresh ways.[59] In particular, it means investigating the mechanisms by which realism maintained its status as chief genre of the probable throughout the period. Realism is not necessarily more probable – in any sense of the term – than other genres. The novelists in this book exhibit notable lapses from probabilistic grace (consider Thackeray's fanciful satire, Collins's lurid plots, Eliot's gothic and melodramatic episodes, Hardy's wild coincidences), and such violations can be traced back to the very beginning of the (realist) novel form in the eighteenth century.[60] There is more variance in the realist canon than we conventionally allow. From the perspective of generic dynamism, my reading of Collins alongside canonical realists can be justified in much the same way as other critics have denominated Eliot a sensation novelist.[61] The more important point, however, is that in engaging scientific, rhetorical, and legal discourses of probability, as I argue it did, realism declared itself the dominant literary space for thinking about and representing uncertainty, by continually insisting on the adjudication of standards of likeness and likelihood, and by policing what Fielding termed the "bounds of probability."[62] If we take realism's wide spectrum as an organizing principle, I think we can better understand its relationship to uncertainty.

The stakes of my analysis – for how we think about literary genre and novel form and how we practice critical judgment – correspond roughly to the two parts of the book, though in practice these matters are addressed throughout. Part II questions our received views of genre by describing different articulations of probable realism. Less a distinct subcategory than a reorientation of the genre's conceptual bases, probable realism restores to visibility what has always been a silent predicate in the practice and analysis of realism (the probable).[63] The term queries what else we might see in realism by provisionally suspending its familiar relationships (to truth, mimesis, representation, language, reference, history, and perspective, among others) and contemplating instead its other conceptual kin (hypothesis, counterfact, approximation, and so on).[64] It explores, moreover, how we might view realism when such generic hallmarks as stylistic indirection and self-consciousness about referential indeterminacy ramify into uncertainties of character, theme, and plot.[65] What emerges is a realism less tethered to the actual, the given, and the status quo; less mired in those well-trodden tenses, present and preterite, by virtue of its restless positing of modal virtuality; and more able to use its engagement with probability to predict and imagine otherwise – particularly in the face of present uncertainties like climate change – than its critics grant.[66] In short, a realism less sure of itself than we usually think deploys uncertainty's changing protocols to explore and reimagine its own confines.

Part I considers how a similarly open-ended vision of critical judgment might emerge by submitting our practices to the framework of uncertainty – for instance, by seeing judgments of probability as participating in a durable project shared with the nineteenth century, rather than as shifting claims of taste.[67] On this view, critical judgment is provisional and corrigible. Without languishing in semantic undecidability and interpretive deferral, on one hand, or staking evaluative claims with finality, on the other, it stresses the many inferences that precede interpretation.[68] Adopting the dispositions I explore in the chapters below, critical judgment under uncertainty is by turns hesitant and comparative, hypothetical and counterfactual, iterative and composite. It makes self-conscious use of both faces of the dual form of probability, aleatory and epistemic. It navigates between individual and aggregate – between the targeted inferences of close reading and its intuitive appraisals of sound and sense, and the combined judgments of genre analysis, methodological positioning, and system-building. In rethinking critical judgment under uncertainty, my account converses with other work on the poetics and aesthetics of related phenomena, including suspense, surprise, curiosity, anticipation, speculation, and play.[69] It builds connections to kindred models of literary thinking, among them Caroline Levine's exploration of how suspense and "narrative doubt" reprise the hypothetico-deductive methods of science, and Elaine Auyoung's account of how realism's "phenomenological effects" underwrite its "epistemological project of constructing intricate mental representations of the fictional world," by means of "cues that prompt readers to retrieve their existing embodied knowledge."[70] Above all, my vision of critical judgment remains open to revision and reading otherwise.

The Highs and Lows of Number

In this and subsequent sections, I trace the strands of intellectual history I see woven together as a backdrop to the chapters, and offer detailed accounts of the book's principal contexts and motivations. By emphasizing linked histories of uncertainty as they inflect literary spheres, often in ways that lose sight of disciplinary origins, I lay the groundwork for reconsidering how uncertainty shadows literary concepts like probability and realism. I begin by detailing developments in probability as understood in logic and mathematics, extending their remit from specific disciplinary histories to a nineteenth-century cultural arena where the intellectual domains of words and numbers were quite porous. Whewell wrote defenses of mathematics and classics as foundational for grasping inductive methods and producing that mental outlook he saw as vital to a liberal education.[71] Matthew Arnold's polemic "Literature and Science" included Isaac Newton's *Principia* and Euclid's *Elements* in the first category.[72] Lewes's *Principles of Success in Literature* (1872) made clear that science and philosophy, no less than art and literature, rely on the imagination.[73]

The major contributions in the history of probability, by figures from Bernoulli and De Moivre to Laplace and Poisson, were published in scientific venues or circulated among like-minded thinkers. Yet this field's demotic origins in solutions to games and wagers, and its continuing practical applications (from insurance instruments to techniques for assessing witness credibility), ensured a wider audience. Looking back to the eighteenth century from early in the nineteenth, Thomas De Quincey highlighted the intellectual prominence of practices usually "slighted as inconsiderable arts," marveling at how betting and wagering "rose suddenly into a philosophic rank" when thinkers cast the "light of a high mathematical analysis upon the whole doctrine of Chances."[74] Much of this "high mathematical analysis" was carried out, early in the nineteenth century, by mathematicians in Europe, reaching Britain through newly flourishing scientific societies and periodicals even as homegrown work found its footing. Charles Babbage, Augustus De Morgan, Thomas Galloway, John Herschel, and later Mill, Boole, and Venn were among those mediating developments in the British context. As the field gained traction, original contributions sat alongside summaries, reviews, and encyclopedia articles.[75] The ideas of thinkers like Laplace, Poisson, and Quetelet were domesticated, mathematical ideas simplified, and intellectual cognates spotlighted – in law, theology, history, and literary criticism. Readers might tackle De Moivre's technical problems in *The Doctrine of Chances* (1718) or settle for his more practical *Annuities upon Lives* (1725), both updated several times into the Victorian period. Laplace's voluminous *Théorie analytique des probabilités* (1812) was complemented by the brief *Essai philosophique sur les probabilités* (1814), condensed from earlier lectures. Quetelet's *Sur l'homme et le développement de ses facultés* (1835, translated 1842) could also be grasped through his *Instructions populaires sur le calcul des probabilités* (1828, translated 1839) or his published letters in the *Théorie des probabilités* (1846, translated 1849), originally written when he was tutor to the young Prince Albert. Reviews often took up both authoritative treatises and accessible digests, and when addressing the latest mathematical ideas were content to speak in wide terms of "probability" and "statistics" with nary a number in sight. In a further sign of entrenchment, the discipline also became conscious of its history. A century before Hacking's work, a synoptic account was available in *History of the Mathematical Theory of Probability from the Time of Pascal to That of Laplace* (1865), by the mathematician Isaac Todhunter. From the vantage point of the history of mathematics, theoretical developments in statistics and (to a lesser extent) probability did not make much headway in Britain until later in the nineteenth century, but these topics were still broadcast in practical and culturally trenchant ways.[76]

What Theodore Porter has described as the "rise of statistical thinking" gave this mathematical work further cultural traction from the early decades of the century. Quetelet took graspable, public information – "vital statistics" (rates of birth, development, and death) and "moral statistics" (rates of behavior, criminal or otherwise) – and inferred objective states of affairs from its regularities, thereby undergirding "a numerical social science of laws, not just of facts."[77] Quetelet's prescriptions about the possibility of "social physics" were straightforward to comprehend (or challenge), and gave impetus to British statistical societies forming in the 1830s, in concert with the reformism of that decade.[78] As statistics broadened its sphere of influence and application through mid-century, "proportions and percentages were referred to as matters of common parlance" and the field faced outward "in an almost utopian spirit as the indispensable foundation of public knowledge, of reason in the public sphere."[79] Already a broader promulgator than his mathematical forebears (Hacking dubs him the era's "greatest regularity salesman"), Quetelet's ideas were deployed in yet more popular fashion by the introduction to Henry Buckle's *History of Civilization in England* (1857), with its famous (and fiercely criticized) vision of statistical determinism applied to history.[80] The key figures in statistics were "widely read generalists" who often espoused nontechnical approaches, using "no abstruse mathematical manipulations"; indeed, statistical rhetoric was often supplemented by narrative particulars more common in realist novels.[81] At the same time, there were sharp criticisms of statistical thinking from figures like Thomas Carlyle, Ruskin, and Charles Dickens, whose attack on "hard facts" in *Hard Times* (1854) singles out statistics ("stutterings"), where the calculative knowledge of the aggregate is set against the mysterious, intuitive knowledge of the individual units.[82] The complex reception of these ideas presents myriad pathways of influence between mathematics and literature, but also explains why historians of science mention literary examples (if at all) in merely instrumental ways, as passing witnesses to historical ruptures.[83]

Returning to the terms introduced earlier, we might say that in nineteenth-century culture, residual knowledge about mathematics (specifically probability) coexisted alongside emergent and dominant ideas. We see this clearly in the rising tide of scientific popularization.[84] In a tradition dating back at least to John Arbuthnot's "An Essay on the Usefulness of Mathematical Learning" (1701), ideas about probability were promoted in textbooks and juvenile works, and in newspapers, periodicals, and pamphlet publications.[85] Widely respected articles such as Herschel's "Quetelet on Probabilities" (1850) continued to mediate Continental innovations for the public, while work geared at lay readers ingrained the ideas of prior generations.[86] The resuscitation of formal logic, after a period of diminished interest from roughly the mid-seventeenth century to the early nineteenth, saw the publication of both commanding treatises (foremost among them Mill's hugely successful *System of Logic*) and accessible works like the text that introduced Hardy to the *Art of Reasoning*.[87] Primers, guides, and digests were ubiquitous: a review in the 1870s encompassed fifteen such introductions to logic.[88] Many discussed probability's dual form explicitly, treating it as an epistemic problem (a question of subjective beliefs and their evidentiary proportioning) while also mentioning its aleatory dimension (a matter of numerical frequencies and their statistical instantiation). Even so rarefied a topic as the nature of scientific induction could be said to have attained a degree of popularization in the public debate carried on by Whewell and Mill.[89] If works like Mill's *System of Logic* (1843), Whewell's *Philosophy of the Inductive Sciences* (1840), Boole's *Investigation of the Laws of Thought* (1854), and Venn's *Logic of Chance* (1866) and *Principles of Empirical or Inductive Logic* (1889) occupied the high ground in the Victorian intellectual landscape, and accessible introductions like William Stanley Jevons's *Elementary Lessons in Logic* (1870) a middle territory, the wider plains were populated by works that freely combined material on logic, mathematics, rhetoric, and grammar: Henry Kett's *Logic Made Easy* (1809), James Gilbart's *Logic for the Million* (1851) and *Logic for the Young* (1855), Alexander Ellis's *Logic for Children* (1882), and Alfred Swinbourne's *Picture Logic* (1875).

In a practical vein, sober works on calculating probability, such as Babbage's *Comparative View of the Various Institutions for the Assurance of Lives* (1826), De Morgan's *Essay on Probabilities and on Their Application to Life Contingencies and Insurance Offices* (1838), and Robert Campbell's *Popular Introduction to the Theory of Probabilities* (1865), drew the link between these ideas and their prudent applications, such as financial investment and insurance schemes.[90] The "rhetoric of contingency" in nineteenth-century insurance treatises and prospectuses, as Tina Choi observes, "made generalizable, calculable risks feel personally relevant" yet "promised a measure of insulation from them."[91] By contrast, countless guides to games and gambling actively solicited risk in an only dubiously practical vein. Again, the shift to a numerical age was clear. An eighteenth-century classic by Edmond Hoyle (often enlarged, abridged, improved, and reissued), *Hoyle's Games* acquired a new section in 1835, updating its guidance to reflect the "mathematical analysis of chances" and tabulating odds for various games.[92] Other writers hawking guidance on gambling co-opted titles of celebrated mathematical treatises, like William Rouse's *Doctrine of Chances, or The Theory of Gaming Made Easy to Every Person* (1814) and William Pole's *On Probabilities, as Illustrated by Events Occurring in Games with Cards* (1869). Throughout the century, a plethora of works – legal diatribes, trial reports, religious sermons, moral tracts – warned against the evils of gambling and chance-based institutions like lotteries (abolished by the state in 1826).[93] Later in the century, gambling remained a target of legal and social censure in Joseph Malet Lambert's *Gambling: Is It Wrong?* (1890) and Benjamin Rowntree's *Betting & Gambling: A National Evil* (1905).[94] At the same time, games of chance continued to anchor popular ideas about probability, as in many articles by the astronomer Richard Proctor, and technical research into statistics, as in Karl Pearson's "Science and Monte Carlo" (1894).[95]

Uncertainty's quantitative intellectual and institutional history thus covers a broad cultural spectrum. Yet beyond the thematic presence of games of chance and annuity schemes from the eighteenth through the early twentieth centuries, novels register the lessons of this variegated mathematical context in complex and formal ways. Novelistic representation works at the cusp between the two modes of probability that have jostled for prominence and still do – what Hacking calls the aleatory and the epistemic: accounts that address ratios and regularities ("frequencies") that empirically obtain across long series of events, and might be thought to track properties (or "propensities") of the physical world, and accounts that measure our degrees of belief and try to model our assessment of single outcomes by adjusting personal predictions in light of new information. The aleatory and epistemic have been mapped onto a closely related distinction, between *objective* and *subjective*, which historians take to mark, roughly speaking, the nineteenth-century transition from one regime of probability (the classical), where objective and subjective were held together, to another (the statistical) around 1840, where these poles came apart.[96] But again, a relatively clear divide in the history of mathematics appears jagged and uneven in literary history. By preserving residual concepts while engaging with emergent and dominant ideas, novels open a space where intellectual contest in the wider culture can be navigated and questioned. And by inscribing such contest in the judgments, decisions, and actions of characters, they record a durable way of thinking about uncertainty (and the objective/subjective tension) that remains useful today. Novels chart events that occur to individuals or social groups, starting their characters (and readers) off, like Hardy's logical lovers, in conditions of subjective uncertainty. At the same time, they attempt to represent, or at least refer to, objective events taking place at larger natural and social scales. Emphasizing the formal tensions engendered by a culture of numbers, my readings will thus be attentive to probability's complex duality – as both aleatory and epistemic, objective and subjective, frequency and degree of belief, "modelling and inference" – and also to moments where these poles blur together.[97]

Chance Collisions

The numerical approaches to uncertainty discussed in the previous section sought to provide rational frameworks for inference. Concepts of mathematical probability thus came into contact, and occasionally conflict, with long-standing philosophical ideas about mental operation and empirical judgment, in particular, the British school of thought known as *associationism*, which in turn inspired specifically literary ways of thinking about thinking, conjecturing, and imagining in the nineteenth century. The associationist tradition offers a neat example of the back-and-forth between mathematical and philosophical domains, and of the myriad channels along which ideas about uncertainty reached the literary sphere. Associationism presents a model of mental operation – predicated on the materialization of chance in our thinking tissue – that meshed with mathematical ideas in the eighteenth century, underwrote descriptions of the poetic mind in the early nineteenth century, and influenced later Victorian developments in psychology that mark the representation of uncertain inference in novels.

Formulated in the fourth edition of Locke's *Essay Concerning Human Understanding* (1700) and generalized in Hume's *Treatise of Human Nature*, the association of ideas was a widely influential approach to explaining cognition.[98] Especially in its later formulations, its tenets were aleatory and material. Sensations, emotions, and ideas were all understood as aggregate products of experience, forming connections and grooving paths in the brain and nervous system according to habit. External events, regularities, and patterns – things happening out there in the world and impinging iteratively on cognition via discrete sense-data – were thought to shape the internal material substrate with which we sense, feel, think, believe, judge, and, crucially, imagine. The world, for the associationist, is quite literally in our heads. Association, moreover, was linked with mathematics in its vision of the mind as a "counting machine that automatically tallied frequencies of past events and scaled degrees of belief in their recurrence accordingly."[99] The external and internal poles of associationist theory are similar to the concepts of objective and subjective probability: aleatory events (in the world) and epistemic judgments (in our heads). They came together, in the eighteenth century, under association's umbrella. As Daston has argued, associationism co-opted both objective and subjective probability, merging mathematical views into updated accounts of inference.[100] Important figures in the associationist tradition were scientifically and mathematically informed. David Hartley's *Observations on Man* (1749), for example, incorporated mathematical notions into a radical version of the associationist model of mind.[101] Hartley argued that "the human body is composed of the same matter as the external world" and so "its component particles should be subjected to the same subtle laws."[102]

In the 1830s, associationism lost traction along with the classical interpretation of probability when the French mathematician Poisson "broke up the classical triumvirate of experience, probability, and belief by separating objective frequencies and subjective beliefs."[103] Until the century's close, as the "world teemed with frequencies," objective standards held sway over subjective degrees of belief.[104] But if the "smooth meshing between the world of things and the world of the mind" was no longer tenable, associationist psychology and its account of mental function remained important in residual ways.[105] Its aleatory underpinnings continued to inform philosophical, psychological, and literary writers. Associationist ideas percolated from eighteenth-century novels and criticism through early Romantic poetics and its theories of imagination.[106] William Hazlitt thought Wordsworth exemplified "in an eminent degree the power of *association*," having "dwelt among pastoral scenes, till each object has become connected with a thousand feelings, a link in the chain of thought, a fibre of his own heart."[107] In the 1805 *Prelude*, Wordsworth described how nature impressed "Rememberable things" into his mind, "By chance collisions and quaint accidents."[108] He and Coleridge were much taken with Hartley's ideas, which appear in the Preface to *Lyrical Ballads* (1800), even if Coleridge later reversed course in *Biographia Literaria* (1817), where his iconic discussion of fancy and imagination follows a "masterful demolition" of associationism.[109]

From Wordsworth's picture of the poet's mind as formed by "quaint accidents" to Conrad's comment that a "philosophical mind is but an accident," the literary discourse of uncertainty drew on associationist tropes, in the process reinforcing the link between literary imagination and psychological inquiry.[110] In philosophy, associationism was one component of Mill's promotion of empiricism and his attack on Whewell's intuitionist account of scientific inference.[111] As in the earlier period, association had a strong affinity with probability: on the basis of prior sensations, in Mill's account, we develop an "expectation" about "possible sensations" that would likely be registered in similar situations.[112] In Victorian psychology, thinkers from James Mill forward linked associationist ideas (in particular, the doctrines of Hartley) with research on the physiological structures of nervous tissues, structures, and reflexes.[113] Above all in the work of Bain, these efforts yielded a more embodied account of mental function, often referred to as physiological psychology.[114] Associationism tended to be linked with philosophical radicalism and "relativistic anti-absolutism," especially in the younger Mill and Bain, but it was also echoed in the cognitive practices of liberal subjectivity.[115] Its depictions of embodied mentation maintained influence – and were picked up by writers like Eliot and Hardy – through the later nineteenth century, when William James dispensed with associationism's simplifications in promoting his vision of the "Stream of Thought."[116]

This intellectual lineage is important for my account in several ways. First, it shows how a current of philosophical thinking about mental operations branched out to absorb ideas from mathematical probability, then eddied back and issued in literary and philosophical tributaries downstream. Associationism was enmeshed with the wider epistemological shift that, as noted earlier, gave us the problem of induction and was coeval with the rise of the novel. It forms a part of the shared genealogy of conjectural reasoning and fictive imagining. Indeed, the prevalent literary theory of the Augustan period was built on associationist assumptions, as Douglas Patey has shown: it characterized the "literary work as a structure of probable signs" and "interpretation as a probabilistic process of sign-inference."[117] Mid-eighteenth-century science and fiction shared the terrain of hypothesis, John Bender has suggested, even as the novel's "manifest fictionality" could be seen to underwrite science's "mantle of factuality," both practices "defining 'truth' in terms of verisimilitude or probability" and describing "the most accurate representations of reality as those that contextualized empirical, sense-based 'facts' by arraying them in probable explanatory networks."[118] Accounts tracing the inauguration of "fictionality" to this period, by Bender, Catherine Gallagher, Ian Duncan, and Sarah Kareem, have invoked Hume's associationist epistemology.[119]

The associationist lineage shows, moreover, how highly abstract models of mental operation can have a vividly material basis – how inductive reasoning might mirror the aggregative patterns that channel pathways through our thinking matter, how predictive thinking might be activated like a habit or gut feeling, and how "chains" or "trains" of ideas (as they were often described) might be linked by powers of imagination. The felt character of uncertainty in this psychological tradition is couched in perceptual and experiential terms that bring its descriptions close to literary representation and critical judgment. To return to my opening image, the daily rhythm of light and dark forms the basic figurative nexus for describing perception (bright or blurry) and knowledge (sharp or shadowy)

in the associationist tradition. The "twilight ... of *Probability*" is how
Locke memorably described our partial knowledge, an image reprised
often, as in Venn's description of beliefs shifting in the face of evidence
like "alternations of light and dark in a murky foggy day," leaving us in a
"dim haze of conjecture."[120]

Only for the Most Part

I have moved out from the reflex concern of one logical reader to a range of
materials that informed nineteenth-century understandings of uncertainty
and probability (logical and mathematical, then philosophical and psychological). In this section I discuss how even discourses with a native
connection to literature – treatises on rhetoric, law, grammar, and literary
style – were marked by the epistemological transformation accompanying
the development of mathematical probability. In rhetorical treatises from
the late eighteenth century onward, we can detect an increasing propensity
to widen the category of evidence to include numerical markers of uncertainty. Campbell's *Philosophy of Rhetoric*, a text indebted to Hume's
epistemology and Thomas Reid's "common sense" philosophy, may be
the first to include "calculations of chances" alongside the usual sources of
evidence from experience, analogy, and testimony.[121] Whately's *Elements
of Rhetoric*, influenced by Campbell and Joseph Priestley but also drawing
on his own logical work, was yet more overt in worrying about the effects
on inference of "cases in which the degree of probability is estimated from
a calculation of chances."[122] Bain's *English Composition and Rhetoric*
(1866), surveying the types of proof one might use for persuasion –
deductive, inductive, analogical, and probable – referred to numerical
proportions and observed that "we do always form some vague estimate
of what we consider the force of an inference that is not certain," even if
"exact numbers" are not forthcoming.[123] These ideas permeated language
at a rudimentary level: Bain's *An English Grammar* (1863) included
sections discussing adverbs of belief, certainty, and probability, and con-
junctions for suppositional or conditional statements.[124] Across different
programs – Campbell's "psychological-epistemological" approach, Whately's
"ecclesiastical" and "neo-Aristotelian" project, Bain's psychophysiological
endeavor – we see the same adherence to probability's dual form.[125]
Treatises of rhetoric, primers on logic, and manuals of grammar penned
by both central and adjacent figures in these traditions were impacted
by the wider intellectual culture of probability as both aleatory and
epistemic.[126] What Poovey describes as an early nineteenth-century

opposition between "figures of arithmetic" (numerical abstractions) and "figures of speech" (rhetorical particulars) was actually undercut, I suggest, not only in statistics but also in rhetorical texts that bordered literary production.[127]

Where rhetorical works included chances in considerations of evidence, the related genre of the legal treatise (especially on evidence) set similar concerns alongside numerical concepts. It may seem intuitive to consider the law as an *application* of the science of chance, but historically the opposite was often the case. As with many areas of probability theory, a "mathematical tool shaped, but was also shaped by, its objects."[128] Poisson's celebrated term for a cardinal concept, the "law of large numbers," was coined in the context of jurisprudence (designing a probability model to evaluate juries with differentially reliable jurors).[129] Law was affiliated with statistical thinking in the nineteenth century in ways that other fields, such as medicine, were not.[130] Barbara Shapiro has described how the law participated in the development of categories of knowledge – from mere opinion to graded probability to demonstrable certainty – from the early modern period through the nineteenth century.[131] She notes how legal treatises incorporated elements of British empiricist (often associationist) philosophy and were generally skeptical of probable calculations at law, even though early in the nineteenth century it was "not unusual for a discussion of legal evidence to include or refer to treatises on logic or for general discussions of logic and modes of proof to devote considerable attention to matters relevant to the law."[132] (I discuss this conceptual transfer between legal and logical domains further in Chapter 2.) Between the massive synthetic projects of Jeremy Bentham's *Rationale of Judicial Evidence* (1827), which contains several reflections on the probable and possible, and John Henry Wigmore's *Principles of Judicial Proof* (1913), many legal treatises worked in this mixed mode, incorporating observations from mathematical and rhetorical probability.[133] Indeed, while extending the eighteenth-century interest in using mathematics to assess the problem of "concurrent testimony . . . of several witnesses" and showing how conclusions can emerge from "a combination of data which singly would have had little or no weight," Whately's *Elements of Rhetoric* also bridged the two discourses under discussion: he first "introduced into the corpus of rhetorical theory the [legal] concepts of presumption and burden of proof."[134] In both rhetoric and law, numerical grades of the probable were added to long-standing methods for assessing credibility and inductive evidence. The concepts used to signal such concerns – "fact," "circumstantial evidence," "probable cause," "reasonable doubt," "moral certainty" – took on a renovated sense in the nineteenth century.[135]

Likely Stories

With these accounts of uncertainty in mathematics and psychology, rhetoric and the law, I have established some contextual, conceptual, and cognitive backgrounds to underpin my readings of a group of nineteenth-century novels. Adopting a broad intellectual approach, I hope to shed light on familiar literary-critical categories that share conceptual space with these discourses and have long inflected practices of critical judgment and understandings of genre. One such category, at once vital and treacherous for a discussion of uncertainty in literature, is *probability*. The dynamic contexts above only intensify the difficulties. Ordinary senses of probability and related terms change, albeit unevenly, alongside developments in the history of science and mathematics. But they are often crosshatched with residual meanings. Despite several critical accounts that draw on probability's modern lexicon, the concept has received less attention in narrative theory than *mimesis* and *verisimilitude*, perhaps because it can seem tenuous to predicate a link to large intellectual-historical trends on the basis of small semantic units.[136] Not always does "probability" (or its cognates) conjure up the aleatory (as in the frequent, paradoxical phrase "in all probability"); not everywhere does an explicit invocation of its numerical underpinnings add up (as in a nineteenth-century critic's swipe at *Madame Bovary* as "a literary application of the mathematics of probability").[137] Folk assessments of likelihood, classical (Aristotelian) notions of plausibility or verisimilitude, and modern (both epistemic and statistical) ideas of probability all jostle for prominence in literature and criticism, and have done since at least the seventeenth century.

For literary writers, probability has often been a self-conscious tactic of representation and generic affiliation. For readers and critics, appraisals of probability have expressed judgments of taste, pronouncements about narrative coherence and generic standards, and preferences along a spectrum that places the frequentative "normal" against the "deviation." Historicist accounts of literary probability (and related concepts) have offered various interpretations of these shifts. Standards of *vraisemblance* in French classicism sponsored, via translation, what Patey describes as the "extraordinary vogue" of probability as a concept in Restoration literature.[138] The rise of the novel, Michael McKeon has argued, was eventually secured by a "conception of truth as realism" woven from the "scattered threads of verisimilitude and probability that Renaissance writers had teased out of [Aristotle's] *Poetics*."[139] By the middle of the eighteenth century, in Catherine Gallagher's account, novelists "stressed that probability was a sign of fictionality as well as a mode of reference," claiming (as Fielding did in *Tom Jones*) the terrain of the "probable" and "verisimilar" against the "marvelous."[140]

All these terms recur in the nineteenth century – sometimes to rehash old disputes, at other times to launch new debates – as literary probability encounters the rise of statistics and the shifts in mathematical probability I discussed above. Various interpretations of these developments are possible. Adam Grener has pointed to nineteenth-century shifts in probability to argue for a realism "fundamentally historicist in its aims and commitments," where novelists make strategic use of improbability, chance, and coincidence to "represent cultural specificity, embedded experience, and historical transformation."[141] Michael Tondre has demarcated "figuring alternatives to the actual" as a shared project of literature, mathematics, and the physical sciences in the nineteenth century, drawing on probabilistic discourses to show how novelists forged "a tradition of realism couched in the conditional or subjunctive mood."[142] Tina Choi has addressed aspects of nineteenth-century probability in scientific, literary, and cultural objects that manifest the era's interest in contingency as "an analytical and epistemological tool" for examining causality.[143] "Contingency might admit the uncertainty of the future," Choi writes, yet its Victorian articulations tended to issue in "a finite set of possible outcomes," "transform[ing] a shapeless, unknowable future into an imaginable, knowable realm of expectation, if not of choice."[144] From these accounts, it is clear that probability elicited a range of interpretations and applications, appeared in a variety of cultural venues, and sheltered emergent, dominant, and residual senses in literary contexts. At each historical stage, probability in literature has responded in complex and uneven ways to models of, and changing ideas about, probability drawn from other areas of knowledge.

In narrative theory, however, and in ordinary critical judgments, literary probability has often remained in thrall to the Aristotelian standard encapsulated in the nineteenth century by another lapidary statement of Hopkins's: "likely seeming fiction is better than unlikely seeming fact."[145] Turning now to assumptions about probability in twentieth-century structuralism and nineteenth-century criticism, I aim to show the abiding hold of probability's dual form, even in venues ostensibly committed to other interpretations. For structuralist narratology, the logic of plausibility is referred to standards of common sense or ideologies of taste, decorum, and class. In a key essay, Gérard Genette shows how seventeenth-century practices frame the verisimilar (*vraisemblable*) or probable as tacitly referring to social codes: "a body of maxims accepted as true by the public to which the narrative is addressed" operate "as a system of natural forces and constraints, which the narrative follows as if without perceiving and, *a fortiori*, without naming."[146] What contravenes probability, on this account, are actions or events both "contrary to good manners, and ... contrary to all reasonable foresight: infraction and accident."[147] French classicism's deference to the norms of verisimilitude, in Genette's rough historical typology, gives way to a modernist distaste for probability, expressed in the explanatory opacity of writers such as Stendhal, Fyodor Dostoevsky, and Henry James. Between these poles and their "shared silence with regard to motives and maxims of action," we find the mixed verisimilar character of realist novels that often explain themselves, notably in Honoré de Balzac, by inserting justificatory phrases or commentaries.[148] Alongside the work of Roland Barthes, Tzvetan Todorov, Seymour Chatman, Jonathan Culler, and others, Genette's account has come to inform an abstract logic whereby the probable is understood to be achieved through "naturalization," or what is termed, following the Russian formalists, "motivation": the "mask of causal determination" that lends coherence and credibility by screening "the functionality of a narrative's elements."[149] For structuralism, we might say, probability is epiphenomenal to narrative laws. It concerns what is "believable within the terms of world or plot," and thus governs the *fabula* (or story) more than the *sjuzhet* (or discourse), modulating narrative's general assumptions rather than its specific expressions.[150] Structuralist analysis targets these underlying elements. In realism, it might aim to unmask the "motivation" or "naturalization" that works to guarantee the air of probability, calling out authorial justifications that surface when narrative events run the risk of seeming improbable (in the sense of not conforming to common sense or opinion).

What I want to point out is that whether we are dealing with historical or theoretical accounts of narrative, the dual concept of probability is implicitly at work alongside (and sometimes against) other standards of the verisimilar, plausible, or natural. Genette's literary examples, *Le Cid* (1637) and *La Princesse de Clèves* (1678), are drawn from the crucial moment of modern probability's development. His descriptions of *vraisemblance* are akin to Hacking's interpretation of earlier, nonmathematical notions of the probable as what was "approvable" or "worthy of approval" (referred to accepted authorities or canons).[151] At the same time, in speaking of the "gradation" of *vraisemblance*, juxtaposing "accident" and "reasonable foresight," Genette tacitly invokes probability's aleatory conception as a spectrum of outcomes to guide prediction.[152] When verisimilitude is tethered to discourses of probability in mathematics, logic, rhetoric, and law, it becomes, I would contend, significantly more complex than a "mask which is assumed by the laws of the text and which we are meant to take for a relation with reality."[153] There is a circularity in any theory trying to explain probability in terms of "general verities" (Genette), "reference codes" that "afford the discourse a basis in scientific or moral authority" (Barthes), or the "degree of conformity to a set of 'truth' norms" (Gerald Prince): such verities, codes, and norms have included the tenets of modern probability since at least the seventeenth century.[154] If, according to the structuralist logic of motivation, narratives "depend on the tacit presence of rules and norms that allow a reader to differentiate between what is believable and unbelievable within *and only within* the world of [a] particular plot or genre," such rules and norms cannot simply be cordoned off from the discourse of probability that aids differentiating judgments in the world without.[155] What is striking in novelists who succumb to the "explicatory demon" Genette finds in Balzac – to some extent all those in this book – is not the content but the *form* of their justifications of the probable: they persistently frame realist probability in terms of odds, statistical facts, contrary-to-fact hypotheses, and other offshoots of probability's discourse that surely belong among "the cultural and literary models which make texts readable."[156]

The discourse of uncertainty thus puts pressure on the abstract criteria of narratology – its tendency to read narrative elements according to rigid textual "devices," "laws," "systems," and "canons" – even if such categories cannot simply be subsumed by a historical account.[157] We need to insist on probability's duality as a way to keep narratological and historical explanations in fluid and productive balance. If probability, in Chatman's terms, governs our assessment of *events* (including their causality and temporality) and *existents* (including the consistency of characters and the plausibility of settings), the former could admit of verification by means of aleatory information, whereas the latter might demand epistemic judgments.[158] (The tendency of letters to go astray in Hardy's novels, say, could be referred to the objective regularity of dead letters in the postal system, Laplace's foundational example of statistical stability, whereas the typicality of Tess's actions as a dairymaid might elicit an assessment made on subjective grounds of experience.[159]) Even the most canonical instance of how textual devices effect an air of reality – the barometer Barthes spots in Gustave Flaubert – could be recast as joining narrative to an eminently probabilistic domain with objective and subjective contours: weather prediction.[160] Down to the most incidental detail, realism is inflected by probability's dual form, uniting number and belief.

If structuralist-influenced narrative theory maintains a suspicious attitude toward probability while nonetheless relying on its dual form, as I have proposed, the abundant nineteenth-century examples of what Genette calls "verisimilist criticism" operate in a more naïve manner. Yet here, too, across the ideological spectrum of Victorian novel reviewing, we find probability discussed in blended terms – as folk judgment of likelihood, stance on propriety, determination of factual accuracy, or expression of generic standard.[161] A radical critic like Lewes, reviewing *Jane Eyre* (1847) in otherwise generous terms, grumbles about "too much melodrama and improbability, which smack of the circulating-library"; a prolific conservative critic like Geraldine Jewsbury uses a similar standard of decorum to charge that George Meredith's *The Ordeal of Richard Feverel* (1859), had it not followed "an abstract and entirely arbitrary idea," might have been read "with the feeling that no probability was being outraged."[162] Margaret Oliphant likewise lauds the perfections and verisimilitudes of Jane Austen but complains that characters and events in *Tess of the d'Urbervilles* (1891) cannot be thought likely or even possible, and (perhaps reworking another Humean image for the problem of induction) judges the subtle turns of Meredith's *The Egoist* (1879) "as little true to nature as the existence of one black swan among a multitude of crows."[163] Victorian reviewing offers abundant examples of probability as likelihood wielded in arguments for propriety, as when Lewes treats bad novelists as an average, sharing a "natural affinity" for risible coincidence, "foolish and improbable" incidents, and a "consistent mediocrity which excludes hope."[164]

Alongside judgments of likelihood and propriety, facticity offers another marker of probability in nineteenth-century criticism, albeit a contested one. De Quincey anticipates Barthes in recalling how Daniel Defoe "so plausibly circumstantiated his false historical records as to make them pass for genuine" through details that "by their apparent inertness of effect, [seem] to verify themselves."[165] With the rise of the novel and the gradual dissolution of the "fact/fiction continuum" in the early eighteenth century, which yielded (as many have discussed) a distinct category of fiction, such appeals to factual authenticity underwrote fictional narratives that could not yet rely on audiences to grant credence.[166] Even with a nineteenth-century novel-reading public comfortable with purely fictional invocations of reality, however, "pseudofactual assertions" persisted, and the plausibility of factual details could be an ambivalent standard.[167] Writers from Dickens to Hardy were often charged with too-scrupulous attention to such particularities, to an overrealism Lewes derided as *"detailism,"* which "confounds truth with familiarity" and often focuses on the "vulgarities of life."[168] Generic norms, finally, are where we often confront (and depart from) nineteenth-century standards of probability. Lewes and David Masson juxtapose Thackeray's realism favorably against Dickens's romance (a contrast we might invert): portraits of "life as it is actually and historically" against those in "a world of semi-fantastic conditions, where the laws need not be those of ordinary probability," lessons in the "general relations of things" against characters "speaking a language never heard in life."[169] Similarly, Elizabeth Rigby offers what now seems a weird claim about *Vanity Fair* as less a novel than "a history of those average sufferings, pleasures, penalties, and rewards to which various classes of mankind gravitate," in which Thackeray "has hardly availed himself of the natural average of remarkable events that really do occur in this life," and readers "almost long for a little exaggeration and improbability to relieve us of that sense of dead truthfulness which weighs down our hearts."[170]

The probable claims of Victorian critics perplexed later traditions; they perplex us now. But the main goal of the foregoing examples is to stress that in the nineteenth century, as in later narrative theory, such determinations were intimately related to the aleatory side of probability ("the natural average of remarkable events") even as they simultaneously appealed to the epistemic in the form of intuition or prejudice ("a language never heard in life"). Indeed, nineteenth-century criticism often drew explicitly on probability's dual character, as we have seen in Whately. *Elements of Rhetoric* includes a discussion of plausibility from Aristotle to Campbell – "the chief kind of Probability which poets, or other writers of fiction, aim at" – and mentions verisimilitude, naturalness, and *eikos*, but Whately also counsels writers to "keep clear of the improbable air produced by the introduction of events, which, though not unnatural, have a great *preponderance of chances* against them."[171] Commenting on *Gulliver's Travels*, Walter Scott notes that "there are degrees of probability proper even to the wildest fiction," just as Lewes later speaks of the "degree of verisimilitude" that grades a representation's difficulty and distance from reality.[172] A vivid example of Victorian criticism's continuing reliance on the probability spectrum is given by the legal theorist James Fitzjames Stephen – brother of Leslie Stephen, uncle to Woolf, first cousin of the logician Venn, and a prominent critic of Buckle's statistical determinism.

Arguing that fictions can only be inadequately tethered to fact, Stephen notes that even Austen,

> whose books convey an impression of reality altogether extraordinary, culls out and pieces together a succession of small incidents, so contrived as to develop, step by step, the characters of the persons represented. Each incident, taken by itself, is so exquisitely natural, and so carefully introduced, that it requires considerable attention to detect the improbability of the story. That improbability consists in the sequence of the incidents wanted.[173]

We may take exception to Stephen's overall judgment yet still see how his assumptions fit in with the dual concept of probability: "incidents" are isolable units of event; a "sequence" arbitrates their overall likelihood. Drawing a similar distinction between the "particular" and the "general" or "aggregate," Masson declares a novel's morality to rest "not so much in any specific proposition that can be extracted out of it as its essence . . . as in the whole power of the work in all its parts to stir and instruct the mind, in the entire worth of the thoughts which it suggests, and in the number and intensity of the impressions which it leaves."[174]

Even when the discussion was not so explicit, nineteenth-century critics invoking probability and related terms to guide individual judgment accessed a cultural code that, understood in Hacking's terms, we broadly share as readers and critics today. We may cavil at certain Victorian opinions or expressions of taste – made according to outdated standards – even as we recognize the higher-order move of an appeal to probability in its dual form. It is in the overall conceptual architecture rather than the brief empirical judgment that we can seek a continuity between the Victorians and our own critical practices. Whether we agree or disagree with, say, Oliphant's assessment of the improbability of *Tess of the d'Urbervilles* is less crucial than the recognition that our assessments and hers operate within roughly the same conceptual frame. We still think with many of the tools relied on by nineteenth-century novelists and their critics.

This detour through structuralist narratology and Victorian novel criticism marks out two poles for inquiring into literary probability. Theorists like Genette and Todorov, eschewing the naïve idea that the verisimilar refers to reality, maintain a suspicious position where ideas of probability change merely according to convention or fashion. By contrast, Victorian reviewers, more naïvely consulting a set of implicit norms, did not tend to imagine the real as only accessible in historically contingent ways. Their more conservative position could be summarized in E. M. Forster's quip: "A mirror does not develop because an historical pageant passes in front of it."[175] But probability is never entirely a matter of either dynamic convention or static norm. Of course, standards of probability, aggregated across many literary texts and critical judgments, do calcify into distinct expectations for various genres: our mirrors, to continue with Forster's figure, often acquire "a fresh coat of quicksilver."[176] For instance, allegory operates according to a "magical causation" that violates naturalistic ideas of probability but has its own plausibility or "logical necessity" (hence its frequent recourse to an iconography of "fortune"); sentimental fiction and drama in the eighteenth century have been linked with "a new order of probability" that swaps prudential calculation for sympathetic intuition; farce acquires credibility by presenting actions with a speed that exceeds judgments of likelihood; and the nineteenth-century "novel of purpose" undergirds its reformism by "expanding the domain of representation" across society, "widen[ing] its verisimilitude."[177] We unavoidably judge probability in static terms, according to "the norms of a group of works," and are bothered by generic mismatches, as when events "passably probable in a fast-moving play" seem incredible in a novel's "slower pace."[178] At the same time, such expectations are dynamic. Differing across genres in a given period, they also modulate as genres evolve.[179] Norms of probability – what readers or critics take to be improbable or unreal at a given historical juncture – play a part in these processes. Victorian discourses of logic and probability, with their notions of "sets," "classes," and "members," still fundamentally shape our conceptions of, and familiar images for, genre's mutable categories.[180]

By considering both abstract models and historical norms, narratology and novel reviewing, I believe we can loosen the hold of Aristotelian conceptions of plausibility in favor of a more capacious approach to probability that includes, without entirely ceding ground to, the modern dual concept. Instead of cordoning off literary genres to their own idiosyncratic canons of the probable, we can situate those assumptions in a wider discursive terrain where literature exhibits certain resemblances to (and key differences from) other genres of the probable in science, rhetoric, and law. We can thereby make space for an analysis of uncertainty that foregrounds the distinctive resources and techniques literary genres have at their disposal for constructed effects and naïve judgments that alike appeal to probability. Realism, as I mentioned earlier, is not more probable – however that term is understood – than other genres. But it still merits special attention for its persistent arbitration of the "bounds of probability." It could do this by emphasizing the probability (greater frequency, higher believability) of its represented characters and events, as if annexing the central band of a normal curve and moving other genres to the margins. Or it could do this by spinning the improbability (lesser frequency, lower plausibility) of those characters and events as precisely their guarantor of "truth" or "reality."[181] Both poles are included in the probability spectrum mediated by a realism trading on statistical concepts, and specifically on a tension in the concept of *normal*. Normal could (and perhaps still does) mark both fact and value, an "existing average" or a "figure of perfection," an accepted generality or an aspirational typicality, the preferred or the pathological, the mediocre or the magisterial.[182] The formalist-structuralist approaches mentioned above would ascribe such stances on probability to a text's fealty to internal laws or external generic standards. But a more robust engagement with the discourses surrounding modern probability, this book claims, could open up more complex visions of realism, of novel form, and of critical judgment as they all navigate the spacious realm of uncertainty.

PART I

Provisional Judgments

CHAPTER I

Indecision Theory
Hesitation and Comparison in Eliot

"Who can be wise, amazed, temperate and furious, / Loyal and neutral, in a moment?" In *Daniel Deronda* (1876), George Eliot unmasks the "rhetoric" of Shakespeare's *Macbeth* – its claim "about the impossibility of being many opposite things in the same moment" – as a statement about the "clumsy necessities of action" rather than the "subtler possibilities of feeling."[1] But her last novel has its own rhetoric, elevating complex interiority over active externality, inner potentiality over outward manifestation. "Acting is slow and poor to what we go through within," one character solemnly intones (647). Eliot here delimits felt interior from agentive exterior in modal as well as spatial terms. Action lacks grace because its *necessities* obviate all but one of the many *possibilities* shadowed in mind. It can give vent to only one agent from the plural *we* of hypothetical selves *within*.

Doubtless Eliot has a "problem with action," as Stefanie Markovits observes.[2] Yet to approach uncertainty in *Daniel Deronda* is to recognize its forestalling of categories in which a cogent problem might be formulated in the first place. The novel presses another unsettling thought from *Macbeth* about how understanding and self-consciousness are misaligned in action: "To know my deed, 'twere best not know myself."[3] With one character who knows neither himself nor his prospective deed, another whose vanity opens her to lacerating doubt, the novel contours the problem of action from the inside out. I argue that *Daniel Deronda* models uncertainty as a recursive phenomenon – a convoluted movement between interior and exterior, potentiality and activity. Quarrying the labyrinthine inner spaces of her characters, Eliot explores, and theorizes, the antecedents and adjuncts of action under uncertainty.

Addressing Gwendolen Harleth's plot first, I characterize her self-centered attitude to chance as *inductive vanity*, a stance that dismisses aggregate pattern in favor of willful solipsism and personal luck. This flawed predictive outlook, a generalization of the gambler's fallacy, ramifies in opposing directions in the novel. It sponsors the practical attitude of *hesitation* (in Gwendolen's plot), and reformulates Eliot's long-standing commitment to the intellectual and moral value of *comparison* (in Deronda's plot). In the second section, I analyze Gwendolen's drawn-out decision to marry as a case study in hesitation, drawing on Eliot's engagement with nineteenth-century physiological psychology, its discourse of embodied volition, and its unexpected legacy in later theories of action. Recast in these terms, Gwendolen's faltering attempt to choose fractures into two models of decision – by proxy support and by volitional drift – in a remarkable portrait of hesitation as a state that precedes, accompanies, and even follows choice. Instead of offering a stable diagnosis for this character (as many have done, typically reading her as a "hysteric"), I frame the temptation to diagnosis within more inclusive pathologies of the embodied will. Turning to Daniel Deronda's plot, the last two sections consider Eliot's engagement with "comparative method" as a reflective stance matching the affective physiology of hesitation. I outline how comparison undergirds Eliot's theory of sympathy, and subsequently argue that Deronda's capacity for comparison and his rational model of action as subservient to ends both need affective supports – principally hope and trust – to function effectively.

Gwendolen moves from certainty to doubt, from a vanity that prompts her to do "what is unlikely" to an uncomfortable but productive form of self-distrust. Deronda moves from doubt to certainty, from inquisitive humility to a journey of historical self-discovery that seeks a foundation for trust and resolve. His emerging decision about a future role in Jewish life is framed by, and draws energy from, his long-standing experience of uncertainty about his background. The critical tradition has often used this bifurcated plot to overstate accompanying binaries of theme, characterization, and intellectual concern, predicating readings on one "half" of the novel. Critical evaluation follows the novel's internal fault lines, from early defenses that found Eliot's sympathetic representations of Jewish culture marred by the mundane marriage plot of a self-indulgent woman to F. R. Leavis's proposed extraction of a retitled novel, *Gwendolen Harleth*.[4] Because Eliot's own criticisms of gambling and its kindred modes of thinking and acting are often voiced through her titular character, it can seem that she turns away from Gwendolen and directs moral attention to Deronda, as if his plot existed to supervise hers. This encourages an interest in critical diagnoses that fix the legibility of one plot while unmooring the other for utopian, cosmopolitan, and collectivist projects.[5]

In this chapter, I offer a different approach, attempting to harmonize both plots under the sign of uncertainty, using several contexts mapped by

Eliot's late work. If the individualist career of Gwendolen, invested in the uncertain fortunes of the marriage market, is outdone by the communitarian trajectory of Deronda, united with prophetic certainties and the matrilineal fortunes of cultural identity, it may be more coherent to see these as *intersecting* rather than opposing approaches to acting with imperfect knowledge. The novel's chiasm of epistemic stances traces what Eliot calls the "kinship" (67) between certainty and doubt, through which problems in one "half" become solutions in the other. To the vanity of induction, Eliot offers the solution of comparison. To the challenges of decision, she presents the hesitant will as both pathological state and potential fail-safe, a fault in action mobilized to moral ends. And to the problem of determinism and the aggregate's constraint on individual lives, she offers particularizing affects like trust and hope, which elude statistical calculus and make the limits of knowledge grounds for a new social dispensation. We can see Eliot developing an ambivalent response to cultural shifts of which her own work was both type and sponsor: prevailing uncertainty in matters of religion; insecurities in structures of social regulation (marriage and gendered inheritance); and skepticism in light of the probabilistic unraveling of scientific laws. Sanguine about statistical thinking, Eliot still questioned the coercion exerted by numerical disciplines – the pressure to weigh options and reduce choices to two alternatives, to commit to just one path from a probable array, to accept one's status as an agent among millions.

Engaging Eliot criticism on matters scientific, epistemological, and political, I enlist uncertainty as a unifying rubric – as much a matter of action and inaction as of thought and knowledge.[6] While others have noted the extent of the novel's volitional collapse, perceiving Gwendolen's "crises of motivation," her "radical insecurity," and the resulting "uncertainty about the novel's sources of propulsion," I suggest that a thick description of decision-making in *Daniel Deronda* illuminates the formal and intellectual stakes of this shift.[7] Why would Eliot turn so insistently in her late work to figures of cognitive, psychological, and gestural uncertainty apparently at cross-purposes with narrative control, moral coherence, and formal consistency? Why would she write a novel to counter her earlier treatments of motivation as "a matter of laborious but essentially feasible reconstruction" (analogous to her patient reimagination of historical texture)?[8] *Daniel Deronda*'s fluctuations prompt us to revise our view of Eliot's stern moral strictures, to subject critical viewpoints to productive tension, and to see her as exploring a spacious moral landscape characterized by the provisional, incomplete, "unfolding" qualities her realism was originally designed to capture.

The Vanity of Induction

"One is always liable to mistake prejudices for sufficient inductions," Eliot wrote to Dante Gabriel Rossetti in 1870: "the relations are too subtle and intricate to be detected, and only shallowness is confident."[9] She could have been describing her future character. Gwendolen lapses often into *inductive vanity*, a fallacious attitude to probabilistic reasoning where dogmas of personal exceptionalism and generalized mediocrity underwrite a belief in inherent luck. She rates herself superior while deriding what she takes to be average. Her "personal pre-eminence" and "*éclat*" (273) will not deign to fall into paths grooved by common lives, for "so exceptional a person as herself could hardly remain in ordinary circumstances or in a social position less than advantageous" (23–24). Yet this desire is self-contradictory. Hoping not to end up like others, "being and doing nothing remarkable" (29), Gwendolen is trailed by the shadow of her own average-ness. She feels compromised by an upbringing with an "irksome lack of distinction and superfluity of sisters" (441), her siblings "all of a girlish average that made four units utterly unimportant, and yet from her earliest days an obtrusive influential fact in her life" (32). In this distaste for the average, Eliot embeds the premises of Gwendolen's plot: she cannot opt for "Mr. Middleton" when "Rex" or "Grandcourt" are available; Deronda, "content with [his] middlingness" (411), is a nonstarter. Gwendolen's psychic peculiarities and attempts to succeed in social performances (music, riding, archery, gambling) are best seen, I argue, as instances of this epistemic flaw, which reveals the novel's saturation by discourses of uncertain thinking.

When others show her up as average, Gwendolen's inductive vanity is piqued. She is by turns stubbornly unaffected and viscerally damaged by criticism. The musician Klesmer's judgment of her "mediocrity" – a question of "measuring probabilities" – presents an exemplary "vision of herself on the common level" (259, 262). Prior to meeting with him, she had privileged inexpert flattery and was "disposed to think approval more trustworthy than objection" (53). Seeking his considered opinion, she "somehow had the conviction that now she made this serious appeal the truth would be favourable" (253). But after his dismissal, her "wounded egoism" is "tempted to think that his judgment was not only fallible but biassed" (50, 257). The musician represents "part of that unmanageable world which was independent of her wishes" (251), his judgment espe-cially grating given Gwendolen's annoyance about the plain Catherine Arrowpoint, who lures Klesmer into marriage by dint of musical and "mental superiority" (52). This early obstacle to ambition undermines Gwendolen's delusional decisiveness. It forces her to realize she is "not remarkable enough to command fortune by force of will and merit" (290). After her family's ruin, "there was not a single direction in which probability seemed to flatter her wishes" (272) and she foresees humiliating mediocrity as an actress or governess.

Gwendolen is thus set in satirical opposition to familiar Eliot *doxa*. In *Adam Bede* (1859), the average life is defended in Reverend Irwine's sympathetic treatment of his sisters' "quite superfluous existences": "the existence of insignificant people has very important consequences in the world. It can be shown to affect the price of bread and the rate of wages, to call forth many evil tempers from the selfish, and many heroisms from the sympathetic, and, in other ways, to play no small part in the tragedy of life."[10] Just as in *Felix Holt* (1866) "there is no private life which has not been determined by a wider public life," so in *Daniel Deronda* the aggregate frames individual choices even if its units, like Gwendolen's sisters, "excel in ignorance" (48).[11] "Human beings are always forecasting their lives," Eliot's life-partner George Henry Lewes writes, "and always finding every episode *unlike* what had been forecast." An "eager imagination" unable to make the "future plastic to its wishes," he continues, in what is almost a character sketch of Gwendolen, often confronts the riddle of the aggregate: "we foresee events in the *mass*, but they reach us in *detail*."[12] Nor is Gwendolen able to avoid the opposite problem (formulated years earlier by Eliot): "validity of induction does not depend on mere enumeration; and a single instance is in some matters, and in other matters to some minds, sufficient to authorize the conclusion, to quicken the intuition, to verify the idea."[13] Yet if the novel does not afford Gwendolen the narrative resolution of the bildungsroman and its "inductive connection between the individual and the large number," as Jesse Rosenthal has argued, it nevertheless offers other strategies to correct inductive vanity and navigate between individual and aggregate.[14]

Vain induction characterizes the novel's much-discussed opening in the Leubronn casino, where Gwendolen imagines herself an "empress of luck" (156). Eliot reconstructs ideas from her wide reading – fallacies about chance in Richard Proctor's "Gambling Superstitions" (1872), descriptions of games as superstitious "survivals" in E. B. Tylor's *Primitive Culture* (1871) – to stress the backwardness of this character.[15] Gwendolen has no comprehension of probability's long-run patterns, only the shorter view where the "chances of roulette had not adjusted themselves to her aims" (236). She attributes victory not to chance but to personal luck; when she wins, in Sir Hugo Mallinger's appraisal, she wins "as coolly as if she had known it all beforehand" (161). Her self-conviction in the face of chance extends to other areas where risk and skill are combined. An accomplished equestrian, Gwendolen on horseback "felt as secure as an immortal goddess, having, if she had thought of risk, a core of confidence that no ill luck would happen to her" (72). A skilled archer, she can bring about success by "believing in her own good fortune even more than in her skill" (104). But this fortune that favors her in particular, colluding with her self-possessed unpredictability, is weirdly malleable to external influence. At the archery meeting, where the minds of the audience engage in "imaginative betting" (100), Grandcourt's arrival marks a fortunate turn: "the certainty that he was there made a distinct thread in her consciousness" and her shooting "gained in precision" (106). Grandcourt's virtual sway contrasts that of Klesmer, in whose presence Gwendolen feels "crushed" (103), and of Daniel, who exerts in the casino an "inward compulsion" (330) experienced as "superstitious dread" (329). These approaches to fortune are superstitious in exactly the sense given by the narrator, "an intense feeling about ourselves which makes the evening star shine at us with a threat and the blessing of a beggar encourage us": the prophetic images match the characters (beggar: Grandcourt; evening star: Deronda) and foreshadow how "superstitions carry consequences which often verify their hope or their foreboding" (329–30).

Riding, shooting, gambling: in each sphere, Gwendolen cultivates unlikely conduct. She tries to annex the mercurial patterns of chance for herself, to set her singularity – her air of "*l'imprévu*" (162) – against rational forecasting. Spoiled and overattended, "she naturally found it difficult to think her own pleasure less important than others made it" and when thwarted is given to "one of those passionate acts which look like a contradiction of habitual tendencies" (25). When Rex speaks of his cousin's predictions about Gwendolen, the latter erupts:

> "I can't tell what I shall do till I get there. Clairvoyantes are often wrong: they foresee what is likely. I am not fond of what is likely; it is always dull. I do what is unlikely."

> "So you would have come round to a likelihood of your own sort. I shall be able to calculate on you. You couldn't surprise me.... You see you can't escape some sort of likelihood. And contradictoriness makes the strongest likelihood of all. You must give up a plan." (69)

Gwendolen's effort at guarding unlikely individuality incurs the narrator's sharp rebuke: "a great deal of what passes for likelihood in the world is simply the reflex of a wish" (98). This statement unmasks forecasts based on desire (mocking those in her family who inferred Grandcourt as a likely suitor merely because no one else had yet succeeded), and underlines the link between prediction and volition. "The most obstinate beliefs that mortals entertain about themselves," the narrator opines, "are such as they have no evidence for beyond a constant, spontaneous pulsing of their self-satisfaction – as it were a hidden seed of madness, a confidence that they can move the world without precise notion of standing-place or lever" (250). A similar image earlier rated Gwendolen's knowledge of the world at virtually nil (39). Her idle subjectivism about probability, borne of the "habitual lazy combinations begotten by our wishes" (238), undermines hypothetical thinking, "the other worlds with which she was conversant being constructed with a sense of fitness that arranged her own future agreeably" (267).

The Physiology of Hesitation

Moments after accepting Grandcourt's proposal, Gwendolen entertains the last probabilistic thought in the stream leading to her decision (and unwittingly skewers many a Victorian marriage plot). "Really," she muses, "he was likely to be the least disagreeable of husbands" (305). Yet her nominal consent hardly concludes the novel's train of hesitations. Decision intensifies irresolution. It prompts a succession of mental states that gradually unbalance Gwendolen, setting prideful vanity against nagging remorse at the wronging of Grandcourt's former mistress, Lydia Glasher. Inductive vanity – taking oneself as a model predictor while spurning aggregate knowledge – begins to corrode more general aspects of the psychology of action. Eliot's representations of decision, especially as liable to coercion and as an afterimage of choice, are best understood in terms of *hesitation*. Here I outline a phenomenology of hesitation using literary theory, philosophy of action, and nineteenth-century physiological psychology. After discussing how hesitation takes hold in *Daniel Deronda* as theme and motif, I identify resonances between Eliot's view of uncertain action and later research into its psychology.

In canonical accounts of action, hesitation is a way-stage – a momentary version of more durable reluctance, a lull in action's forward flow. It is conceptually riddling for models of practical rationality requiring "resolute choice" or "intention stability," which allow our "planning agency" to remain coherent through time.[16] If practical reasoning, for the philosopher of action Elizabeth Anscombe, "reveals the order that there is in this chaos [in the word *doing*]," hesitation threatens to reinstate chaos into orderly action.[17] In his phenomenology of "hesitant consciousness," the philosopher Paul Ricoeur outlines how decisions take place against a variable continuum of willing and identifies three areas undermined by hesitation: projects, selves, and motives.[18] Hesitation swerves the grammar of action into a "conditional mode": goals appear tentative, projects "held-up," intentions "disembodied" in relation to agency's normal movement; one struggles to adopt a deciding persona, testing selves in an "inchoate consciousness which has not yet adopted its sphere of responsibility"; and motives lose their ground, remaining neither absent nor in conflict, but indefinitely "in suspension."[19] Hesitation pulls in paradoxical directions, both "a choice being sought" and a "falling short of choice."[20] This tension between faltering and fixity is replicated in the etymology of "hesitation," which blurs intransitive actions connoting stasis (clinging, attaching) with those that stop movement (stalling, being at a loss).[21] A moving statue is hesitation's exemplary representation.

What Ricoeur describes as the experience of having a "will which is and yet is not yet" has compelling analogues in literary theory.[22] Joseph Vogl's account of "tarrying" (*Zaudern*) emphasizes how narrative anomalies and formal hypotheticals reflect a "world of events" shadowed by an "inchoate world" of "[u]nsettled possibilities, blocked determinations, incompossible elements and suspended attributes."[23] For Vogl, tarrying retards action's forward movement to reveal the contingency of plots, the aesthetic centrality of pauses and counterrhythms, and the historical importance of what is contrary to fact.[24] It takes form in literature as a "choice that is undecided between choosing and not-choosing."[25] Gary Morson's concept of "sideshadowing" similarly posits lateral alternatives that branch out from the plot, "deepen[ing] our sense of the openness of time," and Andrew Miller's idea of the "optative" likewise marks a counterfactual tense that narrativizes paths not taken, "lives unled."[26] In distending narrative time and accentuating the interplay between voluntary and involuntary (attentive and distracted) dimensions of decision-making, hesitation also has affinities with the Victorian psychology of reading and narrative suspense respectively described by Nicholas Dames and Caroline Levine.[27] The literary archetypes of uncertainty in action join reflective and gestural faltering in the "hesitant hero": Orestes wavering before killing Clytemnestra in Aeschylus's *Oresteia*; Aeneas pausing before slaying Turnus in Virgil's *Aeneid*; the hero vacillating before Claudius at prayer in Shakespeare's *Hamlet*.[28] From epic or dramatic indecision, Vogl suggests, we can read off a "crisis in the conception of the world and its order," conflicts between regnant models and rebel dispensations of social arrangements, judicial norms, or standards of knowledge.[29]

Daniel Deronda has many links to the literary tradition of hesitation. Hamlet, the Victorian era's model for "autonomous selfhood," is an insistent reference for Deronda in his "reflective hesitation" (180), orphaned suspicion of familial connections, and gendered mode of moralizing.[30] Gwendolen, too, attains the "self-knowledge prompting such self-accusation as Hamlet's" (795) (notably not Ophelia's). Mordecai is characterized by allusion to Goethe's view of Hamlet in *Wilhelm Meister*, his body a "breaking pot of earth around the fruit-bearing tree, whose seed might make the desert rejoice" (497).[31] Eliot's use of hesitant tropes mirrors other literary manifestations in pointing to cultural uncertainty. As I discussed in the Introduction, the nineteenth century saw the rethinking of inductive and hypothetical methods, and what Eliot termed "mastery of calculation" – in fields such as statistics and, later, neoclassical economics – made individual agency an increasingly fraught matter.[32] John Venn's *Logic of Chance* (1866), studied by Eliot and Lewes, distinguishes deductive certainty from inductive probability by stating that logic "knows nothing of hesitation or doubt."[33] In this light, Eliot's appeal to hesitation revises her oft-cited commitment to strict causality and "undeviating law in the material and moral world."[34] Even if motives can be likened to "forms of force or energy," the late Eliot resists crude reductionism as the ultimate "determiner of motives."[35] The vision of progress we find here results from a "sceptical, hesitating, incredulous temper," in the words of the psychologist Alexander Bain.[36] Eliot thinks through motivation in terms of probable paths and inferential plasticity, adopting tenets of an important mid-century discourse that reimagined voluntary action and decision (as well as indecision and irresolution) in psychophysiological terms.

In Britain, the notion of an embodied will was promoted by experimental psychologists, clinicians, and other psychophysiological writers with whom Eliot had close connections, and who published periodical essays, lectures, and books on these topics. Alongside Bain's magisterial *The Senses and the Intellect* (1855) and *The Emotions and the Will* (1859), the first of which Eliot praised as psychology's equal to Mill's *System of Logic*, key contributions came from William Carpenter, Henry Maudsley, Thomas Laycock, and Lewes, whose *Problems of Life and Mind* (1874–79) overlapped with the writing and publication of *Daniel Deronda*.[37] In Carpenter's sketch of the period's scientific developments, Charles Bell's parceling of the nervous system into "sensory" and "motor" functions in the 1820s led to the subsequent recognition of the central nervous system as independently located in the brain stem and spinal cord, and

Marshall Hall's account of reflex action in 1833 prompted investigations into the spectrum of voluntary and involuntary (conscious and automatic) processes and actions.[38] The Victorian psychophysiology of the will was alert to its probabilistic inheritance. As Daston observes, "volition became closely identified with chance in the epistemic interpretation of probability" after the 1840s.[39]

A loose consensus among these thinkers was that any explanation of willing would have to involve a description of how voluntary processes mobilize, direct, and come habitually to resemble involuntary or automatic substrates.[40] The goal was to disprove the assumption, as Lewes quips, that "Instinct, like Chance, is one of the words under which men conceal their ignorance from themselves."[41] Developing an account of the "discrete power or faculty of willing," sometimes framed in terms of emergent "physical notions of force and energy," these thinkers resisted the mechanistic determinisms of "aggressive polemicists" adjacent to their camp, like Thomas Huxley, John Tyndall, and W. K. Clifford, and wrested the moral burden of the will from earlier views that simply identified action with intellect and emotion.[42] The psychophysiology of the will was both a "public discourse about science" and an investigation of "central moral questions of human identity and agency."[43] Like other discourses canvassed in this book, it was "spaciously framed in its address to common issues, and with an audience crossing wide disciplinary interests."[44] Rethinking the will and its penumbra in unwilled processes, this discourse tried to capture the complexity of human volition and its failings. As a power of the body, the will was both suspected and supervised, a target of pathological classification and cultural vigilance. If a "completely-fashioned will is the true mark of a strong mind," Maudsley cites Friedrich Novalis as saying, its incomplete formation or unraveling characterized the pathologically weak.[45] The discourse thus intertwined the idea of a human "power" beyond mechanism, which might "utilize the Automatic agencies to work out its own purposes," and the collapse of that power through "abnormal conditions in which the controlling power of the Will is in abeyance."[46]

Physiological psychology links up with the literary tradition of hesitation, with the "hesitating Dane" whom Eliot labels "speculative and irresolute" as a litmus test.[47] Reviewing John Conolly's *Study of Hamlet* (1863), Maudsley discusses Hamlet's hesitation within a physiological framework, foreshadowing later claims in *Body and Mind* (1870). The tendency of automatic reflexes to become habitual (yielding similar motor responses whether by external stimulation or internal impulse), Maudsley argues, suggests that volition is subtended by "automatic agency."[48] For Maudsley, "reflective indecision" represents a "stage of development through which minds of a certain character pass before they consciously acquire by exercise a habit of willing," the will being an artifact paradoxically "built up by successive acts of volition."[49] Alluding to *Hamlet*, he ends his first lecture musing that "there are many more things in the reciprocal action of mind and organic element than are yet dreamt of in our philosophy," and ends the second (on mental and nervous disorders) by invoking the "tyranny" of physiological factors that "unconsciously and irresistibly shape [our] ends."[50] Carpenter similarly appeals to deliberate repetition, but emphasizes the moral importance of directing our will to control the automatism on which it relies: "From the time when the human being first becomes conscious that he has a power within himself of *determining the succession* of his mental states, from that time does he begin to be a free agent; and in proportion as he acquires the power of *self-control*, does he become capable of emancipating himself from the domination of his automatic tendencies, and of turning his faculties to the most advantageous use."[51] Aware of how the will required "repeated efforts" to channel its "spontaneous impulsive power," Eliot summarizes such psychophysiological ideas in *Impressions of Theophrastus Such* (1879): "One cannot give a recipe for wise judgment: it resembles appropriate muscular action, which is attained by the myriad lessons in nicety of balance and of aim that only practice can give."[52]

With hesitation's literary and physiological contexts in place, we can see how it dictates formal aspects of *Daniel Deronda* from the opening sentence. "Was she beautiful or not beautiful?" (7) alludes to famous hesitant queries: "To be or not to be?" (*Hamlet*); "Did she do it or did she not?" (*Oresteia*).[53] An aesthetic question thus recalls existential and ethical dilemmas at the outset of a novel that saves one character from suicide and acquits another of the will to murder, while opening out narrative alternatives in which such outcomes are perfectly imaginable. Eliot's amendment of *Macbeth*, with which I began, likewise defends affect's subtlety against action's crudeness by sketching the suspended moment that cannot house mutually exclusive actions – "we cannot kill and not kill in the same moment" – but can still contain "room wide enough . . . for the outlash of a murderous thought and the sharp backward stroke of repentance" (42). Beginning in "unrest," hesitant about its own fabricated setting out, the novel's opening establishes what Barbara Hardy calls its "divided sensibility," a quality "less demonstrable in action."[54] The novel glances back to a philosophical touchstone in giving one protagonist, and the opening in general, a "dynamic quality." Eliot's publisher stumbled over "dynamic," "a *dictionary* word to so many people."[55] But his sense of its scientific meaning should be followed to its deeper root in Aristotle's term for potentiality (*dynamis*), that which allows entities to be (or not), persons to do (or not), a modal undercurrent of both action and inaction.[56]

The novel's prurient representations of gambling continue the emphasis on hesitation, with its distraction tantamount to physical stasis and its temporal suspensions opening up a sensory continuum. We read several disapproving positions on gambling, from Sir Hugo's description of a "monotonous" activity that "knits the brain up into meshes" (161) to Deronda's moralizing view of a "disease," a "besotting kind of taste" that reproduces the vices of social inequity against which it warns, there being "enough inevitable turns of fortune which force us to see that our gain is another's loss" (337). Critics often note Eliot's own distaste for gambling while also probing her insights into its core structure ("repetition without completion") and delusion ("that an induction from a limited number of examples will be in any way predictive").[57] But the arch tone of Eliot's statements also conceals salutary possibilities in these suspended mental states. Even when the narrator airs a conventional physiological view of the "gambling appetite" as "more absolutely dominant than bodily hunger," her description holds a floating parenthesis that marks the more complex state of hesitation: the "passion for watching chances – the habitual suspensive poise of the mind in actual or imaginary play – nullifies the susceptibility to other excitation" (773). My account of inductive vanity showed how the misprision of probability could be both mathematical and epistemic, both gambler's fallacy and derailment of inductive logic. The picture of hesitation I have been outlining recasts that vanity within a psychophysiological paradigm that opens up productive ways of thinking about uncertain motivation and action.

Contemporary work in cognitive psychology and behavioral economics has stressed the enduring appeal of gambling as a model for motivational dysfunction – for the types of irrational decision and temporary preference reversal we find in Eliot. In an influential account developed by the psychiatrist George Ainslie, people are prone to warp the way they evaluate future states, preferring rewards that are smaller (but available sooner) over those that are larger (but accessible later). Such "hyperbolic discounting" undergirds Ainslie's provocative vision of the self as a "population" of agents defending their interests with varying intensity over time.[58] In this view, individuals constitute a "population of reward-seeking operations that survive insofar as they actually obtain reward," yielding a "motivational marketplace" where our subpersonal interests bargain with one another, as if they were factions engaged in "partial cooperation" or "limited warfare."[59] For Ainslie the will just is this intertemporal, game-theoretic model of cooperation, the "recursive process that bets the expected value of your future self-control against each of your successive temptations" and that attempts to elicit self-consistency by "subject[ing] your behavior to personal rules and mak[ing] it consistent over time."[60] Building on Ainslie, work at the intersection of economic theory and cognitive science argues that gambling is *the* formal paradigm for other addictions. In behavioral terms, it commandeers the temporal preference for the smaller, sooner reward over the larger, later one; in cognitive terms, it engages neurochemical reactions no different from those in expectation of stimulants. Gambling, like other addictions, effects what Don Ross and colleagues call a "midbrain mutiny" in our reward system, where short-term interests maximize their utility over longer-term ones. The resulting weakness of will is distinct from *akrasia* in the history of philosophy.[61] This research has a strong connection to Victorian psychophysiology (Ainslie mentions Bain, Sully, and James on willpower and personal rules), reestablishing a link that was cut by trends in psychology in the late nineteenth and early twentieth centuries.[62] It complicates philosophical accounts of rational resolve, intention stability, and temporally extended planning, and erodes the emphasis on utility maximization in the motivations of agents.[63]

Two examples from Eliot illustrate how these abstract models echo representations of hesitation and uncertain motivation in the nineteenth century. The first concerns Lapidoth, the wayward father of Mordecai and Mirah, who steals from Deronda. While he entertains alternately a "forecast" and "prospective regret" about how much money to solicit, the prospect of a larger and later reward evaporates in those "airy conditions preparatory to a receipt which remained indefinite" (789). Lapidoth notices Deronda's ring out in the open and "by no distinct change of resolution, rather by a dominance of desire" (790), almost accidentally absconds with it, illustrating Maudsley's claim that "actions for a definite end, having indeed the semblance of predesigning consciousness and will, may be quite unconscious and automatic."[64] In this small-scale vision of the self at odds with itself, the instantly gratified agent thwarts the interests of the expectant one. Lapidoth's impulsivity usurps his longer-term desires. He surrenders to reward in what Eliot elsewhere calls "that pleasureless yielding to the small solicitations of circumstance."[65]

The second example is from *Middlemarch* (1871–72), and concerns that hapless youth and case study in hyperbolic discounting, Fred Vincy. When confronted about raising expectations on Featherstone's probable bequest, Fred is swayed by the prospect of a close reward, it being "almost harder to part with the immediate prospect of bank-notes than with the more distant prospect of the land" (108). In a sequence of moralized mistakes, Fred discounts future states to satiate present desires, talking up an uncertain inheritance to assuage debtors and purchasing a horse in a speculative attempt to recoup assets. Before receiving less money than he expected from Featherstone, his "hopeful disposition" gets the better of him:

> When Fred got into debt, it always seemed to him highly probable that something or other – he did not necessarily conceive what – would come to pass enabling him to pay in due time. And now that the providential occurrence was apparently close at hand, it would have been sheer absurdity to think that the supply would be short of the need: as absurd as a faith that believed in half a miracle for want of strength to believe in a whole one. (131)

Yet Fred also recognizes the ravages of his self-defeating acts. He erects an external safeguard (what Ainslie calls a personal rule), giving most of the money to his mother and so "tak[ing] some security against his own liability" (138). If *Middlemarch* is less engaged with the later novel's perplexing hesitation, it nonetheless models the self as a fluctuating population. Fred's self-rule involves a difference between his "inner self" and its momentary others; Lydgate bears "two selves within him," which "must learn to accommodate each other and bear reciprocal impediments," as if bargaining across time (133, 150). Both examples can, of course, be chalked up to more familiar moral failings like bad faith (the "fantasy of foreclosure" whereby "a desired future is subtly absorbed into the present," in D. A. Miller's reading of *Middlemarch*'s "scripts of desire") or egoism (which "impairs prudence" and "prevents agents from making sacrifices for long-term goals," in Patrick Fessenbecker's account of Lapidoth).[66] Yet hyperbolic discounting, distinct in being chiefly individual and psychological rather than relational and ethical, as well as partly corrigible, offers a sharper model of the challenges hesitation poses to selfhood and moral action.

Where *Middlemarch* observes how "some of us, with quick alternate vision, see beyond our infatuations, and even while we rave on the heights, behold the wide plain where our persistent self pauses and awaits us" (151), *Daniel Deronda* declares no such Nebo of normative consistency.

Its heroine's terror of wide spaces makes clear that no durable self awaits. Using psychophysiological ideas to go beyond realism's "conception of a unified, integrated character," as Sally Shuttleworth notes, Eliot offers us a labyrinthine picture of self-states that evades even the most complex descriptions of hesitation, which still assume resistance in a single direction.[67] Where Vogl writes of a "vestibule of acting" that proceeds to its main structure, and Ricoeur of the process *from* hesitation *to* choice, Eliot presents Gwendolen's as a choice that never resolves "antecedent indetermination" into "univocal project."[68] "Men, like planets, have both a visible and an invisible history," we read, so if narration were akin to astronomy one "would have to thread the hidden pathways of feeling and thought which lead up to every moment of action, and to those moments of intense suffering which take the quality of action" (164). Oddly, *action* is described here in terms that join etymologically with *passivity* (from Latin *patiri*, "to suffer," "to undergo"), and critics have argued that Eliot's analyses of motive sometimes blur agency and passivity, presenting "suffering as a form of activity."[69] On my account of Eliot, hesitation moves beyond this. It is distinct from inaction and the inconsequential states of "uncounted experience" Anne-Lise François calls "recessive action."[70] It disorients the cohesion of single projects and unidirectional action, following the "secret windings and recesses" of inner life (420) to open out a provocative picture of action as a condensation of intensities along a continuum. If inductive vanity models an inept rapidity of prediction and action, hesitation offers a corrective in its dynamic potentiality, its maze of delay. Hesitation is our failsafe in providing neither the will nor the way.

My Minds Are Not My Own

> You see I have two minds, and both are foolish.
> Sometimes a torrent rushing through my soul
> Escapes in wild strange wishes.
>
> —Eliot, *The Spanish Gypsy*[71]

Having outlined Eliot's interest in literary and psychological traditions of hesitation, and its thematic and formal roles in *Daniel Deronda*, I now follow this phenomenon into the recesses of character. Co-opted by hesitation, Gwendolen's resolve fractures into two distinct modes of decision-making. The first, which I characterize as *decision by proxy*, occupies the novel's first third through the realization of Grandcourt's prior relationship and Gwendolen's flight to Europe. Choice is paralyzed by hesitation and requires the intervention of third parties. Gwendolen hovers in volitional energy between scarcity and surplus, and is passively brought to a decision (though not the one sanctioned by her family) through external constraints. The second mode enlists figures of fluidity to frame *decision by drift*. Here, too, hesitation radically undermines decision by extending beyond the moment of choice to retain (and eventually reinstate) prior contingency. Tracing Gwendolen's drift toward acceptance of Grandcourt's proposal and her continuing resistance to the marriage's one-sided power dynamic, I show how her mental state leading up to the fatal accident formally reprises the couple's earliest interactions. Her decision to marry is thus undone through hesitant tenacity rather than intentional action, restoring her to a prior potentiality of choice.

From the outset, Gwendolen's relation to Grandcourt is marked by vacillation. In describing their first meeting, Eliot resorts to an unusual narrative device, a mode of mental transcription Leavis called "psychological notation."[72] As if literalizing the claim, in the epigraph to Chapter 11, that the "beginning of an acquaintance whether with persons or things is to get a definite outline for our ignorance" (111), Eliot reports her character's thoughts in bursts of suspension: "(Pause, during which she imagined various degrees and modes of opinion about herself that might be entertained by Grandcourt)"; "(Pause, during which Gwendolen, having taken a rapid observation of Grandcourt, made a brief graphic description of him to an indefinite hearer)" (112). We follow as she variously "recalled," "decided," "wondered," "reflected," "speculated," and, in the process, "felt the strength of her own insight, supposing the question had to be decided" (112–13). But while these formulaic pauses apparently report mental processes, they satirize what might be gained by such a commentary. They separate out the putative lovers and their appraisals (even in the act of bringing them together), and set in motion the staccato suppositions that continue through the nominal decision.

If we view this scene as reworking Eliot's excursus in *Adam Bede*, "In which the story pauses a little," hesitation – hiatus, suspension, parenthesis – is aligned with realism.[73] The scene reveals the physiological concomitants of voluntary and involuntary response, from the breathtaking shock of Gwendolen's first view of Grandcourt to the "unwonted flush in her cheeks and the sense of surprise which made her feel less mistress of herself than usual" (114). Grandcourt's glancing proposition is conveyed in two bodily timescales: Gwendolen's alternating sensations, "first blushing, and then turning pale," and his dilated "rate of judgment" (133). Temporality is scrambled by jagged pauses and Gwendolen's "uneasy consciousness of divided impulses which threatened her with repentance of her own acts" (133–34), as though anticipating the future that will hold this present in regret. She speaks "hesitatingly" (136), but nothing, she mistakenly imagines, presages "any subjugation of her will" (132). Her uncertainties are internally registered – "I am in doubt myself" (139) – and externally evident, when Grandcourt asks whether she is "as uncertain about yourself as you make others about you" (135).

These hesitations – in bodily reaction and mental operation – show Gwendolen's lapse from inductive vanity, which needed "everyone to understand that she was going to do just as she liked, and that they had better not calculate on pleasing them" (132).[74] At first, she maintains her self-possessive view of probability, thinking that "after all she was not going to accept Grandcourt" (113) moments after being introduced. Later that evening, while dancing and sensing his attentions, she entertains his implicit proposal only as a negative occasion, when "it began to appear probable that she would have it in her power to reject him" (121). Still later, the grammar of her reported thoughts lapses into indecisive repetition: "on the whole she wished to marry him; he suited her purpose; her prevailing, deliberate intention was, to accept him. . . . But was she going to fulfil her deliberate intention? She began to be afraid of herself, and to find out a certain difficulty in doing as she liked" (138). Insofar as Gwendolen becomes unpredictable *to herself*, the consistency required of a "planning agent" is vitiated; the stability of selfhood, understood as a set of "narrated structures that enhance individuals' predictability, both to themselves and to others," undermined.[75] She is overwhelmed by a choice to remove her freedom of choice – a *de-liberation*.[76] Her tarrying becomes vertiginous:

> Even in Gwendolen's mind that result was one of two likelihoods that presented themselves alternately, one of two decisions toward which she was being precipitated, as if they were two sides of a boundary-line, and she did not know on which she should fall. This subjection to a possible self, a self not to be absolutely predicted about, caused her some astonishment and terror; her favorite key of life – doing as she liked – seemed to fail her, and she could not foresee what at a given moment she might like to do. (136)

Akin to the object cast in a geometric probability trial (Eliot lifts the image from Proctor), or perhaps the ball in roulette, Gwendolen is poised between likelihoods whose value she dare not tilt toward either outcome, without standards of comparison to assess her future selves.[77] As the narrator drolly observes, "ignorance gives one a large range of probabilities" (137).[78]

Her difficulties are compounded by the incalculability of Grandcourt, an abstract character for whom the hypothetical is a *modus vivendi*. He is an "almost certain baronet," a "probable peer" (140). His passions are "of the intermittent, flickering kind," an awful counterpoint to Gwendolen's "iridescence" (156, 42). In the "slowly-churning chances of his mind," thoughts are "like the circlets one sees in a dark pool continually dying out and continually started again by some impulse from below the surface" (319).[79] His valet of fifteen years judges him with difficulty, the "probable effect" of general information being "quite incalculable" given his inscrutability in any "particular case" (281). Even the narrator abjures certainty about this "mind made up of moods" (278). A model of the surfeited consumer, as Catherine Gallagher notes, Grandcourt's psyche is characterized by "a suspension of the sequencing necessary for the accomplishment of any goal."[80] His character is saturated with negation in life and in death, when "he is not rescued."[81]

When Grandcourt hesitates, it is between certainties, not doubts. The novel shows how his "tendency to harden under beseeching" (341) has brought difficulties for his mistress Lydia, another woman who "depended on his will" (343). The same holds for Gwendolen:

> He had never admitted to himself that Gwendolen might refuse him, but – heaven help us all! – we are often unable to act on our certainties; our objection to a contrary issue (were it possible) is so strong that it rises like a spectral illusion between us and our certainty; we are rationally sure that the blind worm can not bite us mortally, but it would be so intolerable to be bitten, and the creature has a biting look – we decline to handle it. (130)

Grandcourt thus refuses to act on a flirtatious hint "which the change in her manner made apparently decisive of her favourable intention," because he "would not make his offer in any way that could place him definitely in the position of being rejected" (148, 133). Nonetheless, he "wanted to have done with the uncertainty that belonged to his not having spoken" (131). "The gain of knowing you," he drawls, "makes me feel the time I lose in uncertainty," yet he presses Gwendolen not toward clear intentions but back into opaque equivocation. "Do *you* like uncertainty?" (147) he asks, to which she responds, puzzled, "There is more in it" (148).

Mutual paradoxes of choice frame this vacillating state of affairs. Gwendolen will only give herself over to a choice that retains the pure form of choice, the "power of doing a great deal of what she liked to do" (137). This recalls her earlier assertions of a "spontaneous sense of capability" (40) after the Davilow family's ruin, and her tautologies about retaining decisive power without particular decisions: "I must decide for myself"; "My life is my own affair" (235). Instead of concrete goals, she envisions a continuing capacity to choose, visualizing marriage as a "dreary state, in which a woman could not do what she liked" (39). Grandcourt, by contrast, seeks the pure form of restricting choice. As Gallagher notes, his "sated condition has concentrated his remaining pleasurable sensations in the exercise of willing alone."[82] He looks to be the "master of a woman who would have liked to master him" (320) and refrains from explicit coercion only because "his will must impose itself without trouble" (350).[83] Through deception he treats her instrumentally, taking her goals as means to his ends. He does not reveal his knowledge that Gwendolen has discovered Lydia, nor does he allow her to get away with clandestine meetings with Deronda.[84] These paradoxes are formally replicated in narration, which alternates open-ended pauses and efforts to close down the plot.[85] The narrator says Gwendolen "would willingly have had weights hung on her own caprice" (139), as if dragging her to a decision, while also making clear that she will submit only if limitless possibilities would be thereby guaranteed.

In this first mode of decision – consent by proxy, a framework often applied to those who are not (yet) capable of their own decisions – Eliot allows us to witness internal complexity but drives the plot through the simpler external comportment of (male) characters.[86] If Gwendolen could formerly find "external testimony" (251) by looking in a mirror, she now finds that to "consider what 'anybody' would say, was to be released from the difficulty of judging where everything was obscure to her when feeling had ceased to be decisive." The "verdict of 'anybody'" (298) is more pressing than her own, and her own choices are routed via external agents. Grandcourt's wily strategies foment "assurance" in public opinion about a forthcoming marriage, which in the mind of its representative, Gwendolen's uncle, "converted itself into a resolution to do his duty by his niece" (130). When her mother reports that Gwendolen is "in some uncertainty about her own mind, but inclined on the whole to acceptance," Mr. Gascoigne intervenes with an "admonitory speech": "The ideas it raised had the force of sensations. Her resistant courage would not help her here, because her uncle was not urging her against her own resolve; he was pressing upon her the motives of dread which she already felt; he was making her more conscious of the risks that lay within herself" (142). Gwendolen resists his "control" (31, 97), but this episode sets a pattern of proxy consent that eventually overwhelms her.

No proxy influence is more efficacious than Lydia, whose letter urges Gwendolen to a meeting and claims that if she is "*in doubt*" about accepting Grandcourt, she will discover "*something to decide her*" (149).

The transitive makes Gwendolen the *object* of a decision rather than a deliberating subject. It effects a temporary resolution: "If I am to be miserable, let it be by my own choice" (155). Her previously "indistinct grounds of hesitation" disappear in a "final repulsion" through a "force of impulse" (297). She flees the site of decision and makes her way to Europe, where we encounter her at the novel's outset. Again, Eliot's narrative structure mimics the unstable patterns of this first mode: in the *fabula* the gambling scene follows the indecisive courtship, but it comes first in the *sjuzhet*. A gambling frenzy is thus formally posited as both antecedent to and consequent on dispassionate marital forecasting.

The second mode, decision by drift, is announced in the ominous passive of the subsequent book's title: "Gwendolen Gets Her Choice." Now aware of Grandcourt's mistress and children, Gwendolen has reason enough against the match. But the narrowing of financial options raises the stakes of her "sick motivelessness" (274). So, "against the imperious lot which left her no choice," she reads Grandcourt's letter renewing his suit "with hopeless inward rebellion" and a choice opens out from the "inescapable path of repulsive monotony" (292). She is thrown back in his direction, drifted into a new disposition: "Where was the good of choice coming again? What did she wish? Anything different? No! and yet in the dark seed-growths of consciousness a new wish was forming itself" (292). In merely responding to the letter, Gwendolen feels anew the need for proxy support: the "contradictory desire to be hastened," since "hurry would save her from deliberate choice" (293), gives her a "reason for keeping away from an absolute decision" and "leav[ing] open as many issues as possible" (294).

The motto of the chapter where Gwendolen's decision finally occurs alters the frame from hesitant suspense to liquid dynamics: "Desire has trimmed the sails, and Circumstance / Brings but the breeze to fill them" (296). Alluding to a classical image for action and self-binding (Odysseus and the Sirens), often updated in modern accounts of volition, Eliot presents the will as a physical system where small pressures are "continually entering with cumulative force into a mood until it gets the mass and momentum of a theory or a motive" (228).[87] This recalls an earlier instance of fluid decision-making governing a character of "perverse resolve" in *The Mill on the Floss* (1860).[88] In a chapter entitled "Borne Along by the Tide," Maggie Tulliver is boating with Stephen Guest, carried "by this stronger present that seemed to bear her along without any act of her own will, like the added self which comes with the sudden exalting influence of a strong tonic" (407). They drift along, shrouded by an "enchanted haze," and Stephen rows "idly, half automatically" (407). When he relies on these conditions to press his suit, she responds: "You have wanted to deprive me of any choice" (409). But after identifying her loss of agency, Maggie – like Gwendolen – finds "an unspeakable charm in being told what to do, and having everything decided for her," and is "hardly conscious of having said or done anything decisive" (410). Dramatizing the psychophysiological states subtending action and inaction, the mirage of selves propagated by hesitation, this floating stupor also characterizes consent in the later novel: "All yielding is attended with a less vivid consciousness than resistance; it is the partial sleep of thought; it is the submergence of our own personality by another" (410).[89]

In *Daniel Deronda* decision by drift is diffused across the narrative rather than clustering around an iconic event or proxy individual. As Leavis notes, Eliot creates a "system of pressures so intolerable . . . and so enclosing, that [Gwendolen's] final acceptance of Grandcourt seems to issue, not from her will, but from them."[90] She experiences "perpetually alternating images and arguments for and against the possibility" of marriage, but her former resolve is "no more a part of quivering life than the 'God's will be done' of one who is eagerly watching chances" (297). The image of fluctuating consideration, formerly represented in the spin of the roulette wheel, now appears as an experience of vertigo, as if Gwendolen were aboard a ship whose prow breaks the horizon, "the alternate dip of counterbalancing thoughts begotten of counterbalancing desires [bringing] her into a state in which no conclusion could look fixed" (297). As on a craft steered by another, Gwendolen "only drifted towards the tremendous decision: – but drifting depends on something besides the currents, when the sails have been set beforehand" (303). Her motivating energy, as Gallagher observes, is "backed up like a faulty hydraulic system" and she "tends towards stasis and inactivity."[91] Her decision, finally, comes as a reversal of her earlier resistance to instrumentality: "Other people allowed themselves to be made slaves of," she had scoffed, "and to have their lives blown hither and thither like empty ships in which no will was present," whereas she would "make the very best of the chances that life offered her, and conquer circumstance by her exceptional cleverness" (39). Reverting to a view of herself as incomparable, she accepts Grandcourt and "gets her choice." The character "who had been used to feel sure of herself, and ready to manage others," the narrator summarizes, "had just taken a decisive step which she had beforehand thought that she would not take" (311).[92]

Yet inertial drift, the aftermath state of hesitation, persists. On one hand, Gwendolen can imagine that her "agitating experience" has been set aside and looks forward to "a fuller power of managing circumstance" (355). On the other, "some dim forecast, the insistent penetration of suppressed experience," blends the "expectation of a triumph with the dread of a crisis" (357). From her wedding day on, "her resolution was dogged by the shadow of that previous resolve [about Lydia] which had at first come as the undoubting movement of her whole being" (311). This "uncertain shadow" (430) sees actions as inexorably trailed:

> Deeds are the pulse of Time, his beating life,
> And righteous or unrighteous, being done,
> Must throb in after-throbs till Time itself
> Be laid in stillness, and the universe
> Quiver and breathe upon no mirror more. (698)

Eliot's sententious motto captures what Vogl calls the "phantom" of action, the "state of suspension that remains present in every actualization and realization."[93] The bright line of decision is accompanied by the dazzling afterimages of uncertainty. Where Gwendolen earlier allegorized herself by turns as "Lady Certainty" and "Lady Perhaps" (356), she now contends with more sinister personae: the "two pale phantoms" of "Temptation" and "Dread" (674), and another pair, adopted from a Heinrich Heine poem, "Das Glück" and "Frau Unglück" (736).

The bleakest sections of the novel describe the crushing of Gwendolen's will through Grandcourt's callous foreclosure of her choices. Having sustained her "last great gambling loss" (441) in marriage, where "losing was not simply a *minus*, but a terrible *plus* that had never entered into her reckoning" (598), the "sense of freedom" (303) following decision passes to a "sense of inferiority" (547). Grandcourt may have entered marriage with a "vacillating whim" (584), but he hardly wavers in finding "new objects to exert his will upon" (585). He reduces the relationship to a purely formal contest of will, where Gwendolen is incapable of contradictory impulse and he becomes "a blank uncertainty to her in everything but this, that he would do just what he willed" (426). Eliot's depiction of the marriage turns repeatedly to figures of suffocation, the arid vestiges of volition: Gwendolen lives in a "painted gilded prison" (590), Grandcourt governs her "with bit and bridle" (680), his "words had the power of thumbscrews and the cold touch of the rack" (680), and so forth.

Even as remorse and a sense of responsibility blossom, Gwendolen's continuing uncertainty about her agentive options within marriage repeat the images of proxy decision and the physiological figures of hesitation. One model for renewed purpose is to imagine herself as a rider, to secure "a determination to do as she would do as if she had started on horseback" (313), another classical analogy for the will adopted by Victorian psycho-physiologists.[94] But just as this activity was linked to compromised agency before her decision, Gwendolen now finds that things are "as if she had consented to mount a chariot where another held the reins" (328). Eliot's allusion to Plato's allegory of the soul as a charioteer (managing mind, will, and desire) makes Gwendolen's subjection clear.[95] Again, where she had previously felt drawn to Deronda, after marriage he "in some mysterious way ... was becoming part of her conscience" (415). Her "precipitancy of confidence towards him, in contrast with her habitual resolute conceal-ment" (445) yields more occasions on which she defers to his judgment – "It is you who will decide" (563) – and he becomes almost the only prop for her vertiginous will, "like the firmness of the earth, the only condition of her walking" (796).

If decision by proxy persists after Gwendolen's choice, principally in the person of Deronda, so does decision by drift. In both modes, the persever-ance of hesitation expresses a desire that necessity be reconverted into contingency – that singular outcomes return to plural possibilities of choice. The chapter where Grandcourt drowns in a sailboat accident off the coast of Genoa is prefaced by a quotation from Shelley ("The unwilling brain / Feigns often what it would not") that recalls the fluid tensions within willing, "those fatal meshes which are woven within more closely than without" (668). How to characterize (and hold responsible) a mere wish frames the novel's final sequences. Against Grandcourt's authoritarian control, the "dreamy do-nothing absolutism" (668) of yachting around the Mediterranean simply to subject her to inactivity, Gwendolen generates out of "irritable, fluctuating stages of despair" the "imaginary annihilation of the detested object" (673). These "plans of evil" make her "afraid of her own wishes," circumventing conscious control to take "shapes possible and impossible, like a cloud of demon-faces," "furies preparing the deed that they would straightway avenge" (681). Where her earlier vacillations concerned the decision to begin a marriage, these darker hesitations focus on the prohibited desire for its absolute end.

Recollecting this mental struggle between "two creatures" to Deronda, her confession replays the paratactic style of her first meeting with her husband, confirming the transit – via hesitation – from necessity back to contingency: "I felt beforehand I had done something dreadful, unalter-able – that would make me like an evil spirit" (691); "I fancied impossible ways of – "; "I did kill him in my thoughts" (695). This phenomenology of deferred fancies and mentally rehearsed murder also recalls the structure of decision by proxy: "I know nothing – I only know that I saw my wish outside me" (696). After several male figures – Gascoigne, Klesmer, Grandcourt, Deronda – actively tried to eventuate their wishes in her, Gwendolen now passively witnesses her wishes manifested in a scenario to which she has not causally contributed. Deronda's view that Grandcourt's death was an "accident that [Gwendolen] could not have hindered" (690) unduly normalizes her psychic complexity. He sees her malice afore-thought as restricted to a mental domain – it has "gone on only in your thought" (692) – and his legal assessment is that it is "almost certain that her murderous thought had had no outward effect" (696).[96] But matters cannot be so straightforward given a picture of psychophysiological motiv-ation where, as Lewes notes, "To imagine an act is to rehearse it mentally. By such mental rehearsal the motor organs are ... disposed to respond in act. Hence it is that a long-meditated crime becomes at last an irresistible criminal impulse."[97] Gwendolen confesses to one action she "never undid" (691): procuring a "small and sharp" object (687), locking it in a drawer, and throwing the key overboard. Unlike Eliot's character Caterina in "Mr. Gilfil's Love Story" (1857), who is carrying a dagger when she happens upon the body of the man she wanted to kill, there is no actual liability here. To echo Victorian legal terms Eliot would have known, such an "attempt" (intentionally securing the means for violent action) would be invalidated by the lack of a causal link.[98] Yet in Gwendolen's "one act" (691) of tarrying – leasing then retracting a potential for harm – we see an attempt to restore an earlier potentiality. Through hesitation, Gwendolen may again become, in the deepest sense, *dynamic*.

In Eliot's distinctive moralizing voice, Deronda tries to deflect Gwendolen from worrying about criminality to sublimating her guilty energy in moral action:

> That momentary murderous will cannot, I think, have altered the course of events. Its effect is confined to the motives in your own breast. Within ourselves our evil will is momentous, and sooner or later it works its way outside us – it may be in the vitiation that breeds evil acts, but also it may be in the self-abhorrence that stings us into better striving. (699)

His advice is to "find our duties in what comes to us, not in what we imagine might have been" (701). He wants to curtail Gwendolen's hesita-tions, dismissing her counterfactuals in favor of restitution to Lydia. Her sense that Deronda's outlook offers a "new footing" (430) parallels his own figurative advice. "Turn your fear into a safeguard," he offers, as though keeping on a moral track were like looking around for a handrail on a precipice: "Try to take hold of your sensibility, and use it as if it were a faculty" (452). This disembodied counsel, which makes "self-judgment" into "comparative activity" (451), bears a structural similarity to psycho-physiological writers who recognized that, faced with "temptations to immoral action," willing such thoughts away would only fuel them further, whereas shifting to a "wholesome and useful pursuit" might form the ground of a new moral life.[99] In contemporary terms, we might see Gwendolen being urged to adopt personal rules against preference reversal through "extrapsychic commitment," or to cultivate the intention stability of a planner who "can make a present choice in favor of a valued sequence of future actions or a valued policy to act in certain ways on certain occasions."[100] The novel's summary epigraph poses a different, more radical kind of advice:

> Let thy chief terror be of thine own soul:
> There, 'mid the throng of hurrying desires
> That trample on the dead to seize their spoil,
> Lurks vengeance.....

The counsel to be afraid of one's own terrible capacities matches Deronda's statements. But the genitive flirts with another reading: allow your "chief terror" to belong to you alone. Gwendolen remains in a "state of unconscious reliance and expectation" toward Deronda, a more benign form of proxy action the narrator adapts into a maxim: "We diffuse our feeling over others, and count on their acting from our motives" (771). Yet her hesitation is ineradicable. These lines suggest she should focus less on taking fear of herself as a "safeguard" than on cultivating a more powerful form of autonomy: to have a fear of her own.

Pathologies of the Will

In my argument thus far, hesitancy does double duty as pathological state and moral safeguard: it's a fault of Gwendolen's character that, in the end, renews agentive potential. Many assessments of her character, however, aim to fix her to a single pathology. Jacqueline Rose calls Gwendolen the "original literary hysteric," and many have concurred.[101] Simon During suggests monomania, a term the novel uses to describe Mordechai (494, 510).[102] David Trotter identifies agoraphobia in Gwendolen's fear of unbounded spaces, her sensitive reactions to changes of light, and her "dialectic of outward triumph and inward helplessness."[103] This sort of critical diagnosis, I contend in this section, obscures the value of hesitancy as a practical attitude and limits the novel's exploration of uncertainty in decision-making to medical terms, rather than the wider and more useful rubric of compromised volition.

Diagnostic readings do illuminate aspects of Gwendolen's character. But because they rely on the same vague descriptors that mark out her sensibility as "peculiar" or "unusual" (25, 58), such accounts traffic in an unwarranted conceptual specificity. If Gwendolen reacts with "nervous shock" and "hysterical violence" to Lydia's letter (359), the discourse of hysteria offers only partial answers. Hysterical women were seen as rebellious, "exhibiting more than usual force and decision of character, of strong resolution, fearless of danger, bold riders, having plenty of what is termed *nerve*," as F. C. Skey's 1866 lectures put it.[104] But Gwendolen has both the symptoms and their opposites. She could plausibly fit various diagnostic criteria. Why not "mental alienation" (493), another category mentioned in the novel? If agoraphobia, why not "persecution-madness," a related category that might capture the "self-dread which urged her to flee from the pursuing images wrought by her pent-up impulse" (673)?[105] What about an anthropological cause, given the narrator's identification of her "streak of superstition" as a survival, "a superstition which lingers in an intense personality even in spite of theory and science" (276)?

Alternating diagnoses – alternation *as diagnosis* – seems more apt. We can find a clue to Gwendolen's unpredictable propensities in what James Paget (a clinician who attended Lewes and Eliot) called "nervous mimicry," a hypochondria where the nervous system intensifies the experience of illness through imitation. In Paget's description of the "neuromimesis" of egotism, which Eliot jotted into a notebook and uses in the image of Gwendolen "simply following her antipathy and inclination, confiding in them as she did in the more reflective judgments into which they entered as sap into leafage" (124), he writes that the malady "seems always in an undercurrent, rising at every interval between the distractions of work or play."[106] This nonspecific, essentially hesitant condition is an outgrowth of indecision, and points to a more general approach to character pathology. We should remember that Eliot includes advance warning about categorical specificity. Deronda's nature is praised, when confronted with Mordecai, for being "too large, too ready to conceive regions beyond his own experience, to rest at once in the easy explanation, 'madness'" (494).[107] Eliot disqualifies her novel from what has been termed "disease specificity" – seeing diseases as "entities existing outside their unique manifestations," "defined and legitimated in terms of characteristic somatic mechanisms."[108]

Instead, we could recognize in Gwendolen a family resemblance of *pathologies of the will*. As the historian German Berrios argues, nineteenth-century psychopathology included overlapping dysfunctions, from melancholia, monomania, and mental alienation to pathologized versions of *akrasia* and weakness of will, including aboulia (lack of will-power), agoraphobia (incapacity of will in open spaces), and *folie du doute* (excessive hesitancy).[109] These disorders overlapped. *Akrasia* is a symptom of hysteria for Maudsley, who also describes "quasi-hysterical melancholia" in adolescents as characterized by indefinite spirituality, vague fears, and "morbid fancies."[110] Mental alienation and monomania fall under "uncontrollableness" in Lewes's review of suicidal motives, which discusses literary representations of the "passion of vehement sudden afflux."[111] Monomania, for Lewes, also shades into anxiety, with its "intensity of apprehensiveness" borne of the "diseased activity of the imagination in picturing consequences."[112] In *Daniel Deronda*, such generic pathologies of volition are more useful than precise diagnoses. For instance, what Trotter reads as agoraphobia in Gwendolen's fear of "any wide scene" and of "immeasurable existence" can be recast as volitional default, because when she recovers it is to the "usual world in which her will was of some avail" (63, 64).[113] Since hers is the "will of a creature with a large discourse of imaginative fears" (423), it makes sense that Gwendolen would fall into several categories.

These diagnostic tags recall the psychophysiology of hesitation, characterizing an individual whose inhibition and hierarchical control of volition are compromised, and who embodies a site of resistance to a culture in thrall to rational decision-making. As Vogl notes, "the more systemic action is divorced from the reasoning and the impulses of individuals, the more motivation, cause and reason for acting become individual problems."[114] The most characteristic of Gwendolen's "hysterical" moments draws on the representational history of hesitation. In the *tableau vivant* episode, playing a scene from *The Winter's Tale* where a statue comes alive, she starts when the painted image of a dead face is revealed and becomes "a statue into which a soul of Fear had entered," an emblem of action *in potentia*, neither still nor in motion.[115] This episode is characterized as a hiatus in character, "an unexplained exception from her normal life" that confirms a psychological instability, her "liability . . . to fits of spiritual dread" (63).[116] By reading such a scene in terms of pathologies of the will, we can better capture the novel's psychology of character and reflect on its representations of compromised (not necessarily diseased) volition in light of categories that risk anachronism when treated too exclusively.

We can also discover harmony in critical dissensus. If hesitation dilates the time of decision while also operating through narrative seizures, we can

read the novel as anti-epiphanic (as Sue Zemka and Irene Tucker do) and
register its concurrent interest in shock and surprise, in experiences that
shake characters out of selfish expectation and humdrum imagination (as
Jill Matus and Caroline Levine do).[117] We can track the novel's engulfing
dilemmas of volition, motivation, action, and *akrasia* (in the views of
Stefanie Markovits, Catherine Gallagher, and Andrew Miller), and also
recognize where its heroine "reclaims some modicum of choice" (in Hilary
Schor's view).[118] We can attend to how Eliot uses descriptions of reflexive
or unconscious processes to stress the embodied nature of such dilemmas
(per Vanessa Ryan) while noticing the novel's rational positions, its "cultivation of detachment" (Amanda Anderson) and commitment to the
"omnipotence of thought" (Adela Pinch).[119] Athena Vrettos's claim that
Gwendolen's state forms a "counternarrative ... not fully explained in or
contained by the text's dominant narrative structure," carrying irresolution
beyond the text, can coexist with the fact that her narrative comes to
closure as she is abandoned by Daniel and Mirah, pilgrims for Zion.[120]
Hesitation is a critical stance. It respects the impulses of symptomatic
reading while flattening symptoms as such. Moving between the moral
psychology of individual states and the larger aggregates of probable
outcomes, hesitation elevates the pause into an interpretive attitude.

Comparison, Our Precious Guide

Hesitation as an aftermath state is marked by hypothetical statements
about alternative futures and counterfactual pasts: "if only things could
have been a little otherwise then, so as to have been greatly otherwise
after!" (68). The narrator dismisses this "futile sort of wishing" (68), but it
does constitute a mode of comparative judgment – "comparison between
what might have been" and "what actually was" (429) – that opens out an
ethical stance.[121] Gwendolen's blithe avoidance of principles for inductive
thinking is corrected, at the level of affect and physiology, by hesitation
and volitional pathology, I have been suggesting. By contrast, Deronda's
self-correction, in relation to the past, showcases an aptitude central to
Eliot's visions of sympathy and social progress: *comparison*. Eliot was
familiar with comparison as a feature of inductive method from the outset
of her intellectual career. Drawing on eighteenth-century natural history,
and fusing earlier discourses of comparison (in rhetoric) and analogy (in
natural theology and moral philosophy), the "comparative turn" spurred a
shift of approach in several nineteenth-century disciplines, including philology, history, law, politics, anthropology, and religion.[122] As Devin

Griffiths has shown, Eliot was primed for these developments through her editorial work with the *Westminster Review* and her engagement with biblical criticism and social history.[123] Her understanding of comparison was surely deepened by encountering its different articulations in William Whewell's history and philosophy of scientific reasoning, John Stuart Mill's "methods" of inductive logic, Auguste Comte's "comparative method," and Herbert Spencer's social evolutionism.[124] Comparison functions in Eliot's work, I argue, as a mode of navigating uncertainty that impels sympathy, understood as an expansive power whose reach is guaranteed through "closer comparison between the knowledge which we call rational & the experience which we call emotional."[125]

Eliot constantly mines comparison as philosophical touchstone and imaginative example. Reviewing Otto Friedrich Gruppe's history of German philosophy, she observes of logical generalization that "every judgment exhibits itself as a comparison, or perception of likeness in the midst of difference," and offers a similar point about R. M. Mackay's *Progress of the Intellect* (1851), describing "that wide comparison which is a requisite for all true, scientific generalization."[126] Eliot reuses the phrase in *The Mill on the Floss*, when the narrator mocks Tom Tulliver: "it is only by a wide comparison of facts that the wisest full-grown man can distinguish well-rolled barrels from more supernal thunder."[127] Comparison as method broadens its reach across Eliot's intellectual domains: reading John Lubbock's *Pre-Historic Times* (1865) alongside "that semi-savage poem" the *Iliad*, she quips that "our religious oracles would do well to study savage ideas by a method of comparison with their own."[128] Wryly advising that comparative method adopt a self-reflexive lens, Eliot makes visible the surprising shifts in temporal perspective and generic classification (Homer as "semi-savage") comparison can produce.

Suzanne Graver has shown how Eliot appealed to comparison to enable readers "to perceive contrasts and similarities between social life in the past and present, to make connections between their own lives and the ones portrayed in the novels," to learn how to contribute to progress, and "to correct the conventional responses that inhibit tolerance and fellow-feeling."[129] Amanda Anderson has similarly assessed a type of comparison in reading the dialectic between "cultivated detachment" and engagement as key to Eliot's ethical sensibility.[130] In earlier novels, comparative standards alternately describe characters and appeal to readers. The chapter "Hetty's World," in *Adam Bede*, informs us that her "sphere of comparison was not large," a judgment recalled when readers are exhorted, in *Middlemarch*, "to use your power of comparison a little more effectively," and cautioned, in

Daniel Deronda, against "arriving at conclusions without comparison" (41).[131] In *Impressions of Theophrastus Such*, Eliot's stance is personified as "our precious guide Comparison," who "would teach us in the first place by likeness, and our clue to further knowledge would be resemblance to what we already know," so that observation would provide a "clue or lantern" to detect congruence between oneself and others.[132] Perhaps leaning on Francis Galton's statistical idea of "intercomparison," developed in the 1870s, Eliot asks us to shuttle between individual capacities for inference and social abilities to comprehend difference, underlining comparison as sympathy's mode of instruction.[133] Graver argues that the "positivist principles of observation, description, and comparison work to separate fact from value" and that Eliot needed realism's facticity to sponsor sympathy's value.[134] But Eliot knew, following Mill and Venn, that fact often requires inference, bringing these poles together.[135]

As a way of steering through uncertainty, comparison in *Daniel Deronda* expands the sympathetic project in both temporal and categorical directions. Eliot's bravura epigraph to Chapter 1, which draws a parallel between science and poetry as both starting *in medias res* (from the "make-believe of a beginning"), is a comparative exercise. It theorizes the tension between synchronic categories and temporal contingency, and challenges "inductive certitude," as Shuttleworth observes.[136] Comparison involves measurement and likeness. The epigraph cautions us against reading without recalibrating the way we gauge and liken, by questioning how we calibrate in the first place. A later motto dramatizes a similar interplay where comparison alone pulls us from ignorance to knowledge. Yet Eliot's statement about the "power of Ignorance" could only be grasped by a mind honed by comparison's inferential expansiveness, through repetitions not unlike those that forge a physiological will:

> looking at life parcel-wise, in the growth of a single lot, who *having a practised vision* may not see that ignorance of the true bond between events, and false conceit of means whereby sequences may be compelled – like that falsity of eyesight which overlooks the gradations of distance, seeing that which is afar off as if it were within a step or a grasp – precipitates the mistaken soul on destruction?[137] (227; emphasis mine)

In *Daniel Deronda*, comparison works at some moments as an admonition *not* to take fictional description at face value, since knowledge of a person (or character) "must be completed by innumerable impressions under differing circumstances" (111). At others, it functions as an appeal to search for a wider class of instances, as when the notion that

Mrs. Arrowpoint's characteristics must have some "essential connection" is dispelled, since a "little comparison would have shown that all these points are to be found apart" (44). Comparison provides the "lantern" and fortifies the vision so such classes are beheld in proportion.

Comparative errors are also instructive. The "magic of *quick* comparison" describes Deronda's first, mistaken inferences about his past, and Gwendolen lacks the "confidence of *thorough* knowledge" to obviate Klesmer's withering assessment of her musical prowess (167, 52; emphases mine). Such temporal errors underline how accurate judgment and responsible representation are matters of what *Middlemarch*, a novel likewise obsessed with error correction, calls "a process and an unfolding" (146).[138] Categorical blindness is similarly attacked in matters of religion: "corrective comparison" stalls prejudice against the people Deronda meets in the Judengasse, precluding his "falling into unfairness" (367). In her later essay "The Modern Hep! Hep! Hep!" (1879) Eliot castigates the European attitude toward Jews precisely on these grounds, as confirming the "prevalence of that grosser mental sloth which makes people dull to the most ordinary prompting of comparison – the bringing things together because of their likeness."[139] Writing to Harriet Beecher Stowe, she specified that her goal was "to rouse the imagination of men and women to a vision of human claims in those races of their fellow-men who *most differ* from them in customs and beliefs."[140]

In *Daniel Deronda*, both characters are hindered in their categorical knowledge by their lack of clear origins, their own "make-believe" beginnings: Gwendolen is uprooted in childhood; Deronda is unaware of his Jewish ancestry. They lack the foundation that grants "a familiar unmistakable difference amidst the future widening of knowledge" and makes affection a "blessed persistence" or "sweet habit of the blood" (22). For Gwendolen, inductive vanity is the initial result of this state of affairs, affording no time for comparison in willful decisions that ignore wider classes of example. What allows comparison to emerge from an affective basis – in her character and in narrative form – is the productive state of hesitation that blooms out of her impatience and opens a chasm between inference (however erroneous) and action. For Deronda, a parallel but opposite movement occurs. The mental stance of comparison adopts the felt energies of hesitation, allowing him to join abstract sympathy to the particulars of a full-blooded habit. If Eliot "meant everything in the book to be related to everything else there," this is less an admission of unity than a prompt to think about the *process* of relation, connection, resemblance – in short, comparison.[141]

Fervent Particulars

Deronda's uncertainty models Gwendolen's in reverse. His unclarity concerns past rather than future states: "he had no certainty how things really had been, and ... had been making conjectures about his own history" (168). Unclear about the lives of his parents and gradually suspicious of the orphan narrative peddled by his uncle, Deronda lives from adolescence onward in a diffuse state of "vapourous conjecture" (177). Through what could be seen as an excess of comparison – too much reflection and abstraction – Deronda's uncertainty is at first immobilizing. Just as indecision draws Gwendolen into hesitation, so the affective orientations of hope and trust draw Deronda out into action in his relations with Mirah and her brother Mordecai. In the latter, Deronda experiences a proxy relationship more radical than the social supervision found in Gwendolen's case. Blending two persons into aspects of an organic self and submerging that self into an aggregate will, a persisting physiological inheritance, the relationship between Deronda and Mordecai presents an orthogonal model of coming-to-decision.

Entertaining multiple past options means Deronda resists one future path. He views the past as a locus of suspicion, haunted by the hypothetical retrospect of "dimly-conjectured, dreaded revelations" (167). But he avoids an investigation that might entail "a mean prying after what he was not meant to know" (168). This scenario, all too familiar to the Victorian novel with its pressing pasts and unexpected reconnections of kin, takes on a complex suppositional structure in Eliot. The narrative becomes recursive, looking backward as more information comes to light. That Deronda's father may have been wicked is "already a cutting thought," principally because "such knowledge might be in other minds," and a stray comment that he takes after his mother is a "small incident [that] became information: it was to be reasoned on" (170). In such retrospective inferences "the main lines of character are often laid down" (171), Eliot claims, yet in forgoing discovery in favor of hypothetical visions of past selves, Deronda is engaged in a backward-facing version of Gwendolen's hesitant forecasting. Aware that "in some unaccountable way it might be that his conjectures were all wrong," Deronda multiplies the options rather than identify what actually happened: "While he was busying his mind in the construction of possibilities, it became plain to him that there must be possibilities of which he knew nothing" (173). Alternate selves are posited in the past and not the future. The novel poses a striking thought experiment where uncertainty about past states of affairs is not essentially different from conjecture about the future. To speak of a hypothetical past is not an oxymoron for a character whom Eliot compares to Leibniz, the philosopher of possible worlds, even though he yearns to mimic active men like Pericles or George Washington (173).

Subjecting the past to probability has repercussions for Deronda's character. If his uncertain construal of origins gives "a bias to his conscience, a sympathy with certain ills, and a tension of resolve in certain directions" (175), these figures incline him to abstract activity, not concrete deeds. Abandoning plans to read mathematics at Cambridge and studying law instead is an "apparent decision [that] had been without other result than to deepen the roots of indecision" (185). His unclarity about origins conflicts with action, even when Mirah and Mordecai enter his life: "when it seemed right that he should exert his will in the choice of a destination, the passion of his nature had got more and more locked by this uncertainty" (468). Deronda's talents for comparison are likewise wholly intellectual at first. What should be his "plenteous, flexible sympathy" remains a mode of "reflective analysis which tends to neutralise sympathy" (364).[142] Eliot discovers an immobilizing extreme to her realist creed, a "too reflective and diffusive sympathy" that might "paralys[e] . . . that indignation against wrong and that selectness of fellowship which are the conditions of moral force" (364). Deronda takes the lessons of comparison too far. His "sense of union with what is remote" (366) fosters a statistical compassion that seems inhuman, an impartiality that has been called a "disease of sympathy."[143] Assessments of his character exhaust synonyms for vacuity: R. H. Hutton called him a "moral mist"; a modern critic finds him "inconcrete to the point of vapidity."[144] Eliot's studied assurances that her character is "ardent" and "affectionate" cannot body forth a more solidly felt personage. At times she belies her own effort: two crucial chapters late in the novel begin with the same clumsy locution that leaves her character as a supposition: "Imagine the conflict in a mind like Deronda's"; "Imagine the difference in Deronda's state of mind" (509, 744).

Yet Deronda's lack of concretion expresses a universalism that his political calling (Jewish nationalism) will both draw on and correct.[145] Where Gwendolen clung to her own particularity and scorned the average, his sense of particular injury is subsumed into an impersonal aggregate, "merely reckoned in an average of accidents" (170). She regards the average as a superfluity that offsets her own idiosyncratic brilliance; his anticipatory dislike of being "turned out in the same mould as every other youngster" (183) is less a revolt against generic sameness than a complaint against being merely *one* case. The narrator's critique of Gwendolen's "self-enclosed unreasonableness" doubles as a confirmation of Deronda's world-view: "What passion seems more absurd, when we have got outside it and looked at calamity as a collective risk, than this amazed anguish that I and not Thou, He, or She, should be just the smitten one?" (289).

Where Gwendolen's "inadequate imagination clothes itself in individual cases" and she graduates from "particularized sympathy" to comparison via hesitation's affective energy, Deronda lowers himself from abstract comparison into particular projects, into the "cultivation of partiality."[146] In so doing, he likewise requires emotional support and proxy guides, to drift into decisive momentum a mind that "balance[s] possibilities with so great a subtlety, that there is no resultant force of will."[147] Gwendolen's hesitation helps convert crushing necessity back into contingency, but Deronda initially lacks the dynamism to trace a path out of impartiality because of "spiritual sloth, an unwillingness resolutely to seek out and risk a course of action that is consonant with his nature."[148] He lacks precisely what Gwendolen has in surplus: the *felt* tensions of indecision, the *affective* energies underwriting particular loves or hates. Indeed, it remains perplexing that Eliot's passionate case for a marginalized culture features a protagonist whose openness to Jews is initially as straightforward as his casual anti-Semitism, as though his abstract expansiveness could adopt both positions without issue.[149] Deronda's momentous development showcases not only the conscription of rational comparison in "reflective dialogism" – Anderson's term for cultural identification through "passionate argumentation, not simple embrace" – but also the charging of his abstract stance with affective dynamism.[150]

In the first event that draws his life course away from abstract universalism into cultural particularity – saving Mirah from suicide in Kew Gardens – Deronda's action appears less like saving another person than preserving her in potentiality. Her "look of immovable, statue-like despair" (187) before the water forms a figurative conduit to Gwendolen's "statuesque pose" in the *tableau vivant*: Deronda's attitude to both women notably maintains them in the pregnant moment just prior to action, familiar from the Laocoön tradition. Yet even this prevention of forward motion tilts Deronda's uncertainty from past to future orientation. He had been "occupied chiefly with uncertainties about his own course; but those uncertainties, being much at their leisure, were wont to have such wide-sweeping connections with all life and history that the new image of helpless sorrow easily blent itself" with his resistance to settling into one career path (188). The narrative impulse to hypothesize about Mirah's past – the "probable romance that lay behind that loneliness and the look of desolation" (188) – is displaced into a future mode. He recollects the incident counterfactually, pondering the "possibilities of what had been and what might be," but in terms now suffused "with the warm blood of passionate hope and fear" (205). His experience even verges on Gwendolen's psychic life, with "vague visions of the future" that deposit "their influence in an anxiety stronger than any motive he could give for it" (207).

Listening to Mirah's story of escape from her exploitive father, Deronda catches some of her "fever of hope" (221). Although his friend Hans Meyrick (Mirah's suitor *manqué*) charges Deronda with not knowing the meaning of *hope* because of his "supreme reasonableness, and self-nullification, and preparation for the worst" (643), he moves toward that affective terrain. He learns Mirah's habit of preferring intuited over reasoned grounds for action. She may not have had "enough reason for [her] suspicions" of her father, but this lack of objective warrant meant little given that her "mind had been lit up, and all that might be stood out clear and sharp" (219). Deronda adopts this almost prophetic mode of thinking, entertaining "rapid images of what might be" (207) and conjuring "consciously Utopian pictures of his own future" (324). Thinking in fervent particulars forces his openness to contingency into one necessary course. His sense that anyone else might have saved Mirah is disparaged: "Saint Anybody," Mrs. Meyrick notes, "is a bad saint to pray to" (370), though Deronda has worshipped at this shrine for years.

This shift also drives Deronda's reasoned sense of probability toward crediting outlandish coincidences, and the plot (as many have observed) toward romance.[151] The random discovery of a bookshop bearing the significant name "Ezra Cohen" makes Deronda wary; he falls back on legal reasoning to "convince himself that there was not the slightest warrantable presumption of this Ezra being Mirah's brother" (382–83). But when he asks Mrs. Cohen whether she has a daughter and her reaction provides an "unwelcome bit of circumstantial evidence" (391), his suspicion falters. He experiences "a hesitation which proved how, in a man much given to reasoning, a bare possibility may weigh more than the best-clad likelihood" (385). He is compelled to a trusting acceptance of this narrative path, abjuring the "inclination to rest in uncertainty" (391). Habituated to the comparative affects of hope and trust, Deronda accepts the prophetic certainty of his plot's next phase. Adjusting himself against a "desponding view of probability" that takes wishes as "ominous," Deronda comes to see in them "good and sufficient security for all kinds of fulfilment" (382). He is hence prepared to accept Mordecai's prophetic outlook not as a set of spiritual truths but as a trusting surrender to particularity, and accepts the chain of events leading him to the elder man as "plainly discernible links" (514).

As a mentor, Mordecai holds Deronda "spellbound" like the proxy figures in Gwendolen's plot.[152] However, the lines between mentor and apprentice are blurred by an emotive form of identification as Mordecai's object appears an already-familiar entity:

> the long-contemplated figure had come as an emotional sequence of Mordecai's firmest theoretic convictions; it had been wrought from the imagery of his most passionate life; and it inevitably reappeared – reappeared in a more specific self-asserting form than ever. Deronda had that sort of resemblance to the preconceived type which a finely individual bust or portrait has to the more generalized copy left in our minds after a long interval: we renew our memory with delight, but we hardly know with how much correction. (479)

This odd alignment of a prior model ("preconceived type") and a generic afterimage ("more generalized copy") begins Eliot's striking defense of prophetic logic, or "second-sight" (470). Mordecai is classed among those whose mental, emotional, and volitional life works through "images which have a foreshadowing power" (471). Such representations relocate actions and outcomes in an imaginative recess, where hypotheses are dominant: "the deed they would do starts up before them in complete shape, making a coercive type" (471). As George Levine has shown, Eliot's descriptions of Mordecai link prophetic vision and scientific hypothesis.[153]

Yet Eliot's articulation of a "forecasting ardor" that supplements "even strictly-measuring science" carries further into the territory of "human motives and actions, [where] passionate belief has a fuller efficacy" (513). Her descriptions of Mordecai's psyche recast inductive vanity, the notion that "enthusiasm may have the validity of proof" (513), in a higher key. Eliot redesigns the noncalculative obstinacy for which Gwendolen was censured into a positive, Comtean view of "emotional intellect" against the cold rationalism of a "mathematical dreamland" (514).[154] Where Gwendolen was mocked for her innocence of numerical reason, Mordecai's mathematical thinking receives a dressing-down that could have come from Mill's *System of Logic*: "Men may dream in demonstrations, and cut out an illusory world in the shape of axioms, definitions, and propositions, with a final exclusion of fact signed Q.E.D. No formulas for thinking will save us mortals from mistake in our imperfect apprehension of the matter to be thought about" (514).

When the novel's philosophical outlooks are examined in parallel, Eliot seems to adopt opposing attitudes. But if we attend to their affective tonalities, we see how they converge along the axes of certainty and uncertainty. Deronda, for instance, "felt nothing that could be called a belief in the validity of Mordecai's impressions concerning him or in the probability of any greatly effective issue," but rather a "profound sensibility to a cry from the depths of another soul" (496). Mordecai's position stalls Deronda's usual tendencies to conjecture, suffusing him with the felt aspects of belief in advance of any intellectual commitment. "Your doubts lie as light as dust on my belief," he says (502). His "energetic certitude" and "fervent trust" (509) shake Deronda's doubt, exposing him to an "instreaming of confidence" (506) and the "agitating moment of uncertainty which is close upon decision" (623). Just as the influence of Mirah checked Deronda's rationalizing, so Mordecai's past-facing prophecy of a Jewish mother adds to the logic whereby "life-long conjectures" are dispelled and additional "surmise" or "inference" is rendered "untrustworthy" (617, 620).[155]

Beyond turning Deronda away from abstract comparison, Mordecai more radically transposes his belief into his young protégé. He is to be "a soul – believing my belief – being moved by my reasons – hoping my hope" (499), the mentor no longer directing his charge but sharing with him the reins of a composite self. Hence Eliot's quiet use of a term from the psychological literature on the mind's hierarchical function, making the younger man the "executive self" (473, 510) of the older – his *will*. Mordecai anticipates the "blent transmission" (751) aligning their souls and joins Deronda to a long heritage, discussed in the debate at the Hand and Banner tavern.[156] Eliot essentially inserts a dialogue on politics involving thinly characterized participants, which Rosenthal has explored in relation to the novel's wider statistical obsessions, including the "countability" of Jewish populations and scientific models for social organization.[157] Changes on an abstract and systemic level, concerning social qualities, are seen as taking visceral shape in bodies across generations, reintroducing the physiology of will as a reference point. Discussing the "law of progress," one character draws a social analogue to scientific "laws of development" and expresses a determinism Deronda resists by declaring that the "degrees of inevitableness in relation to our own will and acts" must leave room for contingent resistance (526). Mordecai offers a more emphatic version of the argument: the "strongest principle of growth lies in human choice" (538).

If this antistatistical line allows Deronda to shed his own universalism and learn the terms of Meyrick's mocking charge – "Any blockhead can cite generalities, but the master-mind discerns the particular cases they represent" (643) – the emphasis on individual choice is actually mis-placed.[158] Deronda learns that his life is the unintentional fulfillment of his grandfather's wishes: "Every Jew should rear his family as if he hoped that a Deliverer might spring from it" (662).[159] His coming to decision is thus an uncanny recursion to another fount of certainty in the past, in the person of Daniel Charisi, whose control over his daughter's musical career parallels the novel's other mentors. A "grand" persona "with an iron will" (631), Charisi was no hesitant hero: his trustee-at-large reports his epi-grammatic credo, "Better a wrong will than a wavering" (724). Deronda's acceptance of his Jewish heritage, his potential destiny as a nation-builder, is guaranteed not by his own will but by an "inherited yearning" (750), a Lamarckian volition.[160]

Hence his phrases for decision are tautological, although in different ways from Gwendolen's. He gives a "decisive acknowledgment of his love," a "definite expression of his resolve," but also comes to a "new state of decision" (745) in terms that exceed the single lifespan, making "an epoch in resolve" (725). Where Gwendolen experiences vertiginous uncer-tainty, Deronda's newfound certainty is historically grounded.[161] The "certitude of ties that altered the poise of hopes and fears" (683) skews his abstract outlook in one direction through a "release of all the energy which had long been spent in self-checking and suppression because of doubtful conditions" (745). His formerly indecisive will is submerged in an aggregate will that allows personal choice within certain parameters. Deronda thus belongs to what Mordecai calls a "multitude whose will moves in obedience to the laws of justice and love" (749), wherein the "effects prepared by generations are likely to triumph over a contrivance which would bend them all to the satisfaction of self" (663). These pronounce-ments echo a late acknowledgment by Eliot and Lewes that the "mind is at once individual and an integral part of the general mind."[162]

The trajectory of Deronda's plot is doubly recursive. He moves from an abstract sympathy into a particular commitment that turns out to draw energy from generational laws; his indecision finds its way to a choice that was made decades earlier by someone else; he acquires a will by borrowing volition from another and blending into a transgenerational population of wills; and his past hypotheticals incline to future hopes that can only succeed by trusting specific narratives about the past. The utopian ending of his plot ultimately has more to do with Gwendolen's than at first appears. His insipid advice, to "care about something in this vast world besides the gratification of small selfish desires ... something that is good apart from the accidents of your own lot" (446), can make sense only if there are individual lots to supersede. He is called to a "higher" life that "holds an enthusiasm for something more than our own appetites and vanities" (451), but such a life takes shape in a world where diminutive passions remain a ground to be transcended. Perhaps this is why Gwendolen's letter to him is aired before he departs from England and the pages before us.[163] Gwendolen is left in renewed uncertainty, whereas Deronda leaves for the East with fragile certainty as his guide. The opposition matters less than the "kinship" (67) Eliot establishes between certainty and doubt, states that blur across the novel's settings and maintain its origin and outcome under a hypothetical sign. I have followed Eliot along what one critic identifies as "moral paths through the picturesque maze of human motive," showing how she takes measure of its complexity – of the intricacies of human motivation teased out into action and back into potentiality, of the seams that join psychophysiological state (hesitation) to reflective orientation (comparison).[164] Deronda escapes the "mazes of impartial sympathy" (745) and from Gwendolen's "labyrinth of reflection" (602), one hopes, there will be an Ariadne's thread out.

CHAPTER 2

Unproven Verdicts
Collins and Legal Uncertainty

[A Scot] has no falterings of self-suspicion. Surmises, guesses, misgivings, half-intuitions, semi-consciousnesses, partial illuminations, dim instincts, embryo conceptions, have no place in his brain, or vocabulary. The twilight of dubiety never falls upon him.... Between the affirmative and the negative there is no border-land with him. You cannot hover with him upon the confines of truth, or wander in the maze of a probable argument. He always keeps the path.
—Charles Lamb, "Imperfect Sympathies"[1]

Despite his fondness for outrageous coincidence, improbable characters, and aleatory plots, the novels of Wilkie Collins might be enlisted on the side of certainty rather than uncertainty. Foundational in the kindred genres of sensation and detective fiction, most prominently in *The Woman in White* (1860) and *The Moonstone* (1868), Collins was central to a representational project that introduced uncertainty on several fronts – social and sexual, narrative and normative – only to retreat to stability, closure, and finality in a shoring up of mid-century ideology.[2] A novelist of liberalism and legal reform, in novels such as *No Name* (1862) and *Man and Wife* (1870) he mounted overt critiques of legal oddities like irregular marriages and unfair inheritance provisions for illegitimate children. Collins thus kept company with other Victorian novelists, in pursuit of a justice no legal system could guarantee, who resorted to narrative scripts – the "poetics of wrongful accusation," the "show-trial" – and their familiar logics of accusation and acquittal.[3] In one script, a wrongful charge is leveled, subsequently overturned by fresh "evidence of innocence," and "providential paradigms ... ensure that the accusation is shown to be unfounded at the point of narrative closure." In another, "characters are put on trial for crimes of which they are essentially innocent," and verdicts are subsequently reversed through "scenes of character-testimony."[4] In sympathy with the conviction underpinning many Victorian novels at law, Collins often "keeps the path."

78

In this chapter, I offer an opposing account of Collins, situating him in a long countertradition of legal thinking that challenges modern law's aspirations to certainty. As legal systems developed out of Roman and canon law, they retained and refined elements of what has come to be seen as a mathematical jurisprudence anchored in notions of number and degree. Roman law's practices of partial or fractional proof are a rudimentary way of talking about mathematical likelihood, and its numerical requirements for witnesses persisted in civil and canon law. Logical and legal treatises from the Enlightenment forward speculated about using numbers to assess the credibility of witness testimony or the reliability of judicial decisions. In our time, the tools of statistics and computation are deployed, from policing to sentencing, to judge individuals according to reference classes in which they are deemed to fit.[5] Yet if the law has played a foundational role in the emergence of modern tactics of thinking under uncertainty, its own techniques of judgment have never attained the rigor of the models to which it gave rise. In a historical irony, legal theory retrofits ideas drawn from other disciplines – about subjective probability or explanatory inference, for example – to establish what the law means by "probable cause," "reasonable doubt," and "moral certainty."[6] Even as attempts were made in the Victorian period to graft numerical certainty onto these nebulous concepts, writers on logic and probability such as John Stuart Mill and John Venn criticized the assumption that "different grades of conviction can be marked off from one another with sufficient accuracy for us to be able to refer individual cases to their corresponding classes."[7] While efforts at quantification have only intensified since the nineteenth century, institutionally secured in journals like *Jurimetrics* and *Law, Probability, and Risk*, legal theorists have cautioned against the dangers of "trial by mathematics," "actuarial justice," and "predictive policing."[8]

These tensions have a compelling instance in the law of Scotland, which has long relied on a verdict that undermines numerical ideals by refusing the binary options for a trial's outcome. The so-called Scotch verdict comes back neither "guilty" nor "not guilty" but "not proven." "Not proven" imputes a lack of evidence for conviction but has the force of an acquittal. Derided for its illogical coexistence with the presumption of innocence, defended for its essential clemency in contrast to sterner binary models, "not proven" is still on the books today (despite intense pressure to scrap it) and is returned in about a third of criminal cases. As an official verdict of hesitation, "not proven" inscribes uncertainty into the process of legal decision, calls into question the patterns of inference that lead to binary verdicts, and ratifies the extralegal penumbra of stigma and suspicion that emerges despite a court's final say. Such hesitant verdicts are more attuned to an asymmetry in our moral psychology whereby blame is more tenacious than exoneration: the formal proof expressed in legal verdicts does not always dissolve the unproven but deeply felt recriminations that swirl in the court of public opinion.[9]

Collins's novel *The Law and the Lady* (1875) makes use of this hesitant structure in the narrative of a young-woman-turned-detective who tries to overturn the "not proven" verdict handed down to her husband for the murder of his first wife. The verdict shapes the novel's narrative mechanics and representations of reasoning, introducing uncertainty into patterns of inference common to the genres of sensation and detective fiction. In the first section I lay the groundwork for this argument by sketching the Scotch verdict's accidental genealogy, showing how its historical sources and conceptual framework seep into the novel in ways that have not been adequately described in legal (as opposed to cultural-national) terms. The verdict's form, I argue in the next section, allows Collins to bypass the rational inference of detective fiction and describe instead a search that operates by counterintuitive methods of *trial and error* and *accidental discovery*. In broad terms, Collins critiques the logic of the courtroom, and its models of hypothesis confirmation, as a space supposedly separate from social judgment. The conceptual tangles of the "not proven" verdict, I suggest toward the end, thus underwrite an expansive vision of uncertainty and an ethics of reading predicated on openness and hesitation.

Reframing *The Law and the Lady* as consonant with the legal principle it supposedly criticizes, I reveal at once a complex picture of legal reformism in Collins's work and a potentially wider category of legal (and other) novels that may similarly dispute standards of conviction and closure. That Collins wrote mostly within the framework of what we now think of as sensation fiction makes his work more rather than less compelling for an account of uncertainty in relation to realism, for it is here that "the conventions of fictional realism come to be punctuated with question marks."[10] Collins has rightly been defended as offering a "rich phenomenology of the various ways in which people perceive and deal with the problem of chance in everyday life": the sensation novel, in his hands, articulates the modern conception of probability as a spectrum concept, recognizing that "the improbable was being made more probable," the factual brought closer to the fictional, through the spread of periodicals and newspapers – a dynamic I return to in Chapter 4.[11] Moreover, by placing uncertainty at the core of detective fiction, in whose genealogy he is so central, Collins makes clear that this genre is not simply a fictional elaboration of modern law, but a critical appraisal of its methods and assumptions. *The Law and the Lady* illuminates the felt problems of uncertainty at the hazy border between fact and fiction, legal system and social space, juridical treatise and literary narrative, realism and its generic others, bringing chance back onto a terrain that defines itself by keeping chance at bay.

That Caledonian *Medium Quid*

In this section I offer an overview of the Scotch verdict that emphasizes its status as legal instrument (as opposed to cultural artifact). The accidental history and usage of the verdict down to Collins's time, most notably in the 1857 trial of Madeleine Smith for poisoning her (first) husband, provides a context more compelling as a source of legal uncertainty than as a record of the post-Union relationship between Scotland and England. This historical sketch shows how the nineteenth-century context maps a jurisprudential genealogy we can trace forward to the verdict's controversial influence today. That current arguments for and against "not proven" invoke the same reasoning – indeed, often the same sources and rhetoric – as in Collins's moment underlines the Victorian novel's continuing vitality for thinking about uncertainty. Considering moments where the verdict is explicitly dealt with in the novel, and uncovering sources for Collins's legal knowledge, I contend that his apparent critique of the Scots trial process needs to be distinguished from his presentation of "not proven" as a legal instrument with considerable social value and psychological utility.

According to its modern exponents, "not proven" emerged by happenstance: the verdict has "no common law or statutory definition."[12] Juries in Scotland initially decided on the familiar general verdicts, "guilty" and "not guilty." During the seventeenth century, the combination of complex indictments and ambient political threats resulted in a concentration on verdicts that governed facts alone. For their protection, jurors became responsible for finding facts "proven" or "not proven," leaving the final (perhaps controversial) ascriptions of "guilty" or "not guilty" to judges.[13] After some flux into the early eighteenth century, "proven" merged with "guilty," where the opposite "not proven" remained at a distance from "not guilty," so that three verdicts were available from 1728.[14] By the early nineteenth century and the appearance of the authoritative *Commentaries on the Law of Scotland* (1797) by David Hume (the philosopher's nephew), "not proven" existed as a "general" verdict not restricted to facts and implying insufficient evidence to convict, where "not guilty" was reserved for a true finding of innocence.[15] Functioning as an acquittal that permits no retrial (regardless of new evidence forthcoming), "not proven" was, in the words of a nineteenth-century commentator, "retained as a useful and fitting expedient."[16] It was a "compromise between irresponsible power, constitutional duty, and conscientious conviction," a process that "administered legal authority, while at the same time it left the juror's mind void of offence."[17]

The verdict has historically attracted two charges of conceptual confusion that are still debated. As an acquittal that does not exonerate, "not proven" seems to compromise the rule about presumption of innocence.[18] As a verdict pronounced by a jury structure that does not require unanimity but only a bare majority (at minimum, eight to seven), it seems to weaken the criminal law's standard of beyond reasonable doubt.[19] The verdict's defenders, in the nineteenth century and now, point to its utility in cases where the jury is not fully convinced of innocence, and its clemency in cases where the conviction of guilt may need moderation (especially when a capital sentence is possible) – a "subtle way of 'nullifying' the law."[20] Such proposals often turn the tables on Anglo-American law, arguing that the "severe and unrelaxing alternative" of its standard two-verdict system neither guarantees the presumption of innocence nor "prevents social stigma for unproven charges," since reasonable doubt implies that some "not guilty" verdicts are reached only because of insufficient evidence.[21] Although accidental in its emergence, the verdict could even be taken as characteristic of the "intermediacy" of Scots law, a mixed system (drawing on common law and civilian traditions) often celebrated for versatility and leniency.[22] Scots law, for instance, rejects the jury vetting process known as *voir dire*, preferring juries that are randomly representative of the citizenry.[23] At a more fundamental level, this flexible verdict undercuts what systems theorist Niklas Luhmann describes as the law's logical structure, where "courts have to decide every case submitted to them" according to a "corresponding norm [that] is called – and the double negation of this formulation demonstrates its logic – the prohibition of the denial of justice."[24]

Authoritative treatises in the eighteenth and early nineteenth centuries wrestled with the paradoxical character of the verdict. In *A Summary of the Powers and Duties of Juries in Criminal Trials in Scotland* (1833), William Steele qualifies that the "phrase *not proven* is usually employed to mark a deficiency only of the full measure of evidence to convict the pannel [viz., the accused]; and that of *not guilty* to convey the jury's opinion of his innocence of the charge."[25] Similar statements are made in Hume's

Commentaries and Archibald Alison's *Practice of the Criminal Law of Scotland* (1833).[26] Yet by far the most prominent view of the verdict sweeps such jurisprudential demurral aside to reveal a primal scene that encapsulates the tension between the verdict and the presumption of innocence:

> At Court, and waited to see the poisoning woman. She is clearly guilty, but as one or two witnesses said the poor wench hinted an intention to poison herself, the jury gave that bastard verdict, *Not proven*. I hate that Caledonian *medium quid*. One who is not *proven guilty* is innocent in the eye of the law.[27]

Walter Scott's cantankerous epithet has long haunted the verdict. Yet his curiously unstable account enacts the type of proof – by "presumption," indication, tendency, or hearsay – that "not proven" came to guard against.[28] Scott defends the presumption of innocence while assuming the obvious guilt of the accused, even though he cannot remember basic details of the proceedings (such as the number of witnesses).

Similar divisions between reasonable jurists and melodramatic commentators continued through mid-century, after an 1848 statute simplified the judicial process in Scotland.[29] One of Collins's sources for the novel, J. H. Burton's *Narratives from Criminal Trials in Scotland* (1852), summarizes the debate in a discussion of poisoning cases, recapitulating Scott's paradigms of forensic and moral uncertainty (poisoning and suicide):

> This middle finding is peculiar to Scotland. Some have held it to be a valuable institution, as leaving a stigma of suspicion where there is not sufficient evidence to convict – a stigma which never leaves its object if he is guilty, and is easily removable if any event should occur enabling him to explain suspicious facts and make his innocence apparent. On the other hand, this form has been objected to as a too accessible resting-place for jurors unwilling to incur the responsibility of finding guilty, and unable to reconcile their consciences to a finding of not guilty.[30]

Sources close to Collins were hardly so measured, especially in the wake of the high-profile Smith trial, which only ramified the conceptual indistinction.[31] One trial report saw the verdict as a "negative salve for the consciences of scrupulous men."[32] In Charles Dickens's *All the Year Round*, in the issue following the final installment of *No Name* in 1863, a contributor discussed the Maclachlan case (note the nominal proximity to "Macallan," the indicted husband in Collins's novel), where a Scotch verdict was overturned by the royal prerogative of mercy.[33] Lamenting the "effete forms" and "antique freaks and extravagances of Scotch procedure," the article declares that "the country of Scott and Burns lies overrun with

the brambles and underwood of a detestable jargon and mediæval procedure."[34] In a letter to the *Pall Mall Gazette* in 1872, Collins's friend Charles
Reade used Scott's epithet to fume in similar tones about the Marguerite
Diblanc trial, where the defendant did not receive a Scotch verdict but
was found guilty even though the jury recommended mercy. This travesty,
in Reade's view, represented a "bastard verdict which says 'Yes' with a
trumpet and 'No' with a penny whistle."[35]

The Law and the Lady does not articulate a single position on the verdict
but instead alludes to this range of views, as though adopting the mantra of
juries in Scotland when they speak not unanimously but in majority, "by a
plurality of voices."[36] A moderate explanation of the verdict is offered to
Valeria by Major Fitz-David:

> There is a verdict allowed by the Scotch law, which (so far as I know) is not
> permitted by the laws of any other civilized country on the face of the earth.
> When the jury are in doubt whether to condemn or acquit the prisoner
> brought before them, they are permitted, in Scotland, to express that doubt
> by a form of compromise. If there is not evidence enough, on the one hand,
> to justify them in finding a prisoner guilty, and not evidence enough, on the
> other hand, to thoroughly convince them that a prisoner is innocent, they
> extricate themselves from the difficulty by finding a verdict of Not Proven.[37]

Although these comments insinuate Scottish backwardness, they accurately depict a half-measure expressed by the jury, a "doubt" that remains
"on public record" (101).[38] Valeria (channeling her inner Scott or Reade)
chooses to hear only one side of this definition and reacts by promising to
"change that underhand Scotch Verdict of Not Proven, into an honest
English verdict of Not Guilty" (116). (The ethnic identity of a Guilty
verdict remains leadingly tacit.)

Critics have naturally jumped on this statement to cast aspersions on the
novel's representations of Scottish institutions working in service of an
English civilizing process.[39] This approach can be traced back to Dougald
MacEachen, who first drew attention to the Smith trial as a source for
Collins and argued his reformist attitude toward the verdict.[40] MacEachen
claims that the novel prosecutes an "attack" on the verdict while paradoxically suggesting that the weakness of Eustace's character makes it difficult to
discern "any great injustice" being done.[41] Mapping internal fractures in
Scotland onto similar divisions in England's cultural identity, Anne
Longmuir interprets the verdict as a "disruptive element" and marker of
"epistemological uncertainty" that threatens national unity with irrational
elements.[42] Teresa Traver likewise finds Collins representing Scots law as
"incapable, weak, and uncivilized to the extent that it deviates from the

English system," and Mary Husemann sees in the verdict "a vehicle for criticizing [Collins'] northern neighbors."[43]

Such readings hinge on understanding what one critic calls the "*Scottishness* of the verdict."[44] But I argue we can get closer to Collins's views by wondering about what could be termed the verdict's *verdictness* – that is, the strangeness of how it tries to tell the truth (from the Latin *verum dicere*) by making visible a kind of truth independent from legal fact. In this respect, it is important that the novel is secretive about its sources. When Valeria writes to Eustace of her plans to investigate the verdict, she tells him that she has checked a definition in a standard Victorian authority whose name would seem to underline the colonial and ethnic topoi. "In plain English," she notes, "I have looked into Ogilvie's Imperial Dictionary . . .: 'A verdict of Not Proven only indicates that, in the opinion of the Jury, there is a deficiency in the evidence to convict the prisoner. A verdict of Not Guilty imports the Jury's opinion that the prisoner is innocent'" (116). The formula aligning semantic plainness with legal candor recurs when Valeria scorns the "uncouth language" (125) of the trial report. It is again "plain English" to which she appeals in stating that "the Jury who tried my husband declined to express their opinion, positively and publicly, that he was innocent" (239).

But this quotation is not from the source advertised: editions of *The Imperial Dictionary* Collins could have consulted either omit an entry for the verdict or define it in different terms.[45] Setting aside the irony that consulting a Scottish expansion of an American authority on "plain English" (as declared on the title page of Webster's dictionary) hardly fits the jingoism just mentioned, the text Valeria actually draws on is William Bell's *A Dictionary and Digest of the Law of Scotland* (1838).[46] Bell is more measured in describing the ideal function of "not proven": "A verdict of *not guilty* imports the jury's opinion that the panel is innocent. A verdict of *not proven* only indicates that, in the opinion of the jury, there is a deficiency in the evidence to convict him."[47] Tacitly having his lady detective quote not from a friendly, illustrated source to underline the superiority of England over Scotland, but rather from a formidable tome replete with references to the main legal authorities, such as Hume, Alison, and Steele, Collins is quietly arming his heroine with the tools of an overwhelmingly masculine profession and giving her (and readers) the resources to valorize Scots law – *as law* – between the lines.

Whatever pragmatic critique Collins levels at aspects of Scotland's legal and trial system needs to be seen as distinct from the novel's encoding of the verdict's logical form.[48] His refraction of these contexts holds more than historical interest, since the terms in which he understands the verdict map discussions that continue through the nineteenth century to the present. In an 1877 case about fraud and forgery, recalled by Edward Clarke (later defense counsel in the celebrated Adelaide Bartlett poisoning case), the language of Collins's novel makes an incongruous appearance at the Old Bailey (an English court where "not proven" cannot apply). Clarke appealed to the jury to release the defendant "not with some bastard verdict of Not Proven, to hang round his neck for the rest of his life the irremovable stigma of suspicion and crime; but with the straightforward honest Not Guilty."[49] By contrast, Arthur Conan Doyle prefaces an account of a criminal case by emphasizing the presumption of innocence and benefit of the doubt: "It cannot be doubted that if the Scotch verdict of 'Not proven,' which neither condemns nor acquits, had been permissible in England it would have been the outcome of many a case which, under our sterner law, has ended upon the scaffold."[50] These examples typify the verdict's floating ideological valence. Detached for rhetorical purposes from any concrete use of "not proven," they proffer the verdict as an embodiment of unjust stigma or just clemency without realizing how its flexibility – resulting from the "difference between a legal and moral acquittal" that was "unknown" in the English system – unstably supports either side of the argument.[51]

Styles of Search and Detection

Before analyzing in detail how the Scotch verdict shapes the novel's form, from local details to larger narrative structures, a plot summary may be in order. The protagonist Valeria Brinton has married a man she takes to be called Eustace Woodville. After some unfortunate coincidences, including a chance meeting with her mother-in-law who does not recognize her last name, Valeria realizes that she has been married under false pretenses. Her husband not only was married before, under the name Macallan, but also was charged with the poisoning of his first wife Sara and acquitted by a "not proven" verdict. Unable to bear this shameful revelation, he abandons Valeria and is seen only intermittently until the conclusion. She, by contrast, undertakes a full-scale investigation to establish his innocence, accompanied by a cadre of zany characters: her father's former clerk, Benjamin, who is usefully obsessed with solving newspaper puzzles; a helpful lawyer, Playmore; an aging libertine, Major Fitz-David; and a wheelchair-using figure, Miserrimus Dexter, who subsists on truffles and burgundy and adds a twist of sensation to an otherwise pedestrian narrative.

Collins introduces two modes of detection that work against the familiar operations of sensation and detective fiction (including his own). The novel's representations of *trial and error* and of *accidental discovery* can be read as formal instantiations of the verdict that resist explanation according to standards of precision, noncontradiction, and closure. Instead of stringing clues together in a sequence assured by logical procedures, trial and error gathers alternatives. Instead of moving forward with a rational purpose, accidental discovery moves laterally in the hope that a wider view will turn out to be a clearer one. The novel's preface establishes a connection between these modes of searching and detecting by emphasizing the value of unpredictability and error and by promoting a capacious understanding of literary probability. Collins reminds us

> (First): that the actions of human beings are not invariably governed by the laws of pure reason. (Secondly): that we are by no means always in the habit (especially when we happen to be women) of bestowing our love on the objects which are the most deserving of it, in the opinions of our friends. (Thirdly and Lastly): that Characters which may not have appeared, and Events which may not have taken place, within the limits of our own individual experience, may nevertheless be perfectly natural Characters and perfectly probable Events, for all that.

One review called this "as arrant a preface as ever was prefixed," a claim accurate in the etymological sense of "arrant": wandering, uncertain, open to error.[52] The novel's many binary chapter titles, nested within an earlier partition in the three-volume edition ("Paradise Lost," "Paradise Regained"), likewise send us along a looping track of thinking, searching, discovering, miscalculating, and correcting: "The Bride's Mistake," "The Bride's Thoughts"; "The Landlady's Discovery," "My Own Discovery"; "In the Dark," "In the Light"; "A Specimen of My Wisdom," "A Specimen of My Folly"; and so on. Collins also lapses into a stylistic tic that involves numerical and repetitive tags (typically, twos that expand into threes and subsequent multiples) and either/or patterns and fallacies. By overextending what Tzvetan Todorov calls the "geometric architecture" of detective fiction, Collins calls attention to *addition* as a formal property of the novel.[53]

When Valeria is led to believe that the truth of her husband's past is lodged somewhere in Major Fitz-David's library, she undertakes a search that deploys these methodical enumerations in the mode of trial and error. She maps the room and classifies every object into multiples of two or three before combing through them all: starting with "two shorter walls," she focuses on the doorway abutted by two card tables and two china bowls (76), moves on to "two corners" with "two little chairs" (77), and ends with the opposite wall, where three window compartments are bracketed by two antique cabinets, each with six drawers (77–78). The effect of this exhaustive catalogue is to set up an investigation that works on an additive model, the strangeness of which it would be hard to overstate. It spurns the techniques of early literary detectives (Auguste Dupin, Sherlock Holmes, Sergeant Cuff), whose emphasis on the ratiocinative and sequential – on "deduction" and "induction" – have been profitably compared to methods in logic and the philosophy of science.[54] It seems to resist the canny logic of the "significant trifle" in detective fiction, "the trifling detail that is suddenly invested with immense significance."[55] And it refuses in advance the vocabulary of rapid apprehension – hunches, guesses, flashes of insight – by which such fiction retrospectively characterizes its clues from the vantage of a hypothetical end point, an "inevitable discovery," that explains them.[56] Any number of the items trawled through might suffice for inferential flights of detection: "a passport, a set of luggage labels, a broken silver snuff-box, two cigar-cases, and a torn map of Rome" (78). Yet the novel declines to showcase such details as clues, as matter for logical analysis or sudden insight, instead portraying its detective simply aggregating these details as circumstantial evidence.[57]

The search by trial and error could in principle afford detection through the consideration of counterfactuals or the disclosure of causal sequences. But in practice it merely makes time for the real discoveries, which prove accidental. Valeria wonders about two findings: "fragments of a broken vase" (78) and a photograph of Eustace with another woman, which falls out of an album of Fitz-David's romances she locates in the last bookcase compartment. A second look reveals an inscription that chains these details together, confirming the significance of Fitz-David's stolen glance at the bookcase and "connecting the vase and the bookcase as twin landmarks on the way that led to discovery" (82): "To Major Fitz-David, with two vases. From his friends, S. and E. M." (89). Although these details in duplicate clearly stand as a model of investigation into causes and patterns – Valeria naturally wonders about the "accident" (81) that broke the vase – they do not promote any corresponding inference. At one level, inference is blurred under the pressure of jealousy, since Valeria absurdly resists the conclusion that the photograph shows Eustace with his first wife (S. and E. M. are their initials). She also seems oblivious to the connection between the vases mentioned and those she has found in the library. At a more general level, it is as though Valeria is engaged in a version of what Mill terms "induction improperly so called," where a generalization inferred from specific propositions does not add anything that was not contained in those propositions: she can make no leap that is not already self-evident in the information she has collected.[58]

The apparently less promising discovery, the vase, turns out to be crucial. The Major's current prima-donna confesses that she broke the vase by hurling a book to displace the bouquet of a rival. That book happens to contain the full report of the trial of Eustace Macallan. Methodical perseverance and symbolic connection succeed where causal inference and pattern detection could not. Three elements that initially seem related (vase, photograph, book of trials) are only trivially linked by cause, whereas their figurative relations stitch them together: the photograph indexes two individuals who translate into three initials; these are the benefactors of two vases, one of which is broken by a book that contains a narrative explanation for the metaphorical sundering of these two persons, of which the shattered vase is both sign and memorial. Valeria, "a person who fails to strike the ordinary observer at first sight; but who gains in general estimation, on a second, and sometimes even on a third, view" (11), thus conducts an iterative search that fosters uncertainty and reveals her own person as an embodiment of the verdict's categorical blurring: "neither maid, wife, nor widow" (40).[59]

The search inaugurates the novel's larger tension between trial and error and accidental discovery, between an additive logic of information and findings that occur by chance. On one hand, we witness Valeria's insatiable desire for taxonomic detail: "not in the least impressed by [Playmore's] solemn appeal to the unseen powers of arithmetic and money," she prefers "being fed with more information" (355). On the other, she eventually finds that "what I had done, I had, so to speak, done blindfold," since the "merest accident might have altered the whole course of later events" (396). Critics have characterized Valeria's mode of detection as "feminine" and "sensate" – terms opposing felt intuition to the purportedly masculine brand of rational inference common in detective fiction.[60] I am arguing that Valeria's success owes more to perseverance under uncertainty than to useful irrationality. She is carried along by what the novel variously describes as her "curiosity" (54), "native obstinacy" (314), and "prodigious tenacity of purpose" (69). These presentiments bring her within sight of vital information while precluding correct inferences – or any process of inference whatsoever.

One might expect this strategy – dogged inquiry, serendipitous discovery – to threaten narrative desire. Suspense, as Caroline Levine has argued, "teach[es] us to take pleasure in the activity of stopping to doubt our most entrenched beliefs, waiting for the world to reveal its surprises, its full

unyielding otherness," and is thus "the form of the acquisition of knowledge," "specifically of a skeptical epistemology that insists on testing
authoritative claims to truth."[61] For Levine "it is the pause – the doubtful,
hopeful middle of the process – that lends the scientific method its
legitimacy."[62] Yet in this novel, as I have suggested, the forward propulsion
of hypothetico-deductive processes of confirmation – "the making of
reasonable guesses" as a way to navigate the passage from ignorance to
knowledge – is missing.[63] Suspense is slackened and has to be sustained in
other ways. Collins accomplishes this by introducing counterfactual statements, unaccounted-for sensations, and glaringly improbable events.
When Valeria signs her married and not her maiden name into the register
at the outset, her aunt's superstitious reaction is coupled with a counterfactual hope – "it may turn out that you have chosen well" (9) – that
fosters suspense by multiplying the possibilities that could explain such a
conditional statement. After Eustace's mother does not recognize Valeria's
last name as Woodville, the latter is puzzled and offers a similarly paradoxical reflection: "If I had only myself to think of, I believe I should have
provoked an explanation on the spot" (27). Explanation is forestalled by
the negation of a condition that first generated the desire for explanation:
just married, Valeria does *not* have "only [herself] to think of." "What was
the secret of her despising him, and pitying me?" she wonders. "Where was
the explanation of her incomprehensible apathy when my name was twice
pronounced in her hearing?" (30). Such anxious inquiries after explanation
foment suspense separately from the plodding processes of trial and error
and accidental discovery. They incite readers to venture guesses where
Valeria obdurately does not.

  As the novel's secrets and alternatives proliferate, Valeria has doubts
about her methods: "a certain uneasy sensation" (9), a "sudden sense of
misgiving" (32), a feeling of "hopeless confusion" (37). These sentiments
likewise encourage suspense by flattering readers who can contrast such
unthinking intuition with their own rational acumen.[64] Sifting the novel's
information, we see through Valeria's frantic hostility to inference, as when
she refuses to take "every one of these monstrous improbabilities [Eustace's
mother's actions]" as "facts that had actually happened" (34). The tension
between character and reader could be read as a moral conundrum placed
within the novel's presentation of detective capabilities. Inferential acuity
may require a "narrow-minded" approach (say, of a reader trained on
detective fiction) that leads to moral difficulties. Conversely, the "many-
sidedness" of a capacious moral view (say, of this novel's remarkably
permissive protagonist) may be too broad to sift information.[65]

Yet in being lured by the novel's encouragement of speculation, readers are actually moving further into uncertainty. We may be encouraged to guess, but our conjectures and surmises do not lead to conclusive explanations. Collins presents a model of reading less indebted to rational detection, scientific method, or mystical intuition and more focused on both the diligent aggregation of detail and an openness to serendipity and failure. D. A. Miller has read the detective work of *The Moonstone* as offering multiple points of view on a single case that solidify into the ideological uniformity of "an essentially monological narration," "always speaking through a master-voice that corrects, overrides, subordinates, or sublates all other voices it allows to speak."[66] *The Law and the Lady* works in a direction opposed to this vision of "local uncertainties" building to "a more fundamental readerly certainty."[67] Instead, it generates a foundationally polyvocal narrative that resists the hardening of probability into fact, of alternatives into single outcomes, of informational clutter into significant clue and, in a broader sense to which I return below, of the "deviant" into the "normal."

Unproven at Trial

Having unearthed the trial report, Valeria proceeds to retell its events as a digest that works according to a similar logic as the search, in a mockery of hypothetico-deductive reasoning. The trial focuses on three questions that concern the means, agent, and motive of Sara Macallan's death. In each instance we see a pattern whereby speculations and suppositions are paradoxically followed by material findings. It is as if "loose and unreliable evidence" (128) is meant to confirm the shaky conjectures that preceded it instead of acting as data from which conclusions could be drawn.[68] Collins's reading of nineteenth-century trial reports (the French *Causes célèbres* and English adaptations) displays in this novel "an awareness of the limits of the text's or the trial's ability to convey an unmediated truth," as Bernadette Meyler has argued.[69] Bearing a formal resemblance to such collections in its use of a "retrospective standpoint" to recharacterize circumstantial evidence, the novel "frames the trial in such a way as to render the legal advocates and decision-makers themselves a subject of inquiry."[70] Collins writes broadly in concert with the skepticism at mid-century "that crime would invariably uncover itself."[71] Questions and interruptions are oddly unvoiced in Valeria's condensed record, which underlines the sense that the trial multiplies inferential possibilities in default of establishing actual occurrences. It might not be a stretch to see

Valeria overturning the entire "adversarial" logic of the English trial system in favor of an "inquisitorial" French approach, with herself as primary investigator, in keeping with the mixed nature of Scots law mentioned earlier.[72]

On the question of whether Sara was poisoned, the nurse who attended during the final illness gives a rambling testimony, calling attention to Eustace's two opportunities for delivering the poison (132–33). Valeria's reflections on this testimony stand for a larger pattern in noting how the prosecution "led the Jury to infer that the prisoner had taken those opportunities to rid himself of an ugly and jealous wife" (139). The defense unwittingly validates this character assassination while trying to challenge it, objecting to the evidence only on "technical" grounds (143, 147) and offering merely a different character portrait: "Was this the sort of woman who would exasperate a man into poisoning her? And was this the sort of man who would be capable of poisoning his wife?" (140–41).[73] The hypotheses of the first question are confirmed, in a non sequitur, by medical testimony. The two doctors originally attending, backed up by the postmortem surgeon and two "analytical chemists," produce the "over-whelming testimony" of poisoning by arsenic, actually displaying the compound that was found in the body "in a quantity admittedly sufficient to have killed two persons instead of one" (141).[74] These findings are described using a word that cannily applies to both desire and geometric deduction: "irresistible" evidence (141).

Likewise, the question of the poisoner first casts a shadow over Eustace in order to combine circumstantial evidence found at the scene.[75] The official investigator murkily describes how charges arose against Eustace – "certain discoveries which were reported" to the Procurator-Fiscal resulted in an arrest warrant (142) – and the sheriff's officer reports how a search of Eustace's residence Gleninch discovered a small screw of paper with some white grains and a chemist's label. Two Edinburgh druggists have signed records of Eustace's purchase of arsenic, for domestic purposes (killing insects and rats) his respective household authorities testify to having no knowledge of (146–48).[76] The prosecution uses all this to "prove" in a leading argument "(1) that Eustace had bought the poison; (2) that the reason which he had given to the druggists for buying the poison was not the true reason; (3) that he had had two opportunities of secretly adminis-tering poison to his wife" (152).

The final question is answered by what the novel ominously terms "silent evidence" (156), Sara's letters and excerpts from Eustace's diary, which underline her marital unhappiness and his apparently homicidal

intentions, given the double-bind of being compelled to marry a woman
he dislikes while hankering after another who is married and beyond his
ken. This assessment of motive involves the entire backstory of Eustace
and Sara's accidental marriage, even though much (including Eustace's
supposed attachment to his married cousin, Helena Beauly) is acknow-
ledged as hearsay. The chance occasion that led to their marriage (Sara
visited Eustace and was found in his bedroom) was, like the trial, a matter
of "motives . . . misinterpreted in the vilest manner" (155). Eustace's note
to self – recognizing "how irresistible temptation can be, and how easily,
sometimes, crime may follow it" (161) – may appear damning but is only
another conjectural item to add to the prosecution's "chain of hostile
evidence" (147). Alluding to the wider sense of the term "libel" as denoting
any criminal charge whatever, Collins has Eustace's mother reject the diary
as a "libel on his character," no less so because that libel is "written by
himself" (168), and Dexter agrees that a diary is "nothing but an expression of the weakest side in the character of the person who keeps
it" (174).[77]

When the trial gives us facts, it thus enumerates evidence to make it
seem convincing: two arsenic purchases, two occasions for poisoning, three
letters, five medical witnesses, six diary excerpts. These repetitions parody
the requirement in Scots law, much stricter than in English, for corroborating evidence: if one fact does not suffice, another one will. The trial
digest might also read as a parody of the trend Alexander Welsh identifies
in evidentiary narratives from the eighteenth into the nineteenth century
whereby witness testimony cedes ground to circumstantial evidence.[78]
Many of the hypotheticals introduced work on the model of so-called
similar fact evidence: as in the Madeleine Smith trial, probable patterns
(former purchases of arsenic, previous illnesses after a beverage offered by
the accused) support a causal chain with no basis in reality.[79] There is
enough such evidence here for several trials.

But when the trial departs from fact into its main mode, conjecture, a
bizarre reversal of conditional probability holds sway. Typically, a trial
holds one referential event stable – say, that a murder has taken place – and
uses concrete evidence to reason back to means and motives, to establish a
verdict in relation to the event. Here that reasoning alternates in a
probabilistic manner that runs the chronology in the wrong direction
and focuses more on the evidence: it asks whether a given piece of evidence
is more likely in relation to a murder or in connection with some other
state of affairs.[80] Such an inversion captures how uncertain poisoning cases
were felt to be in the Victorian period. Collins, an adept of the poisoning

plot since *The Woman in White*, may have followed a logic developed in Burton:[81]

> In all charges of this nature the main substantial fact, to which all others are secondary, is, that the death has been caused by poison. It is not necessary that its presence should be actually detected – it may be shown that it has existed though it exist no longer, and it may be proved ... that poison was actually consumed by the deceased. Having separately and as an independent fact proved the death by poison, we have a safe position whence, from the conduct and motives of parties, we may alight on those who have committed the crime.[82]

Having emphatically demonstrated the primary fact, the trial in Collins's representation mocks this apparently secure position for inference by means of "conduct and motives," and through its many conjectures and loose threads raises the specter of another type of death (suicide) as an explanatory framework for the "facts" presented.

Valeria's reading of the trial places the conjectural before the factual because her own investigation aims to find an alternative evidentiary sequence – to depart from what Jessica Maynard has called "forms of reading that legislate for closure."[83] Since she has to "construct a theory that excludes [Eustace] as the perpetrator of the crime" and to set up a "surrogate trial designed to supplant the original," Valeria needs a different construal of facts open to interpretation (including circumstantial detail, character aspersions, and hearsay evidence).[84] She calls into question not only the evidence she has read and recast, but the very logic that guides how evidence is used. As Sara Murphy has suggested, "the idea of a normative forensic subjectivity, the training in argument and skills in the evaluation of evidence, is itself placed on trial."[85] Valeria derides the prosecution's concluding statement, which reminds the jury that they "must be satisfied with the best circumstantial evidence" while admonishing them "against being too ready to trust it! 'You must have evidence satisfactory and convincing to your own minds,' he said; 'in which you find no conjectures – but only irresistible and just inferences.' Who is to decide what is a just inference? And what does circumstantial evidence rest on, *but* conjecture?" (181). This assault on conjecture is likewise directed at the defense's main theory, that Sara used arsenic as a cosmetic tool and died of an accidental overdose, which rests on assertions about Sara's prior awareness of arsenic as a cosmetic remedy (she had even acquired a book on the practice) despite negative answers to leading questions in this vein.[86] "No direct evidence anywhere! Nothing but conjecture!" (178) Valeria scoffs, agreeing with the prosecution's characterization of the defense as "a clumsy subterfuge, in which no reasonable being could discern the smallest fragment of probability" (184). Presented as a contest of conjecture, circumstance, and inference, the trial in *The Law and the Lady* calls attention to what has been described as the "disjunction of probability and acceptability" in judicial fact-finding and decision-making.[87] The verdict arrived at is less "a statement about a past event" than "a statement about the evidence presented at trial"; the proceedings are arranged less "to promote public acceptance" of the verdict than to emphasize the (often numerical) probability of evidentiary data.[88]

Probable verdicts are not always the same as acceptable verdicts. Valeria's practice of reading with an eye to the trial's procedures rather than its occasioning events is a way of foregrounding an acceptable verdict (Eustace's innocence) rather than quibbling over whether the evidence supports a probable one. Indeed, she predicates her analysis so firmly on innocence that she resolves against the logic of the inquiry before reading: "I want no reason! I believe, in spite of the Verdict" (104). Her view again typifies an inverse reasoning that underwrites the trial with counterfactuals: "Evidence in your favour, that might have been found, has not been found. Suspicious circumstances have not been investigated. Crafty people have not been watched" (107) – and, one might add, books about arsenic's cosmetic uses have not been read. Although her practice becomes more critical over the course of the novel, it does confirm the vision of the "naive reader as potentially endowed with characteristics that will enable her to discover 'truth' more effectively than the professional."[89] So "firmly settled in [her] mind" is the "conviction of some dreadful oversight" (107) that her entire approach could be seen as an attempt to underline, again and again, the presumption of innocence from which any case should proceed and which "not proven" automatically disputes. "We know he is innocent" is her mantra: "Why is his innocence not proved? It ought to be, it must be, it shall be! If the Trial tells me it can't be done, I refuse to believe the Trial" (109). This incantatory repetition goes so far as to redact the trial's founding element, the charge, which Valeria refuses to copy out: "The less there is of that false and hateful Indictment on this page, the better and truer the page will look, to *my* eyes" (125).

Investigating by Numbers

For all her resistance to the trial's "not proven" character, Valeria's own investigation uncannily follows the verdict's hesitant structure. She claims there can be "no half-confidences" and "no such refuge as a middle course"

(236), but finds herself saddled between two equally plausible suspects, Miserrimus Dexter and Helena Beauly, who formed respective love triangles with Sara and Eustace. The investigation constantly runs aground because Valeria continues in the mode she adopted in the library, pursuing through trial and error the sorts of additive or numerical approaches that do not necessarily (per the problem of induction) lead to sound inference. It hardly bodes well that her inquiry is curated by one of the suspects, the fascinating Dexter, who embodies the verdict's in-between logic. His first name is a Latin superlative (*miserrimus*, "unhappiest"), the third term in a comparative structure. It may allude to Thomas Love Peacock's narrative poem *Miserrimus* (1833), with its spirited defense of "anomaly," which "enters into the composition of us all; *impar sibi* ["unlike itself"] is the biography of every created being, and *I* have proved no exception to the rule."[90] His surname means "right" (*dexter*) while his character invokes its Latin antonym for "left" (*sinister*) and alludes to a legal term for "one who plays both sides" (*ambidexter*), or "a juror who takes money for his verdict."[91] A duplicate or triplicate entity, Dexter is a fraction: "literally the half of a man" (173), congenitally missing the lower half of the body. Under his tutelage Valeria tries to undo "not proven" by means of halves, doubles, and multiples of fact, only to uncover more labyrinthine narratives of jealousy and deception.

In the parties to the Macallan case, it is Helena who first draws Valeria's jealous attention, sanctioned by what she dubiously sees as "the inevitable result of reading the evidence" (185). She decides that Helena must have administered the second dose of poison and offers backward reasoning just as specious as the prosecution's: "Admit this, and the inference follows that she also gave the first dose in the early morning" (187). Conjectures inform her suspicion: Helena is in love with and recently free to pursue the unhappily married Eustace, was overheard in conspiratorial conversation with him, has been exposed to the idea of arsenic, and has no alibi for the time Sara was alone in her bedroom. Dexter encourages Valeria in this suspicion, making her guess the person he has in mind by infantilizing her detective capacities to a rudimentary level – "What is the first letter of her name? Is it one of the first three letters of the alphabet?" (250) – and then similarly slandering his object according to "degrees of comparison": "I am positively cunning; the devil is comparatively cunning; Mrs. Beauly is superlatively cunning" (252). Dexter's retelling of the fatal evening when he observed Helena summarizes the options for her passage through the house at a crucial moment: "First room, the little study, mentioned in the nurse's evidence. Second room, Mrs. Eustace Macallan's bedchamber.

Third room, her husband's bedchamber" (254). That his inference about Helena's presence and activity in the house would be compromised by having the "worst possible opinion of Mrs. Beauly" (255) is not seen by Valeria, who is taken in by a narrative that frames inference as a numerical sum:

> Where could she be? Certainly in the house, somewhere. Where? I had made sure of the other rooms; the field of search was exhausted. She could only be in Mrs. Macallan's room – the one room which had baffled my investigations; the only room which had not lent itself to examination. Add to this, that the key of the door in the study, communicating with Mrs. Macallan's room, was stated in the nurse's evidence to be missing; and don't forget that the dearest object of Mrs. Beauly's life (on the showing of her own letter, read at the Trial) was to be Eustace Macallan's happy wife. Put these things together in your own mind, and you will know what my thoughts were, as I sat waiting for events in my chair, without my telling you. (256)

Only when she receives a different account of that night's events (from Helena's maid) does Valeria realize the failure of this additive logic. Adding *to* is not the same as adding *up*. Putting things together just produces a bundle of data, "circumstances," and "discoveries" that can be aggregated or disproved in other combinations (257). "I could now see that I had been trebly in the wrong," another of her triple-decker realizations runs, "wrong in hastily and cruelly suspecting an innocent woman; wrong in communicating my suspicions (without an attempt to verify them previously) to another person; wrong in accepting the flighty inferences and conclusions of Miserrimus Dexter as if they had been solid truths" (269).

Having suspected Helena on account of Dexter's attempt to furnish "a perfectly reasonable and perfectly probable motive" (340) for her guilt, Valeria likewise entertains Playmore's charges that Dexter interfered with the police to suppress evidence and acted in a suspicious manner at Gleninch. Again she falls prey to an additive logic, which Playmore encourages by noting that Dexter had made copies of two keys (to Eustace's diary and the drawer where it was kept): "Add to this information Dexter's incomprehensible knowledge of the contents of your husband's Diary; and the product is – that the wax models sent to the old iron shop in Caldershaws, were models taken by theft from the key of the Diary and the key of the table-drawer in which it was kept" (356). Despite the pitfalls of such reasoning, Valeria's commitment to trial and error does provide the tenacity, the narrative duration, by means of which this "Lady who refuses to listen to reason and who insists on having her own way," as Playmore views her, "accidentally" illuminates aspects of the case that the "whole machinery of the Law" could not (277). It is Playmore's "strong persuasion that, if you succeed in discovering the nature of this communication [between Dexter and Sara], in all human likelihood you prove your husband's innocence by the discovery of the truth" (316).

After these alternations and accidents, the inquiry appears as a "darkly-doubtful game which was neither quite for me, nor quite against me, as the chances now stood" (319). Persistently finding herself between options despite her attempts to carve certainty out of the case, Valeria has to face a different dilemma when Eustace reenters the frame (having in the interim gone on an unfathomable jaunt to a war in Spain where, true to character, he is wounded by a stray bullet). There are now "two cruel alternatives": rejecting him to pursue the investigation or returning without the necessary proof of innocence. She dismisses both: "Those two agreeable fiends, Prevarication and Deceit, took me as it were softly by the hand: 'Don't commit yourself either way, my dear'" (362).

The Puzzle to a Solution

The case's explanation emerges when it is revealed that Dexter tried to destroy Sara's suicide note to protect her memory and conceal his own partial responsibility for her death. Characteristically, this solution appears only in a confession, partly recorded in shorthand, which offers a narrative "told in disguise" on a topic "full of snares for the narrator" (337). The note is recovered, however improbably, from the Gleninch dust-heap and pieced together according to a model of inference that has been deceptively hard to execute thus far: "Only get a central bit of it right, and the rest of the Puzzle falls into its place" (370). The fragments of paper are found stuck to a gum bottle (conveniently discarded in the same bin), so that for once in the novel an accidental discovery can be reconstituted into a signifying whole: "The fragments accidentally stuck together, would, in all probability, be found to fit each other, and would certainly (in any case) be the easiest fragments to reconstruct, as a centre to start from" (380).[92]

This forensic discovery is as irreproachable as the medical evidence that reproduced the fatal arsenic at the trial. But in the end it is no inference at all, just one of those "improper" inductions discussed by Mill:

> Suppose that a phenomenon consists of parts, and that these parts are only capable of being observed separately, and as it were piecemeal. When the observations have been made, there is a convenience ... in obtaining a

representation of the phenomenon as a whole, by combining, or as we may say, piecing these detached fragments together.... But is there anything of the nature of an induction in this process?[93]

There is not. This discovery simply allows a construction of the "plainest circumstantial evidence" to confirm it as "identical with the letter which Miserrimus Dexter had suppressed until the Trial was over, and had then destroyed by tearing it up" (381). It literalizes the standard, expressed in the trial, that a "fragment of probability" (184) is all the law seeks.

By this point it will not be a shock to learn that Sara's suicide note is actually two letters: the first an exposé of Dexter's romantic approaches, the second a set of time-stamped updates as she reports live on the effects of arsenic, surely Collins's attempt to forestall a paradoxical "confession" of suicide. The novel ends as a not proven case in several senses. Its solution is a crime (suicide) that notoriously resists the definition of crime. Unexplained deaths in the period often resulted in an inquest where a coroner could register only an "open verdict."[94] The clinching evidence (the reconstructed letter and the corroborating statements about its circumstantial relevance) is sealed up in an envelope and thus puts any feeling of QED in abeyance. Eustace's legal innocence remains in suspension even if his moral probity is (somewhat) assured, since a retrial is technically disallowed (one cannot be tried twice for the same crime even after "not proven") and Playmore is opaque on how a "new legal inquiry," presumably a civil case somehow involving the same facts that underpinned the criminal one, might be undertaken (385). The novel's conclusion elaborates on the qualities evident in its earlier visual reproduction of the signatures in the marriage register: Valeria's confident flourish, Eustace's nervous squiggle. As in the investigation, there is a tension between "legal evidence" and "moral certainty" (251). Valeria may have failed on the former front, since "nothing will persuade Eustace that I think him worthy to be the guide and companion of my life – but the proof of his innocence, set before the Jury which doubts it, and the public which doubts it, to this day" (241). But it may be just as well that she sticks with the private task of persuading him that he is innocent in her eyes, instead of subjecting him to the "public vindication" (412) that may prove too exacting for a man whose own mother thinks him "one of the weakest of living mortals" (196). "I must destroy at its root his motive for leaving me," Valeria decides, noting that her belief in his innocence is less important than proving how "his position towards me has become the position of an innocent man" (311), a category subtle in its difference from a verdict of "not guilty."[95]

If detective fiction is typically marked by a "narrative reconstruction [that] restores the disrupted social order and reaffirms the validity of the system of norms," this novel neither wholly restores nor entirely ratifies such an order.[96] Collins undercuts the conventional inferences of detective fiction, including his own, in order to present approaches to investigation that use repeated trial and error or that wait for a lucky break. "All my ingenuity – as after events showed me – was wasted on speculations not one of which even approached the truth" (243). Further, if detective fiction's "narrative process is about discovery and the creation of a meaningful sequence," a way of "integrating an aberrant past into the present," this novel disrupts such sequential integration.[97] Collins seems to thwart the enjoyment of both "detective fiction and legal argument, ... the satisfaction derived from the demonstration of inevitability: it had to be this way, and no other way."[98] He leaves us with a solution that is frustratingly simple alongside moral and social motives that are inscrutably complex. He scrambles the ideological aim of restoring "social innocence" through a gradual sifting of information, whereby "the fantasy of total relevance yields to the reality of a more selective meaningfulness, the universality of suspicion gives way to a highly specific guilt."[99] Blurring the line between the courtroom and its social milieu to show how the framing of evidence and hypotheses is often biased, Collins abdicates conventional modes of narrative closure or poetic justice and is alert to "other forms of knowledge that could be disruptive to trial procedure."[100] The novel multiplies the experiences of regret, jealousy, and shame at the heart of its plot.[101] It presents not a closed community made "innocent of crime" but an open social world where uncertainty about guilt or innocence is widely dispersed.[102] Valeria tries to enact the definiteness undermined by the verdict, and her failure is telling. It suggests how legal uncertainty is worked out on a social terrain less tolerant of binary assessments of human action. It affords criticism of a legal system dubiously organized by numerical exactness and epistemological precision. In this probabilistic territory, anyone can get the sum wrong or put the wrong puzzle together. And it cautions us against hasty and additive inferences, when trials, accidents, and hearsay might always tell another story, or no story at all.

Reading without Proving

What might the literary vehicle of the hesitant verdict reveal about the wider terrain of legal novels in the period? A "close attention to the law's ideological and semiotic weaknesses," Jan-Melissa Schramm argues, allowed Victorian novels to explore "what lies outside the law," furnishing "a forum for the representation of repressed or excluded material, of that which exceeds restrictive legal taxonomies."[103] Yet in disclosing not weakness but flexibility at the core of legal logic, Collins's novel runs athwart the reform-minded humanism of Victorian novels as varied as Elizabeth Gaskell's *Mary Barton* (1848), Charlotte Yonge's *The Trial* (1864), and George Eliot's *Felix Holt* (1866), with their certain investment in the "right recognition of the innocence of the wrongfully accused."[104] Just as the Scotch verdict undermines what Schramm elsewhere describes as the trend toward certainty in nineteenth-century legal standards, so Collins offers a legal reformism that is diffuse and tentative: he writes less a "novel of purpose" than a novel that is purposive without concrete goals.[105] *The Law and the Lady* ends not with justice but with what the philosopher Stanley Cavell – writing about categories that could plausibly describe this novel: "comedies of remarriage," "melodramas of the unknown woman" – suggestively calls "good enough justice."[106] A conception of justice as "good enough," in Cavell's terms, is related to a picture of selfhood in progress "that projects no unique point of arrival but only a willingness for change, directed by specific aspirations that, while rejected, may at unpredictable times return with new power."[107] The familiar inversions of wrongful accusation and rightful reinstatement yield to more uncertain conclusions in Collins. Eustace has turned out to be a "good enough" husband, Valeria a "good enough" detective.

To see the legal novel as riven by uncertainty is also to contemplate how other works in Collins's oeuvre are given to accidental and serendipitous "methods," to their own instantiations of the unproven verdict. Indeed, the novel claimed by T. S. Eliot, Dorothy Sayers, and P. D. James as the exemplary detective fiction, *The Moonstone*, can be seen to rely on such patterns, as many critics intuit without necessarily questioning its overriding frameworks of rationality, certainty, and closure. In that novel, the "work of detection is prosecuted in large degree as a result of chance and coincidence," and Ezra Jennings, a "detective-historian of true negative capability," solves the case "through sympathy and sheer luck as much as through scientific ratiocination."[108] In *The Woman in White*, the "tendency to madness makes Marian and Walter no less successful in solving mysteries," and guessing, though "sometimes undisciplined, wild, and intuitive," is not "any less productive."[109] And in "The Diary of Anne Rodway," Collins's (female) investigator, like Valeria, "accomplishes more by chance and by perseverance than by the exercise of any particular detective skill."[110]

More broadly, my account opens up the uncertainty of other novels that deploy representations of legal indeterminacy in opposing the norms of narrative closure, social restitution, and moral control. Anthony Trollope's *Orley Farm* (1862) uses the framing topic of forgery to hesitate between the known guilt of the accused, Lady Mason, and the persistent social assumption of her innocence. Trollope probes the instabilities of prejudicially surmising innocence or guilt, and presents a case resolved by moral confession rather than legal prosecution. Mary Braddon's *An Open Verdict* (1878) is a late entry in a career built on plots of suspected poisoning and unexplained death. The novel follows the daughter of a rich and gloomy widower, who seeks to prevent her from marrying her choice, a curate. The father is deemed a "likely subject for suicide" by other characters and appears in one scene writing what could be a suicide note.[111] After his death, the daughter reveals that she had purchased laudanum from "several chemists" to stave off insomnia, claiming she finished the bottle on the fatal night.[112] After an inquest written as an embedded drama, with different actors speaking their parts, the verdict is death by laudanum, "by whom administered there was no evidence to show."[113] The curate retreats from his lover, "not fully assured of her innocence," and Braddon ramps up the plot's conjectural suspense by means of rumor, confirming the suicide only at the very end, with one character's deathbed confession.[114]

The "not proven" frame might also extend to novels not centrally about the law where events, decisions, or representations are irreducibly marked by uncertainty. In *Daniel Deronda*, as we have seen, Gwendolen's guilt over her husband's accidental death has to do less with her failure to rescue him and more with her lingering sense that she had just abandoned a plan to kill him. In Thomas Hardy's *Tess of the d'Urbervilles*, unsubstantiated hearsay competes with fact about a crime whose details are never fully brought to light. Hardy's plot is driven on many levels by rumor, that form of uncertain knowledge registered with the felt certainty of bodily sensation.[115] Many novels concern quasi-legal matters that the law cannot adequately explain, decide, or convert into binary form. Their recourse to social or moral adjudication reveals how legal structures are often built on an epistemological mirage – not on facts but on unproven claims and tacit assumptions. Hearsay evidence might be inadmissible in courts of law, but in novels (and other courts of public opinion) it is always in vogue.

Legal uncertainty thus holds interest for what it reveals about the mechanics of social and moral knowledge in novels distant from the courtroom. Collins uses puzzles about inference and proof to reflect with dark pragmatism about how criminality is a matter of moral luck:

Is there a common fund of wickedness in us all? Is the suppression or the development of that wickedness a mere question of training and temptation? And is there something in our deeper sympathies which mutely acknowledges this, when we feel for the wicked; when we crowd to a criminal trial; when we shake hands at parting (if we happen to be present officially) with the vilest monster that ever swung on a gallows? It is not for me to decide. (329–30)

This reflection harkens back to the early applications of statistics to judicial questions: Quetelet's "assignments of penchants for crime to the average man," for instance, "implied that every individual had some such penchant, if only latently."[116] Collins includes a wide critique of assumptions governing criminal law and a narrow barb at legal quietism ("if we happen to be present officially"). But he puts both under uncertainty, unsettling us into further reflection.

The Law and the Lady's investment in uncertainty moves from questions of individual selfhood to the deeper concern, again in Cavell's terms, that "any actual society exists in a state not of strict but of partial compliance with the principles of justice," even if through compromise it "maintains good enough justice to allow criticism of itself, and reform."[117] With its traffic in hesitant and nonrestrictive taxonomies that emphasize the half, the double, the middle, and the compromise, the novel undoes what Luhmann has described as the "operative closure" of law from its social milieu.[118] Typically, the law's status as an "autopoetic, self-distinguishing system" is guaranteed by the "binarity of its coding" – its logical sorting of phenomena into legal or illegal – although even this leads to uncertainty and "provides certainty only in a conditional and not in a definitively expressed form."[119] But when the law's binary structure gives way, as it does in the case of the "not proven" verdict," confusion is unleashed in social space. Luhmann has argued that modern systems of law are faced with an "awareness of complexity . . . which eclipses the claim that the problems of the world can be worked out logically or even theoretically," making necessary a pragmatic approach that sometimes bypasses "the prohibition of the denial of justice."[120] Referring to a third verdict that existed in Roman law (and is sometimes taken as an ancestor to "not proven"), Luhmann states that "a 'non liquet' cannot be excluded simply on logical grounds," since our "world does not provide any guarantee for logical order and consistency of deductions" and "options must be kept open for new doubts, better insights, and a change in the rules."[121] Collins's novel thus reflects a situation, a limit case toward which other novels tend, where legal and social orders are confronted with mutual and ineradicable elements of openness, uncertainty, and inconsistency.

Rejecting binary decision in favor of suppler modes of appraisal, *The Law and the Lady* also undercuts clean definitions of the "normal" or "average" human subject in its generally valorizing and engaging portrayal of Dexter and his androgyne cousin-servant Ariel – that is, of the marginal and disabled, of those bodies that nineteenth-century statistics and anthropometry first cast as "deviant" or "irregular."[122] If disability studies and queer theory have, in different ways, prompted us to think of our categories as more open and flexible – as "nondualistic" in Eve Sedgwick's phrase – they meet an intriguing analogue in the "not proven" verdict.[123] Here my account dovetails with what Sara Ahmed has called "a politics of the hap," which "open[s] up possibilities for being in other ways, of being perhaps," and "works toward a world in which things can happen in alternative ways."[124] This novel of legal uncertainty stands as a caution against the application of normalizing techniques, centrally statistics, to bend the law toward standards of certainty that would deprive it of contingency and interpretive flexibility, not to mention humanity. That trend is visible in the nineteenth-century inquiry into mathematical probability as a way of sorting witness testimony, which had been developing since the late seventeenth century and acquired momentum after Hume's notorious arguments in his "Essay on Miracles" and the work of Enlightenment thinkers like Nicolas de Condorcet, Pierre-Simon Laplace, and Siméon-Denis Poisson.[125] In the English context, the further analyses of Charles Babbage, Augustus De Morgan, and George Boole (among others) suggested how mathematical probability might effectively produce what could be thought of as a "normal" witness and an "average" juror (or judge) by combining several independent individuals.[126] Such uses of statistics in the law were strongly criticized by Mill and Venn (who rejected the idea of placing witnesses on a "graduated scale of mendacity").[127] Yet even though the specific analysis of witness testimony was "largely discredited" by century's end, the broader logic remained alluring – and remains so still.[128] In our day, statistical methods are ubiquitous: decisions about sentencing make use of the reference class, an inheritance of this moment in Victorian logic, into which the convicted are deemed to fit; and algorithms are similarly available to predict recidivism.[129] Novelistic uncertainty cuts against this appeal of seeing individuals as merely units in a distribution, their peculiarities subsumed by the law of large numbers.

In literary studies, this stance of moral openness, diffident judgment, and unsure classification could double as a model of reading – call it *reading without proving* – that would thrive on hesitancy and endorse the possibility of having knowledge without final proof, of knowing despite being unable to reach a verdict. Reading without proving offers a modest proposal for methodological pluralism, an open-ended response to debates about "the way we read now." It hovers among calls for reading as close or distant, surface or symptomatic, post-critical or uncritical, and indeed innocent or guilty.[130] Hesitant reading fits between doing manifest injustice to texts and, in Sharon Marcus's neatly ambiguous phrase, "just reading" them.[131] It approaches texts with an openness to surface features (the theme of "not proven" might be expected to consort with aspects of narrative, character, and form) and an alertness to hidden dimensions (the legal sources of "not proven" might be subject to concealment or deception). It stays the sentencing hand, in order not to rest in "undecidability" but to commit to uncertain judgments that make time for further evidence, arbitration, and correction.[132]

Part I of this book has emphasized uncertainty primarily at level of individual characters, considering thoughts, judgments, actions, decisions, verdicts, and reading practices marked by hesitation. While keeping these matters in mind, Part II broadens the frame to investigate uncertainty in aggregate terms, studying its patterns across oeuvres and giving shape to probable realism as a generic instantiation of uncertainty. At the fulcrum between individual and aggregate, I end here by venturing that, given the allure of statistical tools and "trial by mathematics" in both literary studies and the law, it would be worth reflecting on how the uncertainty that plagues so many accounts of human action, moral assessment, and critical judgment seems to call out for a correspondingly uncertain mode of reading. If I have been conducting what the Victorian barrister James Fitzjames Stephen called "trial by literature," reading without proving reveals that, in at least some cases, the jury's still out.[133]

PART II

Probable Realisms

CHAPTER 3

Worlds Otherwise
Thackeray and the Counterfactual Imagination

> What queer speculations the "might have beens" are!
> —William Thackeray, *Letters*[1]

Though he passed his life amid imaginary scenes, William Thackeray was curiously unsure of the boundary between fictional and factual worlds:

> O wondrous power of genius! Fielding's men and women are alive, though History's are not.... Is not Amelia preparing her husband's little supper? Is not Miss Snap chastely preventing the crime of Mr. Firebrand? Is not Parson Adams in the midst of his family, and Mr. Wild taking his last bowl of punch with the Newgate Ordinary? Is not every one of them a real substantial have-been personage now?... For our parts, we will not take upon ourselves to say that they do not exist somewhere else; that the actions attributed to them have not really taken place.[2]

Prior to *Vanity Fair* (1847–48), Thackeray penned several statements along these lines, praising the authenticity and actuality of fictional constructs, musing on the properties that apparently allow them to *have been*. In the "reader's soul" characters become "real creatures, ... beings that take their place by nature's own," "real living personages in history."[3]

Yet Thackeray's world is also populated by visions of a different order from this "preoccupation with the actual": nonentities inhabiting the unreal space of what *might have been*.[4] In letters and essays, stories and novels, Thackeray revivifies fact and fiction by conjuring their respective alternatives: an accident that might have happened, a shooting that might have taken place, a child who might have lived, a war that might have been avoided, a republic that could have been proclaimed, a death that might not have occurred.[5] The pure form of this pattern – heads might have been tails – condenses Thackeray's fascination with probable options and irrevocable outcomes.[6] Overtly *counterfactual*, "bringing into being things not previously existing in the world," Thackeray's realism is also *counterfictional*, "displacing the ordinary attributes of imagining – its faintness, two-dimensionality, fleetingness, and dependence on volitional labor – with the vivacity, solidity, persistence, and givenness of the perceptible world."[7]

Thackeray's oeuvre runs against the grain of both fact and fiction, perhaps more so than other nineteenth-century novelists. Readers are to be persuaded that fictions have attained the status of fact, even as they are lured into acts of counterfactual imagining that derealize facticity, subjecting it to imaginative reanimation. When his fiction draws us into entertaining what Thackeray calls the "might-have-beens," we could be said tacitly to grant its factual, "have-been" status.[8] Yet this blurs any originating distinction between fact and fiction, whose domains shade into one another and lead to generic tensions:

> If we want instruction, we prefer to take it from fact rather than from fiction. We like to hear sermons from his reverence at church; to get our notions of trade, crime, politics, and other national statistics, from the proper papers and figures; but when suddenly, out of the gilt pages of a pretty picture book, a comic moralist rushes forward, and takes occasion to tell us that society is diseased, the laws unjust, the rich ruthless, the poor martyrs, the world lop-sided, . . . persons who wish to lead an easy life are inclined to remonstrate against this literary ambuscadoe.[9]

Thackeray's dialectical irony here prefers factual exactitude over the sham productions of fictional moralists (*gilt* pages, *pretty* book) but elsewhere endorses fiction's authenticity and moral purpose against the factual minutiae of history ("mere contemptible catalogues of names and places, that can have no moral effect upon the reader").[10]

In this chapter, I argue that Thackeray's persistent alternation between fact and counterfact, fiction and counterfiction, yields an uncertainty both narrative and generic. Exposing his small-scale narrative grammar to the uncertainty of counterfactual and conditional statements, Thackeray mantles realism in a generic mirage. He swerves from sketch to satire, pantomime to parody, critical review to ironic squib, historical romance to "A Novel without a Hero." He convenes fictional characters, historical actors, canonical authors, and narratorial guises, steering them in and out of historical events and fictional spaces and recognizing them in reality. He speculatively reframes history against the penumbra of its alternative possibilities but also broods on its inexorable pressures and melancholy achievements. Relying on writing about counterfactuals in philosophy, social psychology, history, and literary theory, I investigate how Thackeray's counterfactual imagination, modeling worlds otherwise, infuses realism with the affects and dictates of uncertainty.

I first establish Thackeray's inchoate thoughts on these topics during his fictional apprenticeship through the 1840s. In what I call his *demonic* mode, Thackeray entertains extremes of improbability, makes casual use of supernatural motifs, and discovers gambling as a theme rich in narrative potential. Thackeray maintains the demonic as a ground of fictional possibility throughout his career, even if its early form is marginalized in the novels and receives fuller expression in minor genres. *Vanity Fair*, treated across the next two sections, domesticates the demonic mode but retains it in the wings of the plot as both narrative and generic alternative. In keeping with one psychological feature of counterfactuals – their spontaneous emergence in atypical scenarios where they regroove psychic and affective norms – the novel conjures the "might-have-beens" to restore realism to its "have-been" authenticity.[11] Where Thackeray's demonic mode involves extravagant futures, a counterfactual undertow pulls the narrative of *Vanity Fair* between moderate sentiments of risk and regret, speculation and retrospect, uncertainty about the future and unease about the past. The novel's "might-have-beens" join its two plots in tension while generating friction between realism and its others.

A third section examines the later intensification of *Vanity Fair*'s remorseful axis. Challenging a critical view of Thackeray as a novelist of fixed memory in *Pendennis* (1848–50) and *Henry Esmond* (1852), I explore the *Roundabout Papers* (1860–63) and their theory of recollection as shaped by virtuality. Thackeray's recurrent problem with memory – where are its objects located? – offers a late version of thinking about fictionality and counterfactuals. Finally, I consider how modal uncertainty usurps narrative attention almost to the exclusion of plot in *Lovel the Widower* (1860), which spurns concrete action to engage in abstract hypotheses on the conditions of narrative imagination. Hypothesis as late style illuminates Thackeray's commodious vision of realism, giving shape to its "profound uncertainty about the nature of reality."[12] He intuits that narratives guided by realist canons of mimesis, probability, decorum, and closure are sustained by the allowance of equally realist commitments to the non-mimetic, improbable, absurd, and open-ended. From a jaunty early mode (sponsoring fantastic plots to get narrative underway) to a jarring later version (using hypotheticals to stall narrative energy), Thackeray's *probable realism* compasses the range of uncertainty's narrative and generic effects.

Chronicling patterns of uncertain thinking in Thackeray, I extend the work of critics who describe his oeuvre in terms of skeptical ambivalence, interpretive variability, relentless irony, referential instability, and tonal fluctuation.[13] Yet I also move beyond an implicit consensus about Thackeray's "aesthetic of uncertainty" (in Amanpal Garcha's phrase) that stops short of a systematic account of its contours or contexts.[14] Although my emphasis here is more internalist, in difference from the book's other chapters, I do consider contextual materials in Thackeray's literary-cultural milieu. He may have squandered his time at Cambridge (where William Whewell was his tutor), spending more time gambling than being coached in mathematics and moral philosophy. But these intellectual materials make an oblique appearance, not least in authorial surrogates like Dobbin, "dull at classical learning, at mathematics ... uncommonly quick."[15] If Thackeray resists "abstract principles" in novels and "prefer[s] romances which do not treat of algebra, religion, political economy, or other abstract science," he still engages such principles on his own terms.[16] I dispute the assertion that his "lack of talent for mathematics" is consonant with a "strange incapacity for abstract thought," and suggest we take his preference for nontechnical knowledge as a credo about realist decorum rather than a blanket censure of abstraction.[17] If Thackeray's narratives are built around a "discernible scaffold of hypothesis and inference" aimed at the "discovery of new ways of talking about reality," that reality includes counterfactual alternatives and the ways we ponder and rationalize them.[18]

Demons of Fact

Thackeray's earliest publications, especially *The Paris Sketch Book* (1840), are replete with wagers on life, representations of gambling, and reversals of fortune. Featuring dreams and demons, familiars and fairies, these tales are often overlooked as productions of an inveterate joker. Yet if Thackeray's demonic characters could grace the pages of *Punch*, they nonetheless underscore a deeper belief: reality's visible manifest is shadowed by invisible presences and unrealized possibilities. I treat these unpredictable demons as the fictional ground that, in normalized or domesticated form, enables the precarious realism of Thackeray's later years. Lengthier and more serious productions rely on the defter and more light-hearted understructure of these sketches, with uncertainty as a linking thread.[19]

One such sketch is "A Gambler's Death" (1840), based on Thackeray's experience but so often reworked it became a fictional staple.[20] Its protagonist is a teller of tales "so monstrously improbable that the smallest boy in the school would scout at them," embedding doubt into the story's fictional logic.[21] When found "tripping in facts," Jack Attwood "unblushingly ... admitted his little errors in the score of veracity," but later in Paris this mentality – truth is a wager, a matter of keeping score – takes an unfortunate turn.[22] Jack mentions "an infallible plan for breaking all the play-banks in Europe" and borrows £5 from Titmarsh (Thackeray's alter ego, like him a regular at the gaming tables).[23] On one occasion he returns after a run of luck; on a later he commits suicide in debt. The sheer pervasiveness of gambling in Thackeray's work may explain why so little criticism takes it into account.[24] Early entries like "A Caution to Travellers" and "A Gambler's Death" (both in *The Paris Sketch Book*) are amplified from *Barry Lyndon* (1856, first serialized in 1844) to *Vanity Fair* and beyond. Gambling is a key locus of narrativity in Thackeray. It shapes kindred topics from the economics of imperialism to the exchange of objects, including the textual commodity he so consciously peddles.[25]

The Kickleburys on the Rhine (1850) is instructive as a continuation of this earlier mode, since it alludes to *Vanity Fair*, and its characters (renamed) reappear in later work. The scene is a casino in the town of "Rougetnoirbourg," a "queer, fantastic, melancholy place" where "strange fortunes" occur (Figure 3.1).[26] We meet the usual suspects of nineteenth-century casinos: winners with "most anxious faces," "poor shabby fellows who have got systems," and an individual who displays high emotion, "not for losing money, but for neglecting to win and play upon a *coup de vingt*, a series in which the red was turned up twenty times running; which series had he but played, it is clear that he might have broken M. Lenoir's bank, and shut up the gambling house."[27] Thwarted potential makes for imaginative continuity, in a digression on the so-called Contrebanque, a Belgian group that descended on Homburg in 1844 with an "infallible system," resulting in an epic contest allegorizing the century's earlier European wars as a tale of two banks.[28] The casino's affective and narrative possibilities compete with other avenues of speculation or amusement, including novel-reading. Titmarsh notes that "until I had lost . . . I was so feverish, excited, and uneasy, that I had neither delectation in reading the most exciting French novels, nor pleasure in seeing pretty landscapes, nor appetite for dinner."[29] An individual who "seemed to have quite a diabolical luck at the table" spotlights the demonic fascination that lures Lady Kicklebury into play, until his luck operates against hers "and he began straightway to win."[30] She loses everything and is shipped home by her chagrined family (a form of social death): so ends this story, which *Lovel the Widower* years later resumes.

A virtual version of the demonic mode, the Faustian bargain, announces the fatal powers of fictionality via wider extremes of contingency (swings of fortune) and necessity (death sentences). Faustian tales confirm that Thackeray's Romantic idealist vision as expressed in *The Newcomes* (1854–55) – art reveals splendors unseen by others, "hidden spirits of

THE INTERIOR OF HADES.

Figure 3.1   William Makepeace Thackeray, "The Interior of Hades," illustration
for *The Kickleburys on the Rhine*, in *The Christmas Books of M. A. Titmarsh*
(London: Smith, Elder, 1868), facing p. 169.
*EC85 T3255 B868c. Houghton Library, Harvard University.

Beauty" – is from the outset ghosted by darker apparitions.[31] In "The Devil's Wager" (1833), a demonic messenger, Mercurius, chauffeurs the condemned soul of Sir Roger de Rollo as he wonders whether his family will say prayers to keep him from hell. "Aves with them are rarae aves" quips Mercurius, and they lay a wager on whether anyone will comply.[32] They visit a number of family members who do not, but Roger is able to trick his brother Ignatius (a prior also bonded to the devil) into saying an *ave*, freeing himself and condemning the latter to hell.[33] "The Painter's Bargain" (1838) recasts this tale in more complex form. The wife of a painter, Simon Gambouge, pawns their possessions and takes to drink. While working, Simon falls into a reverie and fancies an exit. Invoking the devil's help, he is confronted by a creature, Diabolus, who emerges from a tube of crimson lake and requests the "easiest interest in the world": "nothing but the signature of a bond ... and the transfer of an article which, in itself, is a supposition – a valueless, windy, uncertain property of yours."[34] The devil will furnish any desire for seven years – natural desires invisibly, those "out of the course of nature" in person – in exchange for that "supposition," his soul.[35] Simon requests a meal, steals and sells the silver plate, and takes his proceeds to a gambling house, wishing for "half the money that is now on the table upstairs."[36] He places five napoleons on double zero:

> It is a dangerous spot, that o o, or double zero; but to Simon it was more lucky than to the rest of the world. The ball went spinning round – in "its predestined circle rolled," as Shelley has it, after Goethe – and plumped down at last in the double zero.... "Oh Diabolus!" cried he, "now it is that I begin to believe in thee! Don't talk about merit," he cried; "talk about fortune. Tell me not about heroes for the future – tell me of *zeroes*."[37]

The satisfaction of this wish does *not* count as unnatural (Diabolus does not appear), indicating the start of Thackeray's normalization of the demonic in the service of realism, as if anticipating his "Novel without a Hero" (and its many double zeroes). After such excesses, the painter reverts to a norm. He becomes a "capitalist," then repents and turns "abundantly moral."[38] Still vexed by his wife's behavior, he turns the wager on Diabolus, challenging *him* to live with her for six months. The idea is so frightful the devil dissolves the contract and Simon awakes from the reverie, having squeezed crimson lake over himself.[39] It is as if, having exhausted the world of dreams and demons, wagers and wild speculations, Thackeray the realist is ready to *paint*.

Although the demonic mode is subdued after *Vanity Fair*, variations on its extremes – material risk-taking and virtual speculation, real sketches and unreal conceptions – continue to underpin Thackeray's project. Narratives that intermittently rely on the fantastic invariably feature gambling and speculation: *The Great Hoggarty Diamond* (1841) involves a magical ring motivating the ups and downs of an insurance company; *The Diary of Jeames de la Pluche, Esq.* (1845) stars a protagonist who makes his railroad fortune only to lose it and manage a public house, the "Wheel of Fortune." Later narratives resurrect this mode when reversals of fortune are needed: *The Adventures of Philip* (1861–62) tells of an incredible restitution when a will is discovered in a carriage ("fairy chariot") accident.[40] To the end of his career Thackeray relies on the energetic uncertainty and modal perplexity of demonic tales: "Is life a dream? Are dreams facts? Is sleeping being really awake?"[41]

If the novelist's duty is to give convincing shape to demonic presences, it may also be his curse to wonder whether these are phantoms of madness, confusions of actual and invented worlds. Thackeray expresses this concern in one of the *Roundabout Papers*, "De Finibus" (of ends, endings): "Madmen . . . see visions, hold conversations with, even draw the likeness of, people invisible to you and me. Is this making people out of fancy madness? and are novel-writers at all entitled to strait-waistcoats?"[42] The conviction that fictional characters can attain an equivalent status to historical actors becomes *in extremis* a confusion of orders of experience. In what he dubs the "*afflated* style," the author appears as an oracular portal between worlds:

> I have been surprised at the observations made by some of my characters. It seems as if an occult Power was moving the pen. The personage does or says something, and I ask, how the Dickens did he come to think of that? Every man has remarked, in dreams, the vast dramatic power which is sometimes evinced. . . . But those strange characters you meet make instant observations of which you never can have thought previously. In like manner, the imagination foretels things. . . . What if some writer should appear who can write so enchantingly that he shall be able to call into actual life the people whom he invents? What if Mignon, and Margaret, and Goetz von Berlichingen are alive now (though I don't say they are visible), and Dugald Dalgetty and Ivanhoe were to step in at that open window by the little garden yonder? . . . I look rather wistfully towards the window, musing upon these people.[43]

Thackeray cannot believe his eyes and hopes for the truth of what his mind's eye sees. What begins as a reflection on possibility (along with a quip about authorial control: Charles Dickens is prolific enough to write anyone's novel) ends as an incantatory desire for the "suppositional speculation" that has been seen as the core of fictionality.[44] Thackeray's early stylistic and imaginative techniques thus create the sense that fictions have the status of facts (they *could* happen), securing generic acceptability for wild fancies, conferring vivacity on characters, and establishing wagering as formal principle.[45]

Thinking Up and Down

I now turn from the exploration of fictional potential to the investigation of contingency, actual and imagined – from the "have been" to the "might have been." Where Thackeray's demonic mode blurred the sedately referential and the wildly fantastic, *Vanity Fair*'s counterfactual imagination opens a wider space between generic margins and realist center. I describe the novel, in the next section, as an equilibrium point in Thackeray's fictional development, balancing thoughts about what might happen against what might have been, open-ended futures against memory and historical record, predictive and speculative affects against nostalgia and remorse. Siding with "non-combatants" and addressing what "war-chroniclers" omit, the novel's domestic minutiae show what history obstructs from view, even as it deploys a counterfactual mode parasitic on historical writing that enlivens such notional "might-have-beens" with a rich affective and tonal register (293, 308).[46] This section sets up my extended reading of *Vanity Fair* by outlining ideas about counterfactuals in their historical, psychological, and literary significance.

Since David Hume's *Treatise on Human Nature* and John Stuart Mill's *System of Logic*, it has been conventional to note that "implicit in every causal assertion, there is a set of counterfactual implications"; by the same logic, exploring counterfactual statements allows us to hone causal inquiry.[47] Because of their inherent connection to causality, counterfactuals have offered useful resources in the writing of history.[48] In the history of science, counterfactuals have been used to sharpen narratives about scientific development, expand our imagination about the past, and forestall complacency in historical writing – a tradition dating back to Whewell's *History of the Inductive Sciences* (1837).[49] Yet counterfactual reflections in history are not simply, as might be implied by their retrospective gaze, statements about how past circumstances might have differed. They can be unsettling in a more radical sense, distressing the threads of causation that grow from prior conditions into the fabric of later situations. A passing counterfactual thought can be amplified into a full-blown counterfactual history. Thackeray's approach to fictional worlds aligns with this vision of history reimagined from an inflection point, as evidenced by the titles of his historical musings: *The Second Funeral of Napoleon*, "The History of the Next French Revolution," "On a Hundred Years Hence." Still, these forays into "poetic historiography" are not alternate histories.[50] They favor the local tactic of briefly subjecting historical actors and events to contingency, a recurrent move in histories Thackeray admired, including Edward Gibbon's *Decline and Fall of the Roman Empire* (1776–88), Hume's essays and *History of England* (1754–62), its continuation in Tobias Smollett's *Complete History of England* (1758–60) and Thomas Macaulay's magisterial *History of England* (1849–55).[51] The counterfactual reflex in such works has an affective span – from urbane irony to plaintive melancholy – that resonates with Thackeray's emotional range.

Thackeray also engages an uncanny hypothetical in relation to his own history: the work unwritten. He ponders the reality of inexistent writings and restores published works to contingency, perhaps inspired by Macaulay's discussion of how intellects are conditioned by their social milieu: "We extol Bacon, and sneer at Aquinas. But, if their situations had been changed, Bacon might have been the Angelical Doctor, the most subtle Aristotelian of the schools; the Dominican might have led forth the sciences from their house of bondage."[52] Macaulay's essay focuses on the poet John Dryden, wondering what his reputation would have been had he died mid-career, and later imagining "those [works] which he might possibly have written."[53] Ever conscious of being not-Dickens, Thackeray's work is haunted by this concern, visible in his rewriting of narratives under the same narrator, his cross-population of texts with persistent (or quasi-identical) characters, and his interest in prequels and sequels (witness his proposed "continuation" of Walter Scott's *Ivanhoe*).[54] These longer explorations of fictional paths untaken are matched by shorter glimpses of historical and characterological "might-have-beens."

If historical thought experiments compass the wider field of event and outcome, research on counterfactuals in social psychology considers their smaller-scale cognitive, affective, and motivational ramifications.[55] An early statement, part of the research program of judgment under uncertainty, was Daniel Kahneman and Dale Miller's "norm theory," which hypothesized that psychological norms could be seen as retrospective constructs rather than preset schemata, ad hoc reference frames we develop by comparing reality with its alternatives and with memories.[56] Psychologists have since specified the affective direction of counterfactuals (*downward*, *upward*, or *neutral*: things might have been worse, better, or unchanged) and the structural relation such simulations bear to reality (*additive, subtractive,* or *substitutive*: if only *x*, if not for *y*, if only *z* instead).[57] Countless experiments have sharpened the picture of how counterfactuals participate in causal thinking, aid in the construction of meaning and the perception of benefits or deficits, supply predictions and probabilities, and generate "schemata for future action."[58] Such studies typically ask subjects to react to hypothetical narratives, and sometimes exemplify counterfactuals with novelistic characters or describe the essentially literary quality of their alternate realities.[59]

When we entertain counterfactuals, we tacitly manipulate our appraisals of likelihood and modulate our decisions. When confronted with past-facing conditional statements, for instance, subjects have been found to ascribe a higher probability to events that *almost* happened than to events that *actually* occurred ("close-call" counterfactuals).[60] Such "mental undoing" of past facts or events can, paradoxically, calcify our impression of present outcomes as fated, "meant to be," thereby minimizing our sense of contingency and "crystalliz[ing]" an event's significance in a way that direct attempts to generate its meaning cannot."[61] In the same way, future-directed "mental simulation" (a process akin to imagination) shapes decisions through a consideration of the affective states they might entail. Counterfactuals are deeply enmeshed with affective responses: disappointment, surprise, regret, relief.[62] But such "affective forecasting" can go awry.[63] A counterfactual emotion like regret is often anticipated as part of decision-making but is also vulnerable to "misprediction," since it "loom[s] larger in prospect than it actually stands in experience."[64] For my purposes, it is crucial that counterfactuals are likelier to be stimulated by extraordinary scenarios and undesirable outcomes that an ordinary sequence of affairs would have avoided.[65] A different route home results in an accident and the regretful thought, *If only I had gone the usual way*.[66] As a reaction to a deviation, lived or simulated, "counterfactual content recapitulates normality," and reinforces the psychic and affective status quo.[67]

Thackeray's letters and diaries are full of examples echoing the terms of modern experiments. Take this instance of examination regret: "[H]ad I not lost this fortnight," he wrote to his mother, "I might have held a better place" (a *subtractive upward* counterfactual, with *negative* affect . . .) "but it must pass – next year my name will I trust stand a hundred places higher than it does this" (. . . generates *positive* future intentions).[68] Gambling offers rich examples of thinking up and down. Take this frenzy of conditionals:

I mentioned that I had been to Frascati's – but for what went I? to gain?
No – It was a sight I perhaps might never have another opportunity of
seeing, ... it has shewn me that I could not, (as few could) resist the
temptation of gambling, & it therefore has taught me – to keep away from
it – The same motive which would have led me to a Theatre led me to
Frascati's – I was obliged if I went to stake my ten francs at the table instead
of paying at the door – If I had not done so I should never have arrived at a
piece of self knowledge, which I can conscientiously thank God for giving
me. I might have thought ... that it was a pleasant play, into which men
merely entered for amusement and gain – I should not have known that it
was only for the latter. I might at another time [have] been induced to enter
a gaming-house with more money than I had then in my pocket & I should
have as certainly staked it – I have learnt the full extent of the evil.[69]

Learn he did not. A few years later card-sharpers at Cambridge fleeced
Thackeray out of £1500, a loss he would spend years writing to recoup.[70]
Experiences like these, we have seen, underwrite ordinary conditionals in
Thackeray: "except in the fact of his poverty and desperation," we read in
"A Gambler's Death," "was [Attwood] worse than any of us, his compan-
ions, who had shared his debauches and marched with him up to the very
brink of the grave?"[71] Our own counterfactual query in this regard – but
for gambling and misfortune, would we have had *Thackeray*? – underlines
the primacy of this imaginative mode and the link between fiction and
wagering.[72] In 1832, days after breaking another vow against gambling,
Thackeray contemplated his reading of Victor Cousin and confided to his
diary that the "excitement of metaphysics must equal almost that of
gambling." "I found myself," he continued, "giving utterance to a great
number of fine speeches and imagining many wild theories [which]
I found it impossible to express on paper." The entry jars into a report
on the death of a family friend in terms that bend metaphysics toward
melancholy: "had I consented to have gone with my father to Scotland this
valuable man might have been spared to his family – What very trifling
events settle destinies & take away lives."[73] Scales of causation from the
sweep of historical event to the slight inattention that snatches a life,
spectra of affect from rage against past wrongs to twinges of regret at
former follies – such are the historical and psychological resources of
counterfactual thinking Thackeray works into form.

The relationship between literary imagination and counterfactual
thinking has been detailed in compelling fashion by Catherine Gallagher
and Andrew Miller, who examine categories that play off and enrich
fictional representation.[74] Gallagher studies how reference works in diverse
genres of writing. Using the signifier "Napoleon," she argues a

"commonality of referent" across its historical, fictional, and counterfactual deployments.[75] Gallagher's inquiry concerns the types of counterfactual that sustain alternate histories, and her assertion of the difference between such counter-histories and "normal fictions" clarifies the function of ordinary fictional hypothesis.[76] In the case of novelistic characters, she pragmatically states, "we do not take the information we get as a continuous and systematic set of counterfactual hypothetical conjectures": if realist novels "tend to dwell on the unactualized possibilities in a character's history," these remain within the "specified traits" given in the text.[77] Miller addresses such unactualized strata, focusing on the modes of cognitive and affective operation he labels the "optative": thoughts or emotions that stress how the contingency of present arrangements is always environed by the counterfactual and the unrealized.[78] He deftly shows how such experiences of "lives unled" – in which the self appears as doubled, "at once unique and typical," "self-present and contingent" – are vital to realism.[79] "To the extent that realism proposes to give us stories about how things really were," Miller reasons, "a space naturally opens up within that mode to tell us how things might have been, but were not."[80] Counterfactuals aid in realism's descriptive and narrative claims to probability. They might also underline its normative aims in *vraisemblance*: telling us how things *should* have been.[81] Gallagher and Miller shift attention away from technical discussions of counterfactuals, "possible worlds" theory, and related models of literary ontology, returning us to fiction's ordinary imaginative reflexes.[82]

Thackeray could fit straightforwardly into these rubrics. He was intrigued by a recurring protagonist in alternate histories (Napoleon features in *The Paris Sketch Book*) and familiar with a famous entry in the genre, Richard Whately's satire, *Historic Doubts Relative to Napoleon Bonaparte* (1819).[83] Defending the reality of fictional characters, Thackeray notes that "we are inclined to believe in them both as historical personages, and to canvass gravely the circumstances of their lives." "Why should we not?" he continues. "Have we not their portraits? Are they not sufficient proofs? If not, we must discredit Napoleon (as Archbishop Whately teaches), for about his figure and himself we have no more authentic testimony."[84] The particulars of Thackeray's life (persistent professional anxiety, a suspended marriage, an infant lost) make him a case study in Miller's scenarios (social and career mobility, marriage and its others, the death of children).[85] Yet Thackeray's counterfactual mode is materialized in a reflex more diminutive and insistent than the large-scale experiments of the alternate history or the life unled. In his work, the normalizing pressure of counterfactuals is both insistent and uncertain.

The "might-have-beens" mark sites where narrative is solicited by the affective salience of what is extraordinary or unlikely in order to shore up what is understood to be normal or probable, but the alternatives remain on view in the margins. Thackeray's fictionality is precarious, his counterfactuals erratic, distinct from the bold visions of possible lives in Dickens or the complex alternate scenarios in George Eliot and Henry James. They are perhaps more akin to the "alternate-reality effects" of alternate-history novels.[86] Thackeray's writing is less sure of unfettering itself from historical fact, less confident than a realism that, as Miller contends, "tests its own economy" and recognizes "counterfactual possibilities within the story" only to "expel them from the discourse."[87]

Counterfactuals in *Vanity Fair*

In a digression removed in later editions of *Vanity Fair*, Thackeray claims he "might have treated this subject in the genteel or in the romantic or in the facetious manner" (49).[88] Wondering "how this story *might* have been written, if the author had but a mind" (52), such counterfactual gestures both summon and marginalize the narrative and generic possibilities of Thackeray's earlier work. Counterfactuals play a shifting role in *Vanity Fair*. In generic terms, they mark the normalization of the demonic mode, holding its alternatives in the wings of realist possibility. Using the *via media*, a noted tactic of satire – "we must if you please preserve our middle course modestly amidst those scenes and personages" (52) – Thackeray's realism charts a generic course between extremes and a fictional course between divergent models of history.[89] In this nautical figure of the middle way, he imagines shadows to the side of narrative as sirens or demons – both represented in the novel's illustrations – and maintains them as orienting beacons. In narrative terms, counterfactuals track the novel's rotation between speculative and remorseful orientations, charting a course between affective ups and downs. Against the claim that *Vanity Fair* shares the providentialism of pre-1850 fiction where "narrative sequence" is "primarily rhetorical, not historical," with "no open-ended possibilities, no alternative outcomes," "no priority on . . . complex causalities," I argue that the novel's counterfactuals broaden assumptions about what counts as realism, especially in terms of history and reference, causality and closure.[90] As I suggest toward the end, they also link the poised uncertainty of the novel to its external conditions – both proximate (serial publication as manipulation of readerly expectation and retrospect) and distant (war as paradigmatic instance of factual disquiet).

"Are there not little chapters in every body's life," *Vanity Fair*'s narrator muses, "that seem to be nothing and yet affect all the rest of the history?" (52). One function of the novel's counterfactuals is to reconcile narrative scales, causally linking marginal episode and foreground event. Jos Sedley's comic conditionals are a case in point. His inability to propose to Becky is the novel's reason for being – "If he had had the courage ... this work would never have been written" (34) – and is recognized as such by other characters. The counterfactual recurs in Brussels: "There is no knowing what declarations of love and ardour the tumultuous passions of Mr. Joseph might have led him, if Isidor the valet had not made his re-appearance at this minute" (308). The rack punch that inebriates Jos at the Vauxhall party is the "cause of all this history" and "influence[d] the fates of all the principal characters in this Novel without a hero ... although most of them did not taste a drop of it" (56).[91]

Jos's hangover is a familiar, small-scale instance of reasoning about alternatives. But it shares a modal form with the novel's wider elision of history. Referring to "historians on our side," Thackeray conjectures how Napoleon "might have returned and reigned unmolested": "Those who like to lay down the History-book, and to speculate upon what *might* have happened in the world, but for the fatal occurrence of what actually did take place (a most puzzling, amusing, ingenious, and profitable kind of meditation) have no doubt often thought to themselves what a specially bad time Napoleon took to come back from Elba" (277).[92] Implicitly refuting each point of Hamlet's soliloquy ("How weary, stale, flat, and unprofitable / Seem to me all the uses of this world"), Thackeray twists Shakespeare's august query about existence into conditional form, as if the question were: *To have been, or not to have been.* This is an exercise in revisionism akin to (albeit more existentially fraught than) Thackeray's dismissal of history in *Henry Esmond*, where he prefers the "subtext ... of a history *manqué*, history as it might have been, even as it should have been."[93] Tying *Vanity Fair* to a historical nexus, Thackeray's digression on Napoleon highlights the resources of fiction against history: the former can imagine what the latter obviously cannot record. But the metafictional reflection has to remain in proportion to ensure realist continuity. If Napoleon's actions had differed, "what would have become of our story and all our friends, then? If all the drops in it were dried up, what would become of the sea?" (277). This conundrum, less causal than classificatory – can there be a sea without drops of water? – poses a thought experiment that both unsettles and underlines the link between narrative whole (the sea) and constituent parts (*little* chapters, a *drop* of punch).

Thackeray's counterfactual inquiry about history comports with the novel's interest in war memorials for forgotten soldiers, discussed in other texts from the same period ("Waterloo," a travel sketch; "An Essay on Pumpernickel," an unpublished fragment).[94] His lament that "History chooses to forget as too trivial the persons engaged in glorious struggles" recalls *Vanity Fair*'s conditionality.[95] Thackeray asks us to imagine "if a history-book entirely beside the question – made up completely of episodes like *Hamlet* with the part of Hamlet omitted – could be written: it would be a good book to read in, I think, and productive of much moral cogitation."[96] In such a history, "the cause of the war might be omitted altogether." He continues:

> What I would have told would be what actuated Smith, how Brown died, what induced Coddlins to go to war [and] by the above plan [military glory] would be represented more truly than it hitherto has been in the classical works whereof the authors hand us only the results of history, without deigning to trouble themselves with the multiplied little facts of which the results are composed.[97]

Like such engagements with historical counterfactualism, *Vanity Fair* veers in modality, entertains hypotheses about plot, reflects on ways it might have been written, registers such options via tonal oscillation, and understands events to be affected by alternatives small and large. This restless motion can be glimpsed in the epithets used to characterize the two female protagonists: Becky, the devil; Amelia, the angel. Wherever characters appear in Thackeray who are invested with (primarily social) potentiality, the demonic theme is not far off. In the case of Becky Sharp the metaphor moves into overdrive. The narrator's report of her early self-description – "'I'm no angel' – and to say the truth she certainly was not" (10) – introduces several demonic nicknames: Miss Pinkerton sees Becky as a "viper" (14), "rebel," "monster," "serpent," and "firebrand" who laughs "with a horrid sarcastic demoniacal laughter" (15); Jos thinks her "dev'lish" (26); Rawdon remarks, as she snubs George Osborne, "She'd beat the devil, by Jove!" (148).[98] Becky as Satan is further triangulated with Napoleon when the novel records her "greatest blasphemy" at Miss Pinkerton's school: "in those days, in England to say 'Long live Bonaparte,' was as much as to say 'Long live Lucifer'" (10). Likening a fictional character to a cultural emblem for infinite multiformity (Lucifer) and a historical actor who features in alternate histories (Napoleon), this remark establishes Becky as central to *Vanity Fair*'s musing on fictional, historical, and counterfactual imagination.[99]

If "devil" is a surrogate for imaginative potential, the opposing epithet, "angel," embodies achieved necessity. The former is associated with vivacity, energy, and uncertainty in forward propulsion; the latter assumes a position after life, in melancholy retrospect. Thackeray indulges in the fairy-tale logic of his pantomimes and Christmas books to underline this distinction between Becky and Amelia, "the most angelical of young women" (183). Amelia's "kind thoughts" are imagined traveling to George "as if they were angels and had wings," yet arriving at her fiancé's barracks they cannot enter, "so that the poor little white-robed Angel could not hear the songs those young fellows were roaring over the whiskey-punch" (127). Heir to Thackeray's omniscient demons, Becky's thoughts would have no such problem: she is a "superior bad angel" (455). This figurative opposition underlines the future-oriented nature of Becky's plot and its reasoning about alternatives. The aptly named Miss Sharp is ever predicting, speculating, moving onward and upward. Her reflections on paths untaken rethink causation in service of cultivating future plans, and her counterfactual energy even wrests narrative control away from the narrator. After Becky refuses Sir Pitt Crawley's proposal of marriage (being already married to his younger son Rawdon), the baronet's sister thinks she "would have made a good Lady Crawley, after all" (156). Miss Crawley engages in these "conjectures" (156) with the busybody Miss Briggs, who tries "to console [Becky] and prattle about the offer, and the refusal, and the cause thereof" (157). The narrative then focalizes Becky's thoughts:

> And now she was left alone to think over the sudden and wonderful events of the day, and of what had been and what might have been. What think you were the private feelings of Miss, no, (begging her pardon) of Mrs. Rebecca? If, a few pages back, the present writer claimed the privilege of peeping into Miss Amelia Sedley's bed-room, and understanding with the omniscience of the novelist all the gentle pains and passions which were tossing upon that innocent pillow, why should he not declare himself to be Rebecca's confidante too, master of her secrets, and seal-keeper of that young woman's conscience? (158).

The assertion of omniscience is oddly anxious. If the "present writer" knows everything about one character, why not about another? The narrator expresses sympathy with the "regrets" and "disappointment" probably felt by Becky at her refusal of "marvellous good fortune" (158), but does not yet answer his own question by peering into her mind. Instead, he rhetorically aligns himself with a reader's probable reactions: regret is the "natural emotion every properly regulated mind will certainly share"; dejection "deserves and will command every sympathy" (158). As if trying to establish referential stability on a par with Becky's character, the narrator intrudes into the scene. "I remember one night being in the Fair myself," he muses, reflecting on a parallel example, a poor barrister's wife flattered by another woman because she is in line for a baronetcy (158). By juxtaposing this "mere chance of becoming a baronet's daughter" with Becky's having "lost the opportunity" of the same, the narrator steers us back to the main plot, as though only by inference and personal reminiscence could narrative direction be recaptured.

This detour, setting narrator and character in ontological combat, emblematizes how counterfactual thinking is divided in *Vanity Fair*. Becky's plot jettisons thinking otherwise about the past in favor of present and future possibilities. The narrator's opposing interests in Amelia's plot pull against the energy of Becky's upward movement. We have a capsule version of this tension in the same episode. The narrator posits Becky's "very sincere and touching regrets that a piece of marvellous good fortune should have been so near her, and she actually obliged to decline it" (158). But Becky's actual thoughts circumscribe such wallowing:

> Who would have dreamed of Lady Crawley dying so soon? She was one of those sickly women that might have lasted these ten years – Rebecca thought to herself, in all the woes of repentance – and I might have been her lady! I might have led that old man whither I would. I might have thanked Mrs. Bute for her patronage, and Mr. Pitt for his insufferable condescension. I would have had the town-house newly furnished and decorated. I would have had the handsomest carriage in London, and a box at the Opera; and I would have been presented next season. All this *might* have been; but now – now all was doubt and mystery.
>
>   But Rebecca was a young lady of too much resolution and energy of character to permit herself much useless and unseemly sorrow for the irrevocable past; so, having devoted only the proper portion of regret to it, she wisely turned her whole attention towards the future, which was now vastly more important to her. And she surveyed her position, and its hopes, doubts, and chances. (158–59)

The philosopher John Rawls argues that an agent adopting a "rational plan" of life would not experience regret.[100] We see a similar logic here in the thought that regret befits the "properly regulated mind" only in "proper portion."[101] By the same token, counterfactual thinking befits properly regulated *narrative* only by keeping attention trained forward – to "hopes, doubts, and chances," in the serial phrase Thackeray often mocks, "to our next."[102] Events may be subjected to mental manipulation but only in service of a renewed course of action. Whatever might have obtained otherwise, Becky's existing marriage to Rawdon is thus "a great fact," and pondering how to break the news to Miss Crawley she retreats from counterfactual potentiality to realist necessity: "At all events, what use was there in delaying? the die was thrown, and now or to-morrow the issue must be the same" (159).[103] This episode belies the narrator's omniscience, dislodging him as the "master of . . . secrets" in respect of Becky and even of those whose psyches were previously open: of Amelia he later asks, "how do we know what her thoughts were?" (282).[104] Such bounded omniscience has a visual correlative in the chapter's decorative initial, where a devil in voyeuristic surveillance of a weeping figure is formally excluded from the world the letter encloses (Figure 3.2). This is an emblem of demonic potentiality kept to the margins by a character's use of counterfactual thinking to ensure a realist status quo. The narrator is dissociated from Becky's reflections and judgments, even as he demonizes her scheming social mobility from outside.

Like the titular rogue of *Barry Lyndon* who changes his name and social status from chapter to chapter and lives for the future, Becky looks forward, in competition with the narrator's counterfactual mode.[105]

Figure 3.2 William Makepeace Thackeray, decorative initial for *Vanity Fair*, chapter xv
(London: Bradbury & Evans, 1848), p. 129.
Lowell *EC85 T3255 848vb. Houghton Library, Harvard University.

When dealing with the wealthy Miss Crawley, she keeps her options open, thinking that if she "did not forgive them at present, she might at least relent on a future day" (253), whereas the narrator closes off any such alternative: "[Becky and Rawdon] might have gone down on their knees before the old spinster, avowed all, and been forgiven in a twinkling. But that good chance was denied to the young couple, doubtless in order that this story might be written" (163). Retrospective thinking could only hamper the projects of a character whose "superior prudence and foresight" (256) are trained on "visions of the future," whose "castles in the air" (92) are monuments to social ascent.[106] On the morning of Waterloo, Becky sees Rawdon off with "Spartan equanimity," "[k]nowing how useless regrets are, and how the indulgence of sentiment only serves to make people more miserable" (295). Further, "she fell to thinking what she should do if – if anything happened to poor good Rawdon, and what a great piece of luck it was that he had left his horses behind" (324), the real possibility of his death marked by the briefest syntactic hiatus.

"While there is life, there is hope" could be Becky's motto (374). After the war, her calculating efforts to live in the future seem to prevent her from aging. Rawdon becomes a "torpid, submissive, middle-aged, stout gentleman" (456), Amelia has "a silver hair or two marking the progress of time on her head" (459), and Dobbin is in "old-fellow-hood," with "grizzled" hair and "many a passion and feeling of his youth ... grown grey" (578). But Becky's "complexion could bear any sunshine as yet" (476). As troubles mount, she keeps up the façade even against other characters. Her dozing husband cannot "see the face opposite to him, haggard, and weary, and terrible; it lighted up with fresh candid smiles when he woke" (527). Reflecting on her past in reference to future chances, Becky distances herself from prior selves. "I could not go back," she thinks of her childhood days, "and consort with those people now, whom I used to meet in my father's studio" (422).[107] She turns the counterfactual mode against Rawdon, asking, "[W]here you would have been now, and in what sort of a position in society, if I had not looked after you?" (523). Toward the end, revealing that she has kept Jos's portrait, she rejects a return to past possibility – "why speak, – why think, – why look back? It is too late now!" (676) – and, seeing Lord Steyne again in Europe, is taken by the prospect of renewed conquest: "A hundred such touching hopes, fears, and memories palpitated in her little heart" (649).

Although Thackeray rotates Becky's thoughts in a downward direction later in the novel, especially after the confrontation upon Rawdon's return from the sponging house, the move is unconvincing after the reader's experience of Becky on the make. It is hard not to detect sham in her suicidal thoughts, which replay the earlier *Hamlet* allusion: "She thought of her long past life, and all the dismal incidents of it. Ah, how dreary it seemed, how miserable, lonely, and profitless!" (534–35). An exception to this moratorium on looking back proves the rule. In a vault to the future Thackeray gives us a Becky who "has often spoken in subsequent years of this season of her life" – who, after her rendezvous with King George IV, "has owned since that there too was Vanity" (503). Foreshadowing the perplexing narrative voice of *Henry Esmond* and the closural fantasy of *The Newcomes*, this backward glance only assures us of Becky's continuance beyond the boundaries of a novel that is just one stage in her career.[108]

Vanity Fair's other mode – backward-looking, nostalgic, remorseful – takes shape around George Osbourne, intensifying after his early death on the battlefield in Amelia's regret and his father's mourning. The fragility of hindsight becomes a constant motif here, underscored by gambling counterfactuals. If toying with Amelia's affections brings on a "fit of remorse" in George, who confides in Dobbin that "I should have been done but for you," he still admits that "there's no fun in winning a thing unless you play for it" (125). After the collapse of her father's finances, it is unclear whether "[George's] generous heart warmed to [Amelia] at the prospect of misfortune: or that the idea of losing the dear little prize made him value it more" (134). His "remorse and shame" (185) at this juncture are not recalled later, at the Brussels ball, when he commences a "desperate flirtation" with Becky (287). Warnings against gambling are likewise dismissed when the mutual recognition of George's stratagem (a note in a bouquet of flowers) leads to extravagant play. George's betting frenzy disappears as the marching orders for Waterloo arrive and his emotional graph curves down from elation to agent-regret:

> Away went George, his nerves quivering with excitement at the news so long looked for, so sudden when it came. What were love and intrigue now? He thought about a thousand things but these in his rapid walk to his quarters – his past life and future chances – the fate which might be before him – the wife, the child perhaps, from whom unseen he might be about to part. Oh, how he wished that night's work undone! and that with a clear conscience at least he might say farewell to the tender and guileless being by whose love he had set such little store! (292)

Where George's nascent thoughts for the future are pulled downward, Rawdon's similar concerns move in the opposite direction as "he cursed his past follies and extravagances, and bemoaned his vast outlying debts above all," and we sense hollowness in the thought that they "must remain for ever as obstacles to prevent his wife's advancement in the world" (296).

George goes to his death with his thoughts cast backward. Dobbin later recollects how his friend only once "alluded" to his involvement with Becky, "evidently with remorse on his mind" (663).[109] Anticipatory regret affects everyone involved in his plot. Amelia's courtship is fraught with omens: a "mysterious and presentimental" (133) claret-bell announces dinner; her nerves about Mr. Osborne's disapproval lead to a heart "overflowing with tenderness, but it still foreboded evil" (136); and the news of John Sedley's ruin is "only the confirmation of the dark presages which had long gone before" (181). Mr. Osborne's letter vetoing the marriage is "the mere reading of the sentence – of the crime she had long ago been guilty – the crime of loving wrongly, too violently, against reason" (181). Even prior to marriage Amelia mourns the death of her love object, returning George's gifts while keeping his letters. Subsequently, she "lived in her past life – every letter seemed to recall some circumstance of it" (182). She dwells on the "relics and remembrances of dead affection," and "the business of her life, [is] to watch the corpse of Love" (182). Marriage makes a difference in scale, not direction: "What a gulf lay between her and that past life. She could look back to it from her present standing-place, and contemplate, almost as another being, the young unmarried girl absorbed in her love, having no eyes but for one special object" (260). In sharing the melancholy fate "[a]lready to be looking sadly and vaguely back: always to be pining for something which, when obtained, brought doubt and sadness rather than pleasure," these two selves are more coherent than they might seem. They match a third, jealous self, into which "old, old times, griefs, pangs, remembrances, rushed back" when she sees Becky at Pumpernickel, where the "wound which years had scarcely cicatrised bled afresh" (665) with what Miller terms "reminiscent eroticism."[110]

Such unrelenting (I am not the first to say insipid) dejection does make for narrative possibility, particularly late in the novel when Dobbin's devotion becomes the object of inference. When Amelia reflects on why he reacts so strongly to her affection for the piano that George took credit for giving her, she does "not note the circumstance at the time, nor take heed of the very dismal expression which honest Dobbin's countenance assumed; but she thought of it afterwards. And then it struck her" (595). Where the narrative focalizes Becky almost without recollection, in Amelia's case it constantly drifts backward, here to the "memory of [Dobbin's] almost countless services, and lofty and affectionate regard, [which] now presented itself to her, and rebuked her day and night" (677). Her final acceptance of Dobbin is a paradoxical affair. Amelia states the impossibility of loving another – "George is my husband, here and in heaven. How could I love any other but him?" – even as she accepts the love of one who is given a contradictory counterfactual role: "Had you come a few months sooner perhaps you might have spared me that – that dreadful parting" (596).[111]

If Amelia can come to meet the eyes of Dobbin rather than George as she gazes at the past, as when looking out of the latter's childhood room and effectively seeing her way to "the man who had been her constant protector" (612), Mr. Osborne finds a similar solace in his grandson. While his son "stood on the other side of the gulf impassable, haunting his parent with sad eyes" (352), the child Georgy has "the eyes of George who was gone" (358). The older man "would start at some hereditary feature or tone unconsciously used by the little lad, and fancy that George's father was again before him" (566). In later fiction Thackeray overburdens such retrospects, whether in *Pendennis*'s fictional autobiography, which has been read according to the controlling logic of associationist memory; in *Henry Esmond*, with its antiquated historical setting and much-remarked narrative voice from beyond death; or in *The Newcomes*, which sets an epitaphic limit on the imaginative enterprise.[112] *Vanity Fair*, on this account, is a way-stage as the potential of the demonic mode shifts into remorse-laden memorials.

Before passing to late Thackeray, I want to underscore another way *Vanity Fair*'s conditional impulses allow it to confront (not avoid) history via a central experience of modern uncertainty that has long been associated with counterfactual thinking: war.[113] The novel's oscillation between risk and regret, looking forward and back, suggests a homology between (serial) reading and the information economy of war. Both are marked by rumor, belated news, and lagging realization:

> after the announcement of the victories came the list of the wounded and the slain. Who can tell the dread with which that catalogue was opened and read!... Anybody who will take the trouble of looking back to a file of the newspapers of the time, must, even now, feel at second-hand this breathless pause of expectation. The lists of casualties are carried on from day to day: you stop in the midst as in a story which is to be continued in our next. (351)

Thackeray's analogy trades on the capacity of serialization to create an illusion of extraliterary existence, as Juliet McMaster has argued.[114] He breathes life into fictional characters by comparing them to those

who may be discovered as "breathless." In keeping with a tradition Mary
Favret has detailed, where the domestic hearth functions as wartime's locus
of expectancy and dilated temporality, Thackeray often recalls a time when
"ten thousand, a hundred thousand homes in England [were] saddened by
the thought of the coming calamity, and oppressed by the pervading
gloom.... By firesides modest and splendid, all over the three kingdoms,
that sorrow is keeping watch, and myriads of hearts beating with that
thought, 'Will they give up the men?'"[115] The novel likewise recalls the
Napoleonic wars, with "many anxious hearts beating through England ...
and mothers' prayers and tears flowing in many homesteads" (238).
Alongside its wider "narrative syncopation" and "studied vagueness" about
chronology, temporal markers carry us forward while noting events
months apart:[116]

> when war was raging all over Europe, and Empires were being staked –
> when the "Courier" newspaper had tens of thousands of subscribers – when
> one day brought you a Battle of Vittoria, another a Burning of Moscow, or
> a newsman's horn blowing down Russell Square about dinner time
> announced such a fact as "Battle of Leipsic, six hundred thousand men
> engaged, total defeat of the French, two hundred thousand killed." (120)

This paradigm of information – all news is old news – creates a broad fear
of alternate outcomes, echoing England's historical fear of French invasion
after the 1790s. From the aptly named novel *The Invasion, or What Might
Have Been* (1798) to *Vanity Fair*'s recollection of anticipatory militias
formed "to resist the French invasion" (48) to an 1860s article in the
Cornhill Magazine (under Thackeray's editorship) comparing present and
past "Invasion Panics," the disjunction between real-time events and
unpunctual reports fosters counterfactual narratives and alternate histories.[117] In the novel's panicked Brussels, people "rode along the level
chaussée, to be in advance of any intelligence from the army," everyone
asks after "news," and the "prophecies of the French partisans began to
pass for facts" (312).[118] Rumors swirl until the "official announcement" of
an English victory at Quatre Bras (321). Across his work Thackeray uses
this topos to absurd effect, mocking Belgian newspapers that were unaware
of the battle on their soil until they received word from London, and the
French who believed that disastrous campaigns against the Spanish and
English were won by them, so the "real state of things" is "as if it had never
been."[119] But for some the tyranny of old news continues. Dobbin reports
to Amelia "that the action was over, and that her husband was unhurt and
well" (323). His death is then reported.

Wartime's information lag underscores counterfactual links between different narrative scales, as outlined above, where large events play into smaller. John Sedley's misfortunes, for example, take part in the "great roaring war tempest" where "Napoleon is flinging his last stake, and poor little [Amelia] Sedley's happiness forms, somehow, part of it" (178).[120] The "domestic comedy," Thackeray reasons, "would never have been enacted without the intervention of this august mute personage [Napoleon]" (184). Although the actual battle of Waterloo is consigned to the historical past, Thackeray uses it to predict future alternations on the same fields:

> All of us have read of what occurred during that interval. The tale is in every Englishman's mouth; and you and I, who were children when the great battle was won and lost, are never tired of hearing and recounting the history of that famous action. Its remembrance rankles still in the bosoms of millions of the countrymen of those brave men who lost the day. They pant for an opportunity of revenging that humiliation; and if a contest, ending in a victory on their part, should ensue, elating them in their turn, and leaving its cursed legacy of hatred and rage behind to us, there is no end to the so-called glory and shame, and to the alternations of successful and unsuccessful murder, in which two high-spirited nations might engage. Centuries hence, we Frenchmen and Englishmen might be boasting and killing each other still, carrying out bravely the Devil's code of honour. (326)

The narrative possibility of the demonic, the "Devil's code," thus acquires a darker cast.[121] Thackeray upstages the expectations of a reader three decades after Waterloo and gives a bleaker sense to that serial phrase, "our next."

War's intensified present condenses the novel's forward and backward movements, hypothetical and counterfactual modes, thoughts of risk and venture and reflections of regret and retrospect, the expectation of the next narrative and the realization that the last number has already been written. This equilibrium occurs at a brief juncture in Thackeray's oeuvre, but its narrative and temporal logic reveal how keenly invested he is in the uncertainty of close-call counterfactuals, the point of convertibility between just-past and almost-future states. *The Kickleburys on the Rhine* framed gambling as a battle; *Vanity Fair* belabors war as the ultimate wager: "What tremendous hazards of loss or gain! What were all the games of chance he had ever played compared to this one?" (301).[122] Conflict is both source and target of Thackeray's statements on moral luck – on the "mysterious and often unaccountable . . . lottery of life which gives to this man the purple and fine linen, and sends to the other rags for garments and dogs for comforters" (569). Against its accidents he counsels us to be "gentle with those who are less lucky, if not more deserving" (570), given that any individual fate may wander, like George, out of bounds into virtuality:

> Our luck may fail: our powers forsake us: our place on the boards be taken by better and younger mimes – the chance of life roll away and leave us shattered and stranded. Then men will walk across the road when they meet you.... If quacks prosper as often as they go to the wall – if zanies succeed and knaves arrive at fortune, ... sharing ill luck and prosperity for all the world like the ablest and most honest amongst us – I say, brother, the gifts and pleasures of Vanity Fair cannot be held of any great account, and that it is probable ... but we are wandering out of the domain of the story. (385)

To meander into the zone of counterfact is to trespass a limit more fundamental than Henry Fielding's "bounds of probability." It is to threaten realist narrative with a countervailing power it cannot wholly comprehend on its own terms – "who can calculate the might-have-beens?" – even if it is constitutively ghosted by such alternate domains.[123]

Credite Posteri! Memory's Roundabout

The *Roundabout Papers*, brief essays published in the *Cornhill Magazine* under Thackeray's editorship from 1860 to 1863 and later collected into a volume, intensify the remorseful aspects of *Vanity Fair* and have been linked to his "reminiscential" aesthetic and its sense of cyclical time.[124] Critics have taken these eclectic performances to constitute a late mode proper to an author who "loves to remember very much more than to prophesy," who "would rather remember" individuals than "be in love over again."[125] They strike what one critic calls the "low note [that] sounds with a haunting dominance."[126] The lessons of counterfactual thinking – its effect on aesthetic and narrative textures, its interest for causal inquiry – spotlight a different aspect of Thackeray's account of memory. In the late work, I suggest, memory underwrites a mode of hypothetical thinking that contributes to its own attenuation. Read with *Vanity Fair*'s experiments in mind, these marginal entries constitute a provocative vision of Thackeray's melancholy as a fragile mode of prophecy or hope for action. "It is only hope which is real," he once remarked.[127] The reflections of "Mr. Roundabout" take truths of recollected disappointment and vanished youth – that "reality is a bitterness and a lie" – and make them the basis for wisdom that looks in all directions.[128]

The *Roundabout Papers* reprise *Vanity Fair*'s reflections on history and its alternatives, but with an emphasis on negation, fraying the seam that joins fictional and factual worlds. "On Some Late Great Victories" undercuts its upbeat topic with this general reflection: "it has been asserted that Fortune has a good deal to do with the making of heroes; and thus hinted for the consolation of those who don't happen to be engaged in any stupendous victories, that, had opportunity so served, they might have been heroes too."[129] Shifting from military victories to those of the *Cornhill Magazine*, the narrator imagines himself riding in a chariot alongside the editor (Thackeray) and saluting Fortune: "we might have fought bravely, and *not* won. We might have cast the coin, calling 'Head,' and, lo! Tail might have come uppermost."[130] This digression on the lucky conditions keeping the magazine running continues in "Thorns in the Cushion," which likens the *Cornhill Magazine* to a ship navigating a *via media* between "dangers of storm and rock ... and the certain risk of the venture."[131]

Buoyed by victories as both editor and author, perhaps, Thackeray cheekily entertains the converse – the work unwritten – in "On Two Roundabout Papers Which I Intended to Write." The first concerns the topic of good thoughts and how they are diverted by the possibility of bad thoughts: "some of the best actions we have all of us committed in our lives have been committed in fancy."[132] Thus begins a dizzying counterfactual exercise in which we read around both the topic and its abstract moral: "if you could but read some of the unwritten Roundabout Papers," the narrator whimsically offers, "I catch you saying, 'Well, then, I wish *this* was unwritten with all my heart!'"[133] Thackeray prefaces a striking instance of fiction taking over fact by drawing the reader into indirection, in the same way as his journalism on executions never arrives at the object it sets out to document.[134] "Have you ever killed any one in your thoughts?" he asks. "Has your heart compassed any man's death?"[135] The unwritable event in question happened in London, when a client walking into a bank office was confronted by a man shooting a pistol at the wall.[136] Without narration, Thackeray compares this absurd event to the new phenomenon to be found on the boards and in novels: "What a sensation drama this is! What have people been flocking to see at the Adelphi Theatre for the last hundred and fifty nights? ... What is this compared to the real life drama ...?"[137] The story is fodder for a counterfactual moral – "It might have happened to you and to me" – and for a defense of fictional against factual standards: "After this, what is the use of being squeamish about the probabilities and possibilities in the writing of fiction?... After this, what is not possible?"[138]

The tendency of the *Roundabout Papers* to veer into hypothetical reflections turns on memory's virtuality. Often the possibility of a memory that truly takes the self back to an earlier period depends on powers of representation or simulation. Someone looking at a coin minted in George IV's reign "may conjure back his life there"; after gazing on a painting by Van der Helst "you have lived in the year 1648, and celebrated the treaty of Münster."[139] Both experiences are mediated by an image and sponsor an *effet de réel*, despite being historically impossible.[140] Adopting the classical mode of the *ubi sunt*, Thackeray uses memory's precarity to muse on the past's ontological instability. "We who have lived before railways were made, belong to another world," he writes, a world that "has passed into limbo and vanished from under us. I tell you it was firm under our feet once, and not long ago.... Try and catch yesterday. Where is it? Here is a *Times* newspaper dated Monday 26th, and this is Tuesday, 27th. Suppose you deny there was such a day as yesterday?"[141] Recalling similar laments in *Vanity Fair*, where to the "beloved reader's children ... stage-coaches will have become romances," these anxious queries address the future in a forlorn bid for existential ratification, for recognition tomorrow of yesterday's reality, even though the readers of these papers have (as with Whately's Napoleon) nothing but textual representations by which to judge. An allusion to Horace intensifies the thought into an imperative mode: "*Credite posteri*": believe me, you who follow.[142] Thus the essay where these thoughts appear – "De Juventute," on youth – works against its stated topic even as it tries to secure confirmation for its existence. Thackeray finally gives in. Day passes to night, youth to age. But a formal trick holds out hope:

> It is night now: and here is home. Gathered under the quiet roof, elders and children lie alike at rest. In the midst of a great peace and calm, the stars look out from the heavens. The silence is peopled with the past; sorrowful remorses for sins and short-comings – memories of passionate joys and griefs rise out of their graves, both now alike calm and sad. Eyes, as I shut mine, look at me, that have long ceased to shine.[143]

The last sentence encapsulates in its knotted grammar the virtuality of remembering in the *Roundabout Papers*, its combination of present vivacity and pained attenuation. Hovering uncertainly, the eyes first cannot meet their object's gaze (the narrator's are "shut" before the others "look") but then reach the present to "look" before the disqualifying "ceased to shine." The unstable relative clause – associating both "eyes" and "me" with "long ceased to shine" – completes this vaulting movement between reality and interior, present and past. In the guise of Mr. Roundabout, Thackeray thinks back on his own youth in the exact terms, with the same formal lag, as we saw Mr. Osborne in *Vanity Fair* think of his son via his grandson Georgy, with "the eyes of George who was gone" (358).[144] A parallel moment in *Henry Esmond* reflects on the eyes of its heroine Beatrix in comparison to diamonds, only to ask: "Where are those jewels now that beamed under Cleopatra's forehead, or shone in the sockets of Helen?"[145] The querulous *ubi sunt* is addressed to personal recollections (eyes one has known) and the memory of written productions (eyes one has made).

An inherent momentum in the pattern of Thackeray's memory, I am arguing, both defies and participates in the negation of the *ubi sunt*. The sense that melancholy has an upswing allows Thackeray to take risks. He can subject a key trope of counterfactual thinking (gambling) to similar interrogation, as he does musing about the casino in *The Kickleburys on the Rhine*: "Where are the gamblers whom we have read of? Where are the card players whom we can remember in our early days?"[146] He can turn the thought on his own productions, those "old pages" that proffer "anything but elation of mind": "Oh, the cares, the *ennui*, the squabbles, the repetitions, the old conversations over and over again! But now and again a kind thought is recalled, and now and again a dear memory. Yet a few chapters more, and then the last: after which, behold Finis itself come to an end, and the Infinite begun."[147] Beyond the *finis* that closes out his text, Thackeray subtly recommences: the infinite nonetheless begins somewhere and the finite can be stretched beyond its end.[148] The coda of *The Newcomes* similarly undercuts its own logic of closure, and one of the *Roundabout Papers*, "The Last Sketch," asks: "If the Has Been, why not the Might Have Been?"[149] As if rewriting himself as Scheherazade, Thackeray uses the momentum of *roundabout* memory to emphasize both the end and the "yet a few chapters more," the actuality of what *has been* written by his hand and the virtuality of what *might have* issued from the same pen.[150]

The paper most invested in memory and forgetting, "On Some Carp at Sans Souci," operates by tacit counterfactuals. Prompted by meeting a ninety-year-old woman who has been in the workhouse a quarter-century, Thackeray imagines the century she must have witnessed. Chastened by the realization that she registers little of its notables and lives in present hardship, his reflection jumps through an analogy to the long-lived creatures of the title. "Some which Frederick the Great fed at Sans Souci are there now . . . and they could tell all sorts of queer stories, if they chose to speak – but they are very silent, carps are – of their nature *peu communicatives*. Oh! what has been thy long life, old Goody, but a dole of bread and water and a perch on a cage; a dreary swim round and round a Lethe of a pond?"[151] (Perhaps Thackeray has his wife Isabella in mind, who by this point had spent two decades in an asylum, where she would remain a further three decades after his death.) Amazed at creaturely oblivion, Thackeray turns through conditional refrains – "If I were eighty"; "If you were in her place" – in praise of memory, its possibilities, its sudden invigorations.[152] "We may grow old," he writes, "but to us some stories never are old. On a sudden they rise up, not dead, but living – not forgotten, but freshly remembered."[153] In an exercise of sympathetic imagination that justifies the trade-off between memory and present oblivion, history and *sans souci*, the familiar personage of alternate histories walks up to the surface of forgetting: "Those eyes [the carp's] may have goggled beneath the weeds at Napoleon's jack-boots."[154]

The *Roundabout Papers* also showcase simpler accounts of memory, of course. We see musings taken from experience that "have for subjects some little event which happens at the preacher's own gate, or which falls under his peculiar cognizance."[155] These bear out the truth of an address to the writer: "Your sensibility is your livelihood.... You feel a pang of pleasure or pain? It is noted in your memory, and some day or other makes its appearance in your manuscript."[156] Yet even in more overt reminiscences, an imaginative manipulation is at work – as in the advice just quoted, which happens to be voiced by the ghost of Laurence Sterne. Describing Thackeray's cyclical philosophy of time in the *Roundabout Papers*, Richard Oram cites a remark that "we all hold on by love to the past, and by just a little turn of the circle, it becomes the future," so that the "have been is eternal, as well as the will be. We are not only elderly men, but young men, boys, children."[157] Note how this movement is guaranteed only by the capacity to think otherwise – to place the "have been" adjacent to the "will be" in a repetition that is hardly straightforward. In a sophisticated argument about Thackeray's reminiscential vision, Nicholas Dames argues that memory in *Pendennis* and *Henry Esmond* becomes museal: bounded, controlled, edited according to the protocols of mid-century associationist psychology.[158] But within these parameters, counterfactuals still run riot. *Pendennis* is saturated with musings on the unhappened, from Thackeray's framing dedication to Dr. John Elliotson without whom, "in all probability, I never should have risen [from his sickbed] but for your constant watchfulness and skill," to the thoughts that Pen might have been a solicitor or military man, which culminate in his confrontation (in a chapter fitly titled "Fiat Justitia") with Major Pendennis over the latter's knowledge of Blanche Amory's compromised heritage, which has "cursed my career when it might have been – when it might have been so different but for you!," and finally to the comment on the nested fiction, George Warrington's *Leaves from the Life-Book of Walter Lorraine*, which "would never have been written but for Arthur Pendennis's own private griefs, passions, and follies."[159]

To focus on fictional autobiography, as Dames does, omits a recurrent mode of Thackerayan memory: epistemologically riddling, ontologically unlocatable, at once the conditional ground of, and yet vulnerable to, counterfactual manipulations. One does not need a memory of what *was* in order to assess what *might have been*. Actual memory is thus open to censure or revision even as the space of counterfactual imagination appears similar to the no-place of real memories. It is not accidental that Thackeray's meandering reflections on memory are penned in ephemeral venues – periodical reviews, "roundabout" essays, "fugitive literature"[160] – rather than the achieved vehicles of *Pendennis* and *Henry Esmond*, the serial appearance of the first belied by its autobiographical character, the second (as Dames stresses) published first as a volume set.

If Thackeray participates in what Dames calls "the generally *amnesiac* character of mid-Victorian selfhood, a selfhood that continually converts memory into action, remembrance into prediction, the past into promise," the *Roundabout Papers* serve this end by what we might call their *hyper-mnesic* character, pressing memory into frenzy.[161] Both axes of memory and its deficiencies need to be recognized. Indeed, the final paper in the series disparages the habit of "go[ing] through life passionately deploring the irrevocable, and allow[ing] yesterday's transactions to embitter the cheerfulness of to-day and to-morrow."[162] The mnemonic puzzles here are vital to Thackeray's fictional thinking and its ethical import. That the renewed prophecy of the *Roundabout Papers* maintains a melancholy, a "rich suspension of urgency," only adds to the force of its warning to the reader of late Thackeray: use the "might have been" to imagine what might be, to prophesy, to live and love again, in the more deeply registered knowledge that there is no "again."[163]

Hypothesis as Late Style

My argument so far could follow a chronological trajectory from the devilish imaginary of youth to the melancholy recollection of age, following Gordon Ray's picture of Thackeray as shifting from acerbic satire in works like *The Snobs of England* (1846–47) to moral wisdom.[164] Yet in the 1860s, alongside the *Roundabout Papers*, hypothetical thinking breaks through recollection, renewing uncertainty and finding a strand of hope behind the *vanitas* refrain. In its almost total annexation of narrative by thinking otherwise, *Lovel the Widower* embodies the hypotheses (both conceptual and visual) of Thackeray's late style. Adapted from a play never performed in public, *The Wolves and the Lamb* (possibly 1854), and tracing the later history of characters from *The Kickleburys on the Rhine*, *Lovel* owes its riddling openness to a narrator whose erratic tone, wavering attention, and fluctuating self-assessment command the novel's psychological space.[165] The sketchy plot, taking place at the residence of Charles Batchelor's college friend Fred Lovel, records minor intrigues in the widower's domestic life: contretemps between his mother and mother-in-law, scuffles among jealous servants, outrages committed by miscreant children. Batchelor's meandering deferral of the novel's marriage plot – glimpsed only at the conclusion – affords him time to observe, comment, and speculate.

Although written toward the end of his life, *Lovel* marks its connection to Thackeray's demonic mode. Its "scene is in the parlour, and the region beneath the parlour" – the servants' downstairs taking on an infernal quality.[166] Batchelor charts a middle course in an address to readers that underlines the allusion: "We are no heroes nor angels; neither are we fiends from abodes unmentionable, black assassins, treacherous Iagos, familiar with stabbing and poison – murder our amusement, daggers our play-things, arsenic our daily bread, lies our conversation, and forgery our common handwriting" (58). The only dagger here is "used for the cutting open of reviews and magazines" (158). Batchelor's disavowal emphasizes how he is a thoroughly domestic devil, more given to eavesdropping and casual voyeurism than concerted villainy. He fashions himself as "another *Diable Boiteux*, [who] had the roofs of a pretty number of the Shrublands rooms taken off for me" (107). Thackeray alludes to Alain René Le Sage's novel *Le diable boiteux* (1707), where the hero takes a tour with a devil, Asmodeus, who removes the roofs of buildings to narrate their contents without a sense of preceding or following events.[167] Elsewhere in Thackeray this cipher for mobile omniscience ratifies narrative possibility from above, appropriately enough given his self-fashioning as the "Manager of the Performance," an arranger of novelistic puppet shows and pantomimes.[168] Yet Batchelor's case is self-reflexive: peering into other lives, he takes the roof off his own.

Lovel the Widower has two interconnected moments of psychological density. Both are episodes of thwarted love, framed by hypotheticals. Batchelor recollects the first on a visit to his former lodgings in London. He remembers that after his heartbreak at the hands of Glorvina O'Dowd (née Mulligan), the young daughter of his landlady offered sympathy. Batchelor's narcissism obscured the parallel situation of his confidante, Bessy Prior, recently jilted by a captain who had fled to India. Reflecting on these events, he rejects the notion that his confessions gave rise to deeper feelings: "In my case, if a heart is broke, it's broke: if a flower is withered, it's withered. If I choose to put my grief in a ridiculous light, why not? why do you suppose I am going to make a tragedy of such an old, used-up, battered, stale, vulgar, trivial, every-day subject as a jilt . . .?" (84).

This failure of sympathetic communion nonetheless establishes a mutuality between Bessy and Batchelor that the narrative picks up, after an intervening sequence saturated with reflections on alternate outcomes and images of convertibility. Batchelor recalls this episode after visiting Beak Street and having his likeness taken by a photographer who occupies his old lodgings. Where the typical experience in Thackeray would use a youthful keepsake as a talisman for reflecting on time lost, Batchelor reverses this logic and wonders whether his former admirer would want the image to "be reminded of a man whom she knew in life's prime" (82). Just as at Shrublands the eyes of Cecilia's portrait (the deceased wife of Lovel) "followed you about, as portraits' eyes so painted will" (128) and Batchelor senses a "ghost flitting about the place" (129), in his former lodgings he is confronted by "a heap of memories" and "ghosts" of children who used to live there (83, 82).

The episode does not give rise to anything concrete or even conscious. Instead, it generates a cloud of possibilities in excess of the narrative's capacities to substantiate them, in keeping with the psychological maxim that counterfactuals introduce two or more possibilities into mental space.[169] Batchelor's reflections are intensified versions of *Vanity Fair*'s counterfactuals. He wonders why he did not say to Bessy, "We who are initiated, know the members of our Community of Sorrow," and an influx of hypotheticals – "She would have . . .," "We would have . . ." – accompany his thoughts (101). It is notable that Bessy's family name is "Prior": each mention of "Miss Prior" counteracts the narrative's forward movement with a pun about precursors. The chapter titled "Miss Prior Is Kept at the Door" plays up the tautology: the "prior" is always on the point of entering. While Batchelor's hypotheticals move into past possibilities, they also postulate their exact contraries. Enjoying his small pleasures of bachelorhood, he reflects ("Suppose" is a repeated tag) that he might have gained his lover and been unhappy, been kept away from the club, been father to a screaming infant, and so on (104). This tension is a more complex version of Batchelor's uncertain narration, "hedged in by qualifications and by negative definitions that abandon the categories they set up and so fail to function as genuine definitions," floating "romantic possibilities" only "to dematerialize them almost before they present themselves."[170] Every narrative assertion comes with a tacit disclaimer: *this may or may not have happened.*

In the second episode, the narrative has skipped forward and we are at Lovel's home, where Bessy earlier became a governess on Batchelor's recommendation. She has attracted considerable male interest: from Drencher, the local doctor; and Bedford, the butler. As Batchelor's narrative voice muddles toward self-recognition with respect to the feelings disavowed earlier, he is amused yet threatened by Bedford's interest, and then dismayed by the news that Bessy is engaged to Drencher. When the latter engagement is confessed to be a sham – merely in aid of Bessy's respectability in Lovel's household – Batchelor presses his awkward suit. Just as the first episode foundered on an absence of sympathy, the second collapses in a farcical avoidance of action, "permeated with false starts, failed modes, confused ironies."[171] Batchelor's confession prompts Bessy to remove her spectacles to think, making her vulnerable to recognition by Clarence Baker, Cecilia's alcoholic brother whose "pallid countenance told of Finishes and Casinos" (131) and who knew her as a dancer in London. Walking into the morning room where she is alone, Clarence addresses her by her former stage name. In the ensuing ruckus – Clarence becomes aggressive, Bessy punches him, and Bedford comes to her aid – Batchelor slinks away from the French windows and enters the room belatedly, "arriving like Fortinbras in *Hamlet*, when everybody is dead and sprawling, you know, and the whole business is done" (157). This sudden action hardly stalls the narrative's hypothetical mode. The sequence begins with Batchelor's reflections on what he would have done had Clarence run at Bessy or "offered her other personal indignity" (151). He watches while others usurp his possible role, and in place of "heroic speeches" we have excuses entered on his own behalf – "In a strait so odious, sudden, and humiliating, what should I, what could I, what did I do?" – and addresses to the reader – "What would *you* have done? Would *you* have liked to have such a sudden suspicion thrown over the being of your affection?" (152, 154, 153).

Batchelor's hesitation is driven not from "want of courage" – as Bessy assumes, noticing him sneak away – but "error in judgment" (152). The jealousy resulting from Clarence's recognition is a logical operation, based in "cogent and honourable reasons" (152), which arranges and draws a conclusion from the "antecedents" – or priors – of Bessy's "history [that] passed through my mind" (153).[172] These manipulations take place in imagination, as Batchelor draws on other generic conventions to describe his dilemma – "a sudden thought made me drop my (figurative) point: a sudden idea made me rein in my galloping (metaphorical) steed" (152). Similarly, he weighs competing possibilities. "Suppose I had gone in?" he thinks. "But for that sudden precaution, there might have been a Mrs. Batchelor" (152). These thoughts form a chiasmus with the earlier set: "jealous doubt" about whether Bessy would be a good mother of "many possible little Batchelors" (160) takes hold first, and more hopeful musings about the future follow (164–65).

While the narrative lurches forward in time, these patterns establish conjectural eddies where possibilities are raised, entertained, and rejected, introducing a circularity into the "sideshadows" of novelistic space. Much of the novel exists in what Gary Morson calls "hypothetical time," operating "as if every actuality were a mere possibility."[173] Thackeray deploys fiction as an "existential assertion" against temporality, as Ina Ferris argues: his "main target is sequence; his primary strategy, obfuscation."[174] As the oddities of Batchelor's narration become more abstract, they are concretized in visual form. "Where the Sugar Goes" (Figure 3.3), Thackeray's illustration of an otherwise insignificant event, is shadowed by opposed possibilities. The image is meant to capture a petty theft by Bessy's venal mother, Mrs. Prior: Mr. Bedford catches her pilfering dessert. The mirror reflecting them, however, shows an opposite scenario: the female figure stands erect, in portrait, accusatory; the male turns as if discovered. Shadowy quasi-reflections, etched with vertical lines, show us what a mirror could not reflect and perhaps allude to Bedford's secretly held love for Bessy, which compels him to turn a blind eye to the theft. At the end of a long *mise en abyme* of Thackerayan mirrors, this reflection makes visible the recursions that shadow narration.[175] It is a spatial version of the jostling temporalities where "epilogue time" (Morson again) continually ruptures into past narrative moments: "I dine at Lovel's still" (61); "All the house has been altered" (193).[176]

Recasting the patterns of Batchelor's narration as cycles of counterfactual thinking allows us to circumvent critical frustration. Elizabeth Gaskell wondered whether she was "stupid" for judging the novel "a little confusing on account of its discursiveness."[177] Others explain away Batchelor's feints by fixing him in psychological "breakdown," "fragmentation," or "instability."[178] Yet what is striking about Batchelor's narration when viewed as uncertain in form – in its tonal variation, generic or modal unclarity, and allusions to other discourses – is how it settles for coherence

"WHERE THE SUGAR GOES."

Figure 3.3   William Makepeace Thackeray, "Where the Sugar Goes," illustration for *Lovel the Widower*, in *Cornhill Magazine* 1 (January–June 1860): facing p. 330. Widener Library, Harvard University.

in one aspect of content: Batchelor, once and always a bachelor. Following David Kurnick's convincing claim that failure encodes longing in Thackeray, the suppositions and hypotheticals of formal uncertainty show how narration could always underwrite another content.[179] *Lovel the Widower* might more accurately be titled *Batchelor the Unloved*, given the intensity of the narrator's focalization and the marginality of the titular plot. The title also raises the counterfactual possibility of a sequel novel (or play) entitled *Lovel Married*, which would be shadowed by parallel possibilities: *Batchelor in Love* or, in tune with the modal grammar I have outlined, *Batchelor the Lovable*.

To reframe the novel this way is to see gravity behind ironic pronouncements: "That heart may have had its griefs, but is yet susceptible of enjoyment and consolation. That bosom may have been lacerated, but is not therefore and henceforward a stranger to comfort" (103). It is to recognize that assertions of dejection, belatedness, or finality – as when Batchelor reads fragments of Bessy's letter to Drencher: "I might have made a woman happy: I think I should" (138) – are turns in a cycle. If after the eventful day he "lay amidst shattered capitals, broken shafts of the tumbled palace which I had built in imagination ... the ruins of my own happiness" (175), this is to recall the earlier thought that although "my heart may be a ruin – a Persepolis, sir – a perfect Tadmor" there is yet hope: "May not a traveller rest under its shattered columns?" (98).[180] The same "batchelor" connotes (in chivalry or at university) a stage of inexperience: hope springs eternal. At breakfast the day after the tumult in the morning room, Batchelor seems to be at an end like that of *Henry Esmond*'s narrator: "I am dead. I feel as if I am underground, and buried.... I don't belong to the world any more. I have done with it. I am shelved away" (175–76). But to be "shelved away" is to bear the possibility of future reading. Unlike Cecilia's portrait, which stares mutely and is "removed from the post of honour" when the new wife accedes to her place, Batchelor's novel contains his "spirit [which] returns and flitters through the world" (193, 176). That spirit assures the continuity of Thackerayan narrative through the counterfactual energy three decades of writing had not dispelled.

Lovel the Widower confirms the porous nature of Thackeray's fictional worlds, which selectively admit data from the range of discrete literary objects that instantiate it, and from the historical record. The novel is not only a global transformation of a play, but a small-scale reprisal of other fictional worlds. Glorvina O'Dowd, who jilts Batchelor, stands in a curious relationship to the woman of the same name in *Vanity Fair* who, "[u]ndismayed by forty or fifty previous defeats," stages a campaign for the heart of Dobbin (433). *Lovel* continues the Christmas books written around *Vanity Fair*.[181] *Our Street* (1848) has its inveterate snooper (Miss Clapperclaw) with her "eye-glasses ready to spy," and its miserly landlady (Mrs. Cammysole), whose daughter (Flora) the narrator regrets not having approached. Titmarsh (like Batchelor) occupies a second-floor apartment, from which "little nook ... I and a fellow-lodger and friend of mine cynically observe" the street.[182] In *The Kickleburys on the Rhine*, Titmarsh is similarly plagued by self-accusations and "I would have" clauses in respect of Fanny Kicklebury, but also taken by the same hopes: "the sorrows and aspirations of the wounded spirit, stricken and sad, yet not *quite* despairing; still knowing that the hope-plant lurked in its crushed ruins."[183] The earlier tale of the "bachelor condition" displays the narrative desire taken to an extreme in *Lovel*, that of being "a chronicle of feelings and characters, not of events and places."[184]

The circular potential, arcing from hopeful hypotheses to chagrined counterfactuals and vice versa, traces the trajectory of Thackeray's career and finds uncanny expression in his illustrations. The first episode I discussed is accompanied by an image, "Bessy's Spectacles," which freezes the moment of connection between her and Batchelor (Figure 3.4). The lenses figure a pure form that matches their extraneous function in the plot. Blank against the surrounding crosshatching, they run orthogonal to and cut the sightlines of the persons depicted. They frame a stereoscopic space of possibility, inviting us into narrative alternatives. Where Batchelor was figured as an Asmodeus peering down through open roofs, this image delineates the opposite view: looking through blank portals, at an open sky of possibility.

Images of gazing through open portals, the alluring inverse of mirrors, recur often in Thackeray: children examining a diorama in *Vanity Fair*, a scene of absorptive recitation in the *Roundabout Papers*, decorative initials "O" like hoops thrown from text to text (Figures 3.5–3.11). Like the gambler's *double zéro*, these images solicit readers to risks of imagination. They exemplify what Alison Byerly, using Michael Fried's terms, sees as Thackeray's preference for "absorption" over "theatricality," or what Dames relatedly describes as the "distracted reverie" of his representations of reading.[185] These circles recall Thackeray's iconic signature adopted early in his career (spectacles inverted and crossed, visible in Figure 3.2): the means of seeing and sketching transformed into representative content. They fit the sentiment that the "best ink for Vanity Fair use would be one that faded utterly in a couple of days, and left the paper clean and blank, so that you might write on it to somebody else" (192).

BESSY'S SPECTACLES.

Figure 3.4   William Makepeace Thackeray, "Bessy's Spectacles," illustration for *Lovel the Widower*, in *Cornhill Magazine* 1 (January–June 1860): facing p. 233.
Widener Library, Harvard University.

Figure 3.5   William Makepeace Thackeray, title illustration for "On Some Late Great Victories," *Roundabout Papers* (London: Smith, Elder, 1863), p. 50.
*EC85 T3255 863ra. Houghton Library, Harvard University.

Figure 3.6   William Makepeace Thackeray, decorative initial for *Vanity Fair*, chapter xx (London: Bradbury & Evans, 1848), p. 170.
Lowell *EC85 T3255 848vb. Houghton Library, Harvard University.

Figure 3.7   William Makepeace Thackeray, decorative initial for *Vanity Fair*, chapter XLIX
(London: Bradbury & Evans, 1848), p. 393.
Lowell *EC85 T3255 848vb. Houghton Library, Harvard University.

Figure 3.8   William Makepeace Thackeray, decorative initial for *The Adventures of Philip*,
chapter XII, in *Cornhill Magazine* 3 (January–June 1861), p. 568.
Widener Library, Harvard University.

Given this emphasis on openness, it seems fitting that Thackeray left off
in the middle of things. *Lovel the Widower* was one of his last works
published serially and in volume form. He was in process with *Denis
Duval* when, to borrow Batchelor's words, "the fugacious years . . . lapsed,

Figure 3.9   William Makepeace Thackeray, decorative initial for *The Adventures of Philip*, chapter XVIII, in *Cornhill Magazine* 4 (July–December 1861), p. 138.
Widener Library, Harvard University.

Figure 3.10   William Makepeace Thackeray, decorative initial for *The Adventures of Philip*, chapter XXI, in *Cornhill Magazine* 4 (July–December 1861), p. 385.
Widener Library, Harvard University.

my Posthumus!"[186] Four of a projected eight numbers appeared in the *Cornhill Magazine* in 1864, after Thackeray's death. "If, moreover, it after a few months broke short off," Henry James later recalled, "that really gave it something as well as took something away. It might have been as true of works of art as of men and women, that if the gods loved them they died young. 'Denis Duval' was at any rate beautiful, and was beautiful again on

Figure 3.11 William Makepeace Thackeray, decorative initial for *The Adventures of Philip*, chapter XXXIII, in *Cornhill Magazine* 5 (January–June 1862), p. 385.
Widener Library, Harvard University.

reperusal at a later time."[187] With characteristic exactness James praises Thackeray's unfinished work in counterfactual mode. He discerns how an iterative beauty resides in the openness to being otherwise, and registers this novel as "overflowing with possibilities of character."

The living potentiality in Thackeray presses against the mortal inevitability that cannot finally be escaped through counterfactual reasoning. It is striking to observe how his letters typically offer sympathies for another's grief in terms identical to those I have explored: "I have kept back writing, knowing the powerlessness of consolation, and having, I don't know what vague hopes that your brother and Miss Bronson might have been spared."[188] The gesture is bizarre but characteristic: a condolence that restores to contingency the event whose irrevocableness it would assuage. Indeed, counterfactuals remain our familiar mode for reanimating the dead: *she would have loved this novel.* Thinking about that "certain (albeit uncertain) morrow ... about which all of us must some day or other be speculating," Thackeray's counterfactual imagination establishes, in the words of the living, a modal kinship with the dead.[189] "I know Papa was tired & that he did not want to live except for us," wrote his daughter Anne in uncannily similar terms: "yet my heart sickens & aches & I feel that he might have been with us now."[190]

CHAPTER 4

Approximations
Serial and Composite Thinking in Hardy

There are some truly dog-eared books in the novels of Thomas Hardy. The heroine of *Far from the Madding Crowd* (1874) uses one to try her luck at romantic forecasting, its "leaves, drab with age, being quite worn away at much-read verses by the forefingers of unpractised readers in former days." Bathsheba Everdene finds her verse in the book of Ruth, the page marked by a "rusty patch ... caused by previous pressure of an iron substance thereon," where long-vanished predictors placed a key to fulfill the necessary (hardly sufficient) conditions for prophecy.[1] In *A Laodicean* (1881), William Dare's copy of Abraham De Moivre's *Doctrine of Chances* is "as well thumbed as the minister's Bible."[2] Tess Durbeyfield's *Compleat Fortune-Teller* is "so worn by pocketing that the margins had reached the edge of the type."[3]

Whether used to make predictions via superstitious augury or rational calculation, the physical modification of these objects signals the long continuance of repetition: the material encounter with the page just as much as the mental grasp of graphic marks. Worn by constant, customary usage, Hardy's books change in the negative form of attrition (pages thumbed, passages fingered) and in the positive guise of accretion (a verse stained by an elemental trace). In the physicality of reading and handling, their users reenact broader experiences of making inferences from repeated series of events or traces in the material world. At the same time, they engage in activities that depart from physical constraints: constructing images of the future, visualizing possible paths, and weighing outcomes. In *The Mayor of Casterbridge* (1886), a letter's revelation causes Michael Henchard to consider "the paper as if it were a window-pane through which he saw for miles."[4] Reading for prediction becomes abstract: pages fade to windows, pictures supplant words, and mental images mimic the initial overlay of material prop and virtual percept. When characters engage in such counterfactual or suppositional thinking, they perform an immaterial equivalent of accretion or attrition.

In this chapter, I show how Hardy reckons with uncertainty through these two distinct yet complementary modes of thought and representation. In the first, which I term *serial thinking*, he deploys forms of representation and mental operation that take into account long series of events or large classes of instances. Serial thinking emphasizes aggregate patterns, the habitual and the long-run, and is keenly attentive to how repetition is grooved into materiality. In the second mode, *composite thinking*, limited classes of instances or temporally distal events are productively juxtaposed or condensed into images. Composite thinking stresses the family resemblance, the antihabitual and small scale, and is alert to how visualization and conjecture draw us away from the concrete. These modes of representing thought and judgment about uncertain futures show Hardy expanding the terrain of rationality, urging us to attend to the weird ways in which conscious judgment is shadowed by the intuitive and imagistic.

Although Hardy's attraction to material iteration is present from early on, *The Return of the Native* (1878) portrays his most comprehensive examination of serial thinking. In the chapter's first half, I argue that Hardy's descriptions of serial phenomena draw on, even as they surpass in vivacity, one influential account of probability in the period: John Venn's evolutionary vision of chance as a class of outcomes making up a mutable series from which judgments can be drawn. We find arresting images for such series in the novel's palpable setting and in the intuitive knowledge held by individuals, handed down by groups, and indexed in the human body through its natural friction with the world. Games of chance reflect features of such series in unexpected ways. Venn's project is in the spirit of John Stuart Mill's *System of Logic* (1843), with its emphasis on inductive and empirical elements that take priority over deduction and ratiocination in human thinking. If Hardy goes further than these proponents of experience by materializing prediction, he is also sensitive to potential errors of judging under uncertainty by serial methods. His representations of how we attend (or not) to material evidence and are engrossed by errors of perspective yield an account of judgment under uncertainty more flexible than the historical models in logic and philosophy that ground his intuitions.

Where rural plots naturally emphasize knowledge drawn from long-range repetitions, elsewhere in Hardy we see the influence of abstract models for understanding prediction. In *The Mayor of Casterbridge*, he juxtaposes the plot's main antagonists according to their cognitive attitudes – blunt intuition and sophisticated calculation – but also offers a synthetic model of inference under uncertainty where thinking is displaced from the material to the virtual. In the chapter's second half, I link Hardy's later work with the psychological and statistical program of Francis Galton, and especially with his composite photography technique, used to visualize statistical classes and later adapted to allegorize the formation of mental images. I argue that the novel's portrayal of composite thinking – its obsession with counterfactual imagining, family resemblance, and uncanny realization – constitutes another way of operating within the parameters of probable knowledge.

The frameworks I adduce to explain Hardy's serial and composite thinking are fundamentally concerned with selection: Venn's with establishing the relevant instances ("reference classes") from which to make judgments about series, Galton's with choosing the right number of exposures to produce a worthwhile composite. Serial and composite representation also redound to problems of selection in realism. Deciding what counts when evaluating probable arrays or statistical composites is akin to determining what counts for inclusion in the novelistic rendering of a "real" world. These axes of uncertain thinking, manifest in formal and narrative techniques, can be used to reassess Hardy's generic commitments. In the chapter's final part, I demonstrate how Hardy's version of *probable realism* emerges as a coherent project when serial and composite thinking are used to analyze his many proclamations about genre. In descriptions that call attention to repetition, aggregation, and process, Hardy selects for representation a worn and dated world, a setting that arranges both events that occur to human persons and longer-run series in the time of heath and sky. Alternately, he forges representations through composite images, making transparencies of the world where selected memories and mental states, character suppositions and narrative "sideshadows" are overlayed.[5] Reading Hardy's formal techniques and generic claims via intellectual models related to, though considerably more abstract than his usual scientific contexts (Auguste Comte, Mill, Charles Darwin), I recast his influences within the space of probable knowledge. My readings intersect with work on Hardy, science, and philosophy, updating familiar topoi – coincidence, repetition, determinism, fate – to reveal what is still misconceived in our sense of Hardy's representational project.[6]

Serial Thinking

When James Murray, lead editor of the *Oxford English Dictionary*, asked Hardy to clarify his use of "pair-royal" to refer to a triple throw of dice rather than cards in *The Return of the Native*, the latter offered an anecdote about his childhood experience in a raffle. "Being but a child, & the rest adults," he recalled,

> I was made to throw first (the first thrower being deemed least likely to win). But to the consternation of all I threw a "pair-royal," & won the bird [a cottage hen] – to my great inconvenience as I did not know what to do with it. The event was considered such a direct attempt of the devil to lead one of tender years to ruin that I was forbidden to gamble any more – & as a matter of fact, never did.[7]

Hardy's disinterested pose befits one whose first foray into gaming was so uncannily successful. He elsewhere disdains gambling's psychological allure – "if I had won 100 louis at Monte Carlo I should drop the game before losing them" – but qualifies that "games of chance never interest me, so perhaps I speak in too cold blooded a manner."[8]

Writing to his friend and collaborator Florence Henniker, in the year before his novel-writing came to a close with the volume publication of *The Well-Beloved* (1897), Hardy provides a more detailed account that undercuts such disavowals. Having made the acquaintance of a "veritable gambler," he "for the first time really perceived what it is to be possessed of the gaming fever." This Englishman

> won largely at the tables yesterday before dinner, & at dinner time I persuaded him to leave off; but he would not, & returned to the rooms in the evening. I saw him in the morning looking wild, & he said he had lost everything, except enough to pay his fare to England. The curious thing is that he fully believes in his ultimate success by means of a system, & is going to Monte Carlo in November to retrieve all his losses![9]

Hardy was so taken with this anecdote he offered another version in his *Life*, with the same bemused concern for faltering humanity. He laments that the gambler "believes thoroughly in his 'system,'" which "appears to be that of watching for numbers which have not turned up for a long time" and "yet, inconsistently, believes in luck: e.g., 36 came into his head as he was walking down the street towards the Casino today; and it made him back it, and he won."[10] He might be the last of Hardy's hounded characters, appearing on the morning after his ruin "by comparison with the previous night like a tree that has suddenly lost its leaves."[11]

Hardy may have forsworn raffles and roulette in life, but games of chance – their philosophical and mathematical underpinnings, apparent disruption of natural laws, and suppleness as plot devices – held a long-standing fascination. These recollections enact the mode of Hardy's continual return to chance as *topos* and formal tool – as a node joining reasoned belief and folk superstition, a force that rises into awareness from unconscious strata of personal and communal experience, an instrument of comic possibility and moral derailment.

In *The Return of the Native*, the axes of prediction and probable knowledge have a more precise referent in that one of the novel's key characters shares a name with the Victorian logician John Venn. Venn's work shadows the figurative and narrative aspects of his novelistic namesake, allowing him to stand as a condensation and critique of other modes of thinking in the novel. Akin to Venn's theory, Hardy's articulation of probable knowledge is enmeshed in structures of habit and repetition, intuition and perceptual acuity. Yet these representations of *serial thinking* also concede that personal views can never attain to the completeness of a statistical panorama: even a theory of chance grounded in the operations of the physical world founders on the bounded rationality of the individual perspective.

As phenomena from births to bank robberies, and deaths to dead letters were shown to fall into regular patterns, mathematicians in the early nineteenth century retooled accounts of probability in order to make sense of the mass of statistical data. The so-called *frequency* theory of probability, nascent in the work of Mill, Robert Leslie Ellis, Antoine Cournot, and Jakob Fries, held that an event's probability expresses the limit of its frequency of occurrence across a large number of instances. The probability of throwing a given number with a die expresses the limiting frequency of that outcome – 1/6 – across a large number of throws; it is not a predictive statement, but describes an emerging pattern.[12] Venn's elaboration of the frequency theory (which he is credited with formalizing) sought to correct a bias in the prior generation's work. Venn decoupled the science of probability from any pretense to objectivity, and criticized the cultural penchant for statistical determinism given notorious form in Henry Buckle's *History of Civilization in England* (1857–61) (discussed in the Introduction).[13] Probability for Venn was less a mathematical field dealing in stable truths than "a branch of the general science of evidence which happens to make much use of mathematics," drawing on experience not logic alone.[14] Venn's theory, articulated in his influential *Logic of Chance* (1866), and later lectures *On Some of the Characteristics of Belief, Scientific and Religious* (1870), sketches a view of serial thinking that joins the numerical abstractions of chance games to more concrete modes of repetition and aggregation. Venn was instrumental in giving institutional credence to probability theory via the Moral Sciences Tripos at

Cambridge, and his work was widely reviewed in the periodicals Hardy was combing while drafting *The Return of the Native*.[15]

Venn's theory rests on the term *series*. The proper aim of probability is to establish a group or class of instances (not always in temporal succession) that "combines individual irregularity with aggregate regularity."[16] Given such a class, we will find in its *frequency* or "long succession of instances ... a numerical proportion, not indeed fixed and accurate at first, but which tends in the long run to become so."[17] The patterns of this frequency form the basis for drawing inferences about this particular series (not necessarily any other). In prior examples of the so-called law of large numbers – from Pierre-Simon Laplace's calculations on the probability of sunrise to the statistical measurement of social phenomena conducted by Adolphe Quetelet and Siméon-Denis Poisson – the *tendency* of events to fall into regular patterns was taken to imply that they conformed to *laws* and could be identified as stable, objective types.[18] Taking Alfred Tennyson's lines about nature from *In Memoriam* (1850) as his epigraph, Venn begins in similar vein: "So careful of the type she seems, / So careless of the single life."[19] Yet his account departs from fixed types and objective laws, arguing instead that serial patterning forms *changeable* types. The "uniformity which is found in the long run, and which presents so great a contrast to the individual disorder," he points out, "though durable is not everlasting. Keep on watching it long enough, and it will be found almost invariably to fluctuate, and in time may prove as utterly irreducible to rule, and therefore as incapable of prediction, as the individual cases themselves."[20]

Venn's "evolutionary" logic emphasizes the shifting, mutable nature of chance series for two reasons. First, he stresses that our knowledge must rely on experience – "our sole guide" – and dismisses earlier views of probability as a feature of the physical world on which we calculate in advance.[21] He critiques those in the framework of what Lorraine Daston calls "classical" probability, who took the science as deductive and objective and proceeded from a priori principles, and later thinkers who modeled natural and social phenomena after the "*ideal* series" of games of chance.[22] Second, Venn's empirical account meshes with his view of logic as a *material* science that takes cognizance "of laws of things and not of the laws of our own minds in thinking about things," setting him apart from logical treatises like Augustus De Morgan's *Formal Logic* (1847) and George Boole's *The Laws of Thought* (1854).[23]

Within this view of probability as empirical, Venn emphasizes the "physical foundations" that give rise to irregularity in individual cases and tend to (shifting) regularity in the mass.[24] He points to the "influence of agencies" operating as causes that exert a serializing pressure on human activities.[25] These include natural forces and human actions: social averages are inflected by causes "in reality numerous, indeterminate, and fluctuating."[26] Stressing experience as the ground of probable knowledge, Venn asserts that physical conditions need to be kept in mind even in games. "The turning up . . . of a particular face of a die is the result of voluntary agency, but it is not an immediate result. There has been an intermediate chaos of conflicting agencies, which no one can calculate before or distinguish afterwards."[27] Abjuring prediction in advance and explanation in hindsight, Venn insists that even a priori thinking about games operates by a "tacit assumption which can never be determined otherwise than by direct experience."[28]

However critical of probability as an objective discipline, Venn hardly swings back to a subjectivist view. He disputes that our beliefs under uncertainty can be assigned accurate numerical ratios and rejects the quantifiability of "partial belief."[29] Our "belief-meter" is susceptible to confusion by the passions, those "distorting media of hope and fears."[30] Adumbrating his later thinking on evidence as "multiform,"[31] Venn develops a nuanced phenomenology of belief:

> our conviction generally rests upon a sort of chaotic basis composed of an infinite number of inferences and analogies of every description, and these moreover distorted by our state of feeling at the time, dimmed by the degree of recollection of them afterwards, and probably received from time to time with varying force according to the way in which they happen to combine in our consciousness at the moment.[32]

The chaos of coming to belief matches the disorder of causes giving rise to serial fluctuations. Similar complexities that exist both outside and inside our minds still cannot help *one* mind sift through the disarray and account for what the *many* might reveal.

In sum, where the work of his predecessors assumed that natural and even social frequencies tended to deterministic laws, Venn saw only the *appearance* of law-like regularities in a specified series; where they saw stable types in an emerging taxonomy of the world, Venn saw *flexible* types that evolved, however imperceptibly, as more instances came into view; and where the prevailing view cordoned off probability as a logico-mathematical discipline, Venn sought to characterize it as part of the wider consideration of *evidence*. His supple account of serial thinking emphasizes how inference must be based on frequency. It shows how our attitudes are prone to emotional bias, our views flickering "without any conscious alteration of the evidence" like "those alternations of light and dark in a murky foggy day."[33]

Venn's phenomenology of belief has striking parallels with Hardy's perceptual universe. If coming to conviction is "like being dazzled by a strong light; the impression still remains, but begins almost immediately to fade away," it is also like trying to perceive shapes in a dark room and later realizing that "a little more light or a more careful inspection has altogether transformed what we were inclined to call our facts."[34] Venn's work on series elucidates one of Hardy's characteristic tactics of representation: descriptions of objects and persons that notice attrition and other outcomes of repetitive or habitual action.[35]

To illustrate both what Venn's theory militates against and why Hardy's representations follow him in revising earlier models, consider a gambling scene from Hardy's *A Laodicean*. In Monaco a character appropriately named Dare tries out a system for roulette ("my theory of chances and recurrences") he has concocted from an early textbook of probability, De Moivre's *Doctrine of Chances* (1717).[36] He loses steadily and begs one of the novel's central characters, the architect George Somerset, for money, claiming that his "certainty" of winning is "almost mathematical" – that the hundreds of times he has already lost can be treated as a "vast foundation of waste chances" that will eventually "recoup" his expenditure.[37] His theory minimally refers to De Moivre's definition of the expected value of a game.[38] But Dare's notion that the "mathematical expectation of six times at least" is interlaced with his previous losses – that his "waste chances" are *investments* – is nonsensical.[39]

Somerset exposes his wrongheadedness:

> You might persevere for a twelvemonth, and still not get the better of your reverses. Time tells in favour of the bank. Just imagine for the sake of argument that all the people who have ever placed a stake upon a certain number to be one person playing continuously. Has that imaginary person won? The existence of the bank is a sufficient answer.[40]

Hardy's critique of the gambling frenzy in this "phantasmagoria" of a casino, through a character who draws his (faulty) system from a deliberately antiquated textbook, confirms that his dismissal of chance games hinges on our tendency to see them in abstract, numerical terms.[41] The notion of an "imaginary person," too, offers a version of Venn's intriguing thought that on the basis of *sympathy*, an "enlarged fellow-feeling," we might come to include the beliefs and predictions of others in our own sense of odds for or against an outcome, as long as we can conceivably use "evidence drawn from that class."[42] When viewed in Venn's empirical terms the gambler's "system" looks faulty in its premise, assuming that roulette gives stable, prior probabilities for each outcome. Dare ignores experience and trusts in number. In subsequent sections, I show how Hardy's vision of chance matches Venn's in its material and empirical character. His version of serial representation – yoked to the complexities of ordinary ways of appraising and predicting on the basis of fluctuating evidence – joins diminutive examples of chance to wider concerns of probable knowledge in perceptual, character, and narrative structures.[43]

Chance Materialized

Turning from the green baize tables of Monte Carlo to the brown furze of Egdon Heath, a different sequence of chance events anchors the plot of *The Return of the Native*. Things begin when Mrs. Yeobright trusts the fearful Christian Cantle with one hundred guineas to be divided between her son and niece, Clym and Thomasin Yeobright, wedding gifts despite their both having married against her better counsel. Christian is sidelined by a raffle at the inn, which he agrees to attend only "if there's nothing of the black art in it, and if a man may look on without cost or getting into any dangerous wrangle."[44] He wins – throwing a "pair-royal" – in a reprisal of Hardy's childhood victory. Imagining that he has unearthed a seam of fortune, Christian keeps the dice, alternately seeing them as sympathetic bearers of fortune ("magical machines") and vehicles of his former fear ("devil's playthings") (284). Confiding his newfound desire of "multiplying money" (282) to Thomasin's husband Wildeve – whom Mrs. Yeobright did not trust with her gift – Christian reveals his secret consignment. Wildeve lures him to further play, enticing him with stories of gambling that turn on fantastic winnings from low stakes or massive swings from ruin to success (284–85).

The game functions as a control against which subsequent extremes will be measured. On one hand, it fluctuates above and below an even narrative line, an "average [that] was in Wildeve's favour" (286), making clear – in his dismissal of the dice as "only cut out by some lad with a knife" (282) – the physical conditions of this numerical narrative. On the other, it frames Wildeve's changing intentions to show how chance might be wrenched into line by a will unaware of its own aims, "drawn from . . . intentions even in the course of carrying them out," so that "it was extremely doubtful . . . whether Wildeve was conscious of any other intention than that of winning for his own personal benefit" (287). In such a mood Wildeve is confronted by Diggory Venn, the itinerant figure who has been watching the whole scene from the shadows and replaces Christian in this rudimentary casino.

Venn materializes the aggregate regularities of his namesake's theory. Frequent contact with reddle (the substance of his trade in dyeing sheep) has gradually marked his aspect. He is "not temporarily overlaid" but "permeated" to an overall "lurid red" (58). Memorably described as a ghost "dipped in blood" (77), one of those "Mephistophelian visitants" (131) haunting the communal imaginary, Venn is a changeable type, the embodiment of serial repetition and accretion. At one with Hardy's wild setting, the prehistoric heath where changes are registered in glacial time and manmade structures are "almost crystallized to natural products by long continuance" (54), Venn is a figure of methodical, iterative action in the novel. We see him darning (130) and note his frequent rereading of a letter from Thomasin, "to judge from the hinge-like character" of the "worn folds" (133) on its packet (Figure 4.1). He is both exemplar and ground of a mode of knowledge that privileges aggregate regularities over isolated instances.

When Venn replaces Christian he bets, significantly, with sovereigns (coins in circulation) where Wildeve uses Mrs. Yeobright's "spade-guineas" (271) (coins historically out of production since the late eighteenth century), "unworn" (278) and obsolete.[45] The resumption of the game sees Damon Wildeve – his name sonically akin to *A Laodicean*'s William Dare – in a gambling frenzy. Where Wildeve is frenetic, Venn is stately. He sits "with lips impassively closed and eyes reduced to a pair of unimportant twinkles," like "an automaton" or "a red-sandstone statue but for the motion of his arm with the dice-box" (290). His eventual victory suggests that the proper mode of navigating the vagaries of chance is to spurn the individual viewpoint, discarding wild hope and vain belief, reducing awareness, imagining oneself a gaming automaton or Venn's composite "imaginary person." Hardy perhaps anticipates Walter Benjamin's later observation that gambling, like factory work, involves automaticity and "drudgery."[46]

This game initially proceeds as before – it "fluctuated, now in favour of one, now in favour of the other, without any great advantage on the side of either" – but then undergoes a passive shift: "a change had come over the game" (290). Venn wins steadily, throwing higher than Wildeve up to the maximum "triplet of sixes" (291). This angers his opponent, who mimics his vacillating fortunes at an affective level, throwing the dice and box away in anger but then affirming that he means "to have

The reddleman re-reads an old love-letter.

Figure 4.1   Arthur Hopkins, "The Reddleman Re-Reads an Old Love-
Letter," frontispiece for Thomas Hardy, *The Return of the Native*, in *Belgravia* 35
(March–June 1878).
Widener Library, Harvard University.

The stakes were won by Wildeve.

Figure 4.2   Arthur Hopkins, "The Stakes Were Won by Wildeve," frontispiece for
Thomas Hardy, *The Return of the Native*, in *Belgravia* 36 (July–October 1878).
Widener Library, Harvard University.

another chance yet" (291). The game continues despite bizarre events
and strange details of setting: heath-croppers wander in as though to
kibitz, a moth kills their candle and forces them to continue by the light
of "thirteen glowworms" (292) (Figure 4.2). Ensconced in obscure
conditions and playing with a single die, Wildeve proposes modifying
the game so that "the lowest point shall win the stake" (293). But Venn's
luck holds in this direction too, the physical world conspiring to have
him throw lower than an ace – nothing, a blank:

> [T]he die was seen to be lying in two pieces, the cleft sides uppermost.
> "I've thrown nothing at all," he said.
> "Serves me right – I split the die with my teeth. Here – take your money.
> Blank is less than one." (294)

The sequence of events in this chapter – "A New Force Disturbs the
Current" – is more complex than has usually been thought.[47] Even critics
who have noticed the nominal homage to John Venn have not taken into
account its main thrust. Gillian Beer argues that Diggory's win is a "fore-

ordained recuperation," the satirical inverse of Wildeve's tales about gambling, suggesting that "a half-assurance has been proffered to the reader that Venn must win" since the "whole is determined."[48] She uses Venn's work to offer a moralized account of the scene that exemplifies her notion of reading as wagering.[49] Helen Small finds Venn's ideas in Diggory as "an objective quasi-statistical observer" whom Hardy compromises by having him interfere in the plot.[50] She agrees with Beer in reading the gambling scene as a mock of probability theory that hinges on the reader: "the inevitable non-neutrality of plot puts the scene outside the reader's sense of what is probable. For the sake of the narrative, Venn needs to win."[51] These readings illuminate much about the discourse of probability and its pressures on the novel, but they are tangential to the philosophical view they sketch (and criticize). Beer draws her example of readerly uncertainty from a section in which John Venn explicitly sidelines subjective probability, and she invokes a determinism he rejected. Small helpfully shows how Venn's *neutrality* is satirized by Hardy,[52] but she conflates neutrality with objectivity and speaks of *laws* of chance that the *Logic* never sanctions.[53] Emphasizing the *narrative* stakes of this scene, both rely on probability in its literary and epistemic senses. In another reading, Adam Grener observes that the scene "operates on a different order of causality" from the main plot, splitting off Diggory's "idealized position of abstraction" from the novel's "causal structures."[54]

The scene *might* be read as parody, as though Hardy mocked up a fictional response to De Moivre's framing example: "[W]e may suppose two Men at Play throwing a Die, each in their Turns, and that he is to be reputed the Winner who shall first throw an Ace."[55] But the scene ends by recalling Venn's insistence that even games depend on physical conditions whose outcomes cannot be determined objectively, a priori, but only by experience, even if their uniformities *do* seem more fixed than the aggregate regularities of natural or social series. Hardy's fractured die, thrown by a character who actualizes repetition on the surface of his body, is a vivid image for this material substrate. The cleft die alters, then abolishes numerical odds, dispensing with objective mathematics and subjective predictions. Instead of writing the highs and lows of number as he saw them in Monte Carlo, Hardy materializes chance – and then literally breaks the bank.

Countermoves

To follow John Venn's theory into a wider reading of the novel is not, I contend, to complain about how such chains of events signal the plot's departures from credibility or neutrality, nor to belabor what is predetermined by Hardy. Such views seem no more immune than others to Anthony Trollope's dismissal of valuing *telos* over process in reading or criticism: "take the third volume if you please – learn from the last pages all the results of our troubled story, and the story shall have lost none of its interest."[56] It is, rather, to track Hardy's dramatization of probable thinking at the level of small-scale narrative mechanics, to recognize that what converges in this dimly lit scene is present in even dimmer lighting elsewhere, and that repetitions in description and characterization form an interlocking series with this bravura vignette. Here I offer a fuller account of Diggory Venn as a supple predictor, focusing on his perceptual acuity, his attention to figure/ground relations, and his reliance on serial instances.

Venn's plot machinations accrue significance only in aggregate. He is invested in a longer, more regular game than other characters (including perhaps himself) can see. His strategies often involve a mindless repetition that continues even after early results come in. A demonic surrogate with uncanny powers of perception, Venn's eye is "keen as that of a bird of prey" (59).[57] He discerns different qualities of light in a dark landscape, to the distance of a few hundred yards (433), and needs only a brief sound to infer that silk-clad Eustacia has passed by his van (432).[58] His first appearance as an exemplary predictor mobilizes these capacities. He scans the landscape as though it were a graphical display, a "gradual series" of elevations and depressions against the pattern of which his eye is drawn to the "noteworthy object" that turns out to be Eustacia silhouetted on the barrow (62). Watching her outline, which forms a "unity" with, and "obvious justification" for the dark formation, Venn's inference about a significant feature in the landscape transfers into the realm of social judgment. Perceiving an unexpected movement – a "discontinuance of immobility," a "strange phenomenon" – as Eustacia moves off and is replaced by a sequence – "a third, a fourth, a fifth" – of heathfolk who ascend the barrow, Venn singles her out as "more likely to have a history worth knowing" (63). This model of detecting a departure from habitual patterns and drawing probable conclusions is a persistent dimension of Venn's "watchful intentness" (54). When he later descries Wildeve leaving Eustacia, we witness no mere perception but a probabilistic sample from a class of possible events, his character's "keen eye" having seen what was "within the limits of the probable" (327). Hardy offers such scenes through intense visualization, as if challenging us to read according to Venn's mode of pattern recognition, taking in the page's graphical marks and the fibers they overlay.

To have a reasonable class of instances from which to extract a model series, discern a pattern, or make a judgment, Venn needs a store of repeated observations, a background with a convenient stasis. He undertakes a concerted surveillance operation near Rainbarrow, where Wildeve and Eustacia meet in secret, and is not put off by an initial lack of success, "look[ing] upon a certain mass of disappointment as the natural preface to all realizations" (135). His vigil continues for six days and meets with success on the seventh. We infer that his regular watch has continued in the narrative's background, because Venn later reports to Eustacia that Wildeve waited while she was off pursuing a newfound infatuation with Clym (207). Similarly, it is "not by accident" that Venn shadows Wildeve and Thomasin to the church where they are finally married, and makes sure to bring Eustacia, having "with the thoroughness which was part of his character ... determined to see the end of the episode" (220).

Requiring more than one instance to corroborate a judgment, Diggory alternates an almost inhuman fixity with energetic persistence. When he decides to "reconnoitre" along the road leading from Wildeve's home to Clym's (329), he lingers in the dark like a signpost or milestone. By contrast, persuading Eustacia to desist with Wildeve, he uses several lines of attack and then "play[s] the card of truth" (145). His methodical nature is later turned to his own account when, after the Maypole dance, he looks for a glove he knows to be Thomasin's, borrowed and lost by one of the maids. He searches by moonlight, "walking in zigzags right and left till he should have passed over every foot of the ground" (455), as if in anticipation of an image designed to capture randomness in a later edition of *Logic of Chance* (Figure 4.3). Still, this predictive diligence hardly amounts to an omniscient view. Hardy is careful to suture details together to maintain partiality to Venn's information. Crucially, he emerges from the background in the gambling scene *after* Christian has stated that the guineas are a shared trust, so when Wildeve admits the first guinea is not his own Venn mistakenly concludes they are all destined for Thomasin (295–96).

Venn operates by "strategy," "scheme," "method," "system" (135, 143, 148). When one route fails he turns to whichever "channel remain[s] untried" (150). This allies or opposes him to other characters, depending on their place in his designs. What to Wildeve appear as interfering "countermoves" (328) are to Mrs. Yeobright a "providential countermove" (333) in safeguarding her guineas. Venn typically appears as an isolated figure, often invisible to others' notice. During the raffle, he sits outside the circuit of men in a "receding seat," "absolutely unobserved" (283). As a spectator he remains covert, lurking in the shadows or embedding himself

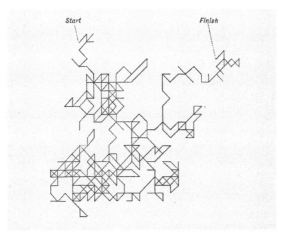

Figure 4.3   Untitled illustration of "a very fair graphical indication of randomness" in John Venn, *The Logic of Chance*, 3rd ed. (London: Macmillan, 1888), p. 118. The image represents approximately 500 decimal places in the value of π, restricted to integers 0 through 7, mapped as compass points.
Widener Library, Harvard University.

in the landscape, covering himself with turves (sections of matted grass) in order to watch at closer range. At other moments he becomes sinister, setting traps and tripwires: a *diabolus ex machina* worthy of the early Thackeray. It is from a collective position that the narrator voices this detail – "isolated he was mostly seen to be" (132) – and often points to Venn's peculiarity as a character. In a novel where *every* principal character is described as singular at least once, Venn receives the appellation several times (143, 208), as though he were a *series* of singularities, sui generis across many different classes, bearing in his face the "ground-work of the singular" (132).[59]

Some Versions of Subjectivism

Venn's acuity serves as a foil for subjective and too-objective prediction in Hardy's novel. He thwarts the excessive subjectivism of Wildeve (impatient with the dictates of probability and dreaming of lucky futures) and his companion in probable knowledge, Eustacia (whose "unpractical mind" is a romantic jumble with "no middle distance in her perspective" [420, 120]). Wildeve, who "threw away his chance" (73) of being an engineer to manage the Quiet Woman Inn on the heath, is a volatile and sentimental figure, "car[ing] for the remote" while "dislik[ing] the near" (274). D. H. Lawrence memorably described his character as an "eternal assumption."[60] Rejecting present facts and "cursed with sensitiveness," he is opposed to Venn, haunted by "blue demons" (95), not red. Akin to Sergeant Troy in *Far from the Madding Crowd* – "a man to whom memories were an encumbrance, and anticipations a superfluity" – Wildeve loses money betting on horses and gambles only with a view to the next throw.[61] When he *does* anticipate future outcomes, he responds with apathetic paralysis. Before the crisis at Shadwater Weir in which he loses his life, he senses the "anticipated futility" of either lover obeying their own will "in the face of a mutual wish that they should throw in their lot together" and so does not "dwell long upon these conjectures, maxims, and hopes" (435).

Eustacia's similar obsession with the world out of immediate view prompts her to wander the heath with a telescope (106), cutting an artificial path to objects of desire in the "near but unattainable foreground."[62] Conversely, she turns such technological framing to her own emotional life, her "colourless inner world" becoming "as animated as water under a microscope" (164) after eavesdropping on Clym. Every quality in her affective range emphasizes fluctuation: "petulant" (111) and "perfervid" (174), she swings from "anxiety" and "impatience" to "triumphant pleasure" (112). Eustacia lives in a world where imperfect knowledge is fleshed out by romance. She knows "by prevision what most women learn only by experience," that "love was but a doleful joy" (122), that it has no "continuance" and will "evaporate like a spirit" (255). This leads her to self-fulfilling prophecy and to vain disregard for past information. Her belief in the need to love Clym, having just met him, prompts an analogy to those "who have dreamed that they were to die on a certain day, and by stress of morbid imagination have actually brought about that event" (199). But when she begins the romance the past is suddenly a "blank" (245), both an empty form and a losing ticket to be discarded.[63] This *carpe diem* philosophy (265) is formulated in these terms: "Only I dread to think of anything beyond the present. What is, we know. We are together now, and it is unknown how long we shall be so: the unknown always fills my mind with terrible possibilities" (258). Hardy's ironic appeal to the language of certainty underlines the flaw in exchanging unknown futures for those one dreams up in advance. Had Eustacia "calculated to such a degree on the probability of success" in her scheme to persuade Clym to move to Paris, she might have taken into account his careful protests to the contrary before settling on this plan "in all likelihood" (300). Her impetuous dislike for waiting contrasts Diggory's methodical observation. Looking down at the Yeobright household to catch a glimpse of the native returned, she "inferred that the guest had not yet come" and leaves minutes later (171). Equally impatient are her attempts to bring about a coincidental meeting with Clym: she walks the heath on five occasions, and only after she gives up does the providential "opportunity" (175) arise for meeting him, by a ruse, at his family's Christmas party. The predictive incompetence of these characters results from their limited experience with serial thinking. Wildeve and Eustacia know only one mode of repetition: cultivation. He inherits land redeemed from the heath (87); she displays "exquisite finish" (319). When they dance, the "hard beaten surface of the sod, when viewed aslant towards the moonlight, shone like a polished table" (322) – a seriality that functions, atypically, as an instrument of vain self-distortion, not prudent self-preservation.[64] Neither understands the "disinterestedness" (209) of Venn's long-run strategy, which seems "counter to [Venn's] own interests" (210). It is not accidental that they meet their demise beneath a reflective surface.

Venn's serial thinking is more congruent with the measured probabilism of Mrs. Yeobright, whose intuition is uncanny but prone to errors of limited information. She has the "well-formed features of the type usually found where perspicacity is the chief quality enthroned within" (83) and is described as "far too thoughtful a woman to be content with ready definitions" (234). Hardy's term for Mrs. Yeobright's predictive skill – "intuition," having a "singular insight into life, considering that she had never mixed with it" – draws on a philosophical tradition concerning the problem of knowledge apart from perceptual experience (248). Drawing allusions from Edmund Burke, Hardy links Mrs. Yeobright to historical figures who were blind from an early age, like the mathematician Nicholas Sanderson, and others who "can watch a world which they never saw, and estimate forces of which they have only heard" (248).[65] An alternate form of reasoning under uncertainty, intuition differs from Venn's materialization of aggregate regularities. It infers unseen forces behind social events just as one imagines the vibrating particles behind movements of dust. "What was the great world to Mrs. Yeobright?" Hardy asks:

> A multitude whose tendencies could be perceived, though not its essences. Communities were seen by her as from a distance; she saw them as we see the throngs which cover the canvases of Sallaert, Van Alsloot, and others of that school – vast masses of beings, jostling, zigzagging, and processioning in definite directions, but whose features are indistinguishable by the very comprehensiveness of the view. (248)

Intuition's visualizing and foreshortening capacity turns human agents into particles, vectors of movement. Mrs. Yeobright sees "issues from a Nebo denied to others around" (83).[66]

Yet the distance that hones her predictive power impairs its granularity, compelling her to supplement what she cannot see by engaging in a mode of prophecy that is both temporal and spatial.[67] On the morning of her son's wedding, her gaze is "listlessly directed towards the open door," through which we follow her across miles to a "domestic drama" that is "but little less vividly present to her eyes than if enacted before her" (275). J. Hillis Miller likens her "wide scope of vision" to Hardy's in *The Dynasts* (1904–8): "The accurate, comprehensive view ... is the supreme Promethean temerity of claiming the sun's wide, inclusive vision of things. Such vision is, in fact, its own punishment, since it is blind to the distinct features of things that make them seem uniquely valuable and uniquely desirable."[68] Her outlook matches a note on creativity Hardy penned in 1866, where he muses that a "widely appreciative mind mostly fails to achieve a great work from pure far-sightedness," because the "very clearness with which he discerns remote possibilities is, from its nature, scarcely ever co-existent with the microscopic vision demanded for tracing the narrow path that leads to them."[69]

Mrs. Yeobright adopts Diggory's own strategic predictions in trying to keep Wildeve from interfering with a possible love interest between Thomasin and the reddleman. In conversation with her presumptive nephew-in-law, she takes Venn's stated "chance of winning [Thomasin] round" as a hedging bet against Wildeve's "backward and forward play" (151), trying to divert him by declaring that "upon the whole the probabilities are in favour of her accepting [Venn] in time" (153). Yet her unwitting collusion with Diggory does not preclude failures in their forecasts. Just as Venn does not foresee the chaotic possibilities of Wildeve's irrationality – "that the tendency of his action would be to divert Wildeve's movement rather than to stop it" (333) – so Mrs. Yeobright's strategy takes its "greatest effect ... in a quarter quite outside her view when arranging it" (154), since it sends Wildeve hankering after Eustacia. When she wanders onto the heath to repair her relationship with her son, she makes a fatal error, not recognizing that the scorching day is "one of a series" (337). Her predictions and Venn's are edged by the omniscient view from which they are occluded – from seeing every link in the series of interlocking events whose probable outcomes no single view could know in advance.

An Obsolescent Face

The Return of the Native condenses different views of probable knowledge, from the patient regularities and acute perceptions of Venn, the exemplar of serial thinking, to the engulfing romanticism of Eustacia and Wildeve, to the foreshortened intuition of Mrs. Yeobright. The novel's famous setting operates in tandem with serial thinking: it provides a slowly mutable background for events, blurs temporalities on a number of scales, and furnishes the treacherous conditions that render narration an inferential task. Egdon Heath is seen not as a landscape on which events take place but as a surface altered however imperceptibly by serial events.[70] The heath sets perceptual and epistemological conditions – requiring heightened acuity and slow movement – that suit Venn's qualities. Human actions take place "musingly, and by small degrees," to match the "protracted and halting dubiousness" that was "not the repose of actual stagnation, but the apparent repose of incredible slowness" (62). Similarly, the heath "could best be felt when it could not clearly be seen" (53), and Venn's operations collude with its "obscure watchfulness."[71] In a figure Miller reads as a "perpetually reversing metalepsis," the heath is a *face*, an "imperturbable countenance … which, having defied the cataclysmal onsets of centuries, reduced to insignificance by its seamed and antique features the wildest turmoil of a single man" (388).[72] The face of this landscape looks upward. To follow its expressions is to adopt what might be thought of as a heath's-eye view, the serial corollary to composite views from above, the bird's-eye view we will encounter in *The Mayor of Casterbridge*.[73] The character most attuned to the setting's predictive possibilities might be Clym, who was "inwoven with the heath" (226) when young. After reading hampers his vision and forces him to manual work, he takes up furze-cutting and tends to the face of the land, "fretting its surface in his daily labour as a moth frets a garment" (339). But the returning native has cut a caesura between his present life and his past. Having been in the diamond trade in Paris, handling objects that resist natural alteration, his division from the heath is ironically measured by how close he finds himself to its surface. Clym looks *at* the heath; Venn watches *out*.

The novel's action occurs against incremental changes and mutable temporalities – against a background that obtrudes its face into the foreground and provides obscure conditions for perceiving, supposing, and knowing beyond a ring of firelight. The gambling scene offers a vision of how subjective predictions are subsumed into the fluctuating series typified by the heath and its mysterious visitant, Diggory Venn. The coins at stake materially represent every character – their judgments, hopes, desires – struggling and failing to maintain a fragile 50/50 balance. As both character and condensation of natural frequencies that conspire against human agents, winning out against sentimental luck and frenzied speculation, Venn usurps the narrator's probable outlooks.[74] Hardy's frequent use of what David Herman calls "hypothetical focalization" – subjecting narrative events to a counterfactual perspective – formally aligns the narrator with Venn. We meet the "natural query of an observer" (59), an "imaginative stranger" (62), an "unimpassioned spectator" (440), and many others. Our view is framed by qualifications, assuring us of what "attentive observation ... would have revealed" (78) or what a scene "would gradually disclose ... when silently watched awhile" (249).[75] Such "diegetic indecision," enabled by the reiterated views of a "counterfactual witness," emphasizes the uncertain series within which Venn's long-run approach works.[76]

The eventual victory of this statuesque automaton whom even Hardy called "weird" (464n) suggests that predictions need to account for series of events that change as they accumulate "in succession under our notice."[77] In a note added in 1912, Hardy declared that in his "original conception," Diggory was "to have disappeared mysteriously from the heath" (464n), as though his fate as a character were subject to fluctuation.[78] Hardy frames the predictions of individual agents as working in the face of incalculable outcomes, those causing "more misfortune than treble the loss in money value could have done" (295). Just as Venn's namesake had criticized Mill for thinking probability might be used to forecast human actions, Hardy brings our subjective views into a clearing only to show how probable knowledge is always edged by uncertainty. In a novel of strange events and singular outcomes, against the impersonal heath that flattens persons into points, he showcases both the pathos and the vanity of any theory of chance that stakes certain meaning in the "devil's playthings" as they split and scatter in the dark.

Composite Thinking

Where *The Return of the Native* offers different modes of judgment under uncertainty only to privilege the materialist model of long-run inference I have called serial thinking, *The Mayor of Casterbridge* presents opposed stances on probable knowledge and synthesizes them in a mode of reasoning that relies on the aggregation and manipulation of (mental) images. Such *composite thinking* raises the profile of abstract evidence and of approaches to inference that require imaginative reconstruction. Focusing again on a somewhat peripheral character, the daughter of the eponymous Mayor, I argue that Hardy places her inferential development between the novel's two antagonists and their competing models of thought. I link the representation of this character's thought processes to photographic experiments in statistics that offered Hardy a new way to think through the problems of individual and aggregate, instance and average – a new way to model thinking under uncertainty. After analyzing the stages and resources of composite thinking in Elizabeth-Jane, I return to the familiar opposition between Michael Henchard and Donald Farfrae to recharacterize their styles of thinking – felt knowledge, rational calculation – as complementary epistemologies sharing certain features with, and in many ways completed by, composite thinking. As in the earlier novel, all remain (to differing extents) limited by the bounded rationality of their perspective.

In the 1870s, in response to suggestions from his cousin Charles Darwin and Herbert Spencer, the psychologist and statistical pioneer Francis Galton developed a technique for projecting photographs of faces onto a single plate. He called the result a *composite photograph*, a "generalised picture . . . that represents no man in particular, but portrays an imaginary figure possessing the average features of any given group."[79] Such an "averaged portrait" – an "aggregate result" revealing "typical characteristics" – had clear uses as a statistical tool.[80] The "amount of blur" in the hazy outlines measured "the tendency of the components [of the face] to deviate from the common type," in contrast to the "common humanity" visible in the clearer details, so composites could be taken as visualizations of a given group's statistical *norm* and *deviation*.[81] Galton's highly contentious uses for such anthropometric images (defining racial types, predicting criminality), in line with his notorious promotion of eugenics, have left a controversial legacy that is still with us in the biases of facial recognition tools. More innocuous applications included drawing a "probable likeness" of historical figures and producing more flattering self-portraits.[82] But these necessary critiques have obscured how Galton and nineteenth-century thinkers used composites in a more fundamental way to model the work of thinking – to visualize how the mind works to aggregate sensory data into images, associations, and concepts. Composites offered an expedient allegory for inference and concept formation, later taken up by Charles Sanders Peirce, Sigmund Freud, and Ludwig Wittgenstein,

Figure 4.4   Francis Galton, "Illustrations of a Family Likeness," 1882. Composite photographs of individuals in an unidentified family: male (left), female (right), and overall (center).

Galton Papers 2/8/1/1/1. UCL Special Collections.

whose notion of "family resemblances" among concepts owes much to Galton (Figures 4.4 and 4.5).[83]

On one hand, composites worked against the "analytical tendency of the mind," which, Galton wrote, "is so strong that out of any tangle of superimposed outlines it persists in dwelling preferably on some one of them, singling it out and taking little heed of the rest."[84] Composites similarly visualized the lessons of statistics, setting the individual in a wider probable array and correcting our natural fondness for the *one* unit. Conversely, they constituted a sharp analysis of the mind's unrigorous tendency to "generic images" and "blended memories,"[85] impressions formed not "by any process of reasoning" but by "blending together a large number of similar incidents" without proportion or precision.[86] Aggregate impressions across all senses would be skewed by "extreme elements," more vividly registered, while moderate elements were "not present in sufficient number to overpower them."[87] In this way, "undue consideration is inevitably given ... to all exceptional cases," to what is "marvellous" and "miraculous," yielding "fertile sources of superstition and fallacy."[88] Resisting both selective analysis and lazy aggregation, composite images neatly figure the work of literary imagination. Hardy came across

Figure 4.5   Francis Galton, "Illustrations of a Family Likeness," 1882. Composite photographs of an unidentified family (left) and original photographs (right) of individual members (male: father, uncle, two sons, cousin; female: mother, two daughters). Galton Papers 2/8/1/1/1. UCL Special Collections.

Galton's work in the 1880s, taking notes on a review of his *Inquiries into Human Faculty and Its Development* (1883).[89] He subsequently relied on these spectral images to describe the dynamics of narrative revelation, the lure of improbability, the mental workings of characters' minds, and the process of fictional representation. We can trace his figural adoption of composites through his changing representations of faces.

Hardy's characters routinely have *mobile* faces. In his earlier novels, such faces are commonly *read* for expressions of emotion or mental activity, in line first with the pseudo-sciences of physiognomy and phrenology and then with Darwin's *Expression of Emotions in Man and Animals* (1872).[90] In *The Return of the Native*, Thomasin's sleeping face registers "her several thoughts and fractions of thoughts ... exhibited by the light to the utmost nicety" (89). Mrs. Yeobright's face, on inquiring whether her niece is married, is one "in which a strange strife of wishes, for and against, was apparent" (220). Clym's face is arresting not "as a picture" but "as a page; not by what it was, but by what it recorded" (225). His face, "overlaid with legible meanings," summarizes the "modern type" marked by "mental concern" (225), the body used by the mind as a "waste tablet whereon to trace its idiosyncrasies" (194). When the inhabitants of the heath – itself "A Face on Which Time Makes but Little Impression" (53) – cluster round a bonfire, an uncanny disarrangement of faces obscures not history or heredity but a "permanent moral expression" (67). As faces shimmer and disappear in the firelight, characters "whom Nature had depicted as merely quaint became grotesque, [and] the grotesque became preternatural" (68).

Prior to his engagement with Galton, then, Hardy's governing model for thinking about faces was *expression*. By contrast, in later work the key features of composites – their relationship to conceptual images, their visualization of statistical knowledge, and their accidental revelations – provide new possibilities for faces at the level of both figure and plot. Consider the story "For Conscience' Sake" (1891), which has echoes of *The Mayor of Casterbridge*. A man makes good on an earlier "unfulfilled promise," marrying a woman in part because a respectable situation might aid the prospects of their illegitimate daughter, Frances, who is being wooed by a young curate.[91] The traces of heredity conspire against them when the family goes sailing with the suitor, and their shared proneness to seasickness makes their relations apparent:

> Nausea ... has this marked effect upon the countenance, that it often brings out strongly the divergences of the individual from the norm of his

race, accentuating superficial peculiarities to radical distinctions. Unexpected physiognomies will uncover themselves at these times in well-known faces; the aspect becomes invested with the spectral presence of entombed and forgotten ancestors; and family lineaments of special or exclusive cast, which in ordinary moments are masked by a stereotyped expression and mien, start up with crude insistence to the view. (425)

Hardy's description alludes to several features of composite photographs: their technological requirements (they could be made by stereotyping), their association with both statistical knowledge (*divergences*, *norm*) and the related science of heredity (*individual, race*), and their tendency to yield uncanny effects. The scene typifies heredity as haunting, a metaphor Galton recognized in describing the "ghosts of stray features" in his photographs.[92] When the "elemental lines" in the faces of father and daughter are revealed, a "mysterious veil" is lifted for the curate, whose mind proceeds to suspicious realizations, to "a strange pantomime of the past" (426). His subsequent disinclination to marriage prompts Frances to realize her parents' secret history.

Hardy's late poem, "Heredity," neatly personifies the connections that surface through composite images – links between facial expression, family history, and narrative recognition:

> I am the family face;
> Flesh perishes, I live on,
> Projecting trait and trace
> Through time to times anon,
> And leaping from place to place
> Over oblivion.[93]

The suppleness of composite images offered new possibilities for Hardy's aesthetics. His changed attitude to facial signification exemplifies a broader narrative and representational shift to composite thinking.

An Art of Conjecture

In *The Mayor of Casterbridge*, a minor but pivotal character, Elizabeth-Jane, develops a composite technique to examine her own mental makeup, using blurred representations to build theories about what those around her are thinking and concealing. Taking what few instances are at hand and subjecting them to mental manipulation and material experiment, she produces further information for reasoning not by means of serial iteration but by imaginative supposition and counterfactual hypothesis. Further, her own face and person become a locus of realization according to the logic of composite images. In offering a detailed account of Elizabeth-Jane's mental operations, I want to correct a superficial view of a character who has divided critical attention. One reviewer called her "excellent, but rather more than a trifle dull," whereas William Dean Howells saw "a very beautiful and noble figure . . . with her unswerving right-mindedness and her never-failing self-discipline," the more so because we "see into her pure soul."[94] Even noting her "quietly judicious perception" as an "extended metaphor for divining the truth," as later critics have, hardly does justice to the synthetic manner of thinking that makes her a striking corollary to that impassive predictor, Diggory Venn.[95]

Initially lacking an adequate number of events from which to draw conclusions, Elizabeth-Jane develops her thinking toward a simple seriality. In the process she makes visible an orthogonal mode of thinking that takes only a couple of instances and subjects them to manipulation, combination, and overlay, yielding inferences that are subsequently tested out in the world. With too little trust in her own intuitions to be aligned with Henchard, too little knowledge to generalize her thoughts like Farfrae, Elizabeth-Jane starts out as a virtual tabula rasa. Hearing the name "Henchard" in Casterbridge, she is "surprised, but by no means suspecting the whole force of the revelation."[96] Indeed, she is in the dark about her mother's prior relationship with the Mayor, even though Susan's every behavior seems to give up the game. "The tremors in Susan Henchard's tone," the narrator notes of her reaction to Henchard's name, "might have led any person but one so perfectly unsuspicious of the truth as the girl was, to surmise some closer connection than the admitted simple kinship as a means of accounting for them" (44). In Elizabeth-Jane we first see an inferential degree zero, a sublime faith in surface appearance matched later when her actual father, Newson, unquestioningly accepts Henchard's misleading truth – that "Elizabeth-Jane," the first daughter with that name, is dead – and just walks away.

The past informing Elizabeth-Jane's outlook is, like Daniel Deronda's, one about which she can have only dim knowledge: "Her conjectures on that past never went further than faint ones based on things casually heard and seen," on "mere guesses" (88). She has "unpractised eyes" in judging the gestural codes of market men (61), and her assessment of others' actions – for instance, noticing when Farfrae does not bid her goodbye – are drawn from single premises. This "simple thought, with its latent sense of slight, had moulded itself out of the following little fact: when the Scotchman came out at the door he had by accident glanced up at her, and then he had looked away again without nodding, or smiling, or saying a word" (58). Hardy characterizes this early stage of knowledge with diminutives: it is "faint," "mere," "simple," "little." Elizabeth-Jane's manner of keeping shyly to her own data – she "seemed to be occupied with an inner chamber of ideas, and to have slight need for visible objects" (93) – is partly described as an emotional stance, one of timidity and "circumspection," "that field-mouse fear of the coulter of destiny despite fair promise, which is common among the thoughtful who have suffered early from poverty and oppression" (85).

Elizabeth-Jane's development and interactions with town life bring "bloom" (84) to her aspect, but casting off residual anxiety and inferential naivety requires unlearning habits. Having been "too early habituated to anxious reasoning to drop the habit suddenly" (85) she is, for instance, prone to judge "lightheartedness" as "too irrational and inconsequent to be indulged in except as a reckless dram now and then" (84). Constrained by a sort of negative seriality, Elizabeth-Jane's manner of appraising the world builds on minimal cues (the "now and then"), undoing habitual anxiety and learning how to discriminate anew – how to draw two distinct perceptions out of what the senses take as one. One condition that allows Elizabeth-Jane to begin acquiring information and making such connections is her position on an upper floor of Henchard's home. From "on high," she has the "opportunity for accurate observation" (87) and is aligned with the zoomed-out view of the town claimed elsewhere by the narrator. Now able to view events at some distance, as well as to catch gossip that drifts up to her window from the market square, she is better positioned to gather data. Like Venn, she remains for much of the novel "out of the game, and out of the group," able to "observe from afar all things" (180).

The uncertain knowledge represented by rumor first ignites her attention. After dancing with Farfrae, "a hint from a nodding acquaintance" implies a social error and Elizabeth-Jane is embarrassed "at the dawning of the idea that her manners and tastes were not good enough for her position" (107). When Farfrae approaches her, she is open in one sense – thinking "there might be something wrong in this; but did not utter any objection" (107) – but unable to see why he would allude to his inability to ask her a question. Her "conjecturing" of these "enigmatic words" and "occult breathings" is slow to inference: she has to recall other events to make this problem "solvable" (109) by a substitution of terms, parsing the evidence to find a salient fact (Farfrae cannot address her because his relationship with Henchard has soured).

This pattern of seeking supplementary confirmation for conclusions she has already come to on her own leads in the direction of composite thinking. Incidentally, it produces some of the novel's more charming moments. By chance, she catches a draft of a letter in Farfrae's hand – a material form of the rumors floating her way. She copies and overlays the greeting so that it reads "Dear Elizabeth-Jane," at the sight of which "a quick red ran up her face and warmed her through, though nobody was there to see what she had done" (109). With vivid literalness, Elizabeth-Jane enacts future prospects and turns conjecture on the contents of her own mind. Instead of isolating herself from the world in timidity, she now develops an "anxiety to know" and can "no longer conceal from herself the cause" (109) of her own emotions. A similar performative experiment shows how she hones conjecture in a fully visual mode:

> To solve the problem whether her appearance on the evening of the dance were such as to inspire a fleeting love at first sight, she dressed herself up exactly as she had dressed then – the muslin, the spencer, the sandals, the parasol – and looked in the mirror. The picture glassed back was, in her opinion, precisely of such a kind as to inspire that fleeting regard, and no more. (110)

What is compelling about these enactments is that they dramatize everyday forms of counterfactual thinking – What if this letter were addressed to me? What would he think if I wore this dress? What about this one? – in terms that suggest the visual overlay of composite images. If ordinarily we entertain such thoughts as mental images – not all probable life paths can be tried on for size – Elizabeth-Jane's imagination literalizes such suppositions, transplanting them from mind to world. This strategy is recalled when she is living with Lucetta, who laments the difficulty of shopping for clothes since each option fashions a "totally different person" – indeed, one that "may turn out to be very objectionable" (166). Lucetta's superficial motive of social vanity is contrasted with Elizabeth-Jane's deeper fascination with becoming a "different person."

As she develops an idiosyncratic art of conjecture, Elizabeth-Jane also acquires the aggregated content with which to forge her cautious inferences: both new information and realizations that emerge from information she previously held in mind as inert data. Her newfound curiosity brings her up against the opaque edges of other minds, which she tries to divine according to her new tools. Consider two scenes where Elizabeth-Jane comes to some realizations about her mistress, Lucetta. In the first, she discerns that Lucetta and Henchard have a private relationship while the three of them marvel at a piece of agricultural equipment:

Then something *seemed* to occur which his stepdaughter *fancied* must really be a *hallucination* of hers. A murmur *apparently* came from Henchard's lips in which she *detected* the words, "You refused to see me!" reproachfully addressed to Lucetta. She *could not believe* that they had been uttered by her stepfather; unless, indeed, they *might have been* spoken to one of the yellow-gaitered farmers near them. Yet Lucetta *seemed* silent; and then all thought of the incident was dissipated by the humming of a song, which sounded *as though* from the interior of the machine. (167; emphases mine)

The passage of "seeming speech" (169) is saturated with the language of appearance and inference. Elizabeth-Jane slowly turns over these odd possibilities in her mind and then comes to a rapid conclusion as to the source of the song, for she "had apprehended the singer in a moment" (168).[97] Where earlier she created a material theater for thinking – forging her own love letter; dressing up to see the reflection of a previous self – she now internalizes that theater in increasingly abstract ways. The peculiarity of her conjectural skill separates her from other characters. She likewise worries about a menacing gesture she sees Henchard make upon entering Farfrae's employ – "or fancied she saw, for she had a terror of feeling certain" – and concerns herself with "what this *might* have meant" (236). Trying to speak to Farfrae, she "felt the difficulty of conveying to his mind the exact aspect of possibilities in her own" (237).

   In the second scene, Elizabeth-Jane's conjectural aptitude looms even larger in consciousness as she observes Lucetta getting ready to leave the house and considers her other romantic interest, Farfrae:

[Elizabeth-Jane] somehow knew that Miss Templeman was nourishing a hope of seeing the attractive Scotchman. The fact was printed large all over Lucetta's cheeks and eyes to any one who read her as Elizabeth-Jane was beginning to do.... A seer's spirit took command of Elizabeth, impelling her to sit down by the fire, and divine events so surely from *data* already her own that they could be held as witnessed. She followed Lucetta thus mentally – saw her encounter Donald somewhere as if by chance – saw him wear his special look when meeting women, with an added intensity because this one was Lucetta. She depicted his impassioned manner; beheld the indecision of both between their lothness to separate, and their desire not to be observed; depicted their shaking of hands; how they probably parted with frigidity in their general contour and movement.... This discerning silent witch had not done thinking of these things when Lucetta came noiselessly behind her, and made her start.... It was all true as she had pictured – she could have sworn it. (170)

Hardy describes these operations as taking place in "the crystalline sphere of a straightforward mind" (177). But this is actually an intricate sequence of mental hypothesis. Lucetta begins in the forefront of Elizabeth-Jane's perceptual field, is held stable in her mental theater, and circles round to emerge behind her in actual space, as though in a prank. The easy inference from a vision of the face as expressive page – "her eyes met"; "The fact was *printed* large" – is overshadowed by the intense visualization of what the page reveals. Seeing amounts to surveillance (Elizabeth-Jane not only "saw," "depicted," and "beheld" but also "followed") and allows for a sense of conviction so strong as to acquire a legal standing ("held as witnessed," "true," "she could have sworn").

Hardy uses this character, I am arguing, to model an experience that cuts against Venn's linear seriality. Indeed, one description of Elizabeth-Jane modifies the familiar motif for serial iteration so crucial to the symbolic patterns of *The Return of the Native*, and to the discourse of uncertainty more generally. Having learnt the "lesson of renunciation," she is "as familiar with the wreck of each day's wishes as with the diurnal setting of the sun" (178). Modeling a different type of seriality, her "experience had consisted less in a series of pure disappointments than in a series of substitutions," whereby "it had happened that what she had desired had not been granted her, and that what had been granted her she had not desired" (178). If she is thwarted in one instance, her conjectural tenacity (she is "not done thinking") wins out in the end. Although she considers with "an approach to equanimity the now-cancelled days when Donald [Farfrae] had been her undeclared lover, and wondered what unwished-for thing Heaven might send her in place of him" (178), her initial losses are only in service of a victory that ultimately occurs by the composite mode of substitution. Elizabeth-Jane loses Farfrae to Lucetta at first, but wins him over eventually, just as Venn loses at first, then wins one game, then several, and finally the hand of his opponent's wife.

Elizabeth-Jane's dejected lucidity is sharpened by personal tragedies. One is Susan's illness – "a shock which had been foreseen for some time by Elizabeth, as the box-passenger foresees the approaching jerk from some channel across the highway" (114) – and subsequent death. The experience gives this "subtle-souled girl" a somber occasion for turning away from the disappointments of the present (Farfrae's initial preference for Lucetta, Henchard's fall from grace) to ask after the causes of her life in metaphysical terms: "why things around her had taken the shape they wore in preference to every other possible shape"; "what that chaos called consciousness, which spun in her at this moment like a top, tended to, and began in" (116). This inquiry primes her mind for retrospective realizations – for Henchard's proffering of "details which a whole series of slight and unregarded incidents in her past life strangely corroborated" (121) – and the reorientation of her thinking around a "new centre of gravity" (122), namely, the realization of her mother's former marriage to the Mayor. There remain aspects of this past vista that cannot be enacted, either literally or in abstract imagining, even if the past still makes itself *felt* in certain ways.[98] Still, Elizabeth-Jane's attempts to reposition past know-ledge in light of new information resist thought experiments that do not adequately match what she knows. When Henchard earnestly presses a deceptive hypothesis to lure her emotions – "Suppose I had been your real father?" – her response strains after the image but rejects it – "I can't think it . . . I can think of no other as my father except my father" (119).

In her own person, and even in her doubled name, Elizabeth-Jane becomes an embodied source of realization for others in terms that recall Hardy's use of composite images and the arresting revelations of the unconscious body. In one scene, her sleeping face reveals to Henchard the lineaments of Newson's (and not his own) paternity. In "For Conscience' Sake" an abnormal state (nausea) leads to hereditary revela-tion. Here the normal state (sleep) unveils what waking physiology has hidden in plain sight. Hardy uses the scene to make a broader claim about the delusions of waking life, underscoring the transition I posited earlier, from faces as expressing emotion to faces as revealing history and heredity: "In sleep there come to the surface buried genealogical facts, ancestral curves, dead men's traits, which the mobility of daytime animation screens and overwhelms" (124).

I have traced Elizabeth-Jane's trajectory from inferential naivety, through a set of experiments that involve learning judgment by conjecture and counterfactual imagination, to her wise prudence toward the end of the novel. A statement made by the narrator – that "a maxim glibly repeated from childhood remains practically unmarked till some mature experience enforces it" (137) – suggests how, through a recursive pattern, Elizabeth-Jane gathers at once the data and the experience on which her perspicacity later operates. By the end she has almost a narrator's knowledge of the causal structures underlying coincidences in the plot, akin to a Jamesian "central intelligence."[99] She aids Henchard in his terror after seeing the effigy of his own person floating beneath the bridge where he considers suicide. What he takes as an "appalling miracle" presaging his own death she suspects to have a rational explanation. They go back to the water and divine the "natural solution of the mystery" (294). Even the narrator agrees with her manner of judging whether "anything should be called curious in concatenations of phenomena wherein each is known to have its accounting cause" (202).

Gradually widening her vista, Elizabeth-Jane comes to see her own life as part of a composite structure. If in the novel's final sentence she "class[es] herself among the fortunate" she also remembers that through modern *fortuna* one might easily find oneself in a different statistical group through the "persistence of the unforeseen" (322).[100]

Coarse Rivalry, Smooth Ciphering

Elizabeth-Jane's versatile mode of thinking casts into relief the novel's oft-noted archetypes for thinking: Henchard's felt, intuitive, even reflex judgments and Farfrae's dispassionate, reasoned, and calculative decisions. This rigid pairing, a "clash of the moody and unpredictable with the rational and consistent," typifies a pattern in Hardy where choices are "routinely between two mutually exclusive options," tantamount to the mathematical idea of "equipossibility."[101] Yet the plasticity of Elizabeth-Jane's thought processes, emerging through image and overlay, allows us to blend such oppositions into a portrait of complementary modes of knowledge. Both Henchard and Farfrae are drawn out of their styles toward composite thinking.

In Henchard, a "rule o' thumb sort of man" (48), we might see this in the "headstrong faculties" (112) that tell on his face. In relating his story to Farfrae he attempts to hide his expressions but cannot quite cover the "marks of introspective inflexibility on his features" (76). Henchard's inferences are blunt, his assessments of risk simplistic, his manner of deliberation binary, his realizations sudden and all-encompassing, and his contractual language clear-cut ("yea" or "nay"). The morning following the disastrous escalation that ends in the sale of his wife, Henchard considers two items of evidence, the money given in the sale and the ring that indexes her disappearance, which combine to confirm what has happened. "A confused picture of the events of the previous evening seemed to come back to him," followed by the "second verification of his dim memories" (15). This folk probabilism has echoes of the fractional proofs of Roman law, another survival in a novel whose setting "announced old Rome in every street, alley, and precinct" (68).[102] Susan's decision to renew contact with Henchard almost two decades later replays this duplicate structure: "He had been described as a lonely widower; and he had expressed shame for a past transaction of his life. There was promise in both" (58). Abjuring details, Henchard assesses future probabilities with as little accuracy in personal affairs as economic ones. His decision-making is equally rudimentary. Trying to bring Elizabeth-Jane to his side after Susan's death,

Henchard's "mind began vibrating between the wish to reveal himself to her, and the policy of leaving well alone, till he could no longer sit still" (119). Moderate compromise is precluded by extremes.

Yet Henchard's stark realizations can attain the visual immediacy of composite thinking. Reading Susan's confessional letter, which disabuses him of the notion that he is Elizabeth-Jane's father (for she is not the identically named daughter he abandoned), Henchard "regarded the paper as if it were a window-pane" (123). He likewise looks at Lucetta's missive from Jersey "as at a picture, a vision, a vista of past enactments," even if its contents are an "unimportant finale to conjecture" (114). These figures for realization emphasize the sudden capacity for vision and inferential reach. They meet a converse figure more obviously linked to composites: the sudden recognition of facts that have always been staring one in the face. Watching his blond-haired charge sleep, Henchard recognizes her true lineage in her facial features. Toward the end of the novel, his "original make" – an inbuilt hostility to subtle inference and causal attribution, a propensity to believe ironic reversal, superstitious agency, and fetishistic diversion – is "denaturalized" (299) by his sensitivity to Elizabeth-Jane's judgments. Agitated by "jealous grief" (300) at the resumption of her interest in Farfrae, Henchard happens to think that she is, "legally, nobody's child" – the thought comes unbidden in that "outer chamber of the brain in which thoughts unowned, unsolicited, and of noxious kind, are sometimes allowed to wander for a moment prior to being sent off whence they came" (301). If Henchard is routinely at the mercy of such associative randomness, he can only aggregate his perceptions into a sound basis for judgment under Elizabeth-Jane's tutelage.

Farfrae, by contrast, relies on his "native sagacity" (112) and operates with "insight, briskness, and rapidity" (297). His qualities are clearly visible in his efficacy at trade. When he becomes the manager for Henchard, who "had used to reckon his sacks by chalk strokes all in a row like garden-palings, measure his ricks by stretching with his arms, weigh his trusses by a lift, judge his hay by a 'chaw,' and settle the price with a curse," Farfrae institutes a new regime of "smooth ciphering, and machines, and mensuration" (104). Later, when Henchard has relieved him and rehired Jopp, they consider how to outclass the Scot and worry that "he must have some glass that he sees next year in" (182), misgauging the source of his long-range predictions as a prophetic instrument. Seeing Farfrae as "deep beyond all honest men's discerning," they do not understand his calculative knowledge, which draws on a familiarity with developments in agricultural technology. His "knack of making everything bring him fortune" (182) hardly comes from gut feelings.[103] Thus when Farfrae takes over Henchard's failed concern, "scales and steelyards began to be busy where guess-work had formerly been the rule" (219), a modus operandi that must have appealed to Hardy, the autodidact who proudly made his way through practical scientific manuals.[104]

Farfrae is not, however, wholly superior for being scientific. If sophisticated in matters agricultural and commercial, he misses certain features of the world. A detail in Henchard's story is a "complication so far beyond the degree of his simple experiences" (77). His relative lack of intuition occasions disaster when Henchard tries to get him back to the ill Lucetta and realizes, in a surprising moment of sensitivity, how the younger man must suspect his report. Henchard can "almost feel this view of things in course of passage through Farfrae's mind" as trust implodes, for Farfrae "did distrust him utterly" and the former Mayor's "treachery was more credible than his story" (282). This situation typifies what the philosopher Annette Baier has called "pathologies of trust," situations in which trust's usual, undeclarative mode is compromised by injunctions, reminders, and "danger signals," indicating that trust has been "confused with reliance on threats."[105] The dramatic impasse between the two rivals is an example of a "too calculative weighing of the costs of untrustworthiness," especially after the kind of betrayal that can lead to a "lasting inability to partake of" any "trust-dependent good."[106] Farfrae fails to see possible explanations for Henchard's having made his way to him at great speed; he cannot take the fact of Henchard's relaying this information as, in itself, a reason for believing him.[107] He returns "in a state bordering on distraction at his misconception" (284), which culminates in Lucetta's death. Yet it is notable how Farfrae's shallow intuitions acquire depth when Elizabeth-Jane is involved. He becomes "one of those men upon whom an incident is never absolutely lost," and "the impulsive judgment of the moment was not always his permanent one" (238). In "revis[ing] impressions from a subsequent point of view," Farfrae starts to rehabituate himself to trust, and does so in a way that co-opts Elizabeth-Jane's practice of mental rehearsal and conjecture: "The vision of [her] earnest face in the rimy dawn came back to him several times during the day. Knowing the solidity of her character he did not treat her hints altogether as idle sounds" (238).

Something in the Air

These disjunctive modes of handling uncertainty come together, via the figure of the composite, in one of the novel's key topics: forecasting the weather. Henchard and Farfrae crystallize a changing dispensation in the nineteenth century, as Katharine Anderson has described, from "weather prophecy" to modern methods of modeling the atmosphere.[108] The founding of the Meteorological Office in 1854 made the science of the air institutional and standardized methods of collecting weather information. Galton presented one of the first data-driven visualizations of weather patterns across the British Isles in *Meteorographica* (1863). Weather is a system of iterated events that, when studied in aggregate, yields regularities – or at least regularly shifting irregularities ("periodicities").[109] It is also a domain of phenomena that admits of felt estimations and inferences. Weather partakes of the novel's opposed epistemologies: rational knowledge and intuitive judgments (especially those registered by the body), both susceptible to the errors of human beings. Weather determinations rely on ambient and often invisible particulars, and are thus paradigmatic for protean and uncertain inferences: simple observations and complex intellectual currents (ideas carried "in the air" in Matthew Arnold's phrase), happy gossip on the model of pleasant weather and rumors of more menacing aspect.[110]

Hardy's weather knowledge condenses many views in Victorian popular science, in particular, the statements of Andrew Steinmetz, whose *Manual of Weathercasts* (1866) Hardy owned.[111] Steinmetz's work falls neatly between the axes of prophecy and prediction, commonplace and meteorological knowledge, providing information that "can lay claim to the authority of general experience or the sanction of science."[112] He emphasizes intuition and science as two sources of foresight, the former registered by the body in the "feeling of [one's] own instruments" (8), the latter involving calculations on the "varying degree of probability of the occurrence of *any* conceivable event in nature" (32). Where felt knowledge has a wider compass in the natural world, as in the registrations of animals, birds, and plants, as well as humans working closely with them (like shepherds), "natural tokens" need not be "superstitious signs" (23). What Steinmetz calls "practical meteorology" (128) succeeds more often than the thin weather lore of those with a narrow ambit of experience (22–23, 108–14). An entry from *Chambers' Cyclopedia*, which Steinmetz cites (without acknowledgment), provides a thought to which Hardy often returns:

> What vast, yet regular alterations, a little turn of *weather* makes, in a tube filled with mercury, or spirit of wine, or in a piece of string, &c. everybody knows, in the common instance of barometers, thermometers, hygrometers, &c. and it is owing partly to our inattention, and partly to our unequal, intemperate course of living, that we do not feel as great and as regular ones

in the tubes, chords, and fibres, of our own bodies.... [A] great part of the brute creation have a sensibility, and sagacity this way, [but] their vessels are regular barometers ... affected only from one external principle, viz. the disposition of the atmosphere; whereas ours are acted on by divers from within, as well as without; some of which check, impede, and prevent the action of others. (s.v. "Weather")

Resituating meteorological technologies within the sensory sphere – for the shepherd all things comprise a "weather-gauge" (22) and those closest to nature are most in tune with its "signals and telegrams" (108) – Steinmetz laments that most humans become "animated barometers" (109) only through bodily damage (scars, rheumatism).

Henchard experiences two iterations of weather regret. Rain and poor planning scupper his plans for Casterbridge's holiday, and he merely "wished he had not been quite so sure about the continuance of a fair season" (102). His more disastrous run is prefaced by the narrator's reflection on the relationship between weather and rural economics:

The farmer's income was ruled by the wheat-crop within his own horizon, and the wheat-crop by the weather. Thus in person, he became a sort of flesh-barometer, with feelers always directed to the sky and wind around him. The local atmosphere was everything to him; the atmospheres of other countries a matter of indifference. The people, too, who were not farmers, the rural multitude, saw in the god of the weather a more important personage than they do now. Indeed, the feeling of the peasantry in this matter was so intense as to be almost unrealizable in these equable days. Their impulse was well-nigh to prostrate themselves in lamentation before untimely rains and tempests. (183)

Reprising Steinmetz's image (and perhaps Venn's "belief-meter"), Hardy makes the farmer at once instrument and insect, attuned to local phenomena and prone to weather superstition. Naturally, Henchard "read a disastrous garnering, and resolved to base his strategy against Farfrae upon that reading," but he curiously stalls in uncertainty: "before acting he wished – what so many have wished – that he could know for certain what was at present only strong probability" (184). He attempts to confirm his hunch by turning to the man known as Fall, who has a "curious repute as a forecaster or weather-prophet" (184). Henchard ignores even the terms of the possible prophecy – that it might be done with "labour and time" – by paying for an instant reading, even though he does not "altogether believe in forecasts" (187). He ignores Fall's hedging as to certainty "in a world where all's unsure," and proceeds to buy "grain

to such an enormous extent that there was quite a talk about his purchases" – his speculation produces speculation – and then the weather
turns so that "an excellent harvest was almost a certainty; and as a
consequence prices rushed down" (187). As he sells, the weather turns
again in a cruel mockery of his decisions, which Hardy recasts as a
foolhardy gamble: he "backed bad weather, and apparently lost" (188).
His experiences of awful weather are figuratively transposed indoors, so
that where "numerical fogs" (74) had to be cleared away from his accounts
by Farfrae, Henchard now faces "gloomy transactions" (188) at the bank in
the form of similar abstract equivalents. Given that the "momentum of his
character knew no patience" (190), Henchard casts around with blunt
instruments, learning little from these events and registering only that
since his wife's arrival, "there had been something in the air which had
changed his luck" (133).

Hardy sets these blunders against successful predictions, not only in
Farfrae's calculative moderation but also in intuitive forecasts by groups of
townsfolk, as on the bright morning of Casterbridge's royal visit when "all
perceived (for they were practised in weather-lore) that there was permanence in the glow" (260). This choral prediction matches other moments in
Hardy where groups concur, as when "twenty pairs of eyes stretched to the
sky to forecast the weather for the day" each morning in *The Woodlanders*
(1887), well ahead of nature's meteorologists, "before a single bird had
untucked his head."[113] Such intuition was recognized in nineteenth-
century meteorology: Galton's *Meteorographica* praises the "glance" as
"an insight different in kind from instrumental or numerical description."[114] Yet ultimately all judgments in this domain remain, so to say,
under a cloud. Certainty is post facto: one "can never be sure of weather till
'tis past" (189), Henchard laments.

Attrition, Overlay, and the View from Above

I have outlined three models of coming to judgment in *The Mayor of
Casterbridge*: Henchard's blunt intuition (which is unable to make discerning forecasts), Farfrae's far-seeing calculation (which falters on matters of
trust), and Elizabeth-Jane's composite mode (which takes time to develop
its imaginative and conjectural tools). If the novel places less emphasis on
the serial repetitions that ground judgment in Hardy's rural settings, from
Far from the Madding Crowd to *The Woodlanders*, its epistemological
frameworks are nonetheless reflected in setting and plot. "Change was
only to be observed in details," the narrator intones about the initial jump

over eighteen years from the wife sale to the present action, "but here it was obvious that a long procession of years had passed by" (19). These details are seen not by an individual but by an aggregate eye, a passive voice, what Hardy names a "casual observer" (3): a "textural change" (19) appears on Susan's skin; Henchard is now "thought-marked," "matured in shape, stiffened in line, exaggerated in traits" (32). The iterative quality of seriality is replaced by the immediate quality of the composite. A "glance was sufficient to inform the eye" (19), Hardy writes of the relation between Susan and Elizabeth-Jane, the former's youthful qualities "transferred so dexterously by Time ... that the absence of certain facts within her mother's knowledge from the girl's mind would have seemed for the moment, to one reflecting on those facts, to be a curious imperfection in Nature's powers of continuity" (19–20). The impartial spectatorship of such appeals – "one reflecting" with no individual mind, a "glance" by no human eye – recalls the counterfactual narration of *The Return of the Native*. Yet the view is no longer serial horizontality but composite verticality. An aerial description of the town, separated from its environs by a "mathematical line" (27), confirms this:

> To birds of the more soaring kind Casterbridge must have appeared ... as a mosaic-work of subdued reds, browns, greys, and crystals, held together by a rectangular frame of deep green. To the level eye of humanity it stood as an indistinct mass behind a dense stockade of limes and chestnuts, set in the midst of miles of rotund down and concave field. (27–28)

This abstracted view appears later in the image of a "chess-board on a green table-cloth" (88), the comparison to a gaming-table confirmed when Henchard wagers on the weather and is "reminded of what he had well known before, that a man might gamble upon the square green areas of fields as readily as upon those of a card-room" (188). The clarity of human plots when seen from distance, sharpened into regular patterns, may be a crude clarity, set apart from the subtler aggregations Hardy's rural characters find in the horizontal view. But it aligns with Elizabeth-Jane's sophisticated model of learning to think from "on high."

To be sure, there are indications of the attrition seen elsewhere in Hardy. Men at market wear "suits which were historical records of their wearer's deeds, sun-scorchings, and daily struggles for many years past" (150); an old shepherd holds a crook "polished to silver brightness by the long friction of his hands" (158); an inn door is "shiny and paintless from the rub of infinite hands and shoulders" (253–54). But the most striking alterations join natural and human materials, so repetitions traceable in one sphere lose their predictive utility in the other. Take the example of bridges that record a natural history of anxiety in their "speaking countenances":

> Every projection in each was worn down to obtuseness, partly by weather, more by friction from generations of loungers, whose toes and heels had from year to year made restless movements against these parapets, as they had stood there meditating on the aspect of affairs. In the case of the more friable bricks and stones even the flat faces were worn into hollows by the same mixed mechanism. (220)

Whatever conclusions we entertain about the fates of these lugubrious figures, the only certain inference from this "mixed mechanism" is that rates of anxiety in a given population remain unhappily stable over time. Likewise, the keystone of the arch over Lucetta's High Place Hall forms an unnatural instance of attrition – a mask with a "comic leer, as could still be discerned," made grotesque by "generations of Casterbridge boys [who] had thrown stones at the mask, aiming at its open mouth" (138). Bridges that record human sighs in their form, an ornament that literalizes the volleys of social judgment – we are far from the heath's inwoven seriality.

In this setting, an "old Roman garrison town, overgrown rather than obliterated by an English *urbs in rure*," natural attrition and human alteration combine in ways more reminiscent of Galton's composite images than Venn's probable series.[115] The image on the sign of the King of Prussia changes in the sun by "warping, splitting, fading, and shrinkage," leaving only an image as a "half invisible film upon the reality of the grain, and knots, and nails" (40). Yet it is still an *image* that remains. Another signpost presents human repetitions as merely surface changes in recalcitrant matter, as Farfrae takes over Henchard's operation: "A smear of decisive lead-coloured paint had been laid on to obliterate Henchard's name, though its letters dimly loomed through like ships in a fog. Over these, in fresh white, spread the name of Farfrae" (219). It is as if Hardy wants us to visualize the composite of just two names: What commonalities and deviations would we see? Composite thinking compels different modes of perceiving, attending, and reading the world. It transforms *series* into *signs* and prises apart the analogies between human events and natural repetitions.

Other avenues of Galton's psychological research offer further clarification of the mode of reading called for by composites. His work on composite photographs and generic images ran alongside investigations into the thresholds of perceptual discrimination in human subjects – an early foray into the scientific study of habit pursued by William James and others. Galton was interested in how much difference was required between two discrete sensations – or levels of sensation – for a subject to notice the change. Calling the unit of such notice the "just-perceptible difference," he pointed to how it allowed perceptions of continuity in discrete phenomena (seeing many dots as a continuous line) and how it took a roughly geometric increase in sensation to compel awareness of a shift (detecting a change in a constantly increasing stimulus).[116] We could see Elizabeth-Jane's early approaches to thinking in these terms, as requiring the disaggregation of habit to compare perceptions in a fresh manner, to consider the surface of the known past and experiment with perceptions in order to locate a "just-perceptible difference" between them. This visual mode of thinking breaks away from seriality – an eminently habitual type of perceiving and cognizing – in a way that brings psychology against other views of aesthetic volition. As though responding to John Ruskin's lament that "WE NEVER SEE ANYTHING CLEARLY" and taking seriously Walter Pater's valorization of the *failure* to form habits as a critical stance, Hardy writes a character who reveals how antihabitual thinking proceeds by way of composite pictures, conjectural reveries, and counterfactual imagining.[117]

Elizabeth-Jane's *composite* model for thinking and predicting is at once an accessory and corrective to the *serial* thinking so prominent in Diggory Venn, and elsewhere in Hardy's fiction. In the absence of a long-range series traceable in the material world, one snapshot is laid over another, slowly building a composite view in which aggregate impressions are gathered and visualized. I have argued that these two modes of uncertain thinking trace a historical development in Hardy's work, but of course they also operate in tandem, joined by other representational tactics from *Desperate Remedies* (1871) through *Jude the Obscure* (1895). Together serial and composite thinking epitomize a dictum found in Hardy's notebooks: "To make a true portrait, you must turn the successive view into the simultaneous."[118]

Probable Realism

How might these modes of thinking illuminate Hardy's views on fiction? In a basic sense, Hardy's theory of art itself emerged in serial and composite fashion, as the evolving self-portrait of a novelist took form out of statements stretching across decades. These include his observations in the *Life*, composed after his novel-writing had ceased but incorporating notes written during his career; his sustained contributions to debates about realism and (French) naturalism in "The Profitable Reading of Fiction" (1888), "Candour in English Fiction" (1890), and "The Science of Fiction" (1891); his prefaces to novels upon initial volume publication, and later in the Osgood, McIlvaine (1895–96) and Wessex editions (1912); his editorial instructions and correspondence on textual matters; and his hurt reactions to early reviewers and later critical studies.

Accounts of these materials fall roughly into aesthetic and political camps. Those who would defend Hardy's realism in an aesthetic sense have to account for how he blends the more stylized aspects of several modes and genres (romance, pastoral, myth, comedy, tragedy, melodrama, sensation, gothic) with more commonly recognized elements of the realist program.[119] Penelope Vigar summarizes the issue in describing Hardy's creation of a world "uncommon and yet credible": "distanced from reality, it is more easily imaginable as fact."[120] George Levine assesses Hardy's "peculiar relation to realism" as both adversarial and recuperative, reflecting on how an "aggressively manipulated narrative" in line with romance also operates an "uneasy but effective conjunction with the traditions of realism."[121] Elsewhere, Levine meditates further on Hardy's "transformation of the materials of realism into patterned artifice," and on the divided loyalties that result – between schematic "parallels, juxtapositions, crossings, and bitter ironies" at some moments, and realist features that undercut such patterns at others.[122] By contrast, political readers in the tradition of Raymond Williams find disruptive strategies in Hardy's novels precisely where they strain against realism as probabilism.[123] Peter Widdowson sees Hardy's improbable antirealism cutting against a discourse of realism as probable, summarized in arch terms: "'plausible' characters are 'convincingly' deployed in relation to the 'credible' processes of the 'real' natural and social world."[124] Tim Dolin suggests that, in the wake of such assessments, critics value Hardy more for his interruptions of realist aesthetics.[125] Those who focus on Hardy's politics within practical, reformist settings seem to have little need for "realism" as a category.[126]

Where aesthetic apologia for Hardy's realism naturalize chance and improbability, political arguments for his antirealism denaturalize chance and see probability as a mystification. The extent to which defenders of realist aesthetics and critics of its ideological artifice converge on topics like chance, coincidence, and probability remains striking. Yet such critics often fall into the patterns of the English gambler: they believe at once in a system governing chance operations and, inconsistently, in luck.[127] Resisting the sense of Hardy as a determinist while pointing out that past repetitions tend to obstruct freedom, Bert Hornback oddly divides coincidences into "chance occurrences" and "causal relationships," the latter functioning to highlight what he terms "moral coincidence."[128] Ian Gregor calls attention to the spurious division into pure coincidence and chance *manqué* in an image that neatly emphasizes such moments as illuminating the mesh of causes always in operation: "[Hardy's] ostentatious use of coincidence is the well-lighted junction where the lines of [his] various plots converge." This is a long-standing way of reconciling chance and determinism in the scientific idea of "intersecting causal lines."[129] We accept Hardy's improbabilities, Gregor suggests, because behind "glaring illogicalities" lies a "subtle network of image and reference in which the mundane is continually expressed in fantastic or incongruous terms, and the extreme is shown as ordinary occurrence."[130]

Bridging these critical discussions, this section canvasses Hardy's many comments on the nature and function of narrative art to show how his concepts, figures, and examples coalesce in an account of realism grounded in probability as a complex representational issue. Exemplifying perhaps the most achieved and self-conscious version of what I am calling probable realism, Hardy defends his oeuvre on the grounds of probability in the several senses I outlined in the Introduction: social plausibility, cultural approvability, generic verisimilitude, statistical likelihood. Hardy's probable realism has four key features, which I address in turn: a defense of the *improbable* that links fictional representation to actual events or recorded realities, thereby unmasking judgments of probability as social codes; a contrasting emphasis on fiction as, so to say, *too probable* on account of its special capacity to renovate the world in distinctive ways; a synthesis of these positions where what is at stake in fiction is declared to be neither real instances nor intensified replications, but a *composite image* of real or nonreal elements; and an updated romanticism that emphasizes *serial impressions*, mutable visions privileging surprise and only operating given substantial credulity. Deliberately offering a speculative reconstruction of Hardy's views, I take his own approximative method as a guide to cut across his statements about fiction – from improbable to too probable, from composite image to serial impression. In so doing, I aim to move beyond a critical impasse caused by the desire to winnow out his works according to conventional realist dictates.

Defending his work against charges of improbability, Hardy often pointed out that his novels were attached to the life of fact, insisting that events deemed "improbable" or "impossible" had a basis in recorded events. He refers to the relevant incidents, places, or people undergirding the probable world of fiction to establish not only their reality as single instances but also the larger reference class of which they formed a part. Apart from his early life in Dorset, such information and documentary evidence came from reading newspapers and periodicals, from the local *Dorchester County Chronicle* to the *Times*, which gave ballast to Hardy's ethnographic interest in his native landscape. He suggests of *A Laodicean* that "its incidents may be taken to be fairly well supported by evidence every day forthcoming in most counties," that *Under the Greenwood Tree* (1872) might be taken as "a fairly true picture, at first hand" of village practices, and that his attention to fact bespeaks an effort "to preserve for my own satisfaction a fairly true record of a vanishing life."[131] In his historical mode, the emphasis on fact is crucial. *The Trumpet-Major* (1880) is described as an account founded on "testimony," "an unexaggerated reproduction of the recollections of old persons ... who were eyewitnesses." *The Dynasts* similarly exhibits – despite its formal innovation – a "tolerable fidelity to the facts ... as they are given in ordinary records."[132] Hardy's views could shift on these matters. His initial preface for *The Hand of Ethelberta* (1876) is an apology, undermining those who attacked the novel's "unexpectedness" ("that unforgivable sin in the critic's sight") and sniffing that a "high degree of probability was not attempted in the arrangement of the incidents."[133] But a later postscript adopts a tone of calm assurance, noting that changed standards in the early twentieth century would see as "reasonable and interesting pictures of life" what was once "deemed eccentric and almost impossible."[134] Writing to a correspondent who had sent him a "melodramatic" story for appraisal, Hardy generalizes this first aspect of his probable realism: "it always happens or nearly always, that the unbelievable parts of a story are real incidents."[135] He wryly twists the Aristotelian line on plausible events (those that "for the most part happen") by referring not to instances of probability *in* fiction but to what happens *outside* fiction in matters of craft.

In *The Mayor of Casterbridge*, this practice of confirming the source of improbable events in real incidents takes on a more iterative or numerical cast. "It may seem strange to sophisticated minds," he notes of the wife sale, "that a sane young matron could believe in the validity of such a transfer; and were there not numerous other instances of the same belief the thing might scarcely be credited."[136] Hardy imputes to his readers a conviction in coincidence that could only emerge through statistics – "she was by no means the first or last peasant woman who had religiously adhered to her purchaser, as too many rural records show" – and juxtaposes such unwilling suspicion against Susan's own felt sense of self-binding after being sold by Henchard.[137] This canny bait was not taken up by early readers, who pointed to the wife sale in calling the novel a "disappointment," "too improbable," "fiction stranger than truth."[138] It required a perceptive reviewer like Howells to defend the incident in Hardy's terms, as "not without possibility, or even precedent."[139] Pointing to facts or conceivable precedents, Hardy exposes the constructed status of judgments that rely on convention to sift the improbable from the verisimilar.

In the second aspect of his probable realism, Hardy develops a fresh defense against improbability by claiming that fiction comprises a species of additive plausibility not found in the world as such. The prior emphasis on actuality becomes, here, a contradictory reassurance: most characters or incidents are so intermixed with fictionality as to be safely unidentifiable. They are "too real to be possible," as though their plausibility were additive, their vividness so probable as to exceed certainty.[140] His "wilful purpose in his early novels until *Far from the Madding Crowd* appeared," he explains in the *Life*, was "to mystify the reader as to their locality, origin, and authorship by various interchanges and inventions."[141] The Baptist minister in *A Laodicean* is a "recognisable drawing . . . though the incidents are invented"; the tranter in *Under the Greenwood Tree* is based on a real person but "not a portrait, nor was the fictitious tranter's kinship to the other musicians based on fact"; Stephen Smith in *A Pair of Blue Eyes* (1873) is an "idealization of a pupil whom Hardy found at Mr. John Hicks's," and his father is "drawn from a mason in Hardy's father's employ, combined with one near Boscastle."[142] Marian in *Tess* may be an exception that proves the rule as "one of the few portraits from life in his works," a dairy-maid Hardy taught in Sunday school.[143] "The Profitable Reading of Fiction" theorizes this position by declaring fiction to be "more true . . . than history or nature can be," since in the latter cases there are always inexplicable elements, "hitches in the machinery of existence."[144] Hardy even gives these terms a normative spin, stating that to earn the conviction of readers one must realize "why fiction must be more probable than history."[145]

To emphasize the probable in fiction with reference to actual events or real people as sources, under these first two aspects, is to invert the terms of the usual charges against Hardy's fiction. He seems to think that the transfer of actual incidents across the porous membrane that separates our world from fictional worlds results in an inversion or idealization. Where the first aspect insisted on referents whose depiction would be declared improbable by accepted standards of taste, the second shows characters, places, and incidents as fused aggregates of actual features and imagined additions. This vision holds across his novelistic oeuvre, even though he was keen to draw his own taxonomy along a probable spectrum, stating that where the (more celebrated) Novels of Character and Environment show "a verisimilitude in general treatment and detail," the Novels of Ingenuity display "a not infrequent disregard of the probable in the chain of events, and depend for their interest on the incidents themselves."[146]

The third feature of probable realism brings us to one of the modes of thinking I have discussed. Hardy repeatedly uses the composite as a figure for aggregates (whether of actual or imagined events) that seem "too real to be possible." As he abandoned novels for poetry and even as he commented on and reshaped the text of his novelistic output, Hardy's manner of describing his imaginative world held tenaciously to the composite. The setting of *Two on a Tower* (1882) is a composite of "two real spots"; Overcombe Mill in *The Trumpet-Major* is a "composite picture" of two separate towns, "containing features of both"; Conjuror Trendle in "The Withered Arm" is a "composite figure of two or three who used to be heard of"; and Mrs. Charmond's house in *The Woodlanders* is not to be mistaken for a referent in the world since it blends several homes.[147] These comments often concern place names, as Hardy retroactively standardized the imaginary world of Wessex. He changed the names of towns in *Desperate Remedies*, for instance, so that they are referred to "by the names under which they appear elsewhere."[148] The "Cliff without a name" in *A Pair of Blue Eyes* was likewise only "*partly* suggested" to him by real cliffs.[149] In the novel's 1895 preface, Hardy demurs so as to maintain the anonymity of the cliff even as he acknowledges a real referent: "Accuracy would require the statement to be that a remarkable cliff which resembles in many points the cliff of the description bears a name that no event has made famous."[150] Whereas the earlier preface speaks of this romance as an "imaginary history" adjoined to "material circumstances" that, even if they *could* be given precisely, occupy in representation a "region of dream and mystery," the later preface of 1912 mentions that Endelstow House is "to a large degree really existent," albeit "several miles south of its supposed site," and therefore a composite of structure and setting.[151] Egdon Heath is not only a historical aggregate but a synchronic one, which "united or typified heaths of various real names, to the number of at least a dozen"; Hardy later maintains this "bringing together of scattered characteristics" in its representation.[152] Communicating revisions for the Indian edition of *The Return of the Native*, almost half a century after its composition, Hardy actually attempts to rewrite such aggregation into the novel, proposing "a combination of some wild tracts" in replacement of the more assertive "a wild tract."[153] In a 1901 interview with William Archer, who identified Hardy's blended representation as a "sort of composite photograph," the novelist concurred and called the human mind a "palimpsest."[154]

This emphasis on composite portraits as generic models is the culmination of a literal emphasis on aggregation present in Hardy's first note on art. In 1865, after publishing the charming vignette "How I Built Myself a House," he reflects on representation as family resemblance: "The form on the canvas which immortalizes the painter is but the last of a series of tentative & abandoned sketches each of which probably contained some particular feature nearer perfection than any part of the finished product."[155] In "The Profitable Reading of Fiction," his critique of novels about the more select strata of society hinges on the claim that "social refinement operates upon characters in a way which is oftener than not prejudicial to vigorous portraiture, by making the exteriors of men their screen rather than their index."[156] Taking only the screen temperature of a face means that the "author's word has to be taken as to the nerves and muscles of his figures," where in representations of more common life "they can be seen as in an *écorché*."[157] Detecting what is composite or hereditary in a face becomes Hardy's cardinal instance of realist sympathy. Hearing a poor and illiterate woman describe how her friend, who lost a child years earlier, bore "the ghost of that child in her face even now," Hardy admires her "power of observation informed by a living heart."[158] He states that "characters, even if they have any truth in them at all, are composite, & impossible to dissect for facts."[159] If, as composite images, characters possess what Galton called a "surprising air of reality," having multiplied the sense of recognition for a single face into a fused overabundance of familiarity, that "reality" cannot be disaggregated into its component parts to be mined for "facts."[160] Hardy's probable realism, then, works by composites, whether actual incidents spliced with imagined ones or aggregates of actual and imagined. He emphasizes both the epistemic status of fiction as a plausible transcription of the world – in its aggregate incidents and overlaid images – and a view that deviates from the norm to insist on curiosities and exceptional incidents.

The relationship between these features of probable realism colludes with its fourth and final aspect, the impression, to which Hardy appeals especially in describing his late novels: *Tess* is "an impression, not an argument"; *Jude the Obscure* "an endeavour to give shape and coherence to ... personal impressions."[161] "Unadjusted impressions have their value," he avers, "and the road to a true philosophy of life seems to lie in humbly recording diverse readings of its phenomena as they are forced upon us by chance and change."[162] In the General Preface to the Wessex Edition, Hardy emphasizes "mere impressions of the moment" as against a consistent worldview, "fugitive impressions which I have never tried to co-ordinate," and in the preface to *Jude* dismisses the "question of their consistency or their discordance, of their permanence or their transitoriness."[163] Commentary on this aspect of Hardy's theory of fiction calls attention to the notion of impression as a para-Romantic tenet, a question of intuited "seemings," appearances, forays beneath the surface of the real. Yet it is striking how impressions (almost always plural) often involve a series of repeated events. If Hardy famously saw *Jude the Obscure* as a "series of seemings," my elaboration of seriality suggests that critical emphasis in thinking about realism needs to be placed more on the first term than the second.[164] *Poems of the Past and the Present* (1901) likewise constitutes "a series of feelings and fancies written down in widely differing moods and circumstances."[165] Such a series needs to be monitored, as Hardy notes elsewhere: "so in life the seer should watch that pattern among general things which his idiosyncrasy moves him to observe, and describe that alone," in a "going to Nature" that results in "no mere photograph."[166]

On one hand, "impressions" and "seemings" make space for circum-stantial details akin to serial representation. Reading for intellectual and moral purposes, one may be interested in "accidents and appendages of narrative," "trifles of useful knowledge, statistics, queer historic fact."[167] The kinship between circumstantial detail and instances of attrition in Hardy's novels is brought out by a comment in the *Life*, which observes how in "a work of art it is the accident which *charms*, not the intention; . . . the amber tones that pervade the folds of drapery in ancient marbles, the deadened polish of the surfaces, and the cracks and the scratches."[168] Selecting such detail for reasons of plausibility is not meant to sponsor what Hippolyte Taine calls "detailism" and Ruskin "copyism," doctrines Hardy mocks by suggesting that scrupulous accuracy is merely "photo-graphic curiousness." It is "trivial," "ephemeral" – "life garniture."[169] Narrative cannot be submitted to "scientific processes," Hardy writes, one key reason being "the impossibility of reproducing in its entirety the phantasmagoria of experience with infinite and atomic truth, without shadow, relevancy, or subordination."[170] If "The Science of Fiction" initially designates a "comprehensive and accurate knowledge of realities" requisite for representation, art – with its pressure on the probable and its "disproportioning ... of realities, to show more clearly the features that matter in those realities" – becomes the operative term once narrative construction gets underway.[171]

On the other hand, impressions can distort in a different direction, as readers find themselves having to suspend disbelief, attempting to find a view in common with the author's vision. Hardy suggests that reading for pleasure requires that an author be "believed in slavishly" despite "marvelous juxtapositions."[172] In a more serious mode he clearly values the qualities of readers who deploy inference and guesswork, who "see what the author is aiming at, and by affording full scope to his own insight, catch the vision which the writer has in his eye."[173] Such mutual harmonizing of agendas for representation also reflects Hardy's conviction that impressions reveal an accuracy beyond direct sensation, in "the mental tactility that comes from a sympathetic appreciativeness of life in all of its manifestations."[174]

From defenses against improbability by resorting to factual authenticity and fictional overabundance, and from the composite image of genre to the serial structure of impression, I offer these four facets of Hardy's probable realism as a way to understand his compelling (if often riddling) aesthetic project. It may be objected that such an account offers only a rearguard defense for a representational project too prone to repetition and restatement, coincidence and wild chains of event, self-correction and recomposition – attended, in short, by "radical disunity."[175] Hardy himself suggests that his emendations may offer only a way to cope with age and forgetting. Correcting a detail about the old woman in "The Withered Arm," in the preface to *Wessex Tales* (1888), he sees it as "an instance of how our imperfect memories insensibly formalize the fresh originality of living fact – from whose shape they slowly depart, as machine-made castings depart by degrees from the sharp hand-work of the mould."[176] In so clearly reprising the vivacity of serial repetition and the uncanniness of a composite overlay even as he laments the fading of an original vision, Hardy makes clear how these figures compose his vision in its most memorable form. The "living fact" constitutes a blood-red thread that runs through Hardy's novels – an artery that carries his visceral attention to the life of sensation. But it is veined with curiosities and incidentals, commentaries and composite memories that embody his own "approximative" approach to realism as a genre of the probable.[177] The vision holds stable despite gauche additions, digressions, and emendations – and despite Hardy's "hesitancy, passivity, [and] a lack of rigour behind the maintaining of literary appearances" – just as blood stays red inside a body that incrementally ebbs away from its cast.[178]

Hardy's thinking expresses what is intuitive about treating realism in relation to discourses of the probable, whether statistical aggregates, factual archives, or averaged portraits. Probable realism replaces the static accuracy and objectivity of number with the mutable precision of impressions gathered through experience. Thinking about Hardy under this rubric offers a corrective to the rigid geometry of his plots, often seen as governed by stern determinism or supernatural designs.[179] If the "determinist lives in a world of occurrences but not of genuine events," probable realism in Hardy provides a counterweight to the causal magnetism of what is fated or determined. We might imagine him taking the logician's caution about long-run series as a representational dogma: "Keep on watching it long enough, and it will be found almost invariably to fluctuate."[180] He does so in order to obviate fixed definitions for fiction, dismissing attempts "to set forth ... in calculable pages" a systematic account of fiction, which could only amount "to writ[ing] a whole library of human philosophy, with instructions how to feel."[181]

Coda

Outside Chance, or The Afterlife of Uncertainty

In "The Darkling Thrush," a poem set at twilight on the nineteenth century's last day, Thomas Hardy crystallizes nineteenth-century uncertainty's rational and affective stances. The poem expresses both lingering doubt and undefined optimism, the speaker's melancholy deliberations on the "Century's corpse" and the thrush's "ecstatic sound," which issues forth a "blessed Hope, whereof he knew / And I was unaware." Though Hardy was obviously unaware of what intellectual shifts would occur in the early twentieth century, he uncannily foreshadows how the redefinition of uncertainty would leave some of its distinctive features behind in the century of his novelistic career. I am far from suggesting (to paraphrase Virginia Woolf) that the character of so complex and multidimensional a phenomenon as uncertainty changed entirely "on or about" 1 January 1900, the day after Hardy's poem.[1] Nor do I claim a comprehensive rupture in its literary manifestations. Yet given how the intellectual and scientific landscape modulates into the modernist years, alongside radical shifts in literary form and expression, the early twentieth century marks a natural end point for this book. Below I offer a rough periodization of uncertainty and a sketch of how modernist writing responds to uncertainty's altered resonance even as it records the residual presence of prior models.

That the modern sense of *uncertainty* is more often referred to the early twentieth century than the Victorian era is a result of major developments in scientific fields, especially the revolution in physics that revealed the constituents of the universe as fundamentally probabilistic, and the technical development of statistics as a mathematical and methodological field central to the practice of science. In the context of quantum mechanics, uncertainty received an additional meaning: it was woven into the fabric of matter as a principle, defined by Werner Heisenberg in 1927, stipulating that the position and momentum of particles cannot be mutually determined. Heisenberg's "uncertainty principle" was one of many breakthroughs that ushered in post-Newtonian or postclassical physics, among them Niels Bohr's related concept of "complementarity" and Albert Einstein's theories of relativity. The various stages and dimensions of this revolution in the physical sciences have been standardly understood as forming a key intellectual-cultural context for modernism in literature and the arts. Although such developments in what Christopher Herbert calls the "modern relativity era" can be seen as part of scientific, philosophical, and cultural trends dating back to the nineteenth century, where the innovations of Victorians like John Stuart Mill, Herbert Spencer, and Alexander Bain stand as precursors to modernist relativity, there is nevertheless a clear shift in the possible valences of uncertainty.[2]

In logical and mathematical arenas, this period also saw the culmination of nineteenth-century trends that had increasingly placed more emphasis on numbers, quantification, and precision. The mathematician Andrey Kolmogorov put probability on a rigorous, axiomatic foundation.[3] The philosophers Gottlob Frege, Bertrand Russell, Alfred North Whitehead, and G. E. Moore similarly aspired to purge language of vagueness and grant it the incontrovertible clarity of formal logic.[4] Following in Francis Galton's footsteps, the next generation of statisticians – including Karl Pearson and W. F. R. Weldon (cofounders of the journal *Biometrika*), Francis Ysidro Edgeworth, George Udny Yule, and R. A. Fisher – developed more precise methods that inaugurated the discipline of mathematical statistics and cemented statistical inference as the key methodological toolkit for the wider social sciences.[5] As Theodore Porter has shown, many social sciences were durably "remade as technical" – that is, understood to achieve objectivity via the "specialized competence" of "closed communities" – through early twentieth-century statistics.[6] It is to this period that we owe the very idea of science's "technicality."[7] In tandem with these refinements in method, uncertainty was for the first time clearly distinguished from risk in the economist Frank Knight's pathbreaking *Risk, Uncertainty and Profit* (1921). Where *risk* is henceforth defined as governing scenarios where outcomes and probabilities are quantifiable, *uncertainty* is relegated to settings where outcomes can be identified but not quantified.

These scientific shifts retroactively confirm a view of uncertainty I have emphasized throughout this book – as a phenomenon linked to, but fundamentally broader and more diffuse than, numerical calculation. From the viewpoint of scientific knowledge and what Porter calls "public reason," the nineteenth century in my account can be roughly characterized as an interregnum – when statistical thinking was more accessible, ordinary, and democratic – between two regimes of expert-driven techno-cracy, embodied in the ideals of Nicolas de Condorcet (in the late eight-eenth century) and Pearson (in the early twentieth).[8] With these later developments in view, the nineteenth-century novel can also be described as an interregnum – when practitioners of realism felt entitled to partici-pate, with seriousness and ambition, in scientific and cultural debates about uncertainty – before modernism's self-conscious cultivation of tech-nicality, difficulty, and innovation.

These modulations in scientific understandings of uncertainty have often been linked to a cultural mood at the fin de siècle that breaks in two directions, one ludic and irreverent, the other stern and authoritarian. As Herbert has catalogued, the culture that extends into modernism was marked by an "antagonism toward every form of dogmatic authority," an "elevation of ironic discrepancy to the level of an essential principle of understanding," and an "almost obsessive love of paradox."[9] As the uni-verse came to seem a great deal more aleatory, down to its most funda-mental particles and patterns, the concept of "randomness" – introduced in the third edition of John Venn's *Logic of Chance* (1888) – promised a mode of chance apparently intractable by statistical method. At the end point of what Ian Hacking describes as the "erosion of determinism," we thus witness the parallel emergence of "a self-conscious conception of pure irregularity, of something wilder than the kinds of chance that had been excluded by the Age of Reason."[10] It was at this cusp between two centuries that the American pragmatist Charles Sanders Peirce embraced indeterminism or what he called "tychism," a philosophy of absolute chance, and the French poet Stéphane Mallarmé's "Un coup de dés" ("A Throw of the Dice") embodied the spirit of irreducible randomness for later practitioners of automatic writing, chance poetry, and other experi-ments in stochastic aesthetics.[11] Instead of fluctuating between the numerical and the narrative, between decision and hesitation, uncertainty in the early twentieth century sponsors radically undecidable forms. At the same time, as Herbert argues, the "comic" stance of a world shaped by relativity has a corresponding "serious" side, a "sense that the sinister principles of totalitar-ianism, absolutism, and concentrated coercive power are in the ascendant, and that the supreme mission of modern thinkers in every domain is to combat such principles by building models of thought (which is to say, models of human relations) radically emancipated from their influence."[12] Even models of thought, though, flirted with the authoritarian. Mathematical statistics warped the liberal ethos of early Victorian thinkers into profoundly illiberal form – Adolphe Quetelet's reformist *l'homme moyen* was usurped by Galton's statistics of elite heredity.[13] These serious and comic sides of uncertainty are entangled. Many modernist experiments in pure chance, as Hacking observes, are akin to random sampling techniques; ludic randomness and statistical rigor come into being as two expressions of a prevailing sense of indeterminacy: "Dada and *Biometrika*: two sides, we might say, of the same coin."[14] This dyad might be taken to encompass some of the extremes of the early twentieth century: the tumult of revolutionary liberation and the torsion of authoritarian control, for instance, might likewise be seen as responses to a corrosive indeterminacy.

Beyond experiments with stochastic form and what Fredric Jameson calls the "narrative logic of the aleatory and the accidental," modernism's uptake of these developments has been identified in its wide commitment to randomness and relativism, contingency and acausality, indeterminism and vagueness.[15] Many twentieth-century texts "assert the objectivity of chance and the arbitrariness of human decisions," as Brian Richardson notes: "The natural development from cause to effect is frequently tampered with or sabotaged in modernist worlds. Voids open between antecedent and consequent, multiple coincidences subvert probability, obscure events produce outlandish results, and familiar causal patterns are supplanted by linguistic, oneiric, or absurdist progressions."[16] As Michael Whitworth argues in *Einstein's Wake*, British modernists including D. H. Lawrence, Woolf, T. S. Eliot, James Joyce, and Aldous Huxley were influenced (however *en passant*) by the new physics and its predecessors in the late nineteenth century. Remarking that Heisenberg's uncertainty principle is "often invoked in relation to the formal quality of uncertainty in modernist literature," however anachronistic the connection, Whitworth argues that nineteenth-century epistemological frameworks – including statistical mechanics applied to thermodynamics – "provided a language in which literary writers could justify the abandonment of the omniscient narrator" and "embrace subjectivism with the full authority of science."[17] Despite a wide hostility to science qua mechanism, modernists adopted aspects of these intellectual developments as metaphor, model, and form, in keeping with physical sciences that "preferred to 'explain' natural phenomena in formal and statistical rather than materialistic and deterministic terms."[18] The direct use of such scientific, logical, and mathematical approaches to read modernist literature results in quite different accounts from mine – for instance, linking Woolf's *The Waves* (1931) to the theory of wave-particle duality.[19]

If modernist writers gleaned perspectives from dominant and emergent intellectual trends, they also relied on the residual. As in the nineteenth century, they made use of outdated tools in the face of uncertainty, including the novel. Science popularization remained culturally vital, promulgated in texts from Pearson's *The Grammar of Science* (1892) to Arthur Eddington's *The Nature of the Physical World* (1928), and by prolific science journalists like J. W. N. Sullivan. Although modernist elitism militated against such works, they were still reviewed in prominent literary journals, and sundry scientific materials found their way into literature.[20] If Joyce's work operates on an "uncertainty principle," as one critic suggests, it is also notable that the Ithaca episode in *Ulysses* (1922) draws on decidedly outdated mathematics and physics textbooks from the earlier century.[21] Treating the nineteenth-century discourse of uncertainty as itself a residual resource – a conceptual fund that can be spent or shelved at will – is one intriguing way in which modernist literature maintains a relationship to the phenomena in this book.

Uncertainty lives on in more quotidian (and less contextually specific) ways, too. Yet for all its variety, modernist uncertainty is distinguished by its self-consciousness and its unflinching suspicion of calculative and instrumental rationality. The first feature often takes a playful form, reminiscent of the ironic deployments of chance, luck, and probability in eighteenth-century fiction (Henry Fielding and Laurence Sterne come to mind). When Joyce uses the surprising accidents of urban life as plot devices, as in the nineteenth century, he mockingly erodes their conceptual basis. Leopold Bloom wanders Dublin and sees, one after another, two people he had been musing on: "There he is: the brother.... Now that's a coincidence. Course hundreds of times you think of a person and don't meet him"; "Now that's really a coincidence: second time. Coming events cast their shadows before."[22] Then another: "Again. Third Time. Coincidence."[23] And so on, as a comic motif is established. The second feature manifests in sweeping rejections of prediction as bureaucratic rationale. In novels that almost define linguistic vagueness and epistemological uncertainty – *The Wings of the Dove* (1902), *The Ambassadors* (1903), and *The Golden Bowl* (1904) – Henry James rejects prediction *tout court* in the name of unconditioned freedom and "radical contingency."[24] As Lisi Schoenbach has argued, James defends risk and "what he calls [in *The Golden Bowl*] 'incalculability,' which both signifies unpredictability in the negative sense and affirms the infinite richness and variety of experience, which can never be properly categorized, summed up, or conclusively judged."[25] E. M. Forster takes a related approach in accident-prone novels like *Howards End* (1910) and *A Passage to India* (1924), musing on the bewildering state of being in a "muddle" and substituting the nineteenth-century assurance of judgment under uncertainty with an ethos of radical unpreparedness: "[Margaret Schlegel] could not explain in so many words, but she felt that those who prepare for all the emergencies of life beforehand may equip themselves at the expense of joy. It is necessary to prepare for an examination, or a dinner-party, or a possible fall in the price of stock: those who attempt human relations must adopt another method, or fail."[26]

***

If uncertainty takes on different qualities as it stretches into the twentieth century, Joseph Conrad's oeuvre offers a schematic vision of how the nineteenth-century tradition of uncertain thinking could be both resisted and reprised. Pervaded by figural obscurity and an obsession with "low vision," committed to impressionism and cautious skepticism, Conrad's narrative technique embodies the modernist intensification of uncertainty.[27] Against the referential solidity of nineteenth-century realism, Conrad fashions "a capricious, unstable reality in which necessary sequence is transformed into unimaginable indeterminacy."[28] Critical commentary routinely identifies hesitation, indecision, approximation, and other motifs of uncertain thinking and representation in Conrad. Marlow's narration in *Heart of Darkness* (1899) and *Lord Jim* (1900) is marked by "equivocal judgments," "hesitancies, ellipses, and repetitions," and Conrad's impressionistic technique aims at "certainty through uncertainty."[29] In some novels, Conrad goes beyond a "hostile view of science," echoing Victorian "anti-mechanical rhetoric," to engage with newer contexts and trends, as in his use of thermodynamics in *The Secret Agent* (1907).[30]

Yet in the novel that would become his unlikely commercial success, Conrad returns with insistence to nineteenth-century motifs.[31] Beyond the themes announced by its title, *Chance* (1914) offers a number of connections to the novels discussed in this book, with its yarn about the "luckless child" of a ruined financier who, after being released from prison, attempts to poison his daughter's husband aboard the ship that was offered to him as sanctuary, only to down the poisoned glass when his malign plan is interrupted.[32] The novel's formal framing holds a commitment to improbable occurrence in tension with an oft-stated guarantee of narratorial probability. I discuss these two poles in turn to note how Conrad's efforts in *Chance* – judged as tortuous by most critics from James onward – express the challenge, within modernism, of retaining an ethos of productive uncertainty within contexts of pervasive indeterminacy.[33]

The improbabilities of Conrad's tale about Flora de Barral come through in a set of nested narratives that self-consciously stage their happenstance nature. At the outset, Captain Roderick Anthony, later Flora's lover, serendipitously adopts Charles Powell as his ship's second mate, the latter having chanced to be present during a last-minute request to the shipping master, coincidentally also named Powell. A "chance acquaintance" (33) with the young Powell years later allows Marlow (Conrad's erstwhile reciter) to spin the yarn of Flora's life after her father's ruin, her quasi-adoption by Mr. and Mrs. Fyne (another "accidental acquaintance" [34]), and her elopement with Anthony (after the two "met somewhere accidentally" [119]). Marlow's connection to Flora's tale gradually becomes more direct, from a chance sighting that (perhaps) saved her from wandering over a cliff to a meeting outside a hotel in Brighton. Further chances and coincidences take hold as events move on board Captain Anthony's ship, the *Ferndale*, including a narrowly averted shipwreck, a later (fatal) collision, and an accident on deck that shatters a window through which Powell (that "completely chance-comer" [315]) happens to spy the hand of de Barral doctoring his son-in-law's nightcap.

Summarized in this way, the plot seems absurd – more Collins than Conrad – and reveals its "debt to popular melodrama."[34] Yet Conrad regularly calls attention to *Chance*'s chance-driven character, to the fact that Flora's tragedy occurs "By the merest chance, as things do happen, lucky and unlucky, terrible or tender, important or unimportant; and even things which are neither, things so completely neutral in character that you would wonder why they do happen at all if you didn't know that they, too, carry in their insignificance the seeds of further incalculable chances" (78). Like Richard Whately a century before him, Conrad identifies "chance" as "incalculable" (79), and goes out of his way to express a graded, balanced vision of uncertainty that would not be out of place in the other novels I have discussed. The term *chance* similarly covers a spectrum of valences in this novel, from random happenstance (the "work of chance," "a most extraordinary chance" [25, 24]) to welcome occasion ("he jumped at the chance," "the most unexpected chance" [22, 143]) to withheld potential.[35] On one level, Conrad distances himself from the novel's aleatory discourse by couching such motifs in Marlow's sententious maxims: "A philosophical mind is but an accident" (10); "Nothing is truer than that, in this world, the luckless have no right to their opportunities" (143); "the science of life consists in seizing every chance that presents itself" (329). But a more fundamental sympathy with judgment under uncertainty is made clear in a 1920 author's note, where Conrad recalls his own "hesitation" and "indecision" about the novel's course, composed after a period of writer's block.[36] He notably reuses the figure we saw in Eliot, of decision at "a fork in the stream":

> I floated in the calm water of pleasant speculation, between the diverging currents of conflicting impulses, with an agreeable but perfectly irrational conviction that neither of those currents would take me to destruction. My sympathies being equally divided and the two forces being equal it is perfectly obvious that nothing but mere chance influenced my decision in the end. It is a mighty force that of mere chance, absolutely irresistible yet manifesting itself often in delicate forms such for instance as the charm, true or illusory, of a human being. (331)

The note wants us to believe in this overpowering force, so characteristic of the modernist era: "chance, fate, providence, call it what you will!" (304). Incidentally, we might wonder whether Conrad protests too much at this moment, after Sigmund Freud's postulation of the unconscious and a logic that reads "chance actions" as "symptomatic acts" or "parapraxes."[37] Whatever we make of the strategy Conrad adopts to explain the novel's genesis, though, his juxtaposition of aggregate and individual, chance and charm, destruction and decision make clear that he knows – and knows how to navigate – the waters of nineteenth-century uncertainty.

At the same time as he flaunts the novel's improbabilities in characteristic modernist fashion, then, Conrad appeals to nineteenth-century tropes. In tandem, he develops a narrative mode fitted to gathering the truth of such an incalculable tale. My schematic summary of the novel's events can hardly capture how buried they are in Marlow's intricate telling, which largely relies on the reported testimony, "recalled experiences," and surmises of various involved parties (the Fynes, Powell), but also on his conjectural reconstruction of what they might have witnessed and wondered (232). *Chance* is "almost entirely the report of a linguistic act, and for long stretches that linguistic act is only reporting other linguistic acts"; even James balked at its "ungoverned verbiage."[38] The novel's internal narratives are recursively nested, often "refuse to move forward," and instead "double back and repeat each other."[39] Half the novel elapses before Marlow directly represents an encounter with the protagonist. A nameless interlocutor opens the novel on the phrase "I believe" and Marlow's last speech closes it with "I expect" (7, 330). In between, verbs of hypothesis multiply, especially in Marlow's telling: he will "think," "believe," "imagine," "suppose," "presume," "guess," "suspect," "take it," and "understand," with the gradation of certainty ranging from tentative ("venture to affirm" [135], "inclined to believe" [242]) to emphatic ("verily believe" [143]). He weighs possibilities and probabilities, deploys averages and analogies, and entertains counterfactuals and questions he "would have liked to ask" (158). He makes constant reference to speculation, prediction, inference, analogy, and realization, thinking of himself as "an investigator – a man of deductions" (242). In difference from *Heart of Darkness* and *Lord Jim*, where these techniques sponsor indeterminacy and irresolution, *Chance* is more invested in the possibility of coming to knowledge through – and acting in the face of – uncertainty. I believe we misunderstand the novel's style by seeing its "elaborate narrative scaffolding" as an "empty formalism," "an endless reverberation of echoes, a series of shells, frames, and haloes."[40] Conrad's commitment to this method is clear in his caustic rebuttal of critics who would have the shorter tale without the sophisticated telling: "No doubt . . . the whole story might have been written out on a cigarette paper" (331). A brief catalog of Marlow's techniques shows how extensively they replay the approaches of nineteenth-century uncertainty, doubling as reflections on how we know, judge, decide, and act in unclear conditions.

First, Conrad emphasizes the epistemological heft of partial views and ad hoc hypotheses, linking "mental conclusions" to "momentary physical sensations" (45). Marlow justifies extrapolating from a single sight of de Barral by defending the "glimpse" as "the proper way of seeing an individuality" (60). He offers a model of inference:

> There were also very few materials accessible to a man like me to form a judgment from. But in such a case I verily believe that a little is as good as a feast – perhaps better. If one has a taste for that kind of thing the merest starting-point becomes a coign of vantage, and then by a series of logically deducted verisimilitudes one arrives at truth – or very near the truth – as near as any circumstantial evidence can do. (66)

Alluding to *Macbeth*, the "coign of vantage" – a jutting corner giving a wide view – models an architecture of inference, blending logic and probability even as the result is still only as convincing as the law's approximate standard for second-hand evidence.

The glimpse, further, affords a mode of narrating without proving that spurns "information" – which Marlow characterizes as "something one goes out to seek and puts away when found as you might do a piece of lead: ponderous, useful, unvibrating, dull" – and valorizes "knowledge" in its fully provisional, mercurial, and associative forms. Gleaned in uncertainty, such knowledge simply "comes to one," "a chance acquisition preserving in its repose a fine resonant quality" (68). The accident that literally offers a window onto events (by breaking one) is attributed, significantly, to "a defective link" that brings ropes and chains crashing down (298). But such knowledge is also acquired by forging causal links and inductive series. Marlow confirms this approach when charging his listener "to remember how many instances of compunction you have seen" (120) or reflecting on "the foolhardiness of the average girl and . . . other instances of the kind" (36). Thus, he supplements glimpses to gather the "secret of the situation" (196) between Flora and Anthony at second hand. In the novel's first half, Marlow's report comes from the Fynes, who watch many of the events on Flora's fateful day from their Brighton hotel, "like a pair of private detectives" (87); in the second half, from Powell's more direct report on board. In both cases, Marlow supplements his inexperienced sources with his own vaunted "sagacity" (103).

Finally, the novel offsets many of its forward-facing uncertainties – as when the Fynes take responsibility for Flora, ignorant of "future complications" and "possible consequences" (99) – by its retrospective certainties. In Marlow's realizations, Conrad makes use of a family of narrative tactics familiar from the nineteenth-century tradition, variously termed "delayed decoding" (between the narrative reporting of impressions and the realization of their import), "epiphanies," "awakenings," and "modernist spot[s] of time."[41] In *Chance*, Marlow's recursions are more specifically thought-laden realizations that do not simply aggregate prior data to reach a conclusion, but recast in an explanatory key what the narrative has already presented in latent form. When Flora disappears, for example, Marlow revises his memory of first meeting her atop the quarry as a sinister clue: "You may be surprised but I assure you I had not perceived this aspect of it till that very moment. It was like a startling revelation; the past throwing a sinister light on the future" (42). Similarly, when he hears the name of her father, Marlow "groped in the darkness of my mind" for things attaching to the name de Barral, "and all at once noise and light burst on me as if a window of my memory had been suddenly flung open on a street in the City" (54). As in Thackeray and Eliot, such retrospections direct uncertain thinking toward the past even as they recharacterize the prospective movement of narrative – and reading – as reiterated judgment in the face of imperfect knowledge.

On many levels, *Chance* remains under a nineteenth-century spell.[42] The novel is perhaps the clearest instance of the fraught continuity of the traditions of British realism in Conrad, whose "attempt at redemption is also an attempt to reassert those traditions."[43] Through sordid family secrets and uncomfortable home truths, sea accidents and suicides averted (and achieved), we have echoes of *Daniel Deronda*, and recognize Eliot's portrayal of Gwendolen's hesitant indecision in Flora, jolted out of "ignorance" and "unconsciousness of the world's ways" (78). Instead of "a gradual process of experience and information ... with saving reserves, softening doubts, veiling theories" (78), the transformation comes through the governess's blunt revelations about her father ("nothing but a thief") and Flora ("a vulgar, silly nonentity") (94), which leave her acting in the face of "a lasting doubt, an ineradicable suspicion of herself and of others" (173). Studying trial reports and "reach[ing] the conclusion of her father's innocence" (149), Flora also echoes Collins's suspicion of legal and moral finality, in a novel similarly partitioned into halves. The counterfactual avenues, hypothetical affects, and "long and roundabout course" (331) of Marlow's narration recall Thackeray's work, particularly in its digressive mode. And Marlow's "unexpected insight" (28) reprises Hardy's probable inferences and impressions.

Conrad flaunts the tale's structuration by chance, serendipity, and happenstance (a typical modernist stance) while stressing the telling's reliance on inference, conjecture, and surmise (a distinctive feature of nineteenth-century narrative). In these two narrative poles, we encounter a *fabula* marked throughout by improbability only by grace of a *sjuzhet* everywhere asserting its air of probability. The reader, like Powell, is held "in a state of wonder which made other coincidences, however unlikely, not so very surprising at all" (232), while also marveling at the technique that inferentially erodes doubt in the "wonderful linking up of small facts" (304). In trying to have it both ways, Conrad inherits the discourse of uncertainty from nineteenth-century realism while working (in the face of his own writerly indecision) to fashion a novel that, through its elaborate nesting and its engagement with randomness, remains true to a modernist vision.

This brief reading marks differences between the nineteenth-century account of uncertain thinking and its attenuated inheritance in modernism, but I do not want to overstate the case. Novels in both periods (and beyond) still reckon with how to carve out a space for individual subjectivity against aggregate pattern – to represent individual thought, judgment, decision, and action in the face of uncertainty, understood as a durably ordinary phenomenon that has received attention from diverse and complex intellectual fields. The prevailing uncertainty of both the nineteenth century and the "modern relativity era" can be traced, inter alia, in late modernism and postwar experimental fiction.[44] The Victorian contexts I have discussed might fray, but aspects of uncertainty, and of probable realism, are inherited and repurposed by other literary forms and critical traditions. I freely admit that this book – and the cluster of ideas it has studied – will open out onto other stories and stakes not envisaged by me, and happily leave it to others to pursue its uncertain lines of flight.

***

I began *The Art of Uncertainty* with the halting emergence of conviction in Hardy's sun-crossed lovers; I end it with his scaled-up statement of their fate. Hardy draws an immense horizon around his characters: "the question how their lives would end seemed the deepest of possible enigmas" to them, even though "to others who knew their position equally well with themselves the question was the easiest that could be asked. – 'Like those of other people similarly circumstanced.'"[45] In the future anterior mode, Cytherea – who might equally stand in for Gwendolen, Valeria, Amelia, Elizabeth-Jane, or Flora – muses on how her friends' judgments will "never realize that it was my single opportunity of existence . . . which they are regarding; they will not feel that what to them is but a thought, easily held in those two words of pity, 'Poor girl,' was a whole life to me."[46] Acknowledging that "unquencheable expectation, which at the gloomiest time persists in inferring that because we are *ourselves*, there must be a special future in store for us, though our nature and antecedents to the remotest particular have been common to thousands," Hardy's auroral logic acknowledges both the lures and limits of uncertainty – the induction that cannot glimpse an emerging totality, the vain self-regard of hypothetical thinking, the melancholy of counterfactual memory, the affective vacuity of the aggregate.[47] In the nineteenth century, I have argued, such "unquencheable expectation" sponsored rich and distinctive accounts of thought, judgment, and action. In the sunrise of the nineteenth-century novel, today was like every day, and anything could happen.

Notes

Introduction

1 *Desperate Remedies*, 32, 33.
2 *Analogy of Religion*, vi.
3 *Enquiry*, 24.
4 *Philosophical Essay on Probabilities*, 19.
5 Campbell, *Philosophy of Rhetoric*, 60; Boole, *Laws of Thought*, 368–70; Mill, *System of Logic*, 1:550–1. See Daston, *Classical Probability*, 205–7, 262–67.
6 *Table Talk*, 1:244–45; quoted in Neil, *Art of Reasoning*, 98.
7 *Correspondence*, 619; to Robert Bridges, 24–25 October 1883. As Shaw glosses Hopkins, faith juxtaposes "a believer's inclusive use of 'both-and'" against "a skeptic's exclusive use of 'either-or'" (*Victorians and Mystery*, 103). Religious doubt constituted a key source of uncertainty for many Victorians, and "nineteenth-century experiments with contingency . . . frequently served as a means of negotiating a still-influential set of Christian narratives and beliefs" (Choi, *Victorian Contingencies*, 9). Yet the inscrutability of faith shields it from logical, mathematical, and psychological analysis, and therefore it seems to me an inapt paradigm for ordinary uncertainty. There *were* rigorous efforts to examine faith through "evidence" and "probability," though they often understood these concepts differently: Butler's *Analogy of Religion*, William Paley's *Natural Theology* (1802), William Whewell's *On Astronomy and General Physics, Considered with Reference to Natural Theology* (1832), Charles Babbage's *Ninth Bridgewater Treatise* (1837), and John Henry Newman's work, from early sermons to *An Essay in Aid of a Grammar of Assent* (1870). There were also satirical exposés of faith, like Francis Galton's "Statistical Inquiries into the Efficacy of Prayer." On faith, doubt, and secularism in nineteenth-century culture, see Shaw, *Victorians and Mystery*, 88–106, 228–50; Larsen, *Crisis of Doubt*; Lane, *Age of Doubt*; Levine, *Realism, Ethics and Secularism*.
8 Hacking, *Taming of Chance*, 1; see 1–15. Victorian literature's response to statistical discourse has been termed the "statistical imagination" (Choi, "Writing the Victorian City," 583; Jaffe, *Affective Life*, 24), the "sociological imagination" (McWeeny, *Comfort of Strangers*, 3), and the "biopolitical

imagination" (Steinlight, *Populating the Novel*, 1–34). See Choi, "Writing the Victorian City," *Anonymous Connections*, 13–32, and *Victorian Contingencies*, 142–82; Reid, "Jamesian Naturalism"; Jaffe, *Affective Life*; Adams, "Numbers and Narratives"; Klotz, "Manufacturing Fictional Individuals"; Hadley, "Nobody, Somebody, and Everybody"; McWeeny, *Comfort of Strangers*, 34–60; Phillips, "Navigating Chance"; Steinlight, *Populating the Novel*; Rosenthal, *Good Form*, 153–90; Womble, "Statistics of Character"; Grener, *Improbability*, 20–28.

9 On the Mill/Whewell debates, see Snyder, *Reforming Philosophy*. On nineteenth-century revisions of Baconian induction, and the new role for hypothesis and imagination in scientific practice, see Smith, *Fact and Feeling*, 11–44. On comparison and analogy, see Griffiths, *Age of Analogy*.

10 On Eliot's reading of Mill, see Pinney, *Essays*, 150n3.

11 For contemporary perspectives, see Kahneman, Slovic, and Tversky, *Judgment under Uncertainty*; Bammer and Smithson, *Uncertainty and Risk*; Gigerenzer and Selten, *Bounded Rationality*; Gigerenzer, *Rationality for Mortals* and *Gut Feelings*.

12 Conrad, *Lord Jim*, 8.

13 Hacking, *Taming of Chance*, 5.

14 Hardy, *Collected Poems*, l. 10.

15 *Holinshed's Chronicles*, 1:242. Related phrases are frequent: "good hap" (24), "euill hap" (152), "sorie hap" (205).

16 Ahmed explores this etymology in her account of the phenomenology, politics, and ethics of happiness, arguing for a return of contingency to "put the hap back into happiness" (*Promise of Happiness*, 222). See 22–33, 217–23.

17 Locke, *Essay*, 652 (emphasis in original).

18 Whately, "Modern Novels," 356.

19 Whately, "Modern Novels," 356.

20 Latin translators rendered Aristotelian probability as *verisimilis* (Newsom, *Likely Story*, 19–20). On *eikos* and *verisimilis*, see Patey, *Probability and Literary Form*, 13–19; for philological discussion, see Hoffman, "Concerning *Eikos*."

21 Morson, *Narrative and Freedom*, 49.

22 Whately, "Modern Novels," 354 (emphasis removed). Whately includes this discussion as an appendix to *Elements of Rhetoric*, 409–11.

23 Aristotle, *Rhetoric*, 1402b.

24 In the history of mathematics, as I discuss in more detail below, probability has been divided into two rough and overlapping frameworks: the *classical* interpretation (1660–1840), ending with Laplace, and the *statistical* (1820–1900); see Gigerenzer et al., *Empire of Chance*, 1–69. In general, I will treat tensions embedded within modern probability as more useful than conflicts between rival interpretations.

25 On the history of probability and statistics, see Byrne, *Probability and Opinion*; Franklin, *Science of Conjecture*; Shapiro, *Probability and Certainty*; Hacking, *Emergence* and *Taming of Chance*; Daston, *Classical Probability*;

Porter, *Rise of Statistical Thinking*; Stigler, *History of Statistics*; MacKenzie, *Statistics in Britain*. For overviews of historical, philosophical, and scientific approaches, see Gigerenzer et al., *Empire of Chance*; Krüger, Daston, and Heidelberger, *Probabilistic Revolution: Ideas in History*; Krüger, Gigerenzer, and Morgan, *Probabilistic Revolution: Ideas in the Sciences*. For work on British statistics and social science, see Cullen, *Statistical Movement*; Collini, "Political Theory and the 'Science of Society'"; Hilts, *Statist and Statistician*; Kent, "Average Victorian"; Carrithers, "Enlightenment Science of Society"; Goldman, *Victorians and Numbers*.

26 Hacking, *Emergence*, 12. On Hacking's thesis, see Garber and Zabell, "On the Emergence of Probability"; Patey, *Probability and Literary Form*, 266–73; Newsom, *Likely Story*, 34–57; Franklin, *Science of Conjecture*, 373–83; Daston, "History of Emergences."

27 Hacking, *Emergence*, 33, 32, 34. On the rise of inductive thinking as a consequence of the emergence of European middle classes, with a corresponding emphasis on everyday judgment, experiential inference, vernacular languages, and the "equality of reason" (163), see Shenefelt and White, *If A, Then B*, 157–84.

28 Hacking, *Emergence*, 176–85. On earlier ideas about induction, see Milton, "Induction before Hume"; Dear, *Discipline & Experience*, 11–31.

29 Hacking, *Emergence*, 63; see 63–72.

30 Hacking, *Emergence*, 82. Even the nineteenth-century "avalanche of printed numbers" could not undergird statistical law without "readers of the right kind, honed to find laws of society akin to those laws of nature established by Newton" (*Taming of Chance*, 35–36).

31 Patey, *Probability and Literary Form*, 198 (on Fielding, see 197–212).

32 In a comparable account of Whately's review, focusing on his comments about Austen, Grener argues that his "rearticulation of probability in quantitative terms enacts a categorical shift" (*Improbability*, 49; see 46–50). See also Wess, "The Probable and the Marvelous in *Tom Jones*."

33 Hacking, *Taming of Chance*, 61; Patey, *Probability and Literary Form*, 149.

34 *Elements of Logic*, 1. Whately played a "central role in revitalizing the study of logic in England," enabling its subsequent placement "on a firm mathematical and scientific foundation" (McKerrow, "Richard Whately and the Revival of Logic," 164, 184). But he did not fully engage with the developments in formal logic for which he paved the way.

35 Poovey, *History of the Modern Fact*, xv. For the culture of statistical thinking in nineteenth-century Britain, see Freedgood, *Victorian Writing about Risk*; Anderson, *Predicting the Weather*; Choi, *Anonymous Connections*; Goldman, *Victorians and Numbers*. In an American context, see Pietruska, *Looking Forward*.

36 Beck, *Risk Society*.

37 For foundational psychological and behavioral-economic research, see Kahneman, Slovic, and Tversky, *Judgment under Uncertainty*. For recent debates and provocations about "predictive processing" in cognitive science,

see Knill and Pouget, "Bayesian Brain"; Bar, *Predictions in the Brain*; Clark, "Whatever Next?" and *Surfing Uncertainty*; Hohwy, *Predictive Mind*. On research into uncertainty at a neuronal level, see Yang and Shadlen, "Probabilistic Reasoning by Neurons."

38 On macroscale risk (its institutions, perception, and management) in nineteenth-century literature and culture, see Freedgood, *Victorian Writing about Risk*; Choi, "Writing the Victorian City" and *Anonymous Connections*, 13–32; Fyfe, *By Accident or Design*, 100–131, 170–210; Steinlight, *Populating the Novel*. For a transhistorical overview of risk in British literature, see Hoydis, *Risk and the English Novel*. On microscale narrative structures that elicit and revise readers' (unconscious) predictive expectations, see Kukkonen, *Probability Designs*.

39 Pattison, "History of Civilization in England"; quoted in Porter, *Rise of Statistical Thinking*, 67.

40 Jaffe, *Affective Life*, 26.

41 On mid-Victorian "liberal cognition" and its "formal ambivalence" in approaching deliberative situations, see Hadley, *Living Liberalism*, 7–12, 55–61. On neoclassical economics, aesthetic culture, and literary choice, see Gagnier, *Insatiability of Human Wants*, 40–60; Garcha, "Narrating Choice" and "Emma's Choices." On finance, see O'Gorman, *Victorian Literature and Finance*; Henry and Schmitt, *Victorian Investments*; Wagner, *Financial Speculation in Victorian Fiction*.

42 See Daston, "Life, Chance & Life Chances." Daston describes a "modern cult of control" that "seeks to stop the wheel [of fortune], once and for all" (12).

43 Whately, *Elements of Rhetoric*, 81.

44 "Faith and the Right to Believe," in James, *Some Problems of Philosophy*, 114.

45 See Nowotny, *Cunning of Uncertainty*.

46 Conrad, *Heart of Darkness*, 5; Ruskin, *Works*, 6:89.

47 Edwards, "Compulsory Providence."

48 Armstrong, *Novel Politics*, 84; Dames, *Physiology of the Novel*, 11; Freedgood, *Worlds Enough*, 32. For Armstrong, the novel's democratic imagination "asks its readers to think in terms of hypotheses" instead of "finite-problem solving or dogma" (84). For Dames, physiological novel theory emphasizes "moment-to-moment affects and processes of reading prolonged narratives" against a static discourse of organic form (12). For Freedgood, various forms of metalepsis fracture Victorian realism's referential designs. Such statements are consonant with earlier, more general views: Levine's account of realism as "always in process" in its "attempt to use language to get beyond language," and Shaw's assessment of realism as a historicist genre, striving "to deal with situations which involve partial knowledge and continual approximation," to "capture the logic and texture of a process," "to place us in history" (*Realistic Imagination*, 12, 6; *Narrating Reality*, 29, 99, 36).

49 *Selected Letters*, 41–42 (to George and Tom Keats, December 1817). On "ephemeral" documents about risk, see Freedgood, *Victorian Writing about Risk*, 121–27.

50 Williams, *Marxism and Literature*, 122.
51 *Daniel Deronda*, 505.
52 Wickman, "Robert Burns and Big Data," 15.
53 Ricoeur, *Freedom and Nature*, 142; Eliot, *Impressions of Theophrastus Such*, 104.
54 Eliot, quoted in Pinney, "More Leaves from George Eliot's Notebook," 364.
55 Tribe, "Trial by Mathematics"; Feeley and Simon, "Actuarial Justice."
56 James, "*Daniel Deronda*: A Conversation," in *Literary Criticism*, 975; Anon., "[Rev. of] *The Law and the Lady*," *Examiner*, 414.
57 Rintoul, "[Rev. of] *Vanity Fair*," 709.
58 Unsigned review, *Athenaeum* (1878); unsigned review, *Saturday Review* (1879), in Cox, *Hardy: The Critical Heritage*, 57, 62.
59 Duff, *Romanticism and the Uses of Genre*, 22.
60 See Hunter, *Before Novels*, 30–35.
61 On Eliot and sensation/melodrama conventions, see Welsh, *George Eliot and Blackmail*, 259–334; Jameson, *Antinomies of Realism*, 154–61; Steinlight, *Populating the Novel*, 149–56. Criticism continues to make productive use of realism's complex antagonisms with generic others: see Dentith, "Realist Synthesis"; Glatt, *Narrative and Its Nonevents*, 13–23, 35–46.
62 Fielding, *Tom Jones*, 392.
63 Critics have used similar epithets without emphasis: McKeon explains how an "emergent division between the 'literary' and the 'historical'" in the early modern period "substitut[ed] for the actual particularity of the claim to historicity the concrete particularity of probabilistic 'realism'"; Fowler briefly mentions "[p]robable realism" in nineteenth-century literature (*Secret History of Domesticity*, 451; *A History of English Literature*, 302). Compare Puskar's related (if more restrictive) epithet, "statistical realism" (*Accident Society*, 219), and Glatt's "hypothetical realism," denoting an "unwritten plot that may be realized within the realist novels of a transformed future" (*Narrative and Its Nonevents*, 140; see 137–74).
64 Prominent defenses and discussions of realism in these terms include Auerbach, *Mimesis*; Lukács, *Studies in European Realism*; Watt, *Rise of the Novel*; Booth, *Rhetoric of Fiction*, 23–64; Levine, *Realistic Imagination*; Ermarth, *Realism and Consensus*, 3–92; Riffaterre, *Fictional Truth*; Furst, *All Is True*; Shaw, *Narrating Reality*, 1–125; Brooks, *Realist Vision*.
65 See Levine, *Realistic Imagination*, 3–22, 131–44, and "Realism," in *Realism, Ethics and Secularism*, 185–209; Morris, *Realism*, 79–87.
66 Here I disagree with Ghosh's argument that nineteenth-century realism is inadequate to the scale of climate disaster because of its affiliation with the probable, ordinary, and (geologically) uniformitarian, as against the improbable, extraordinary, and catastrophist (*Great Derangement*, 16–24). Noting how "a rhetoric of the everyday" emerged alongside "a regime of statistics" (19), Ghosh reprises the structuralist suspicion of verisimilitude I discuss below: "the modern novel, unlike geology, has never been forced to confront the centrality of the improbable: the concealment of its scaffolding of events continues to be essential to its functioning" (23).

67 Throughout I understand *critical judgment* simply to refer to ordinary inferences made by critics in relation to texts. But my account is sympathetic with accounts of *evaluative* or *aesthetic judgment* like Clune's defense of literary-critical judgment as a type of expert practice, "a mode of thought that is itself open to constant revision" and that involves "the capacity to stay with forms or ideas one is currently unable to recognize" (*Defense of Judgment*, 74–75). Clune highlights judgment's "processual, often tacit attentional qualities" (6).

68 In literary criticism, *uncertainty* tends to be flattened into questions of meaning and interpretation (alongside concepts like *ambiguity, indeterminacy,* and *undecidability*): see the essays in Høeg, *Literary Theories of Uncertainty*. On the vitality of "inference" before "interpretation" in understanding fictional narrative, see Chatman, *Story and Discourse*, 27–31; Auyoung, *When Fiction Feels Real*, 1–19.

69 For discussion of these concepts, see Sternberg, "Telling in Time"; Franklin, *Serious Play*; Currie, *The Unexpected*; Levine, "Surprising Realism"; Schor, *Curious Subjects*; Miller, *Surprise*; Rohrbach, *Modernity's Mist*; Tobin, *Elements of Surprise*; Rogers, *Speculation*.

70 Levine, *Serious Pleasures*; Auyoung, *When Fiction Feels Real*, 11, 18.

71 See *Thoughts on the Study of Mathematics as Part of a Liberal Education*; *Mechanical Euclid*, 143–82. On Whewell's educational ideas, see Snyder, *Reforming Philosophy*, 219–21.

72 Arnold, "Literature and Science," 58.

73 *Principles of Success in Literature*, 57–65.

74 "Conversation," 267.

75 See Porter, *Rise of Statistical Thinking*, 74. On these early probabilists, see Richards, "The Probable and the Possible in Early Victorian England." Examples include Babbage, *Games of Chance*; De Morgan's *Encylopædia Metropolitana* entry, two-part review of Laplace's *Théorie analytique des probabilités*, and practical treatise on insurance ("Theory of Probabilities," "Theory of Probabilities (Part I)," "Theory of Probabilities (Part II)," *An Essay on Probabilities*); Galloway, *Treatise on Probability*; and Lubbock and Bethune, *On Probability*.

76 See MacKenzie, *Statistics in Britain*, 7–9.

77 Porter, *Rise of Statistical Thinking*, 41. On Quetelet, see 41–55, 100–109. Compare Hacking, *Taming of Chance*, 105–14; Gigerenzer et al., *Empire of Chance*, 38–45; Goldman, *Victorians and Numbers*, 139–55. On Quetelet's literary influence, see Kent, "Average Victorian"; Jaffe, *Affective Life*, 10–13, 26–30; Tondre, *Physics of Possibility*, 34–35. Kolb posits an inverse impact: Scott's "average men," especially *Waverley*'s "middling hero," made *l'homme moyen* "both accessible and legible to a mass audience" ("In Search of Lost Causes," 61).

78 These included the Statistical Society of London, the Manchester Statistical Society, and the Statistics Section (F) of the British Association for the Advancement of Science; there was also an artisan-founded London Statistical Society. See Porter, *Rise of Statistical Thinking*, 31–33; Goldman, *Victorians and Numbers*, 33–100.

79 Choi, *Victorian Contingencies*, 150; Porter, "Statistics and the Career of Public Reason," 34.

80 On "statistical fatalism," see Hacking, *Taming of Chance*, 115–24. On Buckle and statistical determinism, see Hacking, 125–32; Porter, *Rise of Statistical Thinking*, 60–65, 164–67, 174–75; Goldman, *Victorians and Numbers*, 197–210. Victorian reviews include J. F. Stephen, "Buckle's History of Civilization in England"; L. Stephen, "An Attempted Philosophy of History"; Venn, "Science of History" and "Statistical Averages and Human Actions." Buckle is a touchstone in accounts of literature, probability, and statistics: Small, "Chances Are"; Rosenthal, *Good Form*, 169–73; Tondre, *Physics of Possibility*, 38–40; Grener, *Improbability*, 156–57.

81 Porter, *Rise of Statistical Thinking*, 9, and "Statistics and the Career of Public Reason," 38; Adams, "Numbers and Narratives," 106.

82 See Goldman, *Victorians and Numbers*, 166–77.

83 Hacking calls *Hard Times* Dickens's "finest novel" ("Nineteenth Century Cracks in the Concept of Determinism," 472). Compare Hacking, *Taming of Chance*, 117–19; Porter, *Rise of Statistical Thinking*, 16. Daston briefly mentions Defoe and Fielding (*Classical Probability*, 164–66, 156).

84 See Cantor and Shuttleworth, *Science Serialized*; Lightman, *Victorian Popularizers of Science*; Tondre, *Physics of Possibility*, 18–25.

85 Arbuthnot translated and expanded Huygens's *De ratiociniis in aleae ludo* (1657) as *Of the Laws of Chance* (1692) and claimed to infer divine providence from statistics (Hacking, *Emergence*, 92–93, 167–68; Patey, *Probability and Literary Form*, 67–74).

86 Herschel, "Quetelet on Probabilities." On this review, see Porter, *Rise of Statistical Thinking*, 118–22.

87 Mill's book became "the standard textbook on logic at Oxford" and "widely read" at Cambridge, "not only by the relatively few students taking the moral sciences tripos, for whom it was required, but also by those taking the mathematical and classical triposes, for whom it was not. It went through eight editions during Mill's lifetime, including an inexpensive edition for working-class readers" (Snyder, *Reforming Philosophy*, 99–100). For a synoptic view of this period in logic's history, and its connections to literature, see Blevins and Williams, "Introduction: Logic and Literary Form," 6–13.

88 Hanson, "Logic and Logical Studies in England."

89 Snyder, *Reforming Philosophy*, 202–3.

90 Choi discusses Babbage's early work and actuarial career as prefiguring his later mathematical, computational, and theological projects (*Victorian Contingencies*, 16–55). On nineteenth-century insurance, see Alborn and Murphy, *Anglo-American Life Insurance, 1800–1914*; Alborn, *Regulated Lives*.

91 Choi, *Victorian Contingencies*, 25–26.

92 *Hoyle's Games*, 4–19.

93 See Raven, "Abolition of the English State Lotteries."

94 On the history and sociology of gambling, see Downes, *Gambling, Work and Leisure*; McKibbin, "Working-Class Gambling in Britain 1880–1939"; Itzkowitz, "Victorian Bookmakers and Their Customers" and "Fair Enterprise or Extravagant Speculation"; Clapson, *A Bit of a Flutter*; Munting, *Economic and Social History of Gambling*; Reith, *Age of Chance*. On gambling in literature, see Fabian, *Card Sharps, Dream Books, & Bucket Shops*; Kavanagh, *Enlightenment and the Shadows of Chance* and *Dice, Cards, Wheels*; Franklin, "Victorian Discourse of Gambling"; Flavin, *Gambling*; Richard, *Romance of Gambling*.

95 Proctor's popular articles included "Gambling Superstitions," "Coincidences and Superstitions," "Poker Principles and Chance Laws," and "Luck: Its Laws and Limits."

96 Bernoulli's *Ars conjectandi* (1713), in framing the first limit theorem of modern probability, gave initial form to the difference between subjective and objective (Hacking, *Emergence*, 143–53). The outright distinction is usually dated to the 1840s (in the work of Poisson, Bernard Bolzano, Robert Leslie Ellis, Jakob Friedrich Fries, Mill, and Cournot) and the shift from classical to statistical probability: see Porter, *Rise of Statistical Thinking*, 71–88; Gigerenzer et al., *Empire of Chance*, 6–10, 274–76; Hacking, *Taming of Chance*, 95–99; Daston, "How Probabilities Came to Be Objective and Subjective"; Zabell, "The Subjective and the Objective." For a critique of reading this distinction back into nineteenth-century probabilism, see Verburgt, "The Objective and the Subjective."

97 Hacking, *Taming of Chance*, 98. For other interpretations of the subjective/objective distinction in novels, see Tondre, *Physics of Possibility*, 10–11, 32–34; Grener, *Improbability*, 4–5. These distinctions are evident in narrative theory, even where "probability" just means "plausibility." Currie asks how determinations of likelihood relate to "dictates of objective probability" (*Narratives and Narrators*, 54). Hogan reasons that readerly forecasts "rely on automatic, subjective probability assessments" (*Affective Narratology*, 88).

98 Wright, "Association, Madness, and the Measures of Probability in Locke and Hume." For a synoptic account, see Warren, *History of the Association Psychology*. In fact, Locke's place at the head of this tradition misunderstands his stance on associated ideas, which was narrower and darker than those who followed: "Locke does not believe that mechanistic forces undergird cognition, and holds the association of ideas to be not a general explanatory paradigm but a pathological force" (Tabb, "Locke on Enthusiasm and the Association of Ideas," 77).

99 Gigerenzer et al., *Empire of Chance*, 9.

100 Daston, *Classical Probability*, 188–225.

101 Daston, *Classical Probability*, 203–6.

102 Hartley, *Observations on Man*, 1:64. On Hartley, see Oberg, "David Hartley and the Association of Ideas"; Walls, "Philosophy of David Hartley"; Allen, *David Hartley on Human Nature*.

103 Daston, *Classical Probability*, 219; see 370–86 on the classical interpretation's demise.
104 Hacking, *Taming of Chance*, 97.
105 Daston, "How Probabilities Came to Be Objective and Subjective," 341.
106 See Kallich, *Association of Ideas*, 9–34, 115–32; Engell, *Creative Imagination*, 65–77, 265–76, 331–32; Patey, *Probability and Literary Form*, 252–58; Craig, *Associationism and the Literary Imagination*, 41–83.
107 *Spirit of the Age*, 89.
108 *Thirteen-Book Prelude*, I.616–17.
109 Rylance, *Victorian Psychology*, 63; see 63–65; Hatherell, "Words and Things"; Hamilton, "Deep History."
110 Conrad, *Chance*, 10.
111 Snyder, *Reforming Philosophy*, 129–30, 136–37.
112 Snyder, *Reforming Philosophy*, 129.
113 Huxley, Lewes, and Mill were explicit in their debts to Hartley (Rylance, *Victorian Psychology*, 84–86).
114 Bain's "analysis of motor phenomena was the first union of the new physiology with a detailed association psychology" and "laid the psychological foundations of a thoroughgoing sensory-motor psychophysiology" (Young, *Mind, Brain, and Adaptation*, 114). On associationism's persistence into the Victorian era, and the centrality of Bain, see 94–133; Rylance, *Victorian Psychology*, 55–69, 167–94. For physiological psychology and the novel, see Dames, *Physiology of the Novel*; Ryan, *Thinking without Thinking*.
115 Herbert, *Victorian Relativity*, 42; see 42–49; Rylance, *Victorian Psychology*, 61–63. On associationism and "liberal cognition," see Hadley, *Living Liberalism*, 10n15, 50–51.
116 See James, *Principles of Psychology*, 1:332–41, 457–61, 519–69. In the present, associationism remains alive and well in philosophy and cognitive science. Associations have been characterized, for instance, as "building blocks of predictions" (Bar, "Proactive Brain," 280–81).
117 Patey, *Probability and Literary Form*, 89 (see 84–133 for literature as a "hierarchy of probable signs").
118 Bender, "Enlightenment Fiction and the Scientific Hypothesis," 20. Compare Bender, "Novel Knowledge." On verisimilitude and the rise of the novel, see McKeon, *Origins of the English Novel*, 52–64, 118–28.
119 On Hume's epistemology and "fictionality," see Bender, "Enlightenment Fiction and the Scientific Hypothesis"; Duncan, *Scott's Shadow*, 123–38; Kareem, *Reinvention of Wonder*, 62–67, 75–104. Although Gallagher does not mention Hume, her theory of fictionality as congruent with modern values of "disbelief, speculation, and credit," where fiction operates as a "suppositional speculation" requiring readers' "cognitive provisionality," resonates with his ideas ("Rise of Fictionality," 346–47). For an opposing account, stressing Hume's "anti-cognitivist" view, see Maioli, *Empiricism and the Early Theory of the Novel*, 10–25, 39–60.

120 Locke, *Essay*, 652; Venn, *Characteristics of Belief*, 6, 25. On Locke's ideas about probability, their origins in rhetoric and theology, and their place in his visual epistemology, see Patey, *Probability and Literary Form*, 22–24, 27–34.

121 *Philosophy of Rhetoric*, 56–58. For another numerical invocation, see Priestley, *Oratory and Criticism*, 50. On Campbell's backgrounds, see Bitzer, "Hume's Philosophy in George Campbell's *Philosophy of Rhetoric*"; Agnew, "George Campbell's Rhetoric."

122 *Elements of Rhetoric*, 79; see 76–81 for his discussion of odds. On Whately and prior traditions in logic and rhetoric, see Ehninger, "Campbell, Blair, and Whately Revisited"; Einhorn, "Consistency in Richard Whately"; Van Evra, "Richard Whately and the Rise of Modern Logic"; McKerrow, "Richard Whately and the Revival of Logic"; Snyder, *Reforming Philosophy*, 34–36.

123 *English Composition and Rhetoric*, 235; see 230–36.

124 Bain, *English Grammar*, 44–45, 70–71.

125 Ehninger, "Introduction," xxv, ix; McKerrow, "Richard Whately and the Revival of Logic," 179.

126 See Smith, *Lectures on Rhetoric and Belles-Lettres*; Priestley, *Oratory and Criticism*; Blair, *Lectures on Rhetoric and Belles-Lettres*; Spencer, *Philosophy of Style*; Lewes, *Principles of Success in Literature*.

127 Poovey, *History of the Modern Fact*, 308–17.

128 Gigerenzer et al., *Empire of Chance*, xiv. The probability revolution was thus a "revolution in application" (Cohen, "Scientific Revolutions, Revolutions in Science," 40).

129 Hacking, *Taming of Chance*, 101; see 87–104.

130 Hacking, *Taming of Chance*, 85.

131 Shapiro, *"Beyond Reasonable Doubt" and "Probable Cause,"* 25–41, 116–18, 196–98, 220–41, 253–55; Shapiro, *Probability and Certainty*.

132 *"Beyond Reasonable Doubt" and "Probable Cause,"* 30.

133 Shapiro surveys treatises on evidence in relation to philosophy and mathematics (25–41, 220–41). Her thorough list includes Richard Kirwan, *Logick, or An Essay on the Elements, Principles and Different Modes of Reasoning* (1807), Daniel McKinnon, *The Philosophy of Evidence* (1812), John Gambier, *A Guide to the Study of Moral Evidence* (1834), Thomas Starkie, *Practical Treatise of the Law of Evidence* (1834), William Wills, *An Essay on the Principle of Circumstantial Evidence* (1838), and W. M. Best, *The Principles of the Law of Evidence* (1849).

134 Whately, *Elements of Rhetoric*, 66, 74; Ehninger, "Campbell, Blair, and Whately Revisited," 180.

135 See Shapiro, *"Beyond Reasonable Doubt" and "Probable Cause"*; Poovey, *History of the Modern Fact*; Welsh, *Strong Representations*; Whitman, *Origins of Reasonable Doubt*.

136 On literature and probability from the eighteenth to the twentieth centuries, see Backscheider, *Probability, Time, and Space in Eighteenth-Century Literature*; Patey, *Probability and Literary Form*; Newsom, *Likely Story*; Beer, "Reader's Wager"; Kavanagh, *Enlightenment and the Shadows of*

Chance; Monk, *Standard Deviations*; Richardson, *Unlikely Stories*; Franklin, *Serious Play*; Hamilton, *Accident*; Macpherson, *Harm's Way*; Molesworth, *Chance and the Eighteenth-Century Novel*; Jordan, *Chance and the Modern British Novel*; Campe, *Game of Probability*; Puskar, *Accident Society*; Lee, *Uncertain Chances*; Fyfe, *By Accident or Design*; Tondre, *Physics of Possibility*; Grener, *Improbability*.

137 Edmond Duranty, in Becker, *Documents of Modern Literary Realism*, 97.

138 Patey, *Probability and Literary Form*, 77.

139 McKeon, *Origins of the English Novel*, 128, 120.

140 Gallagher, "Rise of Fictionality," 343. On the "probable" and the "marvelous," see Patey, *Probability and Literary Form*, 147–54. For a contrasting "fictional marvelous . . . defined not by its opposition to, but by its integration with realism" (3), see Kareem, *Reinvention of Wonder*.

141 Grener, *Improbability*, 11, 9.

142 Tondre, *Physics of Possibility*, 2, 4.

143 Choi, *Victorian Contingencies*, 3.

144 Choi, *Victorian Contingencies*, 6.

145 *Correspondence*, 799; to Richard Watson Dixon, 7–9 August 1888.

146 "*Vraisemblance* and Motivation," 242.

147 "*Vraisemblance* and Motivation," 240.

148 "*Vraisemblance* and Motivation," 243; see 242–47. I add Dostoevsky and James following Chatman, *Story and Discourse*, 52n13.

149 "*Vraisemblance* and Motivation," 253. Genette borrows "motivation" from Boris Tomashevsky, who distinguishes three types: *compositional, realistic*, and *artistic* ("Thematics," 78–87). On verisimilitude and motivation, see Barthes, "Reality Effect"; Todorov, "Introduction to Verisimilitude" (*Poetics of Prose*, 80–88), and *Introduction to Poetics*, 17–20; Culler, *Structuralist Poetics*, 131–60; Chatman, *Story and Discourse*, 48–53; Bal, *Narratology*, 41–46; Fludernik, *Towards a "Natural" Narratology*, 31–38, 159–63; Puckett, *Narrative Theory*, 198–204. Such accounts participate in the "rehabilitation" of the Victorian novel, which appears "smoother, more formally impressive" when "annexed to a structuralist idea of French realism" (Freedgood, *Worlds Enough*, 21, 11; see 1–33).

150 Puckett, *Narrative Theory*, 199.

151 Hacking, *Emergence*, 18–23. This earlier usage arises from the Latin *probabilis*, an evaluative term meaning "not evidential support but support from respected people," which was current into the eighteenth century but "began to die out as mathematical probability became more and more successful" (23, 20). For the seventeenth-century French context, see Lyons, *Phantom of Chance*.

152 "*Vraisemblance* and Motivation," 243. As Patey notes, *vraisemblable* had objective and subjective dimensions, denoting "what is most like truth, either in that it resembles truth or that it happens most frequently," and "credibility," "congruence with previously held opinion" (*Probability and Literary Form*, 79). On *vraisemblance* and probability, see 77–84.

153 Todorov, *Poetics of Prose*, 83.

154 "*Vraisemblance* and Motivation," 242; Barthes, *S/Z*, 18; Prince, *Dictionary of Narratology*, 103.

155 Puckett, *Narrative Theory*, 199 (emphasis mine).

156 "*Vraisemblance* and Motivation," 244; Culler, *Structuralist Poetics*, 138.

157 Several thoughtful accounts of probability in literary theory are compromised by their reliance on abstract criteria. Newsom explains the "antinomy of fictional probability," the putative "logical oddity involved in ascribing probability to fiction," by means of readerly code-switching between fact and fiction – between crediting "the conventions of realism" and "recogniz[ing] the fictionality of fiction" – in a "jump from one universe to another" (*Likely Story*, 9, 97; see 90–104, 144–64). Although he dissents from Hacking, declaring "a fundamental unity shared by concepts of probability from Aristotle through the present" (12), Newsom's argument that literary probability is *only* explicable via questions of belief and pretense – that probability ascriptions make sense from "the standpoint in which we actively are moving in and out of the game of make-believe" (155) – surely prioritizes the epistemic. Monk argues that "chance *always* takes on a necessarily fateful quality once it is represented in narrative"; any conception of chance that "can no longer be accommodated by the established narrative system" leads to a "new representational mode that absorbs the anomalous sense of randomness and contingency, constituting in the process a more complex narrative form that again leaves nothing to chance" (*Standard Deviations*, 2, 22). Richardson offers a "paradox of chance in fictional narratives," where chance is either absent or present, and partitions narrative causality into just four "mutually exclusive" models (*Unlikely Stories*, 18, 86). And Kukkonen's predictive processing account of reading as Bayesian inference treats probability judgments as primarily unconscious (*Probability Designs*).

158 Chatman, *Story and Discourse*, 19. On character as a function of predictability, see Todorov, *Poetics of Prose*, 54; Chatman, *Story and Discourse*, 110; Bal, *Narratology*, 120–26.

159 Porter, *Rise of Statistical Thinking*, 51; Hacking, *Taming of Chance*, 117.

160 Barthes, "Reality Effect."

161 "*Vraisemblance* and Motivation," 248.

162 Lewes, "Recent Novels," 692; Jewsbury, "New Novels." If ideas about the psychophysiology of reading linked such ideologically divergent critics as Lewes and Jewsbury, as Dames argues, so did reflex assumptions about probability, despite the fact that physiological novel theory was "unconcerned with the verification of [fictional] events as 'probable' or 'likely'" (*Physiology of the Novel*, 58; see 47–63).

163 Oliphant, "Miss Austen and Miss Mitford," "The Old Saloon," and "New Novels," 404.

164 Lewes, "Realism in Art," 501.

165 De Quincey, "Homer and the Homeridæ," 84.

166 Poovey, *Genres of the Credit Economy*, 77–85, 89–91. On Defoe's complex relation to the fact/fiction continuum, see 93–124. See generally McKeon,

Origins of the English Novel, 25–64; Gallagher, *Nobody's Story,* xv–xviii, 162–74; Davis, *Factual Fictions,* 25–70. Paige questions this gradual disarticulation and places the advent of fictionality proper in the early nineteenth century, following a "pseudofactual" long eighteenth century (*Before Fiction,* 1–33).

167 Paige, *Before Fiction,* 23.
168 *Principles of Success in Literature,* 83, 84, 40.
169 Masson, *British Novelists,* 248, 249; Lewes, "Dickens in Relation to Criticism," 151, 146. Masson's comparison between Thackeray and Dickens builds on an earlier distinction (drawn in terms of probability) between "novel" and "romance" (24–27).
170 Rigby, "*Vanity Fair* – And *Jane Eyre,*" *Quarterly Review* (1848), in Tillotson and Hawes, *Thackeray: The Critical Heritage,* 79–80.
171 Whately, *Elements of Rhetoric,* 48, 48n; see 47–52.
172 Scott, in Williams, *Swift: The Critical Heritage,* 293; Lewes, *Principles of Success in Literature,* 123.
173 Stephen, "Relation of Novels to Life," 166.
174 Masson, *British Novelists,* 11, 13, 118. Compare Whately: "the unnatural is often made to appear, for a time, natural" through "a lively and striking description which is correct in its several *parts,* and unnatural only when these are combined into a *whole*" (*Elements of Rhetoric,* 51). For the relationship between holistic formal standards and Victorian moral thought, see Rosenthal, *Good Form.*
175 Forster, *Aspects of the Novel,* 20.
176 Forster, *Aspects of the Novel,* 20.
177 See, respectively, Fletcher, *Allegory,* 182, 187–88; Chandler, *Archaeology of Sympathy,* 203–28; Patey, *Probability and Literary Form,* 220–51; Brinker, "Farce and the Poetics of the 'Vraisemblable'"; Claybaugh, *Novel of Purpose,* 6–7.
178 Culler, *Structuralist Poetics,* 145; Ford, *Dickens and His Readers,* 142.
179 On probability and genre, see Patey, *Probability and Literary Form,* 175–76. On generic change, see Moretti, *Signs Taken for Wonders,* 262–78; *Distant Reading,* 63–89.
180 Williams, "Slow Fire," 32–35.
181 Culler, *Structuralist Poetics,* 148–49.
182 Hacking, *Taming of Chance,* 168; see 160–79.

Chapter 1

1 *Daniel Deronda,* 42; quoting *Macbeth,* 2.3.109–10. Hereafter cited parenthetically.
2 *Crisis of Action,* 87–128. Markovits understands the "nature and potential of action" in an Aristotelian sense involving ethics and poetics (89), linking the novel's "two kinds of activity" to its realist and romance plots (108–9).
3 Shakespeare, *Macbeth,* 2.2.74.

4 Leavis, *Great Tradition*, 85, 102; see generally 79–125. On Leavis's claims, see Belsey, "Re-Reading the Great Tradition"; Johnson, "F. R. Leavis"; Steinlight, *Populating the Novel*, 161–63. Cases for unity include Beebe, "Visions Are Creators"; Carroll, "Unity of *Daniel Deronda*"; Knoepflmacher, *Religious Humanism*, 128–48; Bayley, "Pastoral of Intellect," 210; Daleski, "Owning and Disowning"; Fleishman, *Fiction and the Ways of Knowing*, 86–109; Qualls, *Secular Pilgrims*, 168–88; Levine, "Marriage of Allegory and Realism"; Caron, "Rhetoric of Magic"; Hardy, *Novels of George Eliot*, 108–14, 153. Some critics counterintuitively see the Jewish part as integrative: Carpenter, *Landscape of Time*, 131–53; Brantlinger, "Nations and Novels." Critics for the opposing case include Beaty, "Unity in Fiction"; Chase, "Decomposition of the Elephants"; Dale, "Symbolic Representation"; Eagleton, *Criticism and Ideology*, 121–25; Moretti, *Way of the World*, 224–27.

5 See Tucker, *Probable State* (on the novel's ending as a model of utopian reading); Anderson, *Powers of Distance*, 9–16, 119–46 (on its cosmopolitanism as balancing universal and particular, detachment and engagement); Kurnick, *Empty Houses*, 94–104 (on the characters as a "cast" who together express Eliot's "theatrical desire," a counterfactual yearning for shared sociality). Even Armstrong's measured account of illegitimacy, "deficit subjects," and the politics of recognition and reversal weighs toward the Deronda side (*Novel Politics*, 162–80).

6 For epistemological readings, see Welsh, *George Eliot and Blackmail*, 300–34; Law, "Transparency and Epistemology"; Levine, "New Epistemology"; Choi, *Victorian Contingencies*, 142–82.

7 Thurschwell, "George Eliot's Prophecies," 99; Goldberg, *Agents and Lives*, 130; Gallagher, *Body Economic*, 132.

8 Bayley, "Pastoral of Intellect," 206.

9 *George Eliot Letters* (hereafter cited as *GEL*), 5:79 (February 1870).

10 *Adam Bede*, 63.

11 *Felix Holt*, 45.

12 Lewes, "Suicide in Life and Literature," 64, 66.

13 "Theology and Philosophy," 1856, 580.

14 Rosenthal, *Good Form*, 156. Rosenthal reads *Daniel Deronda*'s individual/aggregate relation as "a conceptual shift in Eliot's thinking about the relation of the one and the many" after *Middlemarch*, with "laws that operate at the large scale coexisting with unconditioned autonomy at the individual scale – yet with an insurmountable breach between them" (153, 155). On *Middlemarch* and statistical averages, see Jaffe, *Affective Life*, 23–41.

15 See Irwin, *Notebooks*, 280, 283, 308. For Tylor, archery is a survival of hunting and games of chance are survivals of divination (*Primitive Culture*, 66, 70–75).

16 McClennen, *Rationality and Dynamic Choice*, 156–61; Bratman, *Faces of Intention*, 51–52. On Bratman's influential account of planning, see *Intention, Plans, and Practical Reason*; *Faces of Intention*, 15–90; "Reflection, Planning, and Temporally Extended Agency."

17 Anscombe, *Intention*, 80.

18 *Freedom and Nature*, 135–81.

19 Ricoeur, *Freedom and Nature*, 139–40, 142.

20 Ricoeur, *Freedom and Nature*, 137.

21 Glare, *Oxford Latin Dictionary*, s.v. "haereō," "haesitō," and "haesitātiō"; the noun conveys "faltering action" and mental "irresolution." Compare Shulman, *Pale Cast of Thought*, 62–63. Transcribing biblical verbs from J. W. Gibbs's *A Manual Hebrew and English Lexicon*, Eliot noted forms for "to fear, to tremble" and "to shake, hesitate" (*Some George Eliot Notebooks*, 1:122f.).

22 Ricoeur, *Freedom and Nature*, 142.

23 Vogl, *Tarrying*, 55.

24 See Vogl, *Tarrying*, 17–19, 35, 39, 81–82.

25 Vogl, *Tarrying*, 99.

26 Morson, *Narrative and Freedom*, 6; see 117–72; Miller, "Lives Unled in Realist Fiction."

27 Dames, *Physiology of the Novel*, 123–64; Levine, *Serious Pleasures*, 1–17, 101–60.

28 Ziolkowski, *Hesitant Heroes*, 1–8.

29 Vogl, *Tarrying*, 32. On Orestes and Hamlet, see Ziolkowski, *Hesitant Heroes*, 34–53, 74–95; Vogl, *Tarrying*, 23–38. Eliot's Duke Silva embodies such shifts as a "nature half-transformed": "both the lion and the man; / First hesitating shrank, then fiercely sprang, / Or having sprung, turned pallid at his deed / And loosed the prize, paying his blood for nought" (*The Spanish Gypsy*, ll. 1528, 1524–7).

30 Poole, *Shakespeare and the Victorians*, 123. Markovits comments on the *Hamlet* connection (*Crisis of Action*, 207n109). Eliot and Lewes saw a production of *Hamlet* in 1861 (*Journals of George Eliot*, 98; hereafter cited as *GEJ*). Lewes's review praised the actor's "vacillation," noting the "physiological qualities which give the force of animal passion demanded by tragedy" ("Fechter in *Hamlet* and *Othello*," 746).

31 Goethe calls Wilhelm Meister "An oak tree planted in a precious pot which should only have held delicate flowers. The roots spread out; the vessel is shattered" (*Wilhelm Meister's Apprenticeship*, 146). Eliot read Goethe's novel in the 1850s, defending it in "The Morality of *Wilhelm Meister*"; she reread it in the 1870s (see Pinney, *Essays*, 143–47; *GEJ*, 33–36, 141). See Ashton, "Mixed and Erring Humanity"; Shaffer, "George Eliot and Goethe"; Cave, *Retrospectives*, 172–74. Eliot also read Aeschylus' trilogy while composing *Adam Bede* (where it plays a role in the conception of "Nemesis") and again while writing *Felix Holt* (*GEJ*, 70–73, 124–25).

32 *Essays and Leaves from a Note-Book*, 382. Garcha posits a late Victorian "shift in literary representations of decision-making" – from binary choice to multiple "available, commensurable options" – and links it to the advent of consumerism and the development of neoclassical economic theory ("Narrating Choice," 198, 209).

33 *Logic of Chance*, 216. The second edition (1876) was in the Eliot/Lewes library (Baker, *Library*).

34 Pinney, *Essays*, 31.

35 Pinney, "More Leaves from George Eliot's Notebook," 364; *GEL*, 6:99 (to the Hon. Mrs. Henry Frederick Ponsonby, 10 December 1874). Eliot's sense of progress "seems to have been much more about the human potential to will the right things than about the human potential to do the right things" (Markovits, *Crisis of Action*, 90). On determinism and free will in Eliot, see Levine, "Determinism and Responsibility"; Paris, *Experiments in Life*, 120–27; Ermarth, "Incarnations"; Bonaparte, *Will and Destiny*, 48–62; Ryan, *Thinking without Thinking*, 68–71.

36 *The Emotions and the Will*, 583.

37 Eliot, "Theology and Philosophy," 1855, 224–25. Accounts of Eliot and psychophysiological thinkers (especially Lewes) include Collins, "G. H. Lewes Revised"; Levine, "George Eliot's Hypothesis of Reality," in *Realism, Ethics and Secularism*, 25–50; Shuttleworth, *George Eliot and Nineteenth-Century Science*, 175–200; Chase, *Eros and Psyche*, 136–87; Rylance, *Victorian Psychology*, 251–61; Menke, "Fiction as Vivisection"; Wood, *Passion and Pathology*, 132–41; Gallagher, *Body Economic*, 118–55; Matus, *Shock, Memory and the Unconscious*, 121–59; Ryan, *Thinking without Thinking*, 59–77. For volition in British physiological psychology, see Daston, "Theory of Will"; Rylance, *Victorian Psychology*, 194–202 (on Bain's theory); Smith, "Physiology of the Will." For overviews, see Smith, "Background of Physiological Psychology"; Daston, "British Responses to Psycho-Physiology"; Jacyna, "Physiology of Mind"; Danziger, "Mid-Nineteenth-Century British Psycho-Physiology"; Clarke and Jacyna, *Nineteenth-Century Origins of Neuroscientific Concepts*; Young, *Mind, Brain, and Adaptation*; Rylance, *Victorian Psychology*, 70–109.

38 Carpenter, "On the Doctrine of Human Automatism," 398–402. For a similar overview, see Lewes, *Physiology of Common Life*, 2:25–33, 2:165–91.

39 "Theory of Will," 93.

40 This is not to downplay internal differences: Rylance notes Carpenter's resistance to "abolishing the higher faculties, especially the will, in an obsession with mechanism," and Lewes's "genuinely judicious attempts" to qualify outright determinism, although he was "uncompromisingly opposed to automatist theories" like those of Huxley and Tyndall (*Victorian Psychology*, 93, 283).

41 *Physiology of Common Life*, 2:91.

42 Berrios, *History of Mental Symptoms*, 354; Rylance, *Victorian Psychology*, 92. For examples of the materialist/automatist position, see Huxley, "On the Physical Basis of Life" and "On the Hypothesis That Animals Are Automata"; Clifford, "Body and Mind."

43 Smith, "Physiology of the Will," 81.

44 Rylance, *Victorian Psychology*, 7; see 13–17.

45 Maudsley, *Body and Mind*, 187.

46 Carpenter, "Physiology of the Will," 192–93.

47 "A College Breakfast-Party," in *Complete Shorter Poetry*, 25; *The Mill on the Floss*, 353.

48 Maudsley, *Body and Mind*, 12, 21–23. *Body and Mind* and *The Physiology of Mind* (1876) – the first part of *The Physiology and Pathology of Mind* (1868), in its second edition – were in the Eliot/Lewes library (Baker, *Library*). For Maudsley's expanded discussions, see *Physiology of Mind*, 409–62, and *Body and Will*.

49 "Hamlet," 74.

50 *Body and Mind*, 39, 75.

51 Carpenter, "Physiology of the Will," 207–8. On habit in Eliot, its control over action, tendency to usurp volition, and difficulties for accounts of progress, see Markovits, *Crisis of Action*, 93–95.

52 "Theology and Philosophy," 1855, 225; *Impressions of Theophrastus Such*, 105.

53 *Hamlet*, 3.1.56; *The Libation Bearers*, l. 1009.

54 Hardy, *Novels of George Eliot*, 58.

55 *GEL*, 6:183 (John Blackwood to Eliot, 10 November 1875). Hutton and James also criticized the word (Beer, *Darwin's Plots*, 139). Eliot used "dynamic" in *Middlemarch*; perhaps the issue was its placement in the opening sentence. Choi enlists the word to juxtapose Maxwell's statistical mechanics and Eliot's "probabilistic narrative mode of approximating knowledge about human feelings and events": the limits of empirical approaches to knowledge cede to a distributional epistemology she terms "statistical realism" (*Victorian Contingencies*, 145, 174).

56 For accounts of Aristotle's *dynamis* and its fluctuating character, see Agamben, *Potentialities*, 177–84, 243–71; Ricoeur, *Freedom and Nature*, 138.

57 Rosenthal, *Good Form*, 175, 187. Rosenthal offers the richest account of gambling (173–88); others include Bonaparte, *Will and Destiny*, 16–22; Fisher, *Making Up Society*, 211–12; Hardy, *Novels of George Eliot*, 133–34; Gallagher, "The Prostitute and the Jewish Question," 48; Cottom, *Social Figures*, 175–78; Stone, "Play of Chance"; Wagner, "Gambling as Simulation." Eliot's distaste is usually linked to her description of the Homburg *Kursaal*: "Burglary is heroic compared with [gambling]. I get some satisfaction in looking on from the sense that the thing is going to be put down. Hell is the only right name for such places" (*GEL*, 5:312; to Mrs. William Cross, [25 September 1872]).

58 Ainslie, *Breakdown of Will*, 39–44.

59 Ainslie, "Dangers of Willpower," 67; *Breakdown of Will*, 70, 90–104.

60 *Breakdown of Will*, 89, 99. On "intertemporal bargaining," see 73–140. Compare Ainslie, *Picoeconomics*.

61 Ross et al., *Midbrain Mutiny*, 43–105 (on behavioral aspects and hyperbolic discounting), 117–78 (on cognitive or neuroeconomic aspects); Ross, "Economic Models of Addiction." See also Elster, *Ulysses and the Sirens*, *Strong Feelings*, and "Gambling and Addiction."

62 Ainslie, "Dangers of Willpower," 69; *Breakdown of Will*, 79–80. The physiological will was re-psychologized by James in *Principles of Psychology* (1891), and by trends such as experimentalism, psychoanalysis, and behaviorism (see Berrios, *History of Mental Symptoms*, 351–56; Rylance, *Victorian Psychology*, 5–17).

63 For a critique of Ainslie, see Bratman, *Faces of Intention*, 35–57. Using Ainslie's rejection of the equivalence between *reward* and *pleasure*, I differ from Gallagher's reading of Eliot's "models of motivation" according to Bain's simpler calculus of *pleasure* and *pain* and Jevons's theory of marginal utility (Ainslie, *Breakdown of Will*, 58–61; Gallagher, *Body Economic*, 120–23, 130–51). Indeed, Jevons's marginal utility curve, which describes having a commodity until surfeit, is the *opposite* of Ainslie's hyperbolic discount curve, which describes not-having a wanted object until promptly gratified impulse. Despite Ainslie's criticism of utility maximization as an account of human motivation, Jevons was still the first to model temporal discounting: "all future events … should act upon us with the same force as if they were present, allowance being made for their uncertainty" (*Theory of Political Economy*, 76).

64 *Body and Mind*, 9.

65 *Middlemarch*, 772.

66 Miller, *Narrative and Its Discontents*, 138; Fessenbecker, *Reading Ideas*, 166. On Eliot's anticipation of Sartre's *mauvaise foi*, see Jameson, *Antinomies of Realism*, 114–37.

67 Shuttleworth, *George Eliot and Nineteenth-Century Science*, 192; see 184–93. On the self in Eliot as a noncontinuous collection of (Aristotelian) accidents, see Bonaparte, *Will and Destiny*, 51–53.

68 Vogl, *Tarrying*, 32; Ricoeur, *Freedom and Nature*, 164.

69 Markovits, *Crisis of Action*, 99. Compare Hertz, *George Eliot's Pulse*, 135–36.

70 See *Open Secrets*, 1–65.

71 *The Spanish Gypsy*, ll. 2196–98.

72 Leavis, *Great Tradition*, 102–3. John Blackwood thought the scene "like what passes through the mind after each move at a game" (*GEL*, 6:182; to Eliot, 10 November 1875). Tucker reads it as "compositional notes for the conventional realist novel [Eliot] can no longer bring herself to write," focusing on Gwendolen's belief in her autonomous interior (*Probable State*, 80, 115–17).

73 Eliot, *Adam Bede*, 164.

74 For Gwendolen as a critique of Arnoldian liberalism, see Fleishman, *Fiction and the Ways of Knowing*, 92–93.

75 Bratman, *Faces of Intention*, 36–37; Ross, "Economic and Evolutionary Basis of Selves," 249.

76 This pun, deflecting the Latin etymology about weighing choices (*librare*) to questions of freedom (*liberare*), features in various accounts of deliberation – Thomas Hobbes's is a prominent example. See Skinner, *Hobbes and Republican Liberty*, 20–26, 90–91.

77 Eliot transcribed from Proctor the description of an experiment (analogous to urn-drawing or coin-tossing) where objects are cast through parallel slats and the resulting probability distribution observed (Irwin, *Notebooks*, 283). See Seneta, Parshall, and Jongmans, "Nineteenth-Century Developments in Geometric Probability." Choi notes the "language of contingency" in this image (*Victorian Contingencies*, 176).

78 On Gwendolen's volitional compromise, see David, *Fictions of Resolution*, 138–39; Markovits, *Crisis of Action*, 111–18; Gallagher, *Body Economic*, 131–33, 136–40.
79 Shuttleworth links the image to Lewes's metaphor of the mind as a lake (*George Eliot and Nineteenth-Century Science*, 192). Zemka points to Grandcourt's "hedonistic immersion in momentary consciousness" as a type of modern temporality (*Time and the Moment*, 166).
80 *Body Economic*, 135.
81 Fisher, *Making Up Society*, 221; see 217–24.
82 Gallagher, *Body Economic*, 135; see 134–40. Mintz recognizes the issue of "granting or denial of personal liberty" (*Novel of Vocation*, 153). Bonaparte emphasizes egoism and irrational will (*Will and Destiny*, 97–102).
83 Levine sees Grandcourt as a corrupt foil to Mordecai, both "daemonic agents" ("Marriage of Allegory and Realism," 424). Compare Thale, *Novels of George Eliot*, 125–30; Goldberg, *Agents and Lives*, 117–21.
84 Here I rely on a Kantian reading of consent and coercion: "Even the most autonomous cannot genuinely consent to proposals about which they are deceived or with which they are compelled to comply" (O'Neill, "Between Consenting Adults," 259).
85 On the novel's formal contradictions and narrative confusions, see Chase, "Decomposition of the Elephants"; Shuttleworth, *George Eliot and Nineteenth-Century Science*, 175–82; Schor, "Make-Believe of a Middle"; Woloch, "*Daniel Deronda*."
86 For proxy consent in relation to children and the mentally impaired, see Wellman, *Approach to Rights*, 97–104; Feinberg, *Rights, Justice, and the Bounds of Liberty*, 163. This complex has attracted several labels: "paternal admonition," "hero as mentor," "mentor-lover," and "avuncularism" (Tanner, *Adultery in the Novel*, 225–31; Hardy, *Novels of George Eliot*, 57; Menon, *Mentor-Lover*, 163–87; Cleere, *Avuncularism*, 152, 157–59). Compare Chase, *Eros and Psyche*, 175–76; Poole, "Hidden Affinities," 299–302.
87 The image is both individual (in the myth of Odysseus and the Sirens) and political (in the "ship of state"); see Plato, *Republic*, 488a–89; Aristotle, *Politics*, 1276b20–27. Lewes offers a version in *Problems of Life and Mind, Second Series* (1877); see Rylance, *Victorian Psychology*, 285.
88 *The Mill on the Floss*, 401. Cited parenthetically in this paragraph. Markovits also makes this connection, but says the proposal scene is one of "inaction rather than action" (*Crisis of Action*, 115).
89 Ryan also describes the scene in terms of psychophysiology, but argues that its emphasis on the unconscious, reflexive, and automatic *precludes* decision: "Maggie's yielding is not a conscious choice and perhaps not a choice at all" (*Thinking without Thinking*, 67; see 65–71).
90 Leavis, *Great Tradition*, 99.
91 Gallagher, *Body Economic*, 139.
92 Reading the proposal scene, Blackwood reported being "uncertain up to the last moment as to whether [Gwendolen's answer] was to be Yes or No" (*GEL*, 6:186; to Eliot, 17 November 1875).

93 Vogl, *Tarrying*, 28, 27.

94 E.g., in Carpenter: as a rider's will spurs movement by proxy (in a horse's muscles), so volition takes effect through the automatic processes it enlists ("Physiology of the Will," 199; "On the Doctrine of Human Automatism," 398). On Eliot's equestrian images, see Hardy, *Novels of George Eliot*, 227–29; David, *Fictions of Resolution*, 194–95; Shuttleworth, *George Eliot and Nineteenth-Century Science*, 188–89.

95 See Plato, *Phaedrus*, 246a–57.

96 Compare Markovits on Gwendolen's "will unaccompanied by any doing" (*Crisis of Action*, 117). Zemka reads the drowning scene in temporal terms (*Time and the Moment*, 170–72): Gwendolen's shock forecloses deliberation, typifying the instant as "inhospitable to ethical agency" (147).

97 *Problems of Life and Mind, Third Series*, 2:459. Quoting Lewes, Vrettos argues that Gwendolen realizes the "tenuous boundaries between her fantasies and actions" and "assumes full moral responsibility for the crime" (*Somatic Fictions*, 74). On the imagined rehearsal of this crime, see Rodensky, *Crime in Mind*, 166–67; Tucker, *Probable State*, 116–17. On crime and "*wishes* [that] *shape the fields of possibility*" in narrative, see Morson, *Narrative and Freedom*, 141.

98 Austin, *Lectures on Jurisprudence*, 215. Although Eliot probably read Austin in earnest only after *Daniel Deronda*, his discussion of commission and omission haunts the novel (Irwin, *Notebooks*, 229).

99 Carpenter, "Physiology of the Will," 215.

100 Ainslie, *Breakdown of Will*, 84–86; Bratman, *Faces of Intention*, 51–52.

101 *Sexuality in the Field of Vision*, 116. See David, *Fictions of Resolution*, 143–44, 190–97; Stone, "Case History of Gwendolen H"; Ender, *Sexing the Mind*, 229–72; Showalter, *Hystories*, 91–92; Tromp, "Gwendolen's Madness"; Wood, *Passion and Pathology*, 141–62; Flint, "George Eliot and Gender." Jacobus uses Eliot's "The Lifted Veil" (1859) to draw parallels between a pathologized "double consciousness" and the "artist-hysteric" Alcharisi (*Reading Woman*, 272–74). Vrettos, who offers an account of nervous disease and argues that Eliot's depiction drew on scientific developments and literary models, is careful to specify "hysteria" less as a diagnosis than a catch-all for nervous symptoms (*Somatic Fictions*, 197n4; see 48–80).

102 Originated by Jean-Étienne Dominique Esquirol to sharpen symptoms grouped under "melancholy," "monomania" had its moment in the 1840s and thereafter became an imprecise, even tautological category (Berrios, *History of Mental Symptoms*, 142–43, 425–26). See van Zuylen, *Monomania*.

103 Trotter, "Invention of Agoraphobia," 468; see 466–69. Vrettos likewise describes Gwendolen's obsession with containment and expanse: "while locked spaces set tangible boundaries, expansive vistas threaten to disperse her immediate sense of self" (*Somatic Fictions*, 63).

104 Quoted in Showalter, *Female Malady*, 132. Eliot similarly sees hysteria as "constantly creating illusory maladies" (*GEL*, 4:198; to Caroline Hennell Bray, 1865). Still, a brief experience early in life led her to write of "that most wretched and unpitied of afflictions, hysteria" (1:41; to Maria Lewis, [13 March 1840]).

105 Trotter, "Invention of Agoraphobia," 464. For "persecution madness," see Anon., "Du Saulle on Persecution-Madness"; Anon., "The Habit of Fear."

106 Irwin, *Notebooks*, 352. Paget's article was reprinted in *Clinical Essays* (1875), presented to Lewes (352). Lewes discusses imitative phenomena in "Suicide in Life and Literature" and *Problems of Life and Mind, Third Series*, 2:459–60. For discussions of Paget, see Trotter, "Invention of Agoraphobia," 457; Vrettos, *Somatic Fictions*, 83–87, 96–99, 105–10.

107 Such circumspection recalls Eliot's admonition that Maggie Tulliver's "history ... is a thing hardly to be predicted even from the completest knowledge of characteristics" (*The Mill on the Floss*, 352).

108 Rosenberg, "Contested Boundaries," 412, 409. Such resistance to categorical specificity might be seen as another instance of Eliot's interest in "vagueness" as a matter of language and logic; see Wright, *Bad Logic*, 106–41.

109 Berrios, *History of Mental Symptoms*, 357–64, 428; compare Vogl, *Tarrying*, 63. The most influential psychophysiological account of the will and its pathologies, Théodule Ribot's *Les maladies de la volonté* (1883), was written by a psychologist who introduced British empirical methods into France in *La psychologie anglaise contemporaine* (1875) (see Berrios, *History of Mental Symptoms*, 338).

110 *Body and Mind*, 79, 83–84.

111 "Suicide in Life and Literature," 57.

112 Lewes, "Suicide in Life and Literature," 67. Definitions of hysteria Eliot might have found in Lewes's library relate to these wider diagnoses: Carter, *On the Pathology and Treatment of Hysteria* (relying on Carpenter's distinction between "ideo-motor" and willed actions [63–64]); Romberg, *A Manual of the Nervous Diseases of Man* (including many categories as causes or results of nervous disorder).

113 Deronda reacts differently to such scenes and is mentored by one whose "thought went on in wide spaces" (Hardy, *Novels of George Eliot*, 230–31; quoting *Daniel Deronda*, 470).

114 Vogl, *Tarrying*, 64. Vogl places such cultural resistance late in the nineteenth century, citing Ribot (61–63), but the trend is visible much earlier in British psychology. On inhibition (and its lack), see Ziolkowski, *Hesitant Heroes*, 3, 22–26. Rejection of modern systematization has also been linked to motivational problems such as addiction and dissociation (Ainslie, "Dangers of Willpower," 83).

115 For the iconography of a moving statue in Shakespeare's play and classical tradition, see Barkan, "Living Sculptures"; Gross, *Dream of the Moving Statue*, 92–109.

116 Poole links the *tableau vivant* to the gothic topoi of "animated statue" and "haunted portrait" ("Hidden Affinities," 299). Pace sees Gwendolen's terror responding to the panel's representation of "stasis" overlaying "ongoing action," since her character is an "emblem for existence as an ongoing state of potentiality" ("Who Killed Gwendolen Harleth?," 41, 44). For other accounts, see Witemeyer, *George Eliot and the Visual Arts*, 93–94; Stokes,

"An Actress among the Novelists"; Marshall, *Figure of Theater*, 198–201; Litvak, *Caught in the Act*, 183–88; Voskuil, *Acting Naturally*, 104–10.

117 Zemka, *Time and the Moment*, 148–55; Tucker, *Probable State*, 86–88; Matus, *Shock, Memory and the Unconscious*, 142–59; Levine, "Surprising Realism." Zemka defines "anti-epiphanies" as moments that "detach their receivers from their surroundings and attach them to ancient inheritances and future responsibilities" (150).

118 Markovits, *Crisis of Action*, 89–124; Gallagher, *Body Economic*, 118–55; Miller, *Burdens of Perfection*, 54–64, 69–80; Schor, *Curious Subjects*, 214; see 206–18.

119 Ryan, *Thinking without Thinking*, 74–77, 97–101; Anderson, *Powers of Distance*, 119–46; Pinch, *Thinking about Other People*, 139–69.

120 Vrettos, *Somatic Fictions*, 69, 77–79.

121 Compare Eliot on Lisbeth Bede: "To the feminine mind in some of its moods, all things that might be, receive a temporary charm from comparison with what is" (*Adam Bede*, 133).

122 Griffiths, *Age of Analogy*, 3; on comparison vs. analogy, see 12–17, 30–33. Philology: Max Müller, whom Eliot was reading in the 1860s and 1870s (*GEJ*, 107–8; *GEL*, 5:561). Law and political science: Henry Sumner Maine, James Fitzjames Stephen, J. R. Seeley, E. A. Freeman, Henry Sidgwick (see Collini, Winch, and Burrow, *Noble Science of Politics*, 207–46; *Some George Eliot Notebooks*, 1:163–64). Anthropology: E. B. Tylor, John Lubbock, John McLennan, J. G. Frazer (see Stocking, *Victorian Anthropology*, 121–28, 150–69, 174). Eliot read Tylor's *Primitive Culture* in 1872 and *Researches into the Early History of Mankind and the Development of Civilization* in 1874 (*GEL*, 5:288, 6:90).

123 *Age of Analogy*, 173–89.

124 On comparison and analogy in the Whewell/Mill debates, see Griffiths, *Age of Analogy*, 147–56. On Comte's importance for Eliot and Lewes, see Graver, *George Eliot and Community*, 4–6. Eliot started reading Comte's *System of Positive Polity* before *Daniel Deronda* and later took "extensive notes" in the same notebook, including on a section tracing the movement of scientific method through "Observation," "Experiment," and "Comparison" (*GEL*, 6:126; Irwin, *Notebooks*, 226, 187n1).

125 Pinney, "More Leaves from George Eliot's Notebook," 364.

126 Pinney, *Essays*, 36, 152.

127 *The Mill on the Floss*, 118.

128 *GEL*, 4:424; to Sara Hennell, 22 March 1868.

129 *George Eliot and Community*, 47, 70; see 66–71, 298–300. Collins draws on unpublished notebooks to discuss Eliot's skepticism of social evolutionism and comparative method, which posits common ancestors and uniform origins to sociocultural phenomena ("Questions of Method," 392–405).

130 *Powers of Distance*, 3–4, 9–16.

131 *Adam Bede*, 92; *Middlemarch*, 163.

132 *Impressions of Theophrastus Such*, 104.

133 See Galton, "Statistics by Intercomparison." Intercomparison "enable[d] [Galton] to draw exact conclusions from this data as reliably and efficiently as possible" (Porter, *Rise of Statistical Thinking*, 143). Eliot grasped the importance of statistical comparison in describing the rumors about Lydgate's medical style: "some of the particulars being of that impressive order of which the significance is entirely hidden, like a statistical amount without a standard of comparison" (*Middlemarch*, 435). The term was originated by Müller to describe "intercomparison of the grammatical forms of languages" (*OED*).

134 Graver, *George Eliot and Community*, 38–39.

135 Mill, *System of Logic*, 1:7–8; Venn, *Logic of Chance*, 125–27, and *Characteristics of Belief*, 11–14.

136 Shuttleworth, *George Eliot and Nineteenth-Century Science*, 176.

137 The example of distance qua mistaken perception is from Mill (*System of Logic*, 1:7–8): a high bar for the non-ignorant reader. Cottom criticizes Eliot's position on political grounds: "wide understanding depends on an assumption of superiority" figured as "social difference" (*Social Figures*, 112).

138 On comparative errors as underwriting sympathy in *Middlemarch*, see Griffiths, *Age of Analogy*, 189–98.

139 *Impressions of Theophrastus Such*, 143; see Henry, *George Eliot and the British Empire*, 82.

140 *GEL*, 6:301 (emphasis mine).

141 *GEL*, 6:290.

142 For James, "absence of spontaneity" and "excess of reflection" marred Eliot's novels ("The Life of George Eliot," in *Literary Criticism*, 1000).

143 Carroll, "Unity of *Daniel Deronda*," 173. Choi, by contrast, defends sympathy in statistical terms, arguing that the novel's "proliferation of narrative possibilities ... enables ... a willingness to imagine another's range of possible feelings" (*Victorian Contingencies*, 15; see 171–77). Tondre's account of Eliot's engagement with Maxwell's statistical thermodynamics also sees sympathy's power (in *Middlemarch*) as "diffusive" (*Physics of Possibility*, 126–63). Other accounts of sympathy include Welsh, *George Eliot and Blackmail*, 302–5; Stewart, *Dear Reader*, 305–22; Jaffe, *Scenes of Sympathy*, 130–33; Cleere, *Avuncularism*, 165–69; Markovits, *Crisis of Action*, 121–22; Toker, *Ethics of Form*, 120–25.

144 Hutton, "[Rev. of] *Daniel Deronda*," 734; Swann, "Ecumenical Jew," 39.

145 On Deronda's universal and abstract elements, see Swann, "Ecumenical Jew," 39–40; Cohen, "From Home to Homeland"; Gallagher, "The Prostitute and the Jewish Question."

146 Hardy, *Novels of George Eliot*, 125; Anderson, *Powers of Distance*, 121.

147 Maudsley, "Hamlet," 84.

148 Preyer, "Beyond the Liberal Imagination," 50; compare Menon, *Mentor-Lover*, 183–84 (on the paralysis engendered by impartiality).

149 On this aspect, see Baker, "George Eliot's Readings in Nineteenth-Century Jewish Historians" and "George Eliot and Zionism"; Gallagher, "The Prostitute and the Jewish Question"; Brantlinger, "Nations and Novels";

Semmel, *George Eliot and the Politics of National Inheritance*; Ragussis, *Figures of Conversion*, 249–90. Critiques include Said, "Zionism from the Standpoint of Its Victims," 18–22; Meyer, "'Safely to Their Own Borders'"; Novak, "A Model Jew." Cheyette's discussion of "semitic discourse" is a useful corrective to these arguments (*Constructions of "the Jew,"* 1–54).

150 Anderson, *Powers of Distance*, 121; see 129–34.

151 On coincidence and the invisible yet representable causality underlying chance events, see Levine, "Determinism and Responsibility"; Bonaparte, *Will and Destiny*, 36–38, 40–41; Vargish, *Providential Aesthetic*, 241–43; Stone, "Play of Chance," 38–40.

152 For During, Mordecai (like Gwendolen) is figured as a monomaniac, although his mental pathology draws on a discernible somatic condition where hers is more nuanced ("Strange Case of Monomania," 95–100). On Mordecai's psychology, see Thurschwell, "George Eliot's Prophecies," 94–98; Claggett, "George Eliot's Interrogation of Physiological Future Knowledge," 855–61.

153 See Levine, "George Eliot's Hypothesis of Reality," in *Realism, Ethics and Secularism*, 25–50, and *Dying to Know*, 194–95.

154 Stone, "Play of Chance," 40.

155 The biblical book of Daniel is characterized by the relation between prophecy and history. Eliot made notes on research that declared Daniel's author "the first who grasped the history of the world, so far as he knew it, as one great whole, a drama which moves onward at the will of the Eternal One" (Irwin, *Notebooks*, 406).

156 On the abstraction of this heritage and social vision, and its incarnation in the trunk given to Deronda, see Fisher, *Making Up Society*, 212–14.

157 Rosenthal, *Good Form*, 159–73.

158 Lewes damned "uncritical statistics" as the "copious resources of blockheads" ("Suicide in Life and Literature," 70).

159 Deronda's actions negate his mother's resistance to her father's will (David, *Fictions of Resolution*, 147). For Markovits, the social web, the actions of others, and our pasts constrain action and limit choice in Eliot, even as she expresses a belief in free will (Markovits, *Crisis of Action*, 90–93).

160 Compare Eliot's description of musical skill as partly "heritage / From treasure stored by generations past / In winding chambers of receptive sense" (*The Spanish Gypsy*, ll. 1218–20). Lewes offers examples of how "instinctive peculiarities" or "acquired habits" may be inherited, including a penchant for gambling ("Hereditary Influence, Animal and Human," 143). On Eliot and Lamarckian ideas, see Roberts, *George Eliot*, 46–49.

161 Compare Zemka's comments on volition and modern temporality: in Deronda "the will surrenders to the direction of ancestral life"; in Gwendolen it "disintegrates under the pressure of speed" (*Time and the Moment*, 147).

162 Collins, "G. H. Lewes Revised," 479. Mintz discusses how Deronda's "messianic calling" externalizes his self and places him beyond vocation (*Novel of Vocation*, 159–60, 163).

163 Leavis criticized Eliot's endorsement of Deronda, a "paragon of virtue, generosity, intelligence, and disinterestedness [who] has no 'troubles' he needs a refuge from" (*Great Tradition*, 84).

164 Pritchett, *Living Novel*, 91.

Chapter 2

1 "Imperfect Sympathies," in *Elia and the Last Essays of Elia*, 60.

2 See Miller, *Novel and the Police*, 33–57; Brantlinger, "What Is 'Sensational' about the 'Sensation Novel'?" For Miller, *The Moonstone*'s "different points of view, degrees of information, tendencies of suspicion are never allowed to tamper with more basic interpretative securities about character and language" (53). For Brantlinger, sensation novels paradoxically "conclude in ways that liquidate mystery": "The insoluble is reduced to the soluble" (21).

3 Schramm, "Towards a Poetics of Wrongful Accusation"; Schor, "Show-Trials." On nineteenth-century legal reform, see Schramm, *Testimony and Advocacy*; Dolin, *Fiction and the Law*.

4 Schramm, "Towards a Poetics of Wrongful Accusation," 194; Schor, "Show-Trials," 179.

5 On the law and historical developments in probability, see Hacking, *Emergence*, 85–91; Patey, *Probability and Literary Form*, 6–8; Daston, *Classical Probability*, 33–47; Shapiro, *Probability and Certainty* and *"Beyond Reasonable Doubt" and "Probable Cause,"* 116–18, 196–98, 253–55; Zabell, "Probabilistic Analysis of Testimony"; Gigerenzer et al., *Empire of Chance*, 7–8, 26–28, 33–34. On rules for numbers of witnesses, see Wigmore, "Required Numbers of Witnesses." On recent applications of probability, statistics, and decision theory to law, see Cohen, *Probable and the Provable*; Eggleston, *Evidence, Proof and Probability*; Tillers and Green, *Probability and Inference in the Law of Evidence*; Gigerenzer et al., *Empire of Chance*, 258–61, 263–65; Friedman, "Assessing Evidence"; Schum, *Evidential Foundations*; Gastwirth, *Statistical Science in the Courtroom*; Laudan, *Truth, Error, and Criminal Law*. Critical assessments include Tribe, "Trial by Mathematics"; Kaye, "Statistical Significance and the Burden of Persuasion"; Allen and Pardo, "Problematic Value of Mathematical Models of Evidence."

6 For historical accounts of these concepts in relation to scientific and other contexts, see Waldman, "Origins of the Legal Doctrine of Reasonable Doubt"; Shapiro, *"Beyond Reasonable Doubt" and "Probable Cause,"* 1–41, 170–71, "Circumstantial Evidence," 229–41, and "Beyond Reasonable Doubt."

7 Venn, *Logic of Chance*, 327. On legal evidence in relation to modal logic and probability, see 322–31.

8 Tribe, "Trial by Mathematics"; Feeley and Simon, "Actuarial Justice"; Harcourt, *Against Prediction*.

9 On blame as a more persistent moral emotion than praise, even when "unmerited," see Smith, *Theory of Moral Sentiments*, 119–20.

10 Brantlinger, "What Is 'Sensational' about the 'Sensation Novel'?," 11. For general discussion, see Brown, "Realism and Sensation Fiction."

11 Kent, "Probability, Reality and Sensation," 265, 262. On sensation fiction's reliance on newspapers, see Brantlinger, "What Is 'Sensational' about the 'Sensation Novel'?," 3–10.

12 Duff, "Scottish Criminal Jury," 193. I rely on the accounts of Willock, *Origins*, 217–25; Duff, "Not Proven Verdict"; Barbato, "Scotland's Bastard Verdict"; Hope et al., "A Third Verdict Option"; Bray, "Not Proven"; Maher, "Verdict of the Jury." An anonymous nineteenth-century article outlines many of the points made by modern scholars (Anon., "Scotch Verdict"). For broader discussions of Scots law, see Riggs, "Prosecutors, Juries, Judges and Punishment in Early Nineteenth-Century Scotland"; Walker, *Legal History of Scotland*, 20–32, 439–83.

13 Arnot makes this argument about the reign of Charles II (*Celebrated Criminal Trials in Scotland*, 174–75). For a more measured view, see Willock, *Origins*, 219.

14 Anon., "Scotch Verdict," 190. As late as 1800, Hume declares that "the fact is the undoubted and exclusive province of the jury" (*Commentaries on the Law of Scotland*, 2:323; on "general" and "special" verdicts, see 2:288–91).

15 Willock, *Origins*, 217–19; Duff, "Scottish Criminal Jury," 193; Hope et al., "A Third Verdict Option," 246. Special verdicts were "virtually unknown" by mid-century (Maher, "Verdict of the Jury," 42).

16 Anon., "Scotch Verdict," 187. Roman Law's third verdict (*non liquet*) necessitated a further trial. For parallels between *non liquet* and "not proven," see Forsyth, "Criminal Procedure in Scotland and England," 372–75; Pringle, "Verdict of 'Not Proven,'" 434; Willock, *Origins*, 223.

17 Anon., "Scotch Verdict," 184.

18 On the history of the connected notions meant to safeguard this rule, see Shapiro, *"Beyond Reasonable Doubt" and "Probable Cause,"* 1–41.

19 Scottish juries settled at fifteen individuals in the sixteenth century (Willock, *Origins*, 184–90, 226–33). Duff argues that the verdict safeguarded beyond reasonable doubt ("Scottish Criminal Jury," 173, 190–95). Maher points out that the English system, which can result in a hung jury, may present its own difficulties for the beyond reasonable doubt standard, although he argues that "not proven" should be disbanded because it erodes the presumption of innocence ("Verdict of the Jury," 45–49, 50–51).

20 Duff, "Scottish Criminal Jury," 195. Empirical studies suggest jurors would opt for "not proven" when possible, and more acquittals have been hypothesized as a result of what decision theory calls a "compromise effect." See Hope et al., "A Third Verdict Option"; Bray, "Not Proven."

21 Anon., "Scotch Verdict," 182; Bray, "Not Proven," 1300. For a discussion entertaining "not proven" for Anglo-American systems, see Barbato, "Scotland's Bastard Verdict."

22 Barbato, "Scotland's Bastard Verdict," 544.

23 Willock, *Origins*, 193; Duff, "Scottish Criminal Jury," 180–82. On the comparative leniency of the Scottish penal system, historically, see Farmer, *Criminal Law, Tradition, and Legal Order*, 43–44.

24 Luhmann, *Law as a Social System*, 284.

25 Steele, *Juries in Criminal Trials in Scotland*, 211. Where "pannel" usually refers to the jury, in Scots law it designates the trial and/or the individual indicted or brought to trial (see *OED*, "panel, n.1," def. 14a., 15).

26 Hume, *Commentaries on the Law of Scotland*, 2:244–331; Alison, *Practice of the Criminal Law of Scotland*, 2:631–50. Both discuss the "verdict of assize" (i.e., of the trial proceedings).

27 *Journal of Sir Walter Scott*, 1:361 (20 February 1827).

28 Anon., "Scotch Verdict," 185–86; Willock, *Origins*, 201–2. On legal "presumption," see Shapiro, *"Beyond Reasonable Doubt" and "Probable Cause,"* 200–241; Welsh, *Strong Representations*, 2–42.

29 Discussing the statute (11 & 12 Vict. c. 79), one commentator challenges Scott's dismissal: "the respect and submissive deference with which [Scottish] criminal prosecutions are regarded . . .; the frequent use of the verdict by the jury . . .; and the uncomplaining spirit in which it is uniformly received by the conscious persons whom it at once acquits and stigmatizes, testify most powerfully to its convenience and radical justice" (Anon., "Scotch Verdict," 195).

30 Burton, *Narratives from Criminal Trials in Scotland*, 2:61n; see 2:1–78. Discussing the mid-century emergence of secretive methods of poisoning, alongside modern toxicology and medical jurisprudence, Burney suggests that Collins's novels defend toxicology from its critics and dramatize its limits for sensational effect (*Poison, Detection, and the Victorian Imagination*, 179–82). Collins owned key texts in this field, such Alfred Swaine Taylor's *Poisons in Relation to Medical Jurisprudence* (1849) and *On Poisons* (1859).

31 Forsyth, "Criminal Procedure in Scotland and England." On the trial's relationship to sensation novels, see Hartman, "Murder for Respectability"; Helfield, "Poisonous Plots."

32 Anon., "Not Proven."

33 Collins was a frequent contributor to *All the Year Round*, where *The Woman in White* was serialized in 1860.

34 Anon., "Home-Office Inspiration," 465, 466. Similar charges were leveled at the English system: Arthur Hallam, in *The Middle Ages* (1872), calls the requirement of jury unanimity "that preposterous relic of barbarism" (quoted in Willock, *Origins*, 226).

35 "The Legal Vocabulary" (1872) (*Readiana*, 261). Collins corresponded with Reade during the composition and serial run of the novel (see *Collected Letters*, 3:59, 62, 72).

36 For instance, in verdicts recorded by Hume, *Commentaries on the Law of Scotland*, 2:326, 328, 330.

37 *The Law and the Lady*, 101. Hereafter cited parenthetically.

38 As Traver also notes, calling attention to the verdict's use as an avoidance tactic by the jury ("Law and the Nation," 70–71).

39 Harrington calls Valeria's outburst a "patriotic appeal and mission statement" ("From the Lady and the Law to the Lady Detective," 26).

40 MacEachen makes a similar claim for Collins's novels and legal issues: *No Name* focuses on inheritance laws concerning illegitimate children; *Man and Wife* on English marriage laws applying to Ireland, irregular marriages in Scotland, and the legal status of married women in England ("Wilkie Collins and British Law," 125–35). On the novel and the Smith trial, see Murphy, "Inadmissible Evidence."

41 "Wilkie Collins and British Law," 135, 138.

42 Longmuir, "Scotch Verdict and Irregular Marriages," 170.

43 Traver, "Law and the Nation," 68; Husemann, "Irregular and Not Proven," 67.

44 Traver, "Law and the Nation," 70.

45 The 1851 edition mentions only the fact/law and general/special discriminations under "verdict" (2:1165), and under "jury" offers only special cases in which Scots juries must decide unanimously (Ogilvie, *Imperial Dictionary*, 2:1165, 2:16). The verdict is briefly alluded to under "proven" (2:485). In a later edition that entry describes (contra Valeria's definition) "a verdict given by a jury in a criminal case when, although there is a deficiency of evidence to convict the prisoner, there is sufficient to warrant grave suspicion of his guilt" (Ogilvie and Annandale, *Imperial Dictionary*, 3:556–57).

46 *The Imperial Dictionary, English, Technological, and Scientific*, as its full title runs, modifies Webster's phrase to "comprising all the words purely English" on its title page (*Imperial Dictionary*). The locution "in plain English" occurs regularly in Collins, often in contrast to legal jargon: *Armadale*, 146, 164, 473; *The Woman in White*, 153; *The Moonstone*, 41, 113, 170, 256, 335, 356; *No Name*, 346, 441, 501, 730. Briefel suggests another hidden clue: an "Ogilvie" testified in the Smith trial ("Cosmetic Tragedies," 473).

47 *Dictionary and Digest*, 590. Bell's definition cites Alison and Steele and owes some of its phrasing to Hume: "not uncommonly, the phrase *not proven*, has been employed to mark a deficiency only of lawful evidence to convict the pannel, and that of *not guilty*, to convey the jury's opinion of his innocence of the charge" (*Commentaries on the Law of Scotland*, 2:291).

48 On Collins's critique as pragmatic and uninformed, see Traver, "Law and the Nation," 73–74; Husemann, "Irregular and Not Proven," 77–79.

49 "The Detective Case," 382.

50 Doyle, "Strange Studies from Life," 483.

51 Anon., "Scotch Verdict," 183.

52 Anon., "[Rev. of] *The Law and the Lady*," *Examiner*, 414. Collins's prefatory comments often mused on matters ordinary and extraordinary. The preface to *Armadale*, for instance, suggests that the novel "oversteps . . . the narrow limits within which they [viz., readers] are disposed to restrict the development of modern fiction" (5). Such views can be traced back to the preface to *Basil*

(1852) (Martin, "Wilkie Collins and Risk," 189–90); Kent calls this a "sensationalist manifesto" hinging on "probability as subjective belief" ("Probability, Reality and Sensation," 264).

53 "The Typology of Detective Fiction," in *Poetics of Prose*, 45.

54 On the work of Poe and Conan Doyle in relation to logic, science, and semiology, see the essays in Eco and Sebeok, *Sign of Three*. For a different account of Sherlock Holmes and scientific method, see Smith, *Fact and Feeling*, 211–37.

55 Miller, *Novel and the Police*, 27–28. Ginzburg's "conjectural paradigm," traceable from ancient hunting practices to modern medical semiotics and fingerprinting, is an analogous "interpretative method based on taking marginal and irrelevant details as revealing clues" ("Clues and Scientific Method," 101, 86).

56 For "inevitable discovery" and the "retrospectivity of legal narrative" (4), see Brooks, "Clues, Evidence, Detection."

57 An early review praised Collins's ability to "form a puzzle" but complained about the search taking too long to yield "matters of interest indeed, but not of interest to [Valeria]" (Anon., "[Rev. of] *The Law and the Lady*," *Saturday Review*, 357).

58 Mill, *System of Logic*, 1:288–90. On Mill and improper inductions (vs. Whewell's "colligation" and "discoverers' induction"), see Snyder, *Reforming Philosophy*, 101–3.

59 The verdict "has the effect of exposing the fractures in an official identity, marked by a proper name, which sutures a subject to a social order" (Murphy, "Inadmissible Evidence," 173).

60 Harrington, "From the Lady and the Law to the Lady Detective"; Johnston, "Sensate Detection"; Allan, "A Lock without a Key," 50; Murphy, "Inadmissible Evidence," 173. Maynard observes Valeria's use of "imaginative identification, not just inductive reasoning" ("Telling the Whole Truth," 194).

61 Levine, *Serious Pleasures*, 10, 60; see generally 1–17, 37–61.

62 Levine, "An Anatomy of Suspense," 198.

63 Levine, "An Anatomy of Suspense," 200.

64 After the 1850s Collins used "precisely those psychological theories that stressed the unpredictable and unconscious workings of the mind as a key method of creating anxiety, suspense and cognitive uncertainty in his narratives" (Taylor, "Later Novels," 83).

65 I draw this notion from Thomas's account of the logic of liberalism (*Cultivating Victorians*, 3–48).

66 Miller, *Novel and the Police*, 55, 54; see generally 50–57. Duncan critiques Miller's reading of detection as a "double gesture of epistemological totalization and ideological closure" ("*The Moonstone*, the Victorian Novel, and Imperialist Panic," 302). Heller offers a contrasting account of Collins's many-voiced "aesthetics of multiplicity" and the gendered "double voice" of *The Moonstone* (*Dead Secrets*, 37, 151–56).

67 Miller, *Novel and the Police*, 54.

68 A review drily noted "a far greater laxity in admitting evidence than we know of south of the Tweed" (Anon., "[Rev. of] *The Law and the Lady*," *Saturday Review*, 357).

69 Meyler, "Wilkie Collins's Law Books," 136; see 138–48 on Collins's sources.

70 Meyler, "Wilkie Collins's Law Books," 161, 140.

71 Sutherland, "Wilkie Collins and the Origins of the Sensation Novel," 244.

72 On the two systems of trial procedure, see Damaska, "Evidentiary Barriers to Conviction."

73 Farmer comments on a "blurring of the boundaries between guilt and character as a result of the development of new administrative procedures" in nineteenth-century Scots law (*Criminal Law, Tradition, and Legal Order*, 121).

74 The numbers vary in the Smith case; the sense is that the poisoning took several attempts, with enough arsenic to kill anywhere from fifty to a hundred (Hartman, "Murder for Respectability," 398). This chemical technique was highly convincing for both toxicologists and theorists of evidence in the period (Burney, *Poison, Detection, and the Victorian Imagination*, 80–82).

75 The investigation reveals a difference in English and Scottish systems also present in the Smith trial. Where the English system uses coroners to investigate unexplained death (fact), the Scottish, absent a coroner, deploys the Procurator Fiscal to investigate alleged crimes (guilt): the former "proceeds from the facts to the person of the criminal," the latter "from the suspected person to the facts" (Forsyth, "Criminal Procedure in Scotland and England," 350; see 349–52). As Duff notes, this prosecution service is "unaccountable to the police, the courts, the victims of crime, or the accused" ("Scottish Criminal Jury," 176).

76 A detail Collins draws from Burton, who comments on the "vulgar criminal poisoner" who "goes to the nearest chemist to buy arsenic for destroying imaginary rats" (*Narratives from Criminal Trials in Scotland*, 2:1).

77 The damning diary conceit is used to highly self-conscious effect in *Armadale*, where Lydia Gwilt is also charged with murder by poison in echoes of the Smith trial. See Kent, "Probability, Reality and Sensation," 272–73, 276.

78 Scottish procedure holds the prosecution to strict standards of corroboration (Duff, "Scottish Criminal Jury," 189n147). On the widespread genre of circumstantial evidence, see Welsh, *Strong Representations*, 2–42; Meyler, "Wilkie Collins's Law Books," 148–55 (on "factual precedents" guiding jurors).

79 Forsyth, "Criminal Procedure in Scotland and England," 370–72 (noting that such evidence in the Smith trial would have been inadmissible in an English setting). Similar fact evidence "might be admissible if a systematic course of conduct had to be established or intention rather than accident had to be proved or the accused's state of mind had to be established" (Walker, *Legal History of Scotland*, 507).

80 Such backward reasoning about conditional probabilities is criticized in discussions of mathematics and the law. See Friedman, "Assessing Evidence," 1812–16, 1828–35; Tribe, "Trial by Mathematics"; Lempert, "Modeling Relevance."

81 Sutherland, "Wilkie Collins and the Origins of the Sensation Novel," 256.

82 Burton, *Narratives from Criminal Trials in Scotland*, 2:49.

83 Maynard, "Telling the Whole Truth," 193.

84 Reed, "Law and Narrative Strategy," 222, 224.

85 Murphy, "Inadmissible Evidence," 176; see 176–80 on the trial report.

86 Briefel develops an engaging reading of the novel's interest in cosmetics and masquerade ("Cosmetic Tragedies"). Burney discusses the complex regulation of arsenic's medical, cosmetic, and household uses, especially after the Arsenic Act of 1851 (*Poison, Detection, and the Victorian Imagination*, 64–70).

87 Nesson, "The Evidence or the Event?," 1377.

88 Nesson, "The Evidence or the Event?," 1358, 1369; see generally 1377–90.

89 Meyler, "Wilkie Collins's Law Books," 158; see 157–60. Baker reads Valeria's statements in terms of the complex and contradictory relationship between belief and evidence in Victorian law and literature ("Evidence, Belief, and Character in Victorian Fiction," 47–50).

90 *Miserrimus*, 23.

91 *Dictionary and Digest*, 43. Compare "a juror who takes money from both parties for giving his verdict" (*Imperial Dictionary*, 1851 ed., 1:63). The *OED* gives this legal sense as the earliest. Dexter is sometimes true to the allusion: he suggests Valeria bribe Helena's maid, making the case "a matter of pounds, shillings, and pence" (258).

92 As Briefel notes, the vase as symbolic object (with its image of a woman's face) is not reconstructed, whereas the letter as textual confession is in a figurative "recreation of Sara's body" ("Cosmetic Tragedies," 477).

93 Mill, *System of Logic*, 1:292.

94 On the "open verdict," see Anderson, *Suicide in Victorian and Edwardian England*, 230. On inquests as sites of uncertainty, especially when recounted in newspapers, see Fyfe, *By Accident or Design*, 51–61. For an account of suicide's legal and moral perplexity in the period, see Lewes, "Suicide in Life and Literature." On Collins's novel, see Gates, *Victorian Suicide*, 55–60, and "Wilkie Collins's Suicides," 311–12. Magdalen Vanstone's gamble in *No Name* – to kill herself only if an odd number of ships passes her window – reinforces the link between suicide and aleatory phenomena. See Kent, "Probability, Reality and Sensation," 266.

95 On the ambivalence of the letter, which both exonerates and condemns, see Mangum, "Wilkie Collins, Detection, and Deformity," 303; Allan, "A Lock without a Key," 54; Harrington, "From the Lady and the Law to the Lady Detective," 28; Briefel, "Cosmetic Tragedies," 466.

96 Hühn, "Detective as Reader," 452. Other Collins novels have been characterized in similarly open-ended terms: Tondre describes *Armadale*'s "poetics of
postponement," which "stops short of a unified explanation" and "mobilizes
diverse vantages without ever ending in a single, composite claim of truth";
Cohn identifies "doubts about the tenability of the will to knowledge" in *The
Moonstone*, where "a logic of *suspension* defers the urgent pleasures of *suspense*"
(*Physics of Possibility*, 73; "Suspending Detection," 255, 256).

97 Brooks, "Clues, Evidence, Detection," 2, 3.

98 Brooks, "Clues, Evidence, Detection," 14.

99 Miller, *Novel and the Police*, 34.

100 Murphy, "Inadmissible Evidence," 171.

101 Reed discusses the pervasive ambiguity and shame the verdict installs ("Law
and Narrative Strategy," 218–22).

102 Miller, *Novel and the Police*, 36.

103 Schramm, "Towards a Poetics of Wrongful Accusation," 207.

104 Schramm, "Towards a Poetics of Wrongful Accusation," 207.

105 *Testimony and Advocacy*, 192. See Claybaugh, *Novel of Purpose*.

106 Cavell, "The Good of Film," 337, 348.

107 Cavell, "The Good of Film," 337.

108 Miller, *Novel and the Police*, 42; Shaw, *Victorians and Mystery*, 292; Duncan, "*The
Moonstone*, the Victorian Novel, and Imperialist Panic," 301. For a related account
of *The Moonstone* in relation to Victorian psychophysiology and Carpenter's
"unconscious cerebration," see Ryan, *Thinking without Thinking*, 29–43.

109 Levine, "An Anatomy of Suspense," 201.

110 Ashley, "Wilkie Collins and the Detective Story," 50.

111 *An Open Verdict*, 2:26.

112 *An Open Verdict*, 2:46.

113 *An Open Verdict*, 2:81.

114 *An Open Verdict*, 2:101.

115 Williams, "Rumor, Reputation, and Sensation in *Tess of the d'Urbervilles*."

116 Gigerenzer et al., *Empire of Chance*, 47.

117 Cavell, "The Good of Film," 348.

118 Luhmann, *Law as a Social System*, 76–141.

119 Luhmann, *Law as a Social System*, 70, 100.

120 Luhmann, *Law as a Social System*, 285, 284.

121 Luhmann, *Law as a Social System*, 286.

122 Collins alludes to this discourse in describing Dexter as "a man of far more than
average ability" (178). Davis discusses the role of nineteenth-century statistics,
from Quetelet through Galton, in "the construction of normalcy," arguing that
"the novel as a form promotes and symbolically produces normative structures"
(*Enforcing Normalcy*, 23, 41; see 23–49; see also Hacking, *Taming of Chance*,
160–69). Several interpretations engage with (and critique) Collins's representations of disability and the "normal": Taylor, *In the Secret Theatre of Home*,
223–27; Mangum, "Wilkie Collins, Detection, and Deformity"; Denisoff,
"Framed and Hung"; Cothran, "Mysterious Bodies"; Flint, "Disability and

Difference," 155–56; Holmes, "Queering the Marriage Plot"; Reed, "Law and Narrative Strategy," 222–23.

123 Sedgwick, *Weather in Proust*, 19.

124 Ahmed, *The Promise of Happiness*, 223.

125 "The use of mathematical probability to analyze the probative force of testimony was among its earliest applications," as Zabell states in an overview of the historical field ("Probabilistic Analysis of Testimony," 327). See also Hacking, *Taming of Chance*, 87–104.

126 De Morgan, "Theory of Probabilities," 467–73; Babbage, *Ninth Bridgewater Treatise*, 120–31, 192–203; Boole, *Studies in Logic and Probability* ("On the Application of the Theory of Probabilities to the Question of the Combination of Testimonies or Judgments").

127 Venn, *Logic of Chance*, 398; see 394–405 for a critique of probability and testimony. See also Mill, *System of Logic*, 1:538–39. For discussion, see Zabell, "Probabilistic Analysis of Testimony," 332–34.

128 Zabell, "Probabilistic Analysis of Testimony," 327.

129 Colyvan, Regan, and Ferson, "Is It a Crime to Belong to a Reference Class?"; Allen and Pardo, "Problematic Value of Mathematical Models of Evidence."

130 On these terms, see Moretti, *Distant Reading*; Best and Marcus, "Surface Reading"; Love, "Close but Not Deep"; Felski, *Limits of Critique*; Warner, "Uncritical Reading"; Rooney, "Live Free or Describe." Rooney cites Louis Althusser's dictum: "there is no such thing as an innocent reading, we must say what reading we are guilty of" (quoted on 121).

131 Marcus's precursor to "surface reading" "attends to what texts make manifest on their surface," "strives to be adequate to a text conceived as complex and ample rather than as diminished by, or reduced to, what it has to repress," and "accounts for what is in the text without construing presence as absence or affirmation as negation" (*Between Women*, 3, 75).

132 Critics describing the ending's "undecidability" include Allan, "A Lock without a Key," 47; Longmuir, "Scotch Verdict and Irregular Marriages," 171. Others emphasize the ambivalence of leaving the verdict on record: Maynard, "Telling the Whole Truth"; Reed, "Law and Narrative Strategy," 227–28; Meyler, "Wilkie Collins's Law Books," 162; Murphy, "Inadmissible Evidence," 183–84. Other readings of Collins alert to uncertainty qua suspense or delay include Levine, "An Anatomy of Suspense"; Tondre, *Physics of Possibility*, 61–94.

133 Stephen's review of novelists writing about the law, including Dickens, Reade, and Gaskell, accuses the last of assuming "that it is a part of the high commission of literature to try offences which elude the repression of the law" ("License of Modern Novelists," 156).

Chapter 3

1 *Letters*, 3:39 (to Mrs. Carmichael-Smyth, 17–19 April 1852).

2 "Caricatures and Lithography in Paris," in *The Paris Sketch Book* (*Oxford Thackeray*, 2:183–84). Hereafter I refer to this edition of Thackeray's works as

OxT, with citations by volume and page number. For Fielding's influence on Thackeray, see Ray, *Thackeray*, 1:225–26.

3 "A Box of Novels" (*OxT*, 6:413); *Morning Chronicle*, 94 (26 December 1845). Ray argues that Thackeray's *Morning Chronicle* criticism gives the strongest sense of his theory of fiction (*Thackeray*, 1:323–30).

4 Ray, *Thackeray*, 1:394.

5 Drawn from Thackeray, *Letters*, 1:38 (to Mrs. Carmichael-Smyth, 5 March 1829); "On Two Roundabout Papers Which I Intended to Write," in *Roundabout Papers* (*OxT*, 17:528–31); *The Memoirs of Barry Lyndon, Esq.* (*OxT*, 6:279–84); *Letters*, 1:410–11 (to Mrs. Carmichael-Smyth, 18 January 1840); "A Gambler's Death," in *The Paris Sketch Book* (*OxT*, 2:115–25); *Letters*, 1:225–26 (diary entry for 22 August 1832).

6 Thackeray probes the counterfactual coin toss in "On Some Late Great Victories," in *Roundabout Papers* (*OxT*, 17:395).

7 Scarry, *Dreaming by the Book*, 38. Hereafter I include *counterfictional* in the wider term *counterfactual*.

8 *Letters*, 4:154 (to Mrs. Carmichael-Smyth, 1 October 1859).

9 *Morning Chronicle*, 71 (3 April 1845). Quoted in Ray, *Thackeray*, 1:327.

10 "On Some French Fashionable Novels, with a Plea for Romances in General" (*OxT*, 2:93).

11 *Letters*, 4:154 (to Mrs. Carmichael-Smyth, 1 October 1859). For discussions about whether Thackeray *is* a realist, see Rawlins, *Thackeray's Novels*, 111–41; Ortiz-Robles, *Novel as Event*, 127–29.

12 Levine, *Realistic Imagination*, 143; on Thackeray's realism, see 131–66.

13 E.g., Fisher, "Siren and Artist" and *Thackeray's Skeptical Narrative*; Ferris, "Realism and the Discord of Ending," "The Breakdown of Thackeray's Narrator," and *Thackeray*; Fletcher, "The Dandy and the Fogy," "'Mere Outer Works' and 'Fleeting Effects,'" and "'The Foolishest of Existing Mortals'"; Shillingsburg, *Literary Life*; Bonaparte, "Written in Invisible Ink"; Kurnick, *Empty Houses*, 29–66.

14 Garcha, "Forgetting Thackeray and Unmaking Careers," 543.

15 *Vanity Fair*, 45. Hereafter cited parenthetically.

16 *Morning Chronicle*, 71, 78.

17 Ray, *Thackeray*, 1:117, 99.

18 Fletcher, "The Dandy and the Fogy," 395.

19 On the sketch as Thackerayan category, see Carey, *Thackeray*, 34–57; Byerly, "Effortless Art." On his productive improvisation, even carelessness, see Sutherland, *Thackeray at Work*.

20 On the actual incident, see Ray, *Thackeray*, 1:172–73.

21 "A Gambler's Death" (*OxT*, 2:116).

22 "A Gambler's Death" (*OxT*, 2:116).

23 "A Gambler's Death" (*OxT*, 2:118). Gambling losses were a common cause of suicide in nineteenth-century statistics (Hacking, *Taming of Chance*, 76).

24 Thackeray mentions gambling so often that a current textbook on the mathematics of games uses his work to preface chapters on topics like

expectation, house advantage, betting systems, card theory, and martingales (Ethier, *Doctrine of Chances*, e.g., 275–77).

25 For these topics, see Miller, *Novels behind Glass*, 31–40, 46–49; Rosdeitcher, "Empires at Stake"; Flavin, *Gambling*, 108–11.

26 *The Kickleburys on the Rhine* (*OxT*, 10:290).

27 *The Kickleburys on the Rhine* (*OxT*, 10:273).

28 *The Kickleburys on the Rhine* (*OxT*, 10:274; see 10:273–76). The "Contrebanque" was instigated by the French novelist Édouard Suau de Varennes. See Ethier, *Doctrine of Chances*, 310–11, 316, and "Thackeray and the Belgian Progression"; Kavanagh, "Roulette and the *Ancien Régime* of Gambling."

29 *The Kickleburys on the Rhine* (*OxT*, 10:279).

30 *The Kickleburys on the Rhine* (*OxT*, 10:295–96).

31 *The Newcomes*, 112.

32 "The Devil's Wager," in *The Paris Sketch Book* (*OxT*, 2:214).

33 "The Devil's Wager" (*OxT*, 2:221–23).

34 "The Painter's Bargain," in *The Paris Sketch Book* (*OxT*, 2:65).

35 "The Painter's Bargain" (*OxT*, 2:66).

36 "The Painter's Bargain" (*OxT*, 2:68).

37 "The Painter's Bargain" (*OxT*, 2:68).

38 "The Painter's Bargain" (*OxT*, 2:69, 70).

39 "The Painter's Bargain" (*OxT*, 2:77).

40 *The Adventures of Philip*, 515.

41 "The Notch on the Axe," in *Roundabout Papers* (*OxT*, 17:569).

42 "De Finibus," in *Roundabout Papers* (*OxT*, 17:591).

43 "De Finibus" (*OxT*, 17:596–98).

44 Gallagher, "Rise of Fictionality," 346. Ferris writes of "De Finibus" that Thackeray "invokes and inverts realist analogies [and so] destroys the stability of analogical direction," "contaminates history with fiction ... to open up categories, to question distinctions, to ... remain in process" ("Realism and the Discord of Ending," 302). On another view, reflections like these confirm Lukács's dictum: "No writer is a true realist or even a truly good writer, if he can direct the evolution of his own characters at will" (*Studies in European Realism*, 11).

45 Trollope felt that Thackeray's "characters stand out as human beings, with a force and a truth which has not, I think, been within the reach of any other English novelist in any period" (*Autobiography*, 152).

46 Similar phrasing occurs in an earlier review (*Morning Chronicle*, 74); and in *The Four Georges*, where Thackeray would prefer to be "with the mob in the crowd, not with the great folks in the procession" ("George the First," 17).

47 Bunzl, "Counterfactual History," 855.

48 For discussion, see Ferguson, "Virtual History"; Tetlock and Lebow, "Poking Counterfactual Holes in Covering Laws"; Bunzl, "Counterfactual History"; Mordhorst, "From Counterfactual History to Counternarrative History." Ferguson limits counterfactual history to "only those alternatives which we

can show on the basis of contemporary evidence that contemporaries actually considered" (86, emphases omitted).

49 See Hawthorn, *Plausible Worlds*, 1–37; Chang, *Is Water H₂O?*, 62–65; Radick, "Introduction: Why What If?," 548–49.

50 Barnaby, "Thackeray as Metahistorian," 35.

51 Thackeray owned sets of these works (*Catalogue*). He wrote a laudatory review of Macaulay's *Critical and Historical Essays* (1843), "narratives not less exciting than the best fictions of the novelist" (*OxT*, 6:315); and of Burton's *Life and Correspondence of David Hume* (1846) (*Morning Chronicle*, 113–18). Sutherland discusses Thackeray's historical research and similarities with Macaulay (*Thackeray at Work*, 124–32). Ray notes his reading of histories (*Thackeray*, 1:119). See also Douglas, "Thackeray and the Uses of History."

52 Macaulay, "John Dryden," 184.

53 Macaulay, "John Dryden," 221–22, 231. Clive links Macaulay's vivid imagination to his factual exactitude (*Not by Fact Alone*, 66–73). Given this shared technique, Macaulay is unfair on Thackeray as historian, remarking of his lecture on Steele, "Thackeray knows little of those times, & his audience generally less" (quoted in Millgate, "History *versus* Fiction," 48n9).

54 See "Proposals for a Continuation of *Ivanhoe*" (1846) and *Rebecca and Rowena* (1849) (*OxT*, 10:459–572). For Gao, the persistence of characters across the longer novels yields "an experience of fiction as being more persistent than the novel form allows, if nonetheless dependent on the novel as a medium"; he uses *The Newcomes* to explore Thackeray's "contradictory quest to produce literary works and to stay in fictional worlds" (*Virtual Play and the Victorian Novel*, 133, 122; see 104–38).

55 Much of this work builds on technical work on counterfactuals and other conditionals in philosophy, primarily in modal logic and semantics: see Goodman, *Fact, Fiction, and Forecast*; Lewis, *Counterfactuals*.

56 Kahneman and Miller, "Norm Theory."

57 Roese and Olson, "Structure of Counterfactual Thought"; Roese, "Functional Basis of Counterfactual Thinking," "Counterfactual Thinking," "Twisted Pair"; Boninger, Gleicher, and Strathman, "Counterfactual Thinking."

58 Roese, "Functional Basis of Counterfactual Thinking," 806. On causality: Wells and Gavanski, "Mental Simulation of Causality"; Spellman and Mandel, "When Possibility Informs Reality"; Roese and Olson, "Counterfactuals, Causal Attributions, and the Hindsight Bias"; Mandel and Lehman, "Counterfactual Thinking and Ascriptions of Cause and Preventability"; Byrne, *Rational Imagination*, 99–128. On meaning construction and/or preparative intention modeling: Kray et al., "From What *Might* Have Been to What *Must* Have Been"; Kray, Galinsky, and Markman, "Counterfactual Structure and Learning from Experience in Negotiations"; Ruvolo and Markus, "Possible Selves and Performance"; Johnson and Sherman, "Constructing and Reconstructing the Past and the Future in the Present"; McMullen and Markman, "Downward Counterfactuals and Motivation"; Markman and Tetlock, "Accountability and Close-Call Counterfactuals"; Epstude and Roese, "Functional Theory of

Counterfactual Thinking"; McCrea, "Self-Handicapping, Excuse Making, and Counterfactual Thinking"; Nasco and Marsh, "Gaining Control through Counterfactual Thinking."

59 See Gilbert, Driver-Linn, and Wilson, "The Trouble with Vronsky." Kahneman and Tversky note the "Alice-in-Wonderland quality" of simulations that undo the past ("The Simulation Heuristic," in *Judgment under Uncertainty*, 203).

60 Teigen, "When the Unreal Is More Likely Than the Real" and "The Proximity Heuristic in Judgments of Accident Probabilities"; Kray et al., "From What *Might* Have Been to What *Must* Have Been."

61 Kahneman and Tversky, "The Simulation Heuristic," in *Judgment under Uncertainty*, 202; Kray et al., "From What *Might* Have Been to What *Must* Have Been," 114; Lindberg, Markman, and Choi, "Retrospective Meaning Construction through Mental Simulation." A study of historians found that targeted counterfactual exercises heightened their sense of the past's contingency (Tetlock and Lebow, "Poking Counterfactual Holes in Covering Laws").

62 Kahneman and Tversky, "The Simulation Heuristic," in *Judgment under Uncertainty*; Kahneman and Miller, "Norm Theory"; Landman, "Regret and Elation Following Action and Inaction"; Roese and Olson, "Self-Esteem and Counterfactual Thinking"; Markman et al., "The Mental Simulation of Better and Worse Possible Worlds"; Taylor and Schneider, "Coping and the Simulation of Events"; Johnson, "The Knowledge of What Might Have Been"; Gilbert et al., "Looking Forward to Looking Backward"; King and Hicks, "Whatever Happened to 'What Might Have Been'?"; Tykocinski and Pittman, "The Consequences of Doing Nothing"; White and Lehman, "Looking on the Bright Side"; Koo et al., "It's a Wonderful Life."

63 Wilson and Gilbert, "Affective Forecasting."

64 Gilbert et al., "Looking Forward to Looking Backward," 349.

65 Kahneman and Miller, "Norm Theory."

66 Kahneman and Tversky, "The Simulation Heuristic," in *Judgment under Uncertainty*.

67 Roese, "Counterfactual Thinking," 137.

68 *Letters*, 1:83 (to Mrs. Carmichael-Smyth, 3 June 1829). The pattern is described in several studies with examinations as their model: Roese, "Functional Basis of Counterfactual Thinking."

69 *Letters*, 1:96–97 (to Mrs. Carmichael Smyth, 21 August 1829). On Thackeray's gambling, see Ray, *Thackeray*, 1:123–24, 134, 156–57, 159.

70 See Ray, *Thackeray*, 2:134, 156.

71 "A Gambler's Death" (*OxT*, 2:124).

72 On inheritance loss and cyclical fortune, see Miller, *Novels behind Glass*, 27–28.

73 *Letters*, 1:225–26 (diary entry for 22 August 1832). Colby and Shillingsburg credit Thackeray's reading of Cousin with amplifying his moral complexity (*Thackeray's Canvass of Humanity*, 27–52; Shillingsburg, *Literary Life*, 38, 129–30).

74 I cite earlier studies by Gallagher and Miller; their wider accounts are Gallagher, *Telling It like It Wasn't*; Miller, *On Not Being Someone Else*. Also relevant here: Morson's concept of sideshadowing, which involves

subjunctives, hypotheticals, and counterfactuals and the notion that "reality includes what might have happened," but is mostly directed to creating "an open sense of temporality" (*Narrative and Freedom*, 123, 6); Dannenerg's narratological study of coincidence and counterfactuals (*Coincidence and Counterfactuality*); Prendergast's "anthropology" of such thought patterns (*Counterfactuals*); and Freedgood's work on the "world-breaking" figure of metalepsis in Victorian realism, which scrambles fictionality and reference (*Worlds Enough*, 31; see especially 77–114).

75 Gallagher, "What Would Napoleon Do?," 316.

76 Gallagher, "What Would Napoleon Do?," 322. See also Saint-Amour, "Alternate-Reality Effects."

77 Gallagher, "What Would Napoleon Do?," 330; compare *Telling It like It Wasn't*, 72–75.

78 See Miller, "Lives Unled in Realist Fiction," 120–21, "A Case of Metaphysics," 774–75, 778–80, and "For All You Know."

79 Miller, "A Case of Metaphysics," 778, 784. See also Miller, "Lives Unled in Realist Fiction," 122.

80 "Lives Unled in Realist Fiction," 122.

81 On the Platonic ideality of *vraisemblance*, see Genette, "*Vraisemblance* and Motivation," 240; Chatman, *Story and Discourse*, 50.

82 Gallagher dismisses Doležel's arguments for the "uniform fictionality of characters in novels," which would assert a difference between "historical Somebody" and "fictional Nobody," and doubts the utility of possible-worlds semantics for analyzing fictionality ("What Would Napoleon Do?," 318, 319, 331–34). On possible-worlds theory and counterfactuals, see Pavel, *Fictional Worlds*, 35–36, 86–88; Doležel, *Possible Worlds*, 101–26, and *Heterocosmica*, 14, 56. Compare Ryan, who outlines a "principle of minimal departure" to measure the distance between possible and actual worlds (*Possible Worlds, Artificial Intelligence, and Narrative Theory*, 48–61).

83 Napoleon features in what Gallagher describes as the inaugural alternate history, Louis Geoffroy-Château's *Napoléon and the Conquest of the World* (1836) (*Telling It like It Wasn't*, 49–58). Choi discusses Napoleon as a "visual shorthand for contingency" (135) in William Spooner's "protean views" (*Victorian Contingencies*, 135–37).

84 "Caricatures and Lithography," in *The Paris Sketch Book* (*OxT*, 2:184).

85 See Miller, "Lives Unled in Realist Fiction," 123–26, and "A Case of Metaphysics," 784–89.

86 See Saint-Amour, "Alternate-Reality Effects."

87 "Lives Unled in Realist Fiction," 122. Dickens, Eliot, and James are key to Miller's account here and in "A Case of Metaphysics." See also Farina's discussion of "as if" reflexes, which in Dickens "conceptualize reality itself as virtual, as the abstract depth of a character," where Thackeray's "grammar of virtual reality" is contrastingly "diffuse" ("'Dickens's As If,'" 433, 434). Other studies of Victorian counterfactualism include Tondre's account of Meredith, whose *The Ordeal of Richard Feverel* disrupts the linear bildungsroman by

"a field of occluded counterlives" and "finds in nonhappenings the grounds for a more perfect mimesis" (*Physics of Possibility*, 47, 60; see 29–60); Choi's reading of contingency in geology and natural history (*Victorian Contingencies*, 56–93); and Glatt's exploration of "unwritten plots" that elicit (then dispel) "active possibilities" in realist narrative as it negotiates with (and supersedes) other generic conventions (*Narrative and Its Nonevents*).

88 On the genres refuted here (including dramatic action, sentimental romance, apologue, fable, sermon, and satire), see Rawlins, *Thackeray's Novels*, 1–35.

89 Barnaby's account of the *via media* places Thackeray between two historiographic models: subjective (Carlyle) and objective (Langlois) ("Thackeray as Metahistorian," 41–42, 33–34). Relatedly, Scarry describes Thackeray's tendency to bridge extremes at the level of sentence and concept, a "balancing act coordinating critical judgment with sympathetic participation" ("Enemy and Father," 145). McMaster describes the strategy as "making his characters lifelike" by "show[ing] them striking poses that are fictionlike" (*Thackeray*, 32; see 31–36).

90 Ermarth, *English Novel*, 4; see 17–27.

91 Miller mentions this micro-causality in discussing "the paradoxical feeling ... that objects are simultaneously important and insignificant" (*Novels behind Glass*, 32–33).

92 Victorian reviewers thought the counterfactual more puzzling than amusing: Rigby grumbles that Thackeray's Waterloo "brings about only one death, and one bankruptcy, which might either of them have happened in a hundred other ways" (in Tillotson and Hawes, *Thackeray: The Critical Heritage*, 79). For Gallagher, this moment instances how "novelistic fictions often mime counterfactualism" even though "their personae's ontological lack persists" ("What Would Napoleon Do?," 331).

93 Bonaparte, "Written in Invisible Ink," 148.

94 *Little Roadside Travels and Sketches* III, "Waterloo" (*OxT*, 6).

95 "Essay on Pumpernickel," 132. I reproduce Oram's transcription.

96 "Essay on Pumpernickel," 132 (emphasis mine).

97 "Essay on Pumpernickel," 133.

98 On Becky's demonic sexuality contrasted with Amelia's domestic love, see DiBattista, "The Triumph of Clytemnestra," 832–33. On the sirens as allegories for artifice, theatricality, and marketplace lure, in contrast to domestic purity, see Fisher, "Siren and Artist."

99 E.g., in a key example of counterfactual history: Trevelyan, "If Napoleon Had Won the Battle of Waterloo" (1907). Gallagher considers famous mentions of Napoleon in Hegel and Tolstoy in "What Would Napoleon Do?" On Becky and Napoleon, see Daleski, *Unities*, 18–26; Fleishman, *Fiction and the Ways of Knowing*; Lougy, "Vision and Satire"; Fraser, "Pernicious Casuistry"; Hagan, "A Note on the Napoleonic Background of *Vanity Fair*"; Harden, "The Fields of Mars in *Vanity Fair*," 125–26; Gilmour, *Idea of the Gentleman*, 61–64; Marks, "'Mon Pauvre

Prisonnier'"; Hammond, "Thackeray's Waterloo," 34–35. On historical actors in Thackeray's fictional worlds, see Bonaparte, "Written in Invisible Ink," 150.

100 Rawls, *Theory of Justice*, 370–71.

101 Thackeray may be drawing on Watts's project "to lay a foundation for those *rules* which may guide and regulate our conceptions of things" (*Logic*, 75). On Watts and Thackeray, see Colby, *Thackeray's Canvass of Humanity*, 17–22.

102 E.g., *Letters*, 2:633 (to John Douglas Cook, 8 January 1850).

103 Sutherland claims Thackeray had to "oust [Becky] altogether as a narrator": her "co-authorial relationship" had to be revised to produce "a more sophisticated telling and a broader frame of reference" (*Thackeray at Work*, 32–33; "Expanding Narrative," 152, 154).

104 This moment of unstable omniscience is related to Thackeray's tactic of "frequently mov[ing] toward an act of psychological exploration … only to invite us to witness how quickly he then moves away from it" in a "facetious leap back to … social surface" (Scarry, "Enemy and Father," 153). For a critique of the traditional view that Thackeray's narrator is a "historian," aiming at "truth" and properly "omniscient," see Wilkinson, "The Tomeavesian Way of Knowing the World," 374–76.

105 Rosdeitcher, "Empires at Stake," 412, 420.

106 On the opportunism behind Becky's amorous exploits and gambling ventures, see Miller, *Novels behind Glass*, 39–40.

107 Lougy discusses an alternative to the fair (memories of childhood and transport to a less artificial time of life), which Becky is denied ("Vision and Satire," 263–66). Scarry notes how Becky's only version of memory is the recollection of prophecy ("Enemy and Father," 148). McMaster notes her "independence of the past" that guards objects for "future usefulness" ("Thackeray's Things," 82, 83).

108 Ferris argues that Thackeray thus attempts to resist temporality and death ("Realism and the Discord of Ending," 297–300).

109 On the reticence of such remorse, see Redwine, "The Uses of Memento Mori in *Vanity Fair*," 660–61.

110 *Novels behind Glass*, 40.

111 As Garrett-Goodyear puts it, Amelia is a type of Thackerayan character: "too ready to translate situations into incompatible alternatives or intolerable extremes," confirming "ambivalent passions and contradictory emotional drives" as key to his view of human nature ("Stylized Emotions, Unrealized Selves," 179).

112 On *Henry Esmond*'s voice and autobiographical memory, see Dames, *Amnesiac Selves*, 157–64.

113 On counterfactuals and military history, see Gallagher, *Telling It like It Wasn't*, 26–47.

114 McMaster, *Thackeray*, 24–29.

115 "On Half a Loaf," in *Roundabout Papers* (*OxT*, 17:559). See Favret, *War at a Distance*.

116 Sutherland, *Thackeray at Work*, 38, 35. Sutherland labels *Vanity Fair* a "transitional work" because of its complex composition and publishing history ("Expanding Narrative").

117 The anonymous novel is both counterfactual history and romance plot, describing "the invasion of southern England by a nameless foreign power in an unspecified present" (Grenby, *The Anti-Jacobin Novel*, 29). See Higgins, "Invasion Panics."

118 War in the novel is a matter of "jokes, songs, distant noises" (Carey, *Thackeray*, 194).

119 *Little Roadside Travels and Sketches* II, "Ghent – Bruges" (*OxT*, 6:495, 496). Compare "An Invasion of France," in *The Paris Sketchbook* (*OxT*, 2:7).

120 On unconfirmed information and financial uncertainty pre-Waterloo, and the similar instability of the 1840s, see Hammond, "Thackeray's Waterloo," 25–26.

121 Barnaby points to similar statements in *Henry Esmond* as critical of historiography's ideological complicity ("Thackeray as Metahistorian," 48). For different accounts of Thackeray's relation to war and its cultural uses, see Carey, *Thackeray*, 99–100; Hammond, "Thackeray's Waterloo"; Heffernan, "Lying Epitaphs"; Norton, "Colonialism in the Empire of *Vanity Fair*," 128–29; Schad, "Reading the Long Way Round."

122 For Rosdeitcher the link between war and gambling underlines the tension between economics and national identity ("Empires at Stake," 416, 421–26).

123 *Letters*, 4:154 (to Mrs. Carmichael-Smyth, 1 October 1859).

124 See Taube, "Thackeray and the Reminiscential Vision"; Loofborouw, *Thackeray and the Form of Fiction*, 206–11; Carey, *Thackeray*, 125–49; Sudrann, "Thackeray and the Use of Time"; McMaster, *Thackeray*, 39, 56–61; Oram, "Time, Memory, and Repetition in Thackeray's *Roundabout Papers*." Arguments about Thackeray and memory often see him as anticipating Proust: Ray, *Thackeray*, 1:407–8; Carey, *Thackeray*, 82; Sudrann, "Thackeray and the Use of Time," 372, 375; McMaster, "Thackeray's Things," 52–53.

125 "On a Joke I Once Heard from the Late Thomas Hood," in *Roundabout Papers* (*OxT*, 17:460); "On the Benefits of Being a Fogy," in *The Proser* (*OxT*, 8:358). *Roundabout Papers* are hereafter cited by individual title.

126 McMaster, *Thackeray*, 35.

127 "Proposals for a Continuation of *Ivanhoe*" (*OxT*, 10:469).

128 "Proposals for a Continuation of *Ivanhoe*" (*OxT*, 10:469).

129 McMaster, *Thackeray*, 35.

130 "On Some Late Great Victories" (*OxT*, 17:395).

131 "Thorns in the Cushion" (*OxT*, 17:397).

132 "On Two Roundabout Papers Which I Intended to Write" (*OxT*, 17:526).

133 "On Two Roundabout Papers Which I Intended to Write" (*OxT*, 17:528).

134 See "Going to See a Man Hanged" (*OxT*, 3:189–205) and "The Case of Peytel," in *The Paris Sketch Book* (*OxT*, 2:251–79).

135 "On Two Roundabout Papers Which I Intended to Write" (*OxT*, 17:531).

136 The event occurred on Northumberland Street in 1861 (Harden, *Annotations*, 2:490).

137 "On Two Roundabout Papers Which I Intended to Write" (*OxT*, 17:529).

138 "On Two Roundabout Papers Which I Intended to Write" (*OxT*, 17:529–30).

139 "De Juventute," "A Roundabout Journey: Notes of a Week's Holiday" (*OxT*, 17:422, 455). These moments exemplify a mnemonic pattern Dames describes: "pivotal moments of private biography" are solidified through "public facts about the famous" ("Brushes with Fame," 46; see 46–48). Compare *Little Roadside Travels and Sketches* I, "Antwerp" (*OxT*, 6:476–77); and another comment about being "[b]odily ... in 1860 ... but in the spirit ... walking about in 1828" ("A Roundabout Journey: Notes of a Week's Holiday," *OxT*, 17:440).

140 The mediating character of the coin is intensified by Thackeray's many jibes at the emptiness of George IV, mocked in *Vanity Fair* (473–74) and derided as a "great simulacrum" in *The Four Georges* ("George the Fourth," 386). See Barnaby, "Thackeray as Metahistorian," 52–53.

141 "De Juventute" (*OxT*, 17:424–25). In "Memorials of Gormandizing," Thackeray terms "yesterday" the "philosopher's property," and discusses how memory eclipses present experience (Sudrann, "Thackeray and the Use of Time," 374–75).

142 "De Juventute" (*OxT*, 17:427). Thackeray alludes to Horace, *Odes* II, xix.

143 "De Juventute" (*OxT*, 17:435).

144 The Teutonic syntax of these sentences may indicate a German background. Thackeray was fond of quoting the dedication to *Faust*, where likewise "many dear familiar shades emerge" (*Faust*, 1); see *Morning Chronicle*, 179–80.

145 *The History of Henry Esmond*, 182.

146 *The Kickleburys on the Rhine* (*OxT*, 10:279).

147 "De Finibus" (*OxT*, 17:598).

148 On the ambivalence of this conclusion compare Oram, "Time, Memory, and Repetition in Thackeray's *Roundabout Papers*," 162–64.

149 "The Last Sketch" (*OxT*, 17:374). Quoting this essay, Fletcher discusses the aesthetic result of this "sense of the contingency of things past" ("The Dandy and the Fogy," 395). On the conundrums of ending(s) in Thackeray, see Stewart, *Death Sentences*, 131–36, and "Signing Off," 120–24; Ferris, "Realism and the Discord of Ending"; Fletcher, "The Dandy and the Fogy," 385–88.

150 Thackeray was obsessed with the *Arabian Nights*. He owned two editions (*Catalogue*) and wrote a tale in two parts, "Sultan Stork. Being the One Thousand and Second Night" (1842) (*OxT*, 4:181–98). Schad mentions Scheherazade in discussing *Vanity Fair* and reading as the "studied circumvention of a private sadness," a detour "around death" ("Reading the Long Way Round," 30, 31). DiBattista, calling these tales Thackeray's "primary text of childhood," links Becky to Scheherazade and the "sexual subjugation of women" ("The Triumph of Clytemnestra," 837n6).

151 "On Some Carp at Sans Souci" (*OxT*, 17:632).
152 "On Some Carp at Sans Souci" (*OxT*, 17:632–33).
153 "On Some Carp at Sans Souci" (*OxT*, 17:633).
154 "On Some Carp at Sans Souci" (*OxT*, 17:634).
155 "On a Pear-Tree" (*OxT*, 17:609).
156 "Dessein's" (*OxT*, 17:619).
157 Thackeray, *Letters*, 4:225 (to J. F. Boyes, March 1861). Quoted in Oram, "Time, Memory, and Repetition in Thackeray's *Roundabout Papers*," 157.
158 Dames, *Amnesiac Selves*, 125–38, 148–66.
159 *The History of Pendennis*, Dedication, 2:319, 2:24.
160 For this phrase, see "A Brother of the Press on the History of a Literary Man, Laman Blanchard, and the Chances of the Literary Profession" (*OxT*, 6:549).
161 Dames, *Amnesiac Selves*, 166.
162 "Autour de Mon Chapeau" (*OxT*, 17:643).
163 Ferris, *Thackeray*, 117.
164 Ray tracks the contrast in tone between Thackeray's 1837–39 journalism and that of the period 1844–47, preceding *Vanity Fair* (Ray, *Thackeray*, 1:318).
165 By this novel tone has "taken precedence over narrative," McMaster notes, just as the *Roundabout Papers* are "all tone and no narrative" (*Thackeray*, 4). Kurnick ingeniously assesses this feature of *Lovel the Widower* as a failed play, whose "melancholic relation to the lost possibility of performance" leads to "novelistic interiority ... as a container for unaccommodated theatricality" (*Empty Houses*, 32; see 56–66).
166 *Lovel the Widower* (*OxT*, 17:57). Hereafter cited parenthetically.
167 Thackeray may have encountered the translation of Le Sage's novel now established as Tobias Smollett's, *The Devil upon Crutches* (1750, revised 1759), and may also be taking a swipe at Edward Bulwer-Lytton's *Asmodeus at Large*. Thackeray mentions Le Sage alongside Fielding in "A Box of Novels" (*OxT*, 6:413).
168 See Thackeray, *The History of Pendennis*, 1:291, and *The Adventures of Philip*, 280. Jaffe discusses Asmodeus as a model for Dickens's narrators, "remaining present in their narratives but often, effectively, invisible, gaining the advantages but not the limitations of characterological status" ("Omniscience in *Our Mutual Friend*," 95).
169 Byrne, *Rational Imagination*, 34–35, 48–49.
170 Ferris, "The Breakdown of Thackeray's Narrator," 45; Sedgwick, *Epistemology of the Closet*, 191.
171 Ferris, "The Breakdown of Thackeray's Narrator," 38.
172 McMaster describes the pattern of hesitation and action in the successive personas (Titmarsh, Touchit, Batchelor) and compares it to other characters (Dobbin, Warrington, Esmond) who obsess over a woman won by another man (*Thackeray*, 53–56).
173 Morson, *Narrative and Freedom*, 189.
174 Ferris, "Realism and the Discord of Ending," 297. The novel takes to an extreme the patterns of earlier novels, with their "blend of inquiry and

provisional assertion, heuristic in their project to reassess the significance of human action" (Fletcher, "The Dandy and the Fogy," 385).

175 On the mirror topos, see Brink-Roby, "Psyche: Mirror and Mind in *Vanity Fair.*"

176 See Morson, *Narrative and Freedom*, 190–98.

177 *Letters*, 596 (to George Smith, 21 December [1859]).

178 Ferris best describes Batchelor's diffuse style, but draws an unneeded extrapolation to the fragmentation of self and language, arguing that Thackeray cannot disentangle himself from a narratorial surrogate: "technique has opened up the self for investigation and found nothing there"; "Despair vitiates the explorative potential of the late narratives" ("The Breakdown of Thackeray's Narrator," 52). Fisher comments on the aesthetic lassitude of Thackeray's late work, blaming it on the corrupting influence of market demands ("Siren and Artist"). Others liken *Lovel* to the *Roundabout Papers*: James, "Story and Substance in *Lovel the Widower*"; Horn, "Farcical Process, Fictional Product."

179 Kurnick, *Empty Houses*, 29–66.

180 On the narrator's assumed name in the context of nineteenth-century sexual categories, see Sedgwick, *Epistemology of the Closet*, 189–95; Kurnick, *Empty Houses*, 60.

181 Discussing *Lovel*'s composition, Harden points out that the manuscript makes Pendennis the narrator, which adds another layer (*The Emergence of Thackeray's Serial Fiction*, 220–40). Ferris comments on the recurrence of characters as a "preference for the openness of continuity over the closural notion of meaning" ("Realism and the Discord of Ending," 300). She also notes this feature of *Lovel* ("The Breakdown of Thackeray's Narrator," 40).

182 *Our Street* (*OxT*, 10:89, 83).

183 *The Kickleburys on the Rhine* (*OxT*, 10:244).

184 *The Kickleburys on the Rhine* (*OxT*, 10:249).

185 Byerly, *Realism, Representation, and the Arts in Nineteenth-Century Literature*, 60–62; Dames, *Physiology of the Novel*, 121; see generally 73–122.

186 *Lovel the Widower* (*OxT*, 17:138).

187 James, "Winchilsea, Rye, and *Denis Duval*" (in *Literary Criticism*, 1290). Sutherland agrees there is "nothing tired about [*Denis Duval*], it promises in fact a recovery in age of the powers of youth" (*Thackeray at Work*, 110).

188 *Letters*, 3:399 (to William Bradford Reed, 8 November 1854).

189 *Vanity Fair*, 190.

190 *Letters*, 4:303 (Anne Thackeray to Mrs. Baxter, 24 October 1864).

Chapter 4

1 *Far from the Madding Crowd*, 84.

2 *A Laodicean*, 139.

3 *Tess of the d'Urbervilles*, 23.

4 *The Mayor of Casterbridge,* 123.

5 See Morson, *Narrative and Freedom.*

6 For work on Hardy and chance, especially in scientific contexts, see Ebbatson, *Evolutionary Self,* 15–16; Robinson, "Hardy and Darwin"; Wickens, "Literature and Science"; Morrell, "Hardy, Darwin and Nature"; Beer, *Darwin's Plots,* 236–58, and "Reader's Wager"; Dessner, "Space, Time, and Coincidence in Hardy"; Monk, *Standard Deviations,* 157–66; Richardson, "Hardy and Biology"; Faulkner, "Coincidence, Causality, and Hardy's Inconsistent Inconsistency"; Richardson, "Hardy and Science"; Ortiz-Robles, "Hardy's Wessex and the Natural History of Chance"; Grener, *Improbability,* 149–73.

7 *Letters,* 3:69–70 (to James Murray, 9 July 1903).

8 *Letters,* 1:189 (to Lady Grove, 9 April 1898).

9 *Letters,* 2:130 (to Florence Henniker, 24 September 1896).

10 *Life,* 300. These details of a gambling Englishman echo a text Hardy owned (Polson, *Monaco and Its Gaming Tables,* 37).

11 *Life,* 300.

12 On Venn and the frequency theory, see Salmon, "John Venn's Logic of Chance"; Hacking, *Emergence,* 53–54, and *Taming of Chance,* 126–27; Eden, *Evolutionary Logic of Chance*; Wall, "John Venn's Opposition to Probability as Degree of Belief"; Verburgt, "John Venn's Hypothetical Infinite Frequentism and Logic."

13 See Eden, *Evolutionary Logic of Chance,* 2–5 (noting that frequentism relied on universals like species, genus, kind, and class).

14 *Logic of Chance,* vii.

15 Wall, "John Venn, James Ward, and the Chair of Mental Philosophy and Logic at the University of Cambridge." Both editions were reviewed in the *Saturday Review* and *Westminster Review*; the first was also noted in the *Athenæum* and *Reader*; the second, more extensively, in the *London Quarterly Review* and the *British Quarterly Review.*

16 *Logic of Chance,* 4.

17 *Logic of Chance,* 5.

18 Eden notes Venn's rejection of Bernoulli's theorem (adapted by Laplace and Poisson), an objective account positing a "link between the probability of a single event and limiting frequencies" (*Evolutionary Logic of Chance,* 23). See Laplace, *Essai philosophique sur les probabilités*; Quetelet, *Sur l'homme*; Poisson, *Recherches sur la probabilité des jugements.* On Quetelet's concept of "statistical law" and its warm reception in Britain, see Porter, *Rise of Statistical Thinking,* 5–6, 40–70, 100–109.

19 Tennyson, *Major Works,* LV, ll. 7–8.

20 *Logic of Chance,* 13–14.

21 *Logic of Chance,* 74; see 74–95.

22 *Logic of Chance,* 95. See Daston, *Classical Probability,* 33–36, 49–111, 218–23. Daston discusses those who wanted to reduce uncertainty to a calculus, "a mathematical rendering of pragmatic rationality" (108), according

to the classical "creed" wherein "all events are necessary, so probabilities measure the partial certainty upon which we ill-formed mortals must ground rational belief and action" (35).

23 *Logic of Chance*, x. Venn calls such accounts *formal* or *conceptualist*: they see probability as a matter of "formal inferences in which the premises are entertained with a conviction short of absolute certainty" (ix).

24 *Logic of Chance*, 40.

25 *Logic of Chance*, 54, 63–64.

26 *Logic of Chance*, 94.

27 *Logic of Chance*, 67.

28 *Logic of Chance*, 76.

29 *Logic of Chance*, 140; see 119–66 for his critique of subjective probability and measurement of belief. Venn likewise resists inverse probability (179–86), as discussed by De Morgan, because its artificial experiments (predicting draws from an urn) are unlike the regularities of ordinary inference. See Wall, "John Venn's Opposition to Probability as Degree of Belief." On the language of belief in Venn's discipline, see Cohen, "Reasoning and Belief in Victorian Mathematics" and *Equations from God*, 1–13.

30 *Logic of Chance*, 125, 156.

31 Venn, *Characteristics of Belief*, 11.

32 *Logic of Chance*, 126–27.

33 Venn, *Characteristics of Belief*, 6.

34 *Logic of Chance*, 127; *Characteristics of Belief*, 14.

35 For related accounts, see Scarry, *Resisting Representation*, 49–90; Ward, "*The Woodlanders* and the Cultivation of Realism."

36 *A Laodicean*, 286. Commenting on the use of De Moivre's probability theory, Richardson notes Hardy's "analogy between sexual relationships and games" ("Hardy and Science," 160). See also Kolb, "Plot Circles," 602–4.

37 *A Laodicean*, 286–87.

38 "If upon the happening of an Event, I be entitled to a Sum of Money, my Expectation of obtaining that Sum has a determinate value before the happening of the Event" (De Moivre, *Doctrine of Chances*, 2).

39 *A Laodicean*, 287.

40 *A Laodicean*, 287.

41 *A Laodicean*, 283.

42 *Logic of Chance*, 149.

43 For Grener, also drawing on Venn's theory, the novel's "improbable aesthetic cultivates a historicist perspective attuned to ... problems of causality" in the wake of evolutionary thought – an aesthetic that emphasizes contingency and "attests ... to the absence of transhistorical structures of order" (*Improbability*, 154).

44 *The Return of the Native*, 279. Hereafter cited parenthetically.

45 *OED*, s.v. "guinea."

46 Eiland and Jennings, "On Some Motifs in Baudelaire," 330: "The jolt in the movement of a machine is like the so-called *coup* in a game of chance."

47 Bailey notes that the die is broken by a "natural cause" but still reads the event in magical terms where Venn is the "natural means through which the supernatural works" ("Hardy's 'Mephistophelian Visitants,'" 1155n46). Compare Langbaum, *Thomas Hardy in Our Time*, 100–102.

48 Beer, "Reader's Wager," 120, 121; see 118–22.

49 Beer sees gambling and reading as "acts of desire whose longing is to possess and settle the future, but whose pleasure is in active uncertainty" (111).

50 Small, "Chances Are," 80.

51 Small, "Chances Are," 80.

52 Small, "Chances Are," 80–81.

53 See Small, "Chances Are," 70–71 (on Venn's devaluing of psychology). Small mentions an "insistence on objectivity," but for Venn there is "really nothing which we can with propriety call an objective probability" (*Logic of Chance*, 91).

54 Grener, *Improbability*, 170–71.

55 De Moivre, *Doctrine of Chances*, vii (emphasis removed).

56 *Barchester Towers*, 143–44.

57 On Diggory and other demonic tricksters, see Bailey, "Hardy's 'Mephistophelian Visitants,'" 1156–65.

58 On Hardy's attentiveness to the senses in this novel, see Coombs, "Reading in the Dark."

59 Clym's face is "singular" (194) in its thoughtfulness and he is described as "invading some region of singularity" (226); Wildeve's "grace of . . . movement was singular" (93). Venn is associated with singular figures like the devil, the first murderer (reddle "stamps unmistakably, as with the mark of Cain, any person who has handled it" [131]), and the last of an extinct species (the dodo).

60 Lawrence, *Study of Thomas Hardy*, 24.

61 *Far from the Madding Crowd*, 145.

62 Barrell, "Geographies of Hardy's Wessex," 106.

63 *OED*, s.v. "blank," def. 4.

64 Reading material attrition in *The Woodlanders*, Ward links polishing, finishing, and varnishing to cultivation, noting that "effacement is always on the other side of polish" ("*The Woodlanders* and the Cultivation of Realism," 874).

65 Sanderson was an early figure in the area of probability concerned with subjective judgments; see Stigler, "Who Discovered Bayes's Theorem?"

66 On Nebo and the "Pisgah sight," see Landow, *Victorian Types, Victorian Shadows*, 201–31.

67 I draw the idea of spatial prophecy from John Berger; see Soja, *Postmodern Geographies*, 21–24.

68 *Topographies*, 38, 43.

69 *Life*, 56.

70 On the heath, see Hornback, *Metaphor of Chance*, 17–23; Gregor, *Great Web*, 81–85; Fleishman, *Fiction and the Ways of Knowing*, 110–22; Miller, *Topographies*, 19–56; Barrell, "Geographies of Hardy's Wessex"; Cohen, "Faciality and Sensation," 446–47; Bullen, "Imaginative Geography."

71 Miller, *Topographies*, 33.

72 Miller, *Topographies*, 21.

73 On Hardy's scalar alternation, see Lodge, "Thomas Hardy and Cinematographic Form"; Alcorn, *Nature Novel*, 9–11; Gregor, *Great Web*, 108.

74 Bailey reads Venn as "symbolic," "typifying a force" ("Hardy's 'Mephistophelian Visitants,'" 1150–55). For Cohen, he represents the "collapse of external world and sensate individual" ("Faciality and Sensation," 448).

75 Herman, "Hypothetical Focalization." Critics have ascribed various functions to such hypotheticals: they prompt readers to perform the mental feat of suspending "general knowledge to discover the local" (Barrell, "Geographies of Hardy's Wessex," 114); offer narrative surrogates for Hardy's "real self-consciousness about his presence on the scene" in society (Grossman, "Thomas Hardy and the Role of Observer," 636); embody his wider use of speculative syntax (Pane, "The Unreal Path to a Real Place," 67–73); and paradoxically "foreground the embodied, situated nature of perception while also abstracting the action from its immediate context," inscribing a tension between contingent social milieus and "underlying historical continuities" (Grener, *Improbability*, 163, 154).

76 Herman, "Hypothetical Focalization," 232, 237.

77 *Logic of Chance*, 8.

78 The note is often read as expressing Hardy's "continuing disturbance" about the demands of serial publication, his "genuine uncertainty about what does constitute the appropriate ending" (Dalziel, "Anxieties of Representation," 110; Gregor, *Great Web*, 105).

79 "Composite Portraits," 132–33.

80 "Composite Portraiture," 140; "Composite Portraits," 132.

81 "Composite Portraits," 134, 135. On Galton's composites, see Hacking, *Taming of Chance*, 180–88; Porter, *Rise of Statistical Thinking*, 139–40; Pearl, *About Faces*, 186–212.

82 "Composite Portraits," 141. For discussions of Galton's contributions to statistical theory, including his notorious eugenic commitments, see MacKenzie, *Statistics in Britain*, 15–18, 51–72; Porter, *Rise of Statistical Thinking*, 128–46, 270–96; Stigler, *History of Statistics*, 265–99; Goldman, *Victorians and Numbers*, 257–95.

83 See Ginzburg, "Family Resemblances and Family Trees"; Hookway, "Pragmatism, Ideas, and Schematism." Galton's peers already saw the link: Minto describes the "mental picturing" involved in concept formation and suggests parallels to composites (*Logic*, 126–29).

84 "Composite Portraits," 140.

85 "Generic Images," 158.

86 "Generic Images," 158.

87 "Generic Images," 167.

88 "Generic Images," 168, 158.

89 Hardy took notes on a *Spectator* review of Galton's book, which summarizes composite photography (*Literary Notebooks*, 1:154–55; *Inquiries*, 8–19, 354–63). Another curious connection: Hardy and Galton received readings from the same phrenologist (Richardson, "Hardy and Science," 163). For Hardy and the science of heredity, see Ebbatson, *Evolutionary Self*, 25–26; Richardson, "Heredity."

90 On the human face in Hardy, see Bullen, *Expressive Eye*, 97–98; Tytler, "Physiognomy in Thomas Hardy's Fiction"; Cohen, "Faciality and Sensation."

91 *Collected Short Stories*, 417. Hereafter cited parenthetically.

92 Galton, "Composite Portraiture," 145.

93 *Collected Poems*, ll. 1–6. For a discussion of various nineteenth-century overlay techniques that also mentions Hardy's poem in the context of Galton's work, see Emmott, "Parameters of Vibration, Technologies of Capture," 473–77.

94 Unsigned review, *Saturday Review* (1886), in Cox, *Hardy: The Critical Heritage*, 143; Howells, "Editor's Study," 962.

95 Vigar, *Illusion and Reality*, 165; Grossman, "Thomas Hardy and the Role of Observer," 619. Calling her Hardy's "most objective observer" (619), Grossman likens Elizabeth-Jane (in more general terms) to Venn and his "effective observation from a distance," noting their shared "perspicacity [that] lies in the ability to calculate what kind of action best suits what they observe" (632).

96 *The Mayor of Casterbridge*, 32. Hereafter cited parenthetically.

97 Noting how her mind almost merges with "authorial consciousness of the veiled narrator," Gregor reads this scene as forging Elizabeth-Jane as a shrewd interpreter with "sympathetic detachment" (*Great Web*, 124, 125). Hornback suggests that Hardy uses her to minimize his editorializing tendencies (*Metaphor of Chance*, 112–13).

98 The pressure of the past is a familiar *topos* in Hardy criticism, especially on *The Mayor of Casterbridge*. See Miller, *Distance and Desire*, 96–102, 144–50; Edmond, "'The Past-Marked Prospect'"; Johnson, *True Correspondence*, 76–83; Wolfreys, "Haunted Structures."

99 Langbaum, *Thomas Hardy in Our Time*, 138–40.

100 Gregor points to Elizabeth-Jane's final mediating function in the narrative, both in Henchard's will and in the closing reflections (*Great Web*, 128–29). Vigar observes how Henchard's death is "bounded by the sturdy rationality of [Elizabeth-Jane's] thoughtful realization, in the face of her own unforeseen happiness, that good fortune is not equally distributed among men" (*Illusion and Reality*, 167).

101 Vigar, *Illusion and Reality*, 153; Kolb, "Plot Circles," 598; on Hardy's narrative equipossibility, see 597–605.

102 See Daston, *Classical Probability*, 3–48.

103 Franklin, "'Market-Faces' and Market Forces," 59.

104 *Life*, 29.

105 Baier, "Trust." Compare Baier, "Trust and Antitrust" and "Trusting People."

106 Baier, "Trust," 112, 130.

107 See Lipton's argument about testimonial knowledge on the model of "inference to the best explanation" ("Alien Abduction").

108 Anderson comments on "weather wisdom," in particular, the "visual epistemology associated with popular forms of weather knowledge" and the conflict between such modes and formal scientific knowledge gathered by way of observatories and instruments ("Looking at the Sky," 305–8, 301). See generally Anderson, *Predicting the Weather*.

109 *OED*, s.v. "periodicity." The coinage is Herschel's.
110 "The Function of Criticism at the Present Time," 261.
111 Anderson surveys similar details in *The Mayor of Casterbridge* and *Far from the Madding Crowd*, mentioning a different work by Steinmetz (*Predicting the Weather*, 175–77). Elsewhere, she notes the presence and success of intuitive, traditional forms of weather prophecy in the same two novels, suggesting that such wisdom is akin to what Hardy calls a "flesh-barometer": "As a practical, instant and genuine knowledge . . . weather wisdom operated as a kind of standard for scientific weather prediction – not only for its accuracy, but also as a statement of the way in which useful knowledge emerged from observation" ("Looking at the Sky," 307).
112 *Manual of Weathercasts*, xi. Cited parenthetically in this paragraph.
113 *The Woodlanders*, 23.
114 Anderson, "Looking at the Sky," 308.
115 Unsigned review, *Saturday Review* (1886), in Cox, *Hardy: The Critical Heritage*, 143.
116 "The Just-Perceptible Difference." In contemporary psychology the identical concept is called the "just-noticeable difference"; Dames identifies it in George Meredith's work (*Physiology of the Novel*, 166–206).
117 Ruskin, *Works*, 6:75; Pater, *Studies in the History of the Renaissance*, 120.
118 Hardy, *Literary Notebooks*, 1:162. The statement is from Blanche Leppington's review, "Amiel's Journal," in the *Contemporary Review* (1885).
119 See Hyde, "View of Realism"; Kramer, *Forms of Tragedy*; King, *Tragedy in the Victorian Novel*; Langbaum, "Versions of Pastoral"; Yeazell, *Art of the Everyday*, 125–61; Ward, "*The Woodlanders* and the Cultivation of Realism." Pether writes of Hardy's "generic ferment" ("Sex, Lies and Defamation," 173).
120 Vigar, *Illusion and Reality*, 9.
121 *Realistic Imagination*, 234, 239.
122 Levine, *Dying to Know*, 208, 211.
123 *The English Novel*, 97–116.
124 Widdowson, *Hardy in History*, 17–18, 76. Widdowson shows that Hardy's own novelistic classification and prefatory comments adapt earlier critics on the topic of probability (49–50), and that his comments on art reject realism (159–64). See 70–76, 223–24.
125 Dolin, "On Hardy's Realism, Again," 40–44. Dolin discusses the work of Terry Eagleton, Penny Boumelha, and Noorul Hasan, restating the call for a "critical realism" by taking Hardy's own remarks for realism as a "mode of disenchantment," a "rejection of the conventionalism that marks cultural verisimilitude" (44). He claims that Hardy rejects the "positivism of the naturalists and the facile literality of consumer realism" (49).
126 For instance, Claybaugh disidentifies Hardy with the realist tradition in seeing him as a reformer for the New Woman cause (*Novel of Purpose*, 185–214). Davis sees his agitations for legal reform as emerging from neutral uses of legal themes for plot purposes (*Thomas Hardy and the Law*, 47, 124–25, 164–84).

127 The insistence of these themes, already familiar to critics in Hardy's time, is clearly visible in the index pages of any early study under entries like "accident and coincidence," "chance," "determinism": see Webster, *Darkling Plain*.

128 Hornback, *Metaphor of Chance*, 6. Dessner likewise argues that "probabilities against disconcerting coincidences decrease because a larger number of chances ... have come under surveillance" as space and time are narratively contracted, but he blurs subjective belief with objective frequencies in claiming that Hardy cannot "discriminate between varying degrees of likelihood" ("Space, Time, and Coincidence in Hardy," 162).

129 Hacking, *Taming of Chance*, 12.

130 Gregor, *Great Web*, 27, 46.

131 Preface to *A Laodicean*, January 1896; Preface to *Under the Greenwood Tree*, August 1896; General Preface to the Novels and Poems, Wessex Edition, 1912 (*Personal Writings*, 15, 4, 46).

132 Preface to *The Trumpet-Major*, October 1895; Preface to *The Dynasts*, September 1903 (*Personal Writings*, 13–14, 40). For Hardy the problem in such a historical narrative is to find the "true sequence of events indiscriminately recalled" (14).

133 Preface to *The Hand of Ethelberta*, December 1895 (*Personal Writings*, 11). Compare his comments on this episode in *Life*, 111–12.

134 Preface to *The Hand of Ethelberta*, August 1912 (*Personal Writings*, 12).

135 *Letters*, 1:190 (to Lady Grove, 18 April 1898).

136 *The Mayor of Casterbridge*, 4.

137 *The Mayor of Casterbridge*, 4.

138 Unsigned review, *Saturday Review* (1886), in Cox, *Hardy: The Critical Heritage*, 143.

139 Howells, "Editor's Study," 961. On legal precedents for such a sale, see Davis, *Thomas Hardy and the Law*, 106–14; Suk, "The Moral and Legal Consequences of Wife-Selling in *The Mayor of Casterbridge*."

140 "The Profitable Reading of Fiction" (*Personal Writings*, 117).

141 *Life*, 77.

142 *A Laodicean*, 35; *Under the Greenwood Tree*, 94; *Life*, 76.

143 *Life*, 30.

144 "The Profitable Reading of Fiction" (*Personal Writings*, 117).

145 *Letters*, 1:189 (to Lady Grove, 18 April 1898). This is a familiar apology for fiction – as more abstract than historical particulars, more vivid than philosophical abstractions – from Aristotle to Philip Sidney to Samuel Johnson. Hardy might have found a version in George Campbell's *Philosophy of Rhetoric* (82–85).

146 General Preface to the Novels and Poems, Wessex Edition, 1912 (*Personal Writings*, 44, 45).

147 Preface to *Two on a Tower*, July 1895 (*Personal Writings*, 17); *Letters*, 4:123, 3:285, 3:264, 6:132 (to Norah Acland, A. M. Broadley, Hermann Lea, and Florence Henniker, respectively).

148 Preface to *Desperate Remedies*, February 1896 (*Personal Writings*, 3).

149 *Letters*, 4:210 (to Clement Shorter, [3 April 1912?]).

150 Preface to *A Pair of Blue Eyes*, March 1895 (*Personal Writings*, 7–8).

151 Preface to *A Pair of Blue Eyes*, March 1895, June 1912 (*Personal Writings*, 7, 8). Although Hardy spoke of his "portraiture of fictitiously named towns and villages" as "only suggested by certain real places," he nonetheless – perhaps with a prudent eye on the commercial popularity of "Wessex" – did not discourage "keen hunters for the real" who went looking for correspondences (General Preface to the Novels and Poems, Wessex Edition, 1912 [47]).

152 Preface to *The Return of the Native*, July 1895, April 1912 (*Personal Writings*, 12, 13). Compare Vigar on how the heath "surrounds and incorporates all types and degrees of actuality," so that the "unexpected and the dreamlike contrast vividly with the real and probable" in a whole that has "no single aspect, but is many things at once" (*Illusion and Reality*, 127, 128, 130).

153 *Letters*, 7:163 (to J. H. Fowler, 19 January 1925).

154 "Real Conversations [Interview with William Archer]," 529, 528.

155 *Life*, 50.

156 "The Profitable Reading of Fiction" (*Personal Writings*, 124).

157 "The Profitable Reading of Fiction" (*Personal Writings*, 124–25).

158 "The Science of Fiction" (*Personal Writings*, 138).

159 *Letters*, 5:297 (to the Revd. H. G. B. Cowley, 22 February 1919).

160 "Composite Portraits," 133.

161 Preface to the fifth edition of *Tess of the d'Urbervilles*, July 1892; Preface to *Jude the Obscure*, August 1895 (*Personal Writings*, 27, 32–33).

162 Preface to *Poems of the Past and the Present*, August 1901 (*Personal Writings*, 39).

163 General Preface to the Novels and Poems, Wessex Edition, 1912; Preface to *Jude the Obscure*, August 1895 (*Personal Writings*, 49, 53, 32–33). This need not preclude approaches that emphasize thematic and structural kinship: see Casagrande, *Unity in Hardy's Novels*.

164 Preface to *Jude the Obscure*, August 1895 (*Personal Writings*, 32–33). Compare Ermarth's account of realism (by analogy with painting and geometry) as consensus, where different perspectives are harmonized, identities are "series-dependent" (cognizable only by comparison of partial aspects and particular instances), and realism "insists on the serial expression of truth" (*Realism and Consensus*, 5, 50; see 3–92). For Ermarth, *series* is a purely temporal concept.

165 Preface to *Poems of the Past and the Present*, August 1901 (*Personal Writings*, 38–39). Gregor comments on how such descriptions blend the "unfolding process of event" into "a longer perspective, a hint of pattern," leading to an "always provisional" aesthetic (*Great Web*, 33). Levine summarizes this evasive pronouncement thus: "Art is perhaps the most honest response to the empirical: a setting in order of a set of sensations, not an engagement with the material reality beyond" (*Dying to Know*, 216).

166 *Life*, 158.

167 "The Profitable Reading of Fiction" (*Personal Writings*, 112, 113).

168 *Life*, 199.

169 "The Profitable Reading of Fiction" (*Personal Writings*, 119). Recalling Meredith's comments on the manuscript of his first, never-published novel, *The Poor Man and the Lady*, Hardy was gratified that his "naïve realism in circumstantial details that were pure inventions" was good enough to convince Macmillan and his readers of its "seeming actuality" (*Life*, 63).
170 "The Science of Fiction" (*Personal Writings*, 135).
171 "The Science of Fiction" (*Personal Writings*, 134); *Life*, 239.
172 "The Profitable Reading of Fiction" (*Personal Writings*, 111).
173 "The Profitable Reading of Fiction" (*Personal Writings*, 117).
174 "The Science of Fiction" (*Personal Writings*, 137).
175 Bayley, *Essay on Hardy*, 40.
176 Preface to *Wessex Tales*, April 1896, May 1912 (*Personal Writings*, 22).
177 *Life*, 226.
178 Bayley, *Essay on Hardy*, 4–5.
179 The emphasis on fate in Hardy criticism began early: Rutland, *Study*; Webster, *Darkling Plain*; Cecil, *Hardy the Novelist*. Forster's comment could stand for many later critics: Hardy "arranges the events with emphasis on causality, the ground plan is a plot, and the characters are ordered to acquiesce in its requirements" (*Aspects of the Novel*, 93).
180 Morson, *Narrative and Freedom*, 35; Venn, *Logic of Chance*, 13–14.
181 "The Science of Fiction" (*Personal Writings*, 138).

Coda

1 "Character in Fiction," *Essays of Virginia Woolf, vol. 3: 1919–1924*, 421.
2 Herbert, *Victorian Relativity*, 3.
3 Daston, *Classical Probability*.
4 Quigley, *Modernist Fiction and Vagueness*, 14–20.
5 Porter, *Rise of Statistical Thinking*, 255–319; Stigler, *History of Statistics*, 300–361; Goldman, *Victorians and Numbers*, xx–xxii, 265–66, 278–79.
6 Porter, "Statistics and the Career of Public Reason," 34.
7 Porter, "Statistics and the Career of Public Reason," 35.
8 See Porter, "Statistics and the Career of Public Reason," 34–43.
9 Herbert, *Victorian Relativity*, 10.
10 Hacking, *Taming of Chance*, 10.
11 Porter, *Rise of Statistical Thinking*, 219–27; Hacking, *Taming of Chance*, 200–215.
12 Herbert, *Victorian Relativity*, 10.
13 Goldman, *Victorians and Numbers*, 153; see 267–95.
14 Hacking, *Taming of Chance*, 149.
15 *Political Unconscious*, 211. On the collapse of causality, see Kern, *Modernist Novel*, 62–65, and *Cultural History of Causality*; Herbert, *Victorian Relativity*. On vagueness in logic and philosophy of language, see Quigley, *Modernist Fiction and Vagueness*.

16 Richardson, *Unlikely Stories*, 42, 72.

17 *Einstein's Wake*, 82. On Heisenberg's principle as an extension of "descriptionism," see Whitworth, "The Physical Sciences," 44–45.

18 Whitworth, *Einstein's Wake*, 4; on the centrality of metaphor to his account, see 1–25, 233–234; and on the changed relations between literature and science, see 111–45.

19 On Woolf, see Beer, "Wave Theory and the Rise of Literary Modernism"; Whitworth, *Einstein's Wake*, 153–69; Brown, "Relativity, Quantum Physics, and Consciousness"; Crossland, *Modernist Physics*, 19–69. For additional work on modernism and postclassical physics, see Bohnenkamp, "Post-Einsteinian Physics and Literature"; Albright, *Quantum Poetics*; Thiher, *Fiction Refracts Science*. On modernism and mathematics, see Tubbs, *Mathematics in Twentieth-Century Literature and Art*; Brits, *Literary Infinities*; Rodal, "Patterned Ambiguities"; Engelhardt, *Modernism, Fiction and Mathematics*; Bamford MacKenzie, "Mathematics and Modern Literature." And on logic, see Quigley, *Modernist Fiction and Vagueness*; Blevins and Williams, "Introduction: Logic and Literary Form," 13–15.

20 Whitworth, *Einstein's Wake*, 26–57; see also Bowler, *Science for All*.

21 Herring, *Joyce's Uncertainty Principle*; Chow, "Sifted Science."

22 *Ulysses*, 135. See Choi, "Writing the Victorian City"; Fyfe, *By Accident or Design*.

23 Joyce, *Ulysses*, 217.

24 Schoenbach, *Pragmatic Modernism*, 103. For James and vagueness in relation to pragmatism, see Quigley, *Modernist Fiction and Vagueness*, 21–62.

25 Schoenbach, *Pragmatic Modernism*, 104; on James, see 103–13.

26 Forster, *Howards End*, 234, 51.

27 See Volpicelli, "Modernist Low Vision"; Watt, *Conrad in the Nineteenth Century*, 169–80; Peters, *Conrad and Impressionism*; Wollaeger, *Fictions of Skepticism*.

28 Levine, *Realistic Imagination*, 53.

29 Wollaeger, *Fictions of Skepticism*, 85, 20; Peters, *Conrad and Impressionism*, 6.

30 Whitworth, *Einstein's Wake*, 123. On *The Secret Agent*, see Whitworth, 58–82; Galat, "Joseph Conrad and Scientific Naturalism."

31 Jones, "Modernism and the Marketplace," 105.

32 Conrad, *Chance*, 77. Hereafter cited parenthetically.

33 See James, "The New Novel" (1914), in *Literary Criticism*, 147–53.

34 Jones, "Modernism and the Marketplace," 108.

35 Erdinast-Vulcan, *Modern Temper*, 165.

36 Schwarz, *Conrad: The Later Fiction*, 40–42.

37 See Freud, *Psychopathology of Everyday Life*, in *Standard Edition*, 6:191–216.

38 Hensher, "On *Chance*," 39; James, "The New Novel," in *Literary Criticism*, 152.

39 Hensher, "On *Chance*," 40.

40 Wollaeger, *Fictions of Skepticism*, 182; Erdinast-Vulcan, *Modern Temper*, 172. As Watt notes, "the charge that [*Chance*'s] mode of recital is gratuitously imposed seems itself to be gratuitous" (*Essays on Conrad*, 146; on the critical reception, see 170–73, 179–81). For other negative assessments of the novel, see Schwarz, *Conrad: The Later Fiction*, 40–59; Lothe, *Conrad's Narrative Method*, 21–44.

41 Watt, *Conrad in the Nineteenth Century*, 175–76; Paccaud-Huguet, "Motion That Stands Still."

42 Indeed, I borrow Conrad's epigraph to *Chance* for this book, partly in recognition of his continuities with the Victorian novelists I examine.

43 Levine, *Realistic Imagination*, 47; see 47–54.

44 See Jordan, *Chance and the Modern British Novel* and *Late Modernism and the Avant-Garde British Novel*; Belletto, *No Accident, Comrade*; Serpell, *Seven Modes of Uncertainty*. Serpell looks back to another product of modernist scientific and intellectual contexts – William Empson's *Seven Types of Ambiguity* (1930) – to reclaim *uncertainty* from those hegemonic synonyms that have dominated literary criticism in the twentieth century (*"ambiguity, difficulty, indeterminacy"*) and to probe the ethical stakes of the contemporary novel's "continually thwarted will to know" (18).

45 *Desperate Remedies*, 17.

46 *Desperate Remedies*, 236.

47 *Desperate Remedies*, 17.

Bibliography

Adams, Maeve. "Numbers and Narratives: Epistemologies of Aggregation in British Statistics and Social Realism, c. 1790–1880." In *Statistics and the Public Sphere: Numbers and the People in Modern Britain, c. 1800–2000*, edited by Tom Crook and Glen O'Hara, 103–20. New York: Routledge, 2011.

Aeschylus. *The Oresteia. Agamemnon. The Libation Bearers. The Eumenides.* 3rd ed. Edited by David Grene, Mark Griffith, and Glenn W. Most. Translated by Richard Lattimore. Chicago: University of Chicago Press, 2013.

Agamben, Giorgio. *Potentialities: Collected Essays in Philosophy.* Edited and translated by Daniel Heller-Roazen. Stanford, CA: Stanford University Press, 1999.

Agnew, Lois. "The 'Perplexity' of George Campbell's Rhetoric: The Epistemic Function of Common Sense." *Rhetorica* 18, no. 1 (2000): 79–101.

Ahmed, Sara. *The Promise of Happiness.* Durham, NC: Duke University Press, 2010.

Ainslie, George. *Breakdown of Will.* Cambridge: Cambridge University Press, 2001.

"The Dangers of Willpower." In *Getting Hooked: Rationality and Addiction*, edited by Jon Elster and Ole-Jørgen Skog, 65–92. Cambridge: Cambridge University Press, 1999.

Picoeconomics: The Strategic Interaction of Successive Motivational States within the Person. Cambridge: Cambridge University Press, 1992.

Alborn, Timothy L. *Regulated Lives: Life Insurance and British Society, 1800–1914.* Toronto: University of Toronto Press, 2009.

Alborn, Timothy L., and Sharon Ann Murphy, eds. *Anglo-American Life Insurance, 1800–1914.* 3 vols. London: Pickering & Chatto, 2010.

Albright, Daniel. *Quantum Poetics: Yeats, Pound, Eliot, and the Science of Modernism.* Cambridge: Cambridge University Press, 1997.

Alcorn, John. *The Nature Novel from Hardy to Lawrence.* New York: Columbia University Press, 1977.

Alison, Archibald. *Practice of the Criminal Law of Scotland.* 2 vols. Edinburgh: William Blackwood, 1833.

Allan, Janice M. "A Lock without a Key: Language and Detection in Collins's *The Law and the Lady*." *Clues: A Journal of Detection* 25, no. 1 (2006): 45–57.

Allen, Richard C. *David Hartley on Human Nature*. Albany: SUNY Press, 1999.

Allen, Ronald J., and Michael S. Pardo. "The Problematic Value of Mathematical Models of Evidence." *The Journal of Legal Studies* 36, no. 1 (2007): 1–34.

Anderson, Amanda. *The Powers of Distance: Cosmopolitanism and the Cultivation of Detachment*. Princeton, NJ: Princeton University Press, 2001.

Anderson, Katharine. "Looking at the Sky: The Visual Context of Victorian Meteorology." *The British Journal for the History of Science* 36, no. 3 (2003): 301–32.

   Predicting the Weather: Victorians and the Science of Meteorology. Chicago: University of Chicago Press, 2005.

Anderson, Olive. *Suicide in Victorian and Edwardian England*. Oxford: Clarendon Press, 1987.

Anon. "Du Saulle on Persecution-Madness." *Saturday Review* 33, no. 855 (1872): 341–42.

   "The Habit of Fear." *Saturday Review* 28, no. 731 (1869): 572–73.

   "Home-Office Inspiration." *All the Year Round*, 24 January 1863, 465–68.

   "Not Proven." *The Law Times*, 18 July 1857, 211.

   "[Rev. of] *The Law and the Lady*, by Wilkie Collins." *Examiner*, 10 April 1875, 414–15.

   "[Rev. of] *The Law and the Lady*, by Wilkie Collins." *Saturday Review* 39, no. 1011 (1875): 357–58.

   "The Scotch Verdict of Not Proven." *Law Magazine* 13, no. 25 (1850): 182–99.

Anscombe, G. E. M. *Intention*. 2nd ed. 1963. Reprint, Cambridge, MA: Harvard University Press, 2000.

Aristotle. *The Art of Rhetoric*. Edited and translated by J. H. Freese. Cambridge, MA: Harvard University Press, 1929.

   Politics. Translated by C. D. C. Reeve. Indianapolis: Hackett, 1968.

Armstrong, Isobel. *Novel Politics: Democratic Imaginations in Nineteenth-Century Fiction*. Oxford: Oxford University Press, 2017.

Arnold, Matthew. "The Function of Criticism at the Present Time." In *The Complete Prose Works of Matthew Arnold, vol. 3: Lectures and Essays in Criticism*, edited by R. H. Super, 258–85. Ann Arbor: University of Michigan Press, 1962.

   "Literature and Science." In *The Complete Prose Works of Matthew Arnold, vol. 10: Philistinism in England and America*, edited by R. H. Super, 53–73. Ann Arbor: University of Michigan Press, 1974.

Arnot, Hugo. *A Collection and Abridgement of Celebrated Criminal Trials in Scotland, from A.D. 1536 to 1784*. Edinburgh: William Smellie, 1785.

Ashley, Robert P. "Wilkie Collins and the Detective Story." *Nineteenth-Century Fiction* 6, no. 1 (1951): 47–60.

Ashton, Rosemary. "Mixed and Erring Humanity: George Eliot, G. H. Lewes and Goethe." *George Eliot–George Henry Lewes Studies*, nos. 24–25 (1993): 93–117.

Auerbach, Erich. *Mimesis: The Representation of Reality in Western Literature*. Translated by Willard A. Trask. 1953. Reprint, Princeton, NJ: Princeton University Press, 2003.

Austin, John. *Lectures on Jurisprudence: The Philosophy of Positive Law*. Edited by Robert Campbell. New York: Henry Holt, 1875.

Auyoung, Elaine. *When Fiction Feels Real: Representation and the Reading Mind*. New York: Oxford University Press, 2018.

Babbage, Charles. *An Examination of Some Questions Connected with Games of Chance*. Edinburgh, 1820.

The Ninth Bridgewater Treatise: A Fragment. 1837. 2nd ed. London: John Murray, 1838.

Backscheider, Paula R., ed. *Probability, Time, and Space in Eighteenth-Century Literature*. New York: AMS Press, 1979.

Baier, Annette. "Trust." In *Tanner Lectures on Human Values*. Salt Lake City: University of Utah Press, 1992.

"Trust and Antitrust." *Ethics* 96, no. 2 (1986): 231–60.

"Trusting People." *Philosophical Perspectives* 6 (1992): 137–53.

Bailey, J. O. "Hardy's 'Mephistophelian Visitants.'" *PMLA* 61, no. 4 (December 1946): 1146–84.

Bain, Alexander. *English Composition and Rhetoric: A Manual*. 1866. Reprint, New York: D. Appleton and Co., 1867.

An English Grammar. London: Longman, Green, Longman, Roberts, and Green, 1863.

The Emotions and the Will. 1859. 2nd ed. London: Longmans, Green, 1865.

Baker, Geoffrey. "'I Know the Man': Evidence, Belief, and Character in Victorian Fiction." *Genre* 50, no. 1 (2017): 39–57.

Baker, William. *The George Eliot–George Henry Lewes Library: An Annotated Catalogue of Their Books at Dr. Williams's Library, London*. New York: Garland, 1977.

"George Eliot and Zionism." In *Daniel Deronda: A Centenary Symposium*, edited by Alice Shalvi, 47–63. Jerusalem: Jerusalem Academic Press, 1976.

"George Eliot's Readings in Nineteenth-Century Jewish Historians: A Note on the Background of *Daniel Deronda*." *Victorian Studies* 15, no. 4 (1972): 463–73.

Bal, Mieke. *Narratology: Introduction to the Theory of Narrative*. 3rd ed. Toronto: University of Toronto Press, 2009.

Bamford MacKenzie, Alice. "Mathematics and Modern Literature." *New Left Review* 124 (2020): 107–23.

Bammer, Gabriele, and Michael Smithson, eds. *Uncertainty and Risk: Multidisciplinary Perspectives*. London: Earthscan, 2008.

Bar, Moshe, ed. *Predictions in the Brain: Using Our Past to Generate a Future*. Oxford: Oxford University Press, 2011.

"The Proactive Brain: Using Analogies and Associations to Generate Predictions." *Trends in Cognitive Sciences* 11, no. 7 (2007): 280–89.

Barbato, Joseph M. "Scotland's Bastard Verdict: Intermediacy and the Unique Three-Verdict System." *Indiana International and Comparative Law Review* 15, no. 3 (2015): 543–81.

Barkan, Leonard. "'Living Sculptures': Ovid, Michelangelo, and *The Winter's Tale*." *ELH* 48, no. 4 (1981): 639–67.

Barnaby, Edward T. "Thackeray as Metahistorian, or the Realist *Via Media.*" *Clio* 31, no. 1 (2001): 33–55.

Barrell, John. "Geographies of Hardy's Wessex." In *The Regional Novel in Britain and Ireland, 1800–1990*, edited by K. D. M. Snell, 99–118. Cambridge: Cambridge University Press, 1998.

Barthes, Roland. "The Reality Effect." In *The Rustle of Language*, translated by Richard Howard, 141–48. Berkeley: University of California Press, 1989.

S/Z. Translated by Richard Miller. New York: Hill and Wang, 1974.

Bayley, John. *An Essay on Hardy.* Cambridge: Cambridge University Press, 1978.

"The Pastoral of Intellect." In *Critical Essays on George Eliot*, edited by Barbara Hardy, 199–213. London: Routledge & Kegan Paul, 1970.

Beaty, Jerome. "*Daniel Deronda* and the Question of Unity in Fiction." *Victorian Newsletter* 15 (1959): 16–20.

Beck, Ulrich. *Risk Society: Towards a New Modernity.* Translated by Mark Ritter. London: Sage, 1992.

Becker, George Joseph, ed. *Documents of Modern Literary Realism.* Princeton, NJ: Princeton University Press, 1963.

Beebe, Maurice. "'Visions Are Creators': The Unity of *Daniel Deronda.*" *Boston University Studies in English* 1, no. 3 (1955): 166–77.

Beer, Gillian. *Darwin's Plots: Evolutionary Narrative in Darwin, George Eliot and Nineteenth-Century Fiction.* 1983. 3rd ed. Cambridge: Cambridge University Press, 2009.

"The Reader's Wager: Lots, Sorts, and Futures." *Essays in Criticism* 40, no. 2 (1990): 99–123.

"Wave Theory and the Rise of Literary Modernism." In *Open Fields: Science in Cultural Encounter*, 295–318. Oxford: Oxford University Press, 1996.

Bell, William, and George Ross. *A Dictionary and Digest of the Law of Scotland.* 1838. Reprint, Edinburgh: Bell & Bradfute, 1861.

Belletto, Steven. *No Accident, Comrade: Chance and Design in Cold War American Narratives.* Oxford: Oxford University Press, 2012.

Belsey, Catherine. "Re-Reading the Great Tradition." In *Re-Reading English*, edited by Peter Widdowson, 121–35. London: Methuen, 1982.

Bender, John. "Enlightenment Fiction and the Scientific Hypothesis." *Representations,* no. 61 (1998): 6–28.

"Novel Knowledge: Judgment, Experience, Experiment." In *This Is Enlightenment*, edited by Clifford Siskin and William Warner, 284–300. Chicago: University of Chicago Press, 2010.

Berrios, German E. *The History of Mental Symptoms: Descriptive Psychopathology since the Nineteenth Century.* Cambridge: Cambridge University Press, 1996.

Best, Stephen, and Sharon Marcus. "Surface Reading: An Introduction." *Representations* 108, no. 1 (2009): 1–21.

Bitzer, Lloyd F. "Hume's Philosophy in George Campbell's *Philosophy of Rhetoric.*" *Philosophy & Rhetoric* 2, no. 3 (1969): 139–66.

Blair, Hugh. *Lectures on Rhetoric and Belles-Lettres.* Edited by Harold Harding. 2 vols. 1783. Reprint, Carbondale: Southern Illinois University Press, 1966.

Blevins, Jeffrey, and Daniel Williams. "Introduction: Logic and Literary Form." *Poetics Today* 41, no. 1 (2020): 1–36.

Bohnenkamp, Dennis. "Post-Einsteinian Physics and Literature: Toward a New Poetics." *Mosaic* 22, no. 3 (1989): 19–30.

Bonaparte, Felicia. *Will and Destiny: Morality and Tragedy in George Eliot's Novels*. New York: New York University Press, 1975.

"Written in Invisible Ink: The Deconstruction of History and Historical Narrative in William Makepeace Thackeray's *Henry Esmond*." *Clio* 39, no. 2 (2010): 135–59.

Boninger, David S., Faith Gleicher, and Alan J. Strathman. "Counterfactual Thinking: From What Might Have Been to What May Be." *Journal of Personality and Social Psychology* 67, no. 2 (1994): 297–307.

Boole, George. *An Investigation of the Laws of Thought, on Which Are Founded the Mathematical Theories of Logic and Probabilities*. London: Macmillan, 1854. *Studies in Logic and Probability*. New York: Dover, 2012.

Booth, Wayne C. *The Rhetoric of Fiction*. 2nd ed. Chicago: University of Chicago Press, 1983.

Bowler, Peter J. *Science for All: The Popularization of Science in Early Twentieth-Century Britain*. Chicago: University of Chicago Press, 2009.

Braddon, Mary Elizabeth. *An Open Verdict*. 3 vols. Leipzig: Bernard Tauchnitz, 1878.

Brantlinger, Patrick. "Nations and Novels: Disraeli, George Eliot, and Orientalism." *Victorian Studies* 35, no. 3 (1992): 255–75.

"What Is 'Sensational' about the 'Sensation Novel'?" *Nineteenth-Century Fiction* 37, no. 1 (1982): 1–28.

Bratman, Michael. *Faces of Intention: Selected Essays on Intention and Agency*. Cambridge: Cambridge University Press, 1999.

Intention, Plans, and Practical Reason. Stanford, CA: Center for the Study of Language and Information, 1999.

"Reflection, Planning, and Temporally Extended Agency." *The Philosophical Review* 109, no. 1 (2000): 35–61.

Bray, Samuel. "Not Proven: Introducing a Third Verdict." *University of Chicago Law Review* 72, no. 4 (2005): 1299–329.

Briefel, Aviva. "Cosmetic Tragedies: Failed Masquerade in Wilkie Collins's *The Law and the Lady*." *Victorian Literature and Culture* 37, no. 2 (2009): 463–81.

Brink-Roby, Heather. "Psyche: Mirror and Mind in *Vanity Fair*." *ELH* 80, no. 1 (2013): 125–47.

Brinker, Menachem. "Farce and the Poetics of the 'Vraisemblable.'" *Critical Inquiry* 9, no. 3 (1983): 565–77.

Brits, Baylee. *Literary Infinities: Number and Narrative in Modern Fiction*. London: Bloomsbury, 2017.

Brooks, Peter. "Clues, Evidence, Detection: Law Stories." *Narrative* 25, no. 1 (2017): 1–27.

Realist Vision. New Haven, CT: Yale University Press, 2005.

Brown, Daniel. "Realism and Sensation Fiction." In *A Companion to Sensation Fiction*, edited by Pamela K. Gilbert, 94–106. Malden, MA: Wiley-Blackwell, 2011.

Brown, Paul Tolliver. "Relativity, Quantum Physics, and Consciousness in Virginia Woolf's *To the Lighthouse.*" *Journal of Modern Literature* 32, no. 3 (2009): 39–62.

Browne, Thomas. *Religio Medici*. Edited by James Winny. Cambridge: Cambridge University Press, 1963.

Bullen, J. B. *The Expressive Eye: Fiction and Perception in the Work of Thomas Hardy*. Oxford: Clarendon Press, 1986.

"The Imaginative Geography of Hardy's *The Return of the Native.*" In *Transits: The Nomadic Geographies of Anglo-American Modernism*, edited by Giovanni Cianci, Caroline Patey, and Sara Sullam, 21–29. New York: Peter Lang, 2010.

Bunzl, Martin. "Counterfactual History: A User's Guide." *The American Historical Review* 109, no. 3 (2004): 845–58.

Burney, Ian. *Poison, Detection, and the Victorian Imagination*. Manchester: Manchester University Press, 2006.

Burton, J. H. *Narratives from Criminal Trials in Scotland*. 2 vols. London: Chapman & Hall, 1852.

Butler, Joseph. *The Analogy of Religion, Natural and Revealed, to the Constitution and Course of Nature*. 1736. 3rd ed. London: Printed for John and Paul Knapton, 1740.

Byerly, Alison. "Effortless Art: The Sketch in Nineteenth-Century Painting and Literature." *Criticism* 41, no. 3 (1999): 349–64.

Realism, Representation, and the Arts in Nineteenth-Century Literature. Cambridge: Cambridge University Press, 1997.

Byrne, Edward. *Probability and Opinion: A Study in the Medieval Presuppositions of Post-Medieval Theories of Probability*. The Hague: Martinus Nijhoff, 1968.

Byrne, Ruth. *The Rational Imagination: How People Create Alternatives to Reality*. Cambridge, MA: MIT Press, 2005.

Campbell, George. *The Philosophy of Rhetoric*. Edited by Lloyd F. Bitzer. 1776. Reprint, Carbondale: Southern Illinois University Press, 1998.

Campe, Rüdiger. *The Game of Probability: Literature and Calculation from Pascal to Kleist*, translated by Ellwood H. Wiggins, Jr. Stanford, CA: Stanford University Press, 2012.

Cantor, Geoffrey, and Sally Shuttleworth, eds. *Science Serialized: Representations of the Sciences in Nineteenth-Century Periodicals*. Cambridge, MA: MIT Press, 2004.

Carey, John. *Thackeray: Prodigal Genius*. London: Faber and Faber, 1977.

Caron, James. "The Rhetoric of Magic in *Daniel Deronda.*" *Studies in the Novel* 15, no. 1 (1983): 1–9.

Carpenter, Mary Wilson. *George Eliot and the Landscape of Time: Narrative Form and Protestant Apocalyptic History*. Chapel Hill: University of North Carolina Press, 1986.

Carpenter, William B. "On the Doctrine of Human Automatism." *Contemporary Review* 25 (1875): 397–416.

"The Physiology of the Will." *Contemporary Review* 17 (1871): 192–217.

Carrithers, David. "The Enlightenment Science of Society." In *Inventing Human Science: Eighteenth-Century Domains*, edited by Christopher Fox, Roy Porter, and Robert Wokler, 232–70. Berkeley: University of California Press, 1995.

Carroll, D. R. "The Unity of *Daniel Deronda*." *Essays in Criticism* 9, no. 4 (1959): 369–80.

Carter, Robert Brudenell. *On the Pathology and Treatment of Hysteria*. London: Churchill, 1853.

Casagrande, Peter J. *Unity in Hardy's Novels: "Repetitive Symmetries."* Lawrence: Regents Press of Kansas, 1982.

Catalogue of the Valuable Library of the Late William Makepeace Thackeray, Esq. London: W. Clowes and Sons, 1864.

Cave, Terence. *Retrospectives: Essays in Literature, Poetics and Cultural History.* Edited by Neil Kenny and Wes Williams. London: Legenda, 2009.

Cavell, Stanley. "The Good of Film." In *Cavell on Film*, edited by William Rothman, 333–48. Albany: SUNY Press, 2005.

Cecil, David. *Hardy the Novelist: An Essay in Criticism*. London: Constable, 1943.

Chandler, James. *An Archaeology of Sympathy: The Sentimental Mode in Literature and Cinema*. Chicago: University of Chicago Press, 2013.

Chang, Hasok. *Is Water H₂O? Evidence, Realism and Pluralism*. Dordrecht: Springer, 2012.

Chase, Cynthia. "The Decomposition of the Elephants: Double-Reading *Daniel Deronda*." *PMLA* 93, no. 2 (1978): 215–27.

Chase, Karen. *Eros & Psyche: The Representation of Personality in Charlotte Brontë, Charles Dickens, and George Eliot*. New York: Methuen, 1984.

Chatman, Seymour. *Story and Discourse: Narrative Structure in Fiction and Film*. Ithaca, NY: Cornell University Press, 1980.

Cheyette, Bryan. *Constructions of "the Jew" in English Literature and Society: Racial Representations, 1875–1945*. Cambridge: Cambridge University Press, 1993.

Choi, Tina Young. *Anonymous Connections: The Body and Narratives of the Social in Victorian Britain*. Ann Arbor: University of Michigan Press, 2016.

Victorian Contingencies: Experiments in Literature, Science, and Play. Stanford, CA: Stanford University Press, 2021.

"Writing the Victorian City: Discourses of Risk, Connection, and Inevitability." *Victorian Studies* 43, no. 4 (2001): 561–89.

Chow, Yi Jean. "Sifted Science: James Joyce's Reference to George Albert Wentworth and George Anthony Hill's *A Text-Book of Physics*." *James Joyce Quarterly* 52, nos. 3–4 (2015): 637–54.

Claggett, Shalyn. "George Eliot's Interrogation of Physiological Future Knowledge." *Studies in English Literature* 51, no. 4 (2011): 849–64.

Clapson, Mark. *A Bit of a Flutter: Popular Gambling and English Society, c. 1823–1961*. Manchester: Manchester University Press, 1992.

Clark, Andy. *Surfing Uncertainty: Prediction, Action, and the Embodied Mind.* New York: Oxford University Press, 2015.

——— "Whatever Next? Predictive Brains, Situated Agents, and the Future of Cognitive Science." *Behavioral and Brain Sciences* 36, no. 3 (2013): 181–204.

Clarke, Edward. "The Detective Case." In *Selected Speeches*, 350–82. London: Smith, Elder, 1908.

Clarke, Edwin, and L. S. Jacyna. *Nineteenth-Century Origins of Neuroscientific Concepts.* Berkeley: University of California Press, 1987.

Claybaugh, Amanda. *The Novel of Purpose: Literature and Social Reform in the Anglo-American World.* Ithaca, NY: Cornell University Press, 2007.

Cleere, Eileen. *Avuncularism: Capitalism, Patriarchy, and Nineteenth-Century English Culture.* Stanford, CA: Stanford University Press, 2004.

Clifford, W. K. "Body and Mind." *Fortnightly Review* 16, no. 96 (1874): 714–36.

Clive, John Leonard. *Not by Fact Alone: Essays on the Writing and Reading of History.* New York: Knopf, 1989.

Clune, Michael W. *A Defense of Judgment.* Chicago: University of Chicago Press, 2021.

Cohen, Daniel J. *Equations from God: Pure Mathematics and Victorian Faith.* Baltimore: Johns Hopkins University Press, 2007.

——— "Reasoning and Belief in Victorian Mathematics." In *The Organisation of Knowledge in Victorian Britain*, edited by Martin Daunton, 139–58. Oxford: Published for the British Academy by Oxford University Press, 2005.

Cohen, I. Bernard. "Scientific Revolutions, Revolutions in Science, and a Probabilistic Revolution 1800–1930." In *The Probabilistic Revolution, vol. 1: Ideas in History*, edited by Lorenz Krüger, Lorraine Daston, and Michael Heidelberger, 23–44. Cambridge, MA: MIT Press, 1987.

Cohen, L. Jonathan. *The Probable and the Provable.* Oxford: Clarendon, 1977.

Cohen, Monica. "From Home to Homeland: The Bohemian in *Daniel Deronda.*" *Studies in the Novel* 30, no. 3 (1998): 31–45.

Cohen, William A. "Faciality and Sensation in Hardy's *The Return of the Native.*" *PMLA* 121, no. 2 (2006): 437–52.

Cohn, Elisha. "Suspending Detection: Collins, Dickens, and the Will to Know." *Dickens Studies Annual* 46 (2015): 253–76.

Colby, Robert A. *Thackeray's Canvass of Humanity: An Author and His Public.* Columbus: Ohio State University Press, 1979.

Coleridge, Samuel Taylor. *Table Talk.* Edited by R. A. Foakes. 2 vols. *The Collected Works of Samuel Taylor Coleridge*, vol. 14. Princeton, NJ: Princeton University Press, 1990.

Collini, Stefan. "Political Theory and the 'Science of Society' in Victorian Britain." *The Historical Journal* 23, no. 1 (1980): 203–31.

Collini, Stefan, Donald Winch, and John Burrow. *That Noble Science of Politics: A Study in Nineteenth-Century Intellectual History.* Cambridge: Cambridge University Press, 1983.

Collins, K. K. "G. H. Lewes Revised: George Eliot and the Moral Sense." *Victorian Studies* 21, no. 4 (1978): 463–92.

"Questions of Method: Some Unpublished Late Essays." *Nineteenth-Century Fiction* 35, no. 3 (1980): 385–405.

Collins, Wilkie. *Armadale*. Edited by John Sutherland. 1866. Reprint, London: Penguin, 1995.

The Law and the Lady. Edited by Jenny Bourne Taylor. 1875. Reprint, Oxford: Oxford University Press, 2008.

The Moonstone. Edited by John Sutherland. 1868. Reprint, Oxford: Oxford University Press, 2008.

No Name. Edited by Virginia Blain. 1862. Reprint, Oxford: Oxford University Press, 2008.

The Public Face of Wilkie Collins: The Collected Letters. Edited by William Baker. 4 vols. London: Pickering & Chatto, 2005.

The Woman in White. Edited by John Sutherland. 1860. Reprint, Oxford: Oxford University Press, 2008.

Colyvan, Mark, Helen M. Regan, and Scott Ferson. "Is It a Crime to Belong to a Reference Class?" *The Journal of Political Philosophy* 9, no. 2 (2001): 168–81.

Conrad, Joseph. *Chance: A Tale in Two Parts*. Edited by Martin Ray. 1914. Reprint, Oxford: Oxford University Press, 2002.

Heart of Darkness: Authoritative Text, Backgrounds and Contexts, Criticism. Edited by Paul B. Armstrong. 1899. Reprint, New York: W. W. Norton, 2017.

Lord Jim: A Tale. Edited by J. H. Stape and Ernest W. Sullivan. 1900. Reprint, Cambridge: Cambridge University Press, 2011.

Coombs, David Sweeney. "Reading in the Dark: Sensory Perception and Agency in *The Return of the Native*." *ELH* 78, no. 4 (2011): 943–66.

Cothran, Casey A. "Mysterious Bodies: Deception and Detection in Wilkie Collins's *The Law and the Lady* and *The Moonstone*." *Victorians Institute Journal* 34 (2006): 193–214.

Cottom, Daniel. *Social Figures: George Eliot, Social History and Literary Representation*. Minneapolis: University of Minnesota Press, 1987.

Cox, R. G., ed. *Thomas Hardy: The Critical Heritage*. London: Routledge & Kegan Paul, 1970.

Craig, Cairns. *Associationism and the Literary Imagination: From the Phantasmal Chaos*. Edinburgh: Edinburgh University Press, 2007.

Crossland, Rachel. *Modernist Physics: Waves, Particles, and Relativities in the Writings of Virginia Woolf and D. H. Lawrence*. Oxford: Oxford University Press, 2018.

Cullen, M. J. *The Statistical Movement in Early Victorian Britain: The Foundations of Empirical Social Research*. Hassocks: Harvester Press, 1975.

Culler, Jonathan. *Structuralist Poetics: Structuralism, Linguistics and the Study of Literature*. Ithaca, NY: Cornell University Press, 1975.

Currie, Gregory. *Narratives and Narrators: A Philosophy of Stories*. Oxford: Oxford University Press, 2010.

Currie, Mark. *The Unexpected: Narrative Temporality and the Philosophy of Surprise*. Edinburgh: Edinburgh University Press, 2013.

Dale, Peter. "Symbolic Representation and the Means of Revolution in *Daniel Deronda*." *Victorian Newsletter* 59 (1981): 25–30.

Daleski, H. M. "Owning and Disowning: The Unity of *Daniel Deronda*." In *Daniel Deronda: A Centenary Symposium*, edited by Alice Shalvi, 67–89. Jerusalem: Jerusalem Academic Press, 1976.

Unities: Studies in the English Novel. Athens: University of Georgia Press, 1985.

Dalziel, Pamela. "Anxieties of Representation: The Serial Illustrations to Hardy's *The Return of the Native*." *Nineteenth-Century Literature* 51, no. 1 (1996): 84–110.

Damaska, Mirjan. "Evidentiary Barriers to Conviction and Two Models of Criminal Procedure: A Comparative Study." *University of Pennsylvania Law Review* 121, no. 3 (1973): 506–89.

Dames, Nicholas. *Amnesiac Selves: Nostalgia, Forgetting, and British Fiction, 1810–1870*. Oxford: Oxford University Press, 2001.

"Brushes with Fame: Thackeray and the Work of Celebrity." *Nineteenth-Century Literature* 56, no. 1 (2001): 23–51.

The Physiology of the Novel: Reading, Neural Science, and the Form of Victorian Fiction. Oxford: Oxford University Press, 2007.

Dannenberg, Hilary P. *Coincidence and Counterfactuality: Plotting Time and Space in Narrative Fiction*. Lincoln: University of Nebraska Press, 2008.

Danziger, Kurt. "Mid-Nineteenth-Century British Psycho-Physiology: A Neglected Chapter in the History of Psychology." In *The Problematic Science: Psychology in Nineteenth-Century Thought*, edited by William R. Woodward and Mitchell G. Ash, 119–46. New York: Praeger, 1982.

Daston, Lorraine. "British Responses to Psycho-Physiology, 1860–1900." *Isis* 69, no. 2 (1978): 192–208.

Classical Probability in the Enlightenment. Princeton, NJ: Princeton University Press, 1988.

"The History of Emergences." *Isis* 98, no. 4 (2007): 801–8.

"How Probabilities Came to Be Objective and Subjective." *Historia Mathematica* 21, no. 3 (1994): 330–44.

"Life, Chance & Life Chances." *Daedalus* 137, no. 1 (2008): 5–14.

"The Theory of Will versus the Science of Mind." In *The Problematic Science: Psychology in Nineteenth-Century Thought*, edited by William R. Woodward and Mitchell G. Ash, 88–115. New York: Praeger, 1982.

David, Deirdre. *Fictions of Resolution in Three Victorian Novels: North and South, Our Mutual Friend, and Daniel Deronda*. New York: Columbia University Press, 1981.

Davis, Lennard J. *Enforcing Normalcy: Disability, Deafness, and the Body*. London: Verso, 1999.

Factual Fictions: The Origins of the English Novel. 1983. Reprint, Philadelphia: University of Pennsylvania Press, 1996.

Davis, William A. *Thomas Hardy and the Law: Legal Presences in Hardy's Life and Fiction*. Newark: University of Delaware Press, 2003.

De Moivre, Abraham. *The Doctrine of Chances: Or, a Method of Calculating the Probability of Events in Play*. 1718. Reprint, London: A. Millar, 1795.

De Morgan, Augustus. *An Essay on Probabilities and on Their Application to Life Contingencies and Insurance Offices*. London: Longman, Orme, Brown, Green, and Longmans, 1838.

"Theory of Probabilities." In *Encylopædia Metropolitana; or Universal Dictionary of Knowledge*, edited by E. Smedley, 2:393–490. 1837. Reprint, London: B. Fellowes, 1845.

"Theory of Probabilities (Part I) [Rev. of *Théorie analytique des probabilités*, by Pierre-Simon Laplace]." *Dublin Review* 2, no. 4 (1837): 338–54.

"Theory of Probabilities (Part II) [Rev. of *Théorie analytique des probabilités*, by Pierre-Simon Laplace]." *Dublin Review* 3, no. 5 (1837): 237–48.

De Quincey, Thomas. "Conversation." In *Selected Essays on Rhetoric*, edited by Frederick Burwick, 264–88. Carbondale: Southern Illinois University Press, 2010.

"Homer and the Homeridæ." In *The Collected Writings of Thomas De Quincey*, edited by David Masson, 6:7–93. Edinburgh: Adam and Charles Black, 1890.

Dear, Peter. *Discipline & Experience: The Mathematical Way in the Scientific Revolution*. Chicago: University of Chicago Press, 1995.

Denisoff, Dennis. "Framed and Hung: Collins and the Economic Beauty of the Manly Artist." In *Reality's Dark Light: The Sensational Wilkie Collins*, edited by Maria K. Bachman and Don Richard Cox, 34–58. Knoxville: University of Tennessee Press, 2003.

Dentith, Simon. "Realist Synthesis in the Nineteenth-Century Novel: 'That Unity Which Lies in the Selection of Our Keenest Consciousness.'" In *Adventures in Realism*, edited by Matthew Beaumont and Rachel Bowlby, 33–49. Malden, MA: Blackwell, 2007.

Dessner, Lawrence Jay. "Space, Time, and Coincidence in Hardy." *Studies in the Novel* 24, no. 2 (1992): 154–72.

DiBattista, Maria. "The Triumph of Clytemnestra: The Charades in *Vanity Fair*." *PMLA* 95, no. 5 (1980): 827–37.

Doležel, Lubomír. *Heterocosmica: Fiction and Possible Worlds*. Baltimore: Johns Hopkins University Press, 1998.

Possible Worlds of Fiction and History: The Postmodern Stage. Baltimore: Johns Hopkins University Press, 2010.

Dolin, Kieran. *Fiction and the Law: Legal Discourse in Victorian and Modernist Literature*. Cambridge: Cambridge University Press, 1999.

Dolin, Tim. "On Hardy's Realism, Again." In *Literature as History: Essays in Honour of Peter Widdowson*, edited by Simon Barker and Jo Gill, 39–52. London: Continuum, 2010.

Douglas, Denis. "Thackeray and the Uses of History." *The Yearbook of English Studies* 5 (1975): 164–77.

Downes, David M. *Gambling, Work and Leisure: A Study across Three Areas*. London: Routledge & Kegan Paul, 1976.

Doyle, Arthur Conan. "Strange Studies from Life." *The Strand Magazine* 21, no. 125 (1901): 481–89.

Duff, David. *Romanticism and the Uses of Genre.* Oxford: Oxford University Press, 2009.

Duff, Peter. "The Not Proven Verdict: Jury Mythology and 'Moral Panics.'" *Juridical Review* 41 (1996): 1–12.

"The Scottish Criminal Jury: A Very Peculiar Institution." *Law and Contemporary Problems* 62, no. 2 (1999): 173–301.

Duncan, Ian. "*The Moonstone*, the Victorian Novel, and Imperialist Panic." *Modern Language Quarterly* 55, no. 3 (1994): 297–319.

Scott's Shadow: The Novel in Romantic Edinburgh. Princeton, NJ: Princeton University Press, 2007.

During, Simon. "The Strange Case of Monomania: Patriarchy in Literature, Murder in *Middlemarch*, Drowning in *Daniel Deronda*." *Representations*, no. 23 (1988): 86–104.

Eagleton, Terry. *Criticism and Ideology: A Study in Marxist Literary Theory.* London: Verso, 2006.

Ebbatson, Roger. *The Evolutionary Self: Hardy, Forster, Lawrence.* Sussex: Harvester Press, 1982.

Eco, Umberto, and Thomas A. Sebeok, eds. *The Sign of Three: Dupin, Holmes, Peirce.* Bloomington: Indiana University Press, 1983.

Eden, Berna Kılıç. *John Venn's Evolutionary Logic of Chance.* Berlin: Max-Planck-Institut für Wissenschaftsgeschichte, 1998.

Edmond, Rod. "'The Past-Marked Prospect': *The Mayor of Casterbridge*." In *Reading the Victorian Novel: Detail into Form*, edited by Ian Gregor, 111–27. London: Vision, 1980.

Edwards, W. Walter. "Compulsory Providence." *The Nineteenth Century* 6, no. 33 (1879): 893–903.

Eggleston, Richard. *Evidence, Proof and Probability.* London: Weidenfeld and Nicolson, 1978.

Ehninger, Douglas. "Campbell, Blair, and Whately Revisited." *The Southern Speech Journal* 28, no. 3 (1963): 169–82.

"Introduction." In *Elements of Rhetoric: Comprising an Analysis of the Laws of Moral Evidence and of Persuasion, with Rules for Argumentative Composition and Elocution*, 7th ed., edited by Douglas Ehninger. Carbondale: Southern Illinois University Press, 1963.

Eiland, Howard, and Michael W. Jennings, eds. "On Some Motifs in Baudelaire." In *Walter Benjamin: Selected Writings, vol. 4: 1938–1940*, 313–55. Cambridge, MA: Belknap Press of Harvard University Press, 2006.

Einhorn, Lois J. "Consistency in Richard Whately: The Scope of His Rhetoric." *Philosophy & Rhetoric* 14, no. 2 (1981): 89–99.

Eliot, George. *Adam Bede.* Edited by Carol A. Martin. 1859. Reprint, Oxford: Clarendon Press, 2001.

The Complete Shorter Poetry of George Eliot. Edited by Antonie Gerard van den Broek. London: Pickering & Chatto, 2004.

Daniel Deronda. Edited by Graham Handley. 1876. Reprint, Oxford: Clarendon Press, 1984.

Essays and Leaves from a Note-Book. 2nd ed. Edited by Charles Lee Lewes. Edinburgh: William Blackwood, 1884.

Felix Holt, the Radical. Edited by Fred C. Thomson. 1866. Reprint, Oxford: Clarendon Press, 1980.

The George Eliot Letters. Edited by Gordon S. Haight. 7 vols. New Haven, CT: Yale University Press, 1954.

Impressions of Theophrastus Such. Edited by Nancy Henry. 1879. Reprint, London: Pickering, 1994.

The Journals of George Eliot. Edited by Margaret Harris and Judith Johnston. Cambridge: Cambridge University Press, 1998.

Middlemarch. Edited by David Carroll. 1871–72. Reprint, Oxford: Clarendon Press, 1986.

The Mill on the Floss. Edited by Gordon S. Haight. 1860. Reprint, Oxford: Clarendon Press, 1980.

Some George Eliot Notebooks: An Edition of the Carl H. Pforzheimer Library's George Eliot Holograph Notebooks, MSS 707, 708, 709, 710, 711. Edited by William Baker. Vol. 1. Salzburg: Institut für Englische Sprache und Literatur, Universität Salzburg, 1976.

The Spanish Gypsy. London: William Blackwood, 1868.

"Theology and Philosophy." *Westminster Review* 64 (1855): 205–25.

"Theology and Philosophy." *Westminster Review* 65 (1856): 563–80.

Elster, Jon. "Gambling and Addiction." In *Getting Hooked: Rationality and Addiction*, edited by Jon Elster and Ole-Jørgen Skog, 208–34. Cambridge: Cambridge University Press, 1999.

Strong Feelings: Emotion, Addiction, and Human Behavior. Cambridge, MA: MIT Press, 1999.

Ulysses and the Sirens: Studies in Rationality and Irrationality. Rev. ed. Cambridge: Cambridge University Press, 1984.

Emmott, James. "Parameters of Vibration, Technologies of Capture, and the Layering of Voices and Faces in the Nineteenth Century." *Victorian Studies* 53, no. 3 (2011): 468–78.

Ender, Evelyne. *Sexing the Mind: Nineteenth-Century Fictions of Hysteria.* Ithaca, NY: Cornell University Press, 1995.

Engelhardt, Nina. *Modernism, Fiction and Mathematics.* Edinburgh: Edinburgh University Press, 2018.

Engell, James. *The Creative Imagination: Enlightenment to Romanticism.* Cambridge, MA: Harvard University Press, 1981.

Epstude, Kai, and Neal J. Roese. "The Functional Theory of Counterfactual Thinking." *Personality and Social Psychology Review* 12, no. 2 (2008): 168–92.

Erdinast-Vulcan, Daphna. *Joseph Conrad and the Modern Temper.* Oxford: Clarendon Press, 1991.

Ermarth, Elizabeth Deeds. *The English Novel in History, 1840–1895.* London: Routledge, 1997.

"Incarnations: George Eliot's Conception of 'Undeviating Law.'" *Nineteenth-Century Fiction* 29, no. 3 (1974): 273–86.

Realism and Consensus in the English Novel: Time, Space and Narrative. Princeton, NJ: Princeton University Press, 1983.

Ethier, Stewart N. *The Doctrine of Chances: Probabilistic Aspects of Gambling.* Berlin: Springer, 2010.

"Thackeray and the Belgian Progression." *Mathematical Scientist* 24, no. 1 (1999): 1–23.

Fabian, Ann. *Card Sharps, Dream Books, & Bucket Shops: Gambling in 19th-Century America.* Ithaca, NY: Cornell University Press, 1990.

Farina, Jonathan. "'Dickens's As If': Analogy and Victorian Virtual Reality." *Victorian Studies* 53, no. 3 (2011): 427–36.

Farmer, Lindsay. *Criminal Law, Tradition, and Legal Order: Crime and the Genius of Scots Law, 1747 to the Present.* New York: Cambridge University Press, 1997.

Faulkner, Laura. "'That's Convenient, Not to Say Odd': Coincidence, Causality, and Hardy's Inconsistent Inconsistency." *Victorian Review* 37, no. 1 (2011): 92–107.

Favret, Mary A. *War at a Distance: Romanticism and the Making of Modern Wartime.* Princeton, NJ: Princeton University Press, 2010.

Feeley, Malcolm M., and Jonathan Simon. "Actuarial Justice: The Emerging New Criminal Law." In *The Futures of Criminology*, edited by David Nelken, 173–201. London: Sage, 1994.

Feinberg, Joel. *Rights, Justice, and the Bounds of Liberty: Essays in Social Philosophy.* Princeton, NJ: Princeton University Press, 1980.

Felski, Rita. *The Limits of Critique.* Chicago: University of Chicago Press, 2015.

Ferguson, Niall. "Virtual History: Towards a 'Chaotic' Theory of the Past." In *Virtual History: Alternatives and Counterfactuals*, edited by Niall Ferguson, 1–90. New York: Basic Books, 1999.

Ferris, Ina. "The Breakdown of Thackeray's Narrator: *Lovel the Widower*." *Nineteenth-Century Fiction* 32, no. 1 (1977): 36–53.

"Realism and the Discord of Ending: The Example of Thackeray." *Nineteenth-Century Fiction* 38, no. 3 (1983): 289–303.

William Makepeace Thackeray. Boston: Twayne, 1983.

Fessenbecker, Patrick. *Reading Ideas in Victorian Literature: Literary Content as Artistic Experience.* Edinburgh: Edinburgh University Press, 2020.

Fielding, Henry. *Tom Jones.* Edited by John Bender and Simon Stern. 1749. Reprint, Oxford: Oxford University Press, 2009.

Fisher, Judith L. "Siren and Artist: Contradiction in Thackeray's Aesthetic Ideal." *Nineteenth-Century Fiction* 39, no. 4 (1985): 392–419.

Thackeray's Skeptical Narrative and the "Perilous Trade" of Authorship. Aldershot: Ashgate, 2002.

Fisher, Philip. *Making Up Society: The Novels of George Eliot.* Pittsburgh: University of Pittsburgh Press, 1981.

Flavin, Michael. *Gambling in the Nineteenth-Century English Novel: "A Leprosy Is o'er the Land."* Brighton: Sussex Academic Press, 2003.

Fleishman, Avrom. *Fiction and the Ways of Knowing*. Austin: University of Texas Press, 1978.

Fletcher, Angus. *Allegory: Theory of a Symbolic Mode*. Ithaca, NY: Cornell University Press, 1964.

Fletcher, Robert P. "The Dandy and the Fogy: Thackeray and the Aesthetics/ Ethics of the Literary Pragmatist." *ELH* 58, no. 2 (1991): 383–404.

"'The Foolishest of Existing Mortals': Thackeray, 'Gurlyle,' and the Character(s) of Fiction." *Clio* 24, no. 2 (1995): 113–25.

"'Mere Outer Works' and 'Fleeting Effects': Thackeray's Novelistic Art and the Art of the Novel." *The Journal of English and Germanic Philology* 91, no. 1 (1992): 43–64.

Flint, Kate. "Disability and Difference." In *The Cambridge Companion to Wilkie Collins*, edited by Jenny Bourne Taylor, 153–67. Cambridge: Cambridge University Press, 2007.

"George Eliot and Gender." In *The Cambridge Companion to George Eliot*, edited by George Levine, 159–80. Cambridge: Cambridge University Press, 2001.

Fludernik, Monika. *Towards a "Natural" Narratology*. London: Routledge, 1996.

Ford, G. H. *Dickens and His Readers: Aspects of Novel-Criticism since 1836*. Princeton, NJ: Princeton University Press, 1955.

Forster, E. M. *Aspects of the Novel*. New York: Harcourt, Brace, 1956.

Howards End. 1910. Reprint, London: Penguin, 2000.

Forsyth, William. "Criminal Procedure in Scotland and England." *Edinburgh Review* 108, no. 220 (1858): 343–76.

Fowler, Alastair. *A History of English Literature*. Cambridge, MA: Harvard University Press, 1987.

François, Anne-Lise. *Open Secrets: The Literature of Uncounted Experience*. Stanford, CA: Stanford University Press, 2008.

Franklin, J. Jeffrey. *Serious Play: The Cultural Form of the Nineteenth-Century Realist Novel*. Philadelphia: University of Pennsylvania Press, 1999.

"The Victorian Discourse of Gambling: Speculations on *Middlemarch* and *The Duke's Children*." *ELH* 61, no. 4 (1994): 899–921.

Franklin, James. *The Science of Conjecture: Evidence and Probability before Pascal*. Baltimore: Johns Hopkins University Press, 2001.

Franklin, Michael J. "'Market-Faces' and Market Forces: [Corn-]Factors in the Moral Economy of Casterbridge." *The Review of English Studies* 59, no. 240 (2007): 426–48.

Fraser, Russell A. "Pernicious Casuistry: A Study of Character in *Vanity Fair*." *Nineteenth-Century Fiction* 12, no. 2 (1957): 137–47.

Freedgood, Elaine. *Victorian Writing about Risk: Imagining a Safe England in a Dangerous World*. Cambridge: Cambridge University Press, 2000.

Worlds Enough: The Invention of Realism in the Victorian Novel. Princeton, NJ: Princeton University Press, 2019.

Freud, Sigmund. *The Standard Edition of the Complete Psychological Works of Sigmund Freud*. Edited by James Strachey and Anna Freud. 24 vols. London: Hogarth Press, 1957–74.

Friedman, Richard D. "Assessing Evidence." *Michigan Law Review* 94, no. 6 (1996): 1810–38.

Furst, Lilian R. *All Is True: The Claims and Strategies of Realist Fiction*. Durham, NC: Duke University Press, 1995.

Fyfe, Paul. *By Accident or Design: Writing the Victorian Metropolis*. Oxford: Oxford University Press, 2015.

Gagnier, Regenia. *The Insatiability of Human Wants: Economics and Aesthetics in Market Society*. Chicago: University of Chicago Press, 2000.

Galat, Joshua R. "Joseph Conrad and Scientific Naturalism: Revolutionising Epistemology in *The Secret Agent*." *English Studies* 101, no. 4 (2020): 450–70.

Gallagher, Catherine. *The Body Economic: Life, Death, and Sensation in Political Economy and the Victorian Novel*. Princeton, NJ: Princeton University Press, 2006.

———. "George Eliot and *Daniel Deronda*: The Prostitute and the Jewish Question." In *Sex, Politics, and Science in the Nineteenth-Century Novel*, edited by Ruth Bernard Yeazell, 39–62. Baltimore: Johns Hopkins University Press, 1986.

———. *Nobody's Story: The Vanishing Acts of Women Writers in the Marketplace, 1670–1820*. Berkeley: University of California Press, 1994.

———. "The Rise of Fictionality." In *The Novel, vol. 1: History, Geography, and Culture*, edited by Franco Moretti, 336–63. Princeton, NJ: Princeton University Press, 2006.

———. *Telling It like It Wasn't: The Counterfactual Imagination in History and Fiction*. Chicago: University of Chicago Press, 2018.

———. "What Would Napoleon Do? Historical, Fictional, and Counterfactual Characters." *New Literary History* 42, no. 2 (2011): 315–36.

Galloway, Thomas. *A Treatise on Probability*. Edinburgh: Adam and Charles Black, 1839.

Galton, Francis. "Composite Portraits." *Journal of the Royal Anthropological Institute of Great Britain and Ireland* 8, no. 2 (1879): 132–44.

———. "Composite Portraiture." *The Photographic Journal* 5 (1881): 140–46.

———. "Generic Images." *The Nineteenth Century* 6, no. 29 (1879): 157–69.

———. *Inquiries into Human Faculty and Its Development*. London: Macmillan, 1883.

———. "The Just-Perceptible Difference." *Proceedings of the Royal Institution* 14 (1893): 13–26.

———. "Statistical Inquiries into the Efficacy of Prayer." *Fortnightly Review* 12, no. 68 (1872): 125–35.

———. "Statistics by Intercomparison with Remarks on the Law of Frequency of Error." *Philosophical Magazine* 49, no. 322 (1875): 33–46.

Gao, Timothy. *Virtual Play and the Victorian Novel: The Ethics and Aesthetics of Fictional Experience*. Cambridge: Cambridge University Press, 2021.

Garber, Daniel, and Sandy Zabell. "On the Emergence of Probability." *Archive for History of Exact Sciences* 21, no. 1 (1979): 33–53.

Garcha, Amanpal. "Emma's Choices: Economics and Modern Narratives of Decision-Making." *Novel* 55, no. 2 (2022): 218–39.

"Forgetting Thackeray and Unmaking Careers." *Victorian Literature and Culture* 46, no. 2 (2018): 531–45.

"Narrating Choice in Later Nineteenth-Century Novels and Neoclassical Economics." In *From Political Economy to Economics through Nineteenth-Century Literature: Reclaiming the Social,* edited by Elaine Hadley, Audrey Jaffe, and Sarah Winter, 197–218. Cham: Springer, 2019.

Garrett-Goodyear, Joan. "Stylized Emotions, Unrealized Selves: Expressive Characterization in Thackeray." *Victorian Studies* 22, no. 2 (1979): 173–92.

Gastwirth, Joseph L. *Statistical Science in the Courtroom.* New York: Springer, 2000.

Gates, Barbara T. *Victorian Suicide: Mad Crimes and Sad Histories.* Princeton, NJ: Princeton University Press, 1988.

"Wilkie Collins's Suicides: 'Truth as It Is in Nature.'" *Dickens Studies Annual* 12 (1983): 303–18.

Genette, Gérard. "*Vraisemblance* and Motivation." Translated by David Gorman. *Narrative* 9, no. 3 (2001): 239–58.

Ghosh, Amitav. *The Great Derangement: Climate Change and the Unthinkable.* Chicago: University of Chicago Press, 2016.

Gigerenzer, Gerd. *Gut Feelings: The Intelligence of the Unconscious.* New York: Viking, 2007.

Rationality for Mortals: How People Cope with Uncertainty. Oxford: Oxford University Press, 2008.

Gigerenzer, Gerd, and Reinhard Selten, eds. *Bounded Rationality: The Adaptive Toolbox.* Cambridge, MA: MIT Press, 2001.

Gigerenzer, Gerd, Zeno Swijtink, Theodore Porter, Lorraine Daston, John Beatty, and Lorenz Krüger. *The Empire of Chance: How Probability Changed Science and Everyday Life.* Cambridge: Cambridge University Press, 1989.

Gilbert, Daniel T., Eric Driver-Linn, and Timothy D. Wilson. "The Trouble with Vronsky: Impact Bias in the Forecasting of Future Affective States." In *The Wisdom in Feeling: Psychological Processes in Emotional Intelligence,* edited by Lisa Feldman Barrett and Peter Salovey, 114–43. New York: Guilford Press, 2002.

Gilbert, Daniel T., Carey K. Morewedge, Jane L. Risen, and Timothy D. Wilson. "Looking Forward to Looking Backward." *Psychological Science* 15, no. 3 (2004): 346–50.

Gilmour, Robin. *The Idea of the Gentleman in the Victorian Novel.* London: Allen & Unwin, 1981.

Ginzburg, Carlo. "Family Resemblances and Family Trees: Two Cognitive Metaphors." *Critical Inquiry* 30, no. 3 (2004): 537–56.

"Morelli, Freud, and Sherlock Holmes: Clues and Scientific Method." In *The Sign of Three: Dupin, Holmes, Peirce,* edited by Umberto Eco and Thomas A. Sebeok, 81–118. Bloomington: Indiana University Press, 1983.

Glare, P. G. W., ed. *Oxford Latin Dictionary.* Oxford: Clarendon Press, 1996.

Glatt, Carra. *Narrative and Its Nonevents: The Unwritten Plots That Shaped Victorian Realism.* Charlottesville: University of Virginia Press, 2022.

Goethe, Johann Wolfgang von. *Faust I & II*. Edited and translated by Stuart Atkins. Princeton, NJ: Princeton University Press, 2014.

Wilhelm Meister's Apprenticeship. Edited and translated by Eric A. Blackall in cooperation with Victor Lange. Princeton, NJ: Princeton University Press, 1995.

Goldberg, S. L. *Agents and Lives: Moral Thinking in Literature*. Cambridge: Cambridge University Press, 1993.

Goldman, Lawrence. *Victorians and Numbers: Statistics and Society in Nineteenth Century Britain*. Oxford University Press, 2022.

Goodman, Nelson. *Fact, Fiction, and Forecast*. 3rd ed. Indianapolis: Bobbs-Merrill, 1973.

Graver, Suzanne. *George Eliot and Community: A Study in Social Theory and Fictional Form*. Berkeley: University of California Press, 1984.

Gregor, Ian. *The Great Web: The Form of Hardy's Major Fiction*. London: Faber and Faber, 1974.

Grenby, M. O. *The Anti-Jacobin Novel: British Conservatism and the French Revolution*. Cambridge: Cambridge University Press, 2001.

Grener, Adam. *Improbability, Chance, and the Nineteenth-Century Realist Novel*. Columbus: Ohio State University Press, 2020.

Griffiths, Devin. *The Age of Analogy: Science and Literature between the Darwins*. Baltimore: Johns Hopkins University Press, 2016.

Gross, Kenneth. *The Dream of the Moving Statue*. Ithaca, NY: Cornell University Press, 1992.

Grossman, Julie. "Thomas Hardy and the Role of Observer." *ELH* 56, no. 3 (1989): 619–38.

Hacking, Ian. *The Emergence of Probability: A Philosophical Study of Early Ideas about Probability, Induction and Statistical Inference*. 1975. 2nd ed. Cambridge: Cambridge University Press, 2006.

"Nineteenth Century Cracks in the Concept of Determinism." *Journal of the History of Ideas* 44, no. 3 (1983): 455–75.

The Taming of Chance. Cambridge: Cambridge University Press, 1990.

Hadley, Elaine. *Living Liberalism: Practical Citizenship in Mid-Victorian Britain*. Chicago: University of Chicago Press, 2010.

"Nobody, Somebody, and Everybody." *Victorian Studies* 59, no. 1 (2016): 65–86.

Hagan, John. "A Note on the Napoleonic Background of *Vanity Fair*." *Nineteenth-Century Fiction* 15, no. 4 (1961): 358–61.

Hamilton, Ross. *Accident: A Philosophical and Literary History*. Chicago: University of Chicago Press, 2007.

"Deep History: Association and Natural Philosophy in Wordsworth's Poetry." *European Romantic Review* 18, no. 4 (2007): 459–81.

Hammond, Mary. "Thackeray's Waterloo: History and War in *Vanity Fair*." *Literature & History* 11, no. 2 (2011): 19–38.

Hanson, James. "Logic and Logical Studies in England." *London Quarterly Review* 38, no. 77 (1872): 301–47.

Harcourt, Bernard E. *Against Prediction: Profiling, Policing, and Punishing in an Actuarial Age.* Chicago: University of Chicago Press, 2007.

Harden, Edgar F. *Annotations for the Selected Works of William Makepeace Thackeray: The Complete Novels, the Major Non-Fictional Prose, and Selected Shorter Pieces.* 2 vols. New York: Garland, 1990.

The Emergence of Thackeray's Serial Fiction. Athens: University of Georgia Press, 1979.

"The Fields of Mars in *Vanity Fair.*" *Tennessee Studies in Literature* 10 (1965): 123–32.

Hardy, Barbara. *The Novels of George Eliot: A Study in Form.* London: Athlone, 1985.

Hardy, Thomas. *Collected Poems of Thomas Hardy.* London: Macmillan, 1930.

Collected Short Stories. London: Macmillan, 1988.

Desperate Remedies. Edited by Patricia Ingham. 1871. Reprint, Oxford: Oxford University Press, 2003.

Far from the Madding Crowd. Edited by Rosemarie Morgan and Shannon Russell. 1874. Reprint, London: Penguin, 2000.

A Laodicean. Edited by Jane Gatewood. 1881. Reprint, Oxford: Oxford University Press, 1991.

The Life and Work of Thomas Hardy. Edited by Michael Millgate. Athens: University of Georgia Press, 1985.

The Literary Notebooks of Thomas Hardy. Edited by Lennart A. Björk. 2 vols. New York: New York University Press, 1985.

The Mayor of Casterbridge. Edited by Keith Wilson. 1886. Reprint, London: Penguin, 2003.

"Real Conversations [Interview with William Archer]." *Pall Mall Magazine* 23, no. 96 (1901): 527–37.

The Return of the Native. Edited by George Woodcock. 1878. Reprint, Harmondsworth: Penguin, 1978.

Tess of the d'Urbervilles. Edited by Tim Dolin. 1891. Reprint, London: Penguin, 2003.

Thomas Hardy's Personal Writings. Edited by Harold Orel. Lawrence: University of Kansas Press, 1966.

Under the Greenwood Tree. Edited by Tim Dolin. 1872. Reprint, London: Penguin, 1998.

The Woodlanders. Edited by James Gibson. 1887. Reprint, Harmondsworth: Penguin, 1981.

Harrington, Ellen Burton. "From the Lady and the Law to the Lady Detective: Gender and Voice in Collins and Dickens." *Storytelling* 6, no. 1 (2006): 19–31.

Hartley, David. *Observations on Man, His Frame, His Duty, and His Expectations.* 1749. 5th ed. 2 vols. London: Richard Cruttwell, 1810.

Hartman, Mary S. "Murder for Respectability: The Case of Madeleine Smith." *Victorian Studies* 16, no. 4 (1973): 381–400.

Hatherell, William. "'Words and Things': Locke, Hartley and the Associationist Context for the Preface to *Lyrical Ballads.*" *Romanticism* 12, no. 3 (2006): 223–35.

Hawthorn, Geoffrey. *Plausible Worlds: Possibility and Understanding in History and the Social Sciences.* Cambridge: Cambridge University Press, 1991.

Hazlitt, William. *The Spirit of the Age.* Edited by P. P. Howe. *The Complete Works of William Hazlitt in Twenty-One Volumes,* vol. 11. London: J. M. Dent and Sons, 1932.

Heffernan, Julian Jimenez. "Lying Epitaphs: *Vanity Fair,* Waterloo, and the Cult of the Dead." *Victorian Literature and Culture* 40, no. 1 (2012): 25–45.

Helfield, Randa. "Poisonous Plots: Women Sensation Novelists and Murderesses of the Victorian Period." *Victorian Review* 21, no. 2 (1995): 161–88.

Heller, Tamar. *Dead Secrets: Wilkie Collins and the Female Gothic.* New Haven, CT: Yale University Press, 1992.

Henry, Nancy. *George Eliot and the British Empire.* Cambridge: Cambridge University Press, 2002.

Henry, Nancy, and Cannon Schmitt, eds. *Victorian Investments: New Perspectives on Finance and Culture.* Bloomington: Indiana University Press, 2009.

Hensher, Philip. "On *Chance.*" *The Conradian* 32, no. 2 (2007): 39–42.

Herbert, Christopher. *Victorian Relativity: Radical Thought and Scientific Discovery.* Chicago: University of Chicago Press, 2001.

Herman, David. "Hypothetical Focalization." *Narrative* 2, no. 3 (1994): 230–53.

Herring, Phillip F. *Joyce's Uncertainty Principle.* Princeton, NJ: Princeton University Press, 1987.

Herschel, John F. W. "Quetelet on Probabilities." *Edinburgh Review* 92, no. 185 (1850): 1–57.

Hertz, Neil. *George Eliot's Pulse.* Stanford, CA: Stanford University Press, 2003.

Higgins, Matthew James. "Invasion Panics." *Cornhill Magazine* 1 (1860): 135–49.

Hilts, Victor L. *Statist and Statistician.* New York: Arno Press, 1981.

Høeg, Mette Leonard, ed. *Literary Theories of Uncertainty.* London: Bloomsbury, 2021.

Hoffman, David C. "Concerning *Eikos*: Social Expectation and Verisimilitude in Early Attic Rhetoric." *Rhetorica* 26, no. 1 (2008): 1–29.

Hogan, Patrick Colm. *Affective Narratology: The Emotional Structure of Stories.* Lincoln: University of Nebraska Press, 2011.

Hohwy, Jakob. *The Predictive Mind.* Oxford: Oxford University Press, 2013.

Holinshed, Raphaell. *Holinshed's Chronicles: England, Scotland and Ireland.* Vol. 1. 1587. Reprint, London: Routledge, 1967.

Holmes, Martha Stoddard. "Queering the Marriage Plot: Wilkie Collins's *The Law and the Lady.*" In *Victorian Freaks: The Social Context of Freakery in Britain,* edited by Marlene Tromp, 237–58. Columbus: Ohio State University Press, 2008.

Hookway, Christopher. "'... A Sort of Composite Photograph': Pragmatism, Ideas, and Schematism." *Transactions of the Charles S. Peirce Society* 38, nos. 1–2 (2002): 29–45.

Hope, Lorraine, Edith Greene, Amina Memon, Melanie Gavisk, and Kate Houston. "A Third Verdict Option: Exploring the Impact of the Not

Proven Verdict on Mock Juror Decision Making." *Law and Human Behavior* 32, no. 3 (2008): 241–52.

Hopkins, Gerard Manley. *Correspondence*. Edited by R. K. R. Thornton and Catherine Phillips. 2 vols. Oxford: Oxford University Press, 2013.

Horn, Anne Layman. "Farcical Process, Fictional Product: Thackeray's Theatrics in *Lovel the Widower*." *Victorian Literature and Culture* 26, no. 1 (1998): 135–54.

Hornback, Bert G. *The Metaphor of Chance: Vision and Technique in the Works of Thomas Hardy*. Athens: Ohio University Press, 1971.

Howells, William Dean. "Editor's Study [Rev. of *The Mayor of Casterbridge*, by Thomas Hardy]." *Harper's New Monthly Magazine* 73, no. 438 (1886): 961–67.

Hoydis, Julia. *Risk and the English Novel: From Defoe to McEwan*. Berlin: De Gruyter, 2019.

Hoyle, Edmond. *Hoyle's Games*. London: Longman and Co., 1835.

Hühn, Peter. "The Detective as Reader: Narrativity and Reading Concepts in Detective Fiction." *Modern Fiction Studies* 33, no. 3 (1987): 451–66.

Hume, David. *An Enquiry Concerning Human Understanding: A Critical Edition*. Edited by Tom Beauchamp. 1748. Reprint, Oxford: Clarendon Press, 2000.

Hume, David (Baron). *Commentaries on the Law of Scotland*. Vol. 2. Edinburgh: Bell & Bradfute, 1800.

Hunter, J. Paul. *Before Novels: The Cultural Contexts of Eighteenth-Century English Fiction*. New York: W. W. Norton, 1990.

Husemann, Mary M. "Irregular and Not Proven: The Problem of Scottish Law in the Novels of Wilkie Collins." *Victorian Newsletter* 116 (2009): 66–89.

Hutton, R. H. "[Rev. of] *Daniel Deronda*, by George Eliot." *Spectator* 49 (1876): 734.

Huxley, Thomas Henry. "On the Hypothesis That Animals Are Automata, and Its History." In *Method and Results: Essays by Thomas Henry Huxley*, 199–250. New York: D. Appleton and Co., 1901.

"On the Physical Basis of Life." *Fortnightly Review* 5, no. 26 (1869): 129–45.

Hyde, William J. "Hardy's View of Realism: A Key to the Rustic Characters." *Victorian Studies* 2, no. 1 (1958): 45–59.

Irwin, Jane, ed. *George Eliot's Daniel Deronda Notebooks*. Cambridge: Cambridge University Press, 1996.

Itzkowitz, David C. "Fair Enterprise or Extravagant Speculation: Investment, Speculation, and Gambling in Victorian England." *Victorian Studies* 45, no. 1 (2002): 121–47.

"Victorian Bookmakers and Their Customers." *Victorian Studies* 32, no. 1 (1988): 7–30.

Jacobus, Mary. *Reading Woman: Essays in Feminist Criticism*. London: Methuen, 1986.

Jacyna, L. S. "The Physiology of Mind, the Unity of Nature, and the Moral Order in Victorian Thought." *The British Journal for the History of Science* 14, no. 2 (1981): 109–32.

Jaffe, Audrey. *The Affective Life of the Average Man: The Victorian Novel and the Stock-Market Graph*. Columbus: Ohio State University Press, 2010.

"Omniscience in *Our Mutual Friend*: On Taking the Reader by Surprise." *Journal of Narrative Technique* 17, no. 1 (1987): 91–101.

Scenes of Sympathy: Identity and Representation in Victorian Fiction. Ithaca, NY: Cornell University Press, 2000.

James, David L. "Story and Substance in *Lovel the Widower*." *Journal of Narrative Theory* 7, no. 1 (1977): 70–79.

James, Henry. *Literary Criticism*. New York: Literary Classics of the United States, 1984.

James, William. *The Principles of Psychology*. Edited by Frederick H. Burkhardt, Fredson Bowers, and Ignas K. Skrupskelis. 3 vols. Cambridge, MA: Harvard University Press, 1981.

Some Problems of Philosophy. Edited by Frederick H. Burkhardt, Fredson Bowers, and Ignas K. Skrupskelis. Cambridge, MA: Harvard University Press, 1979.

Jameson, Fredric. *The Antinomies of Realism*. London: Verso, 2013.

The Political Unconscious: Narrative as a Socially Symbolic Act. 1981. Reprint, London: Routledge, 2002.

Jevons, W. Stanley. *The Theory of Political Economy*. London: Macmillan, 1871.

Jewsbury, Geraldine. "New Novels." *Athenæum* 1654 (1859): 48.

Johnson, Bruce. *True Correspondence: A Phenomenology of Thomas Hardy's Novels*. Tallahassee: University Presses of Florida, 1983.

Johnson, Claudia L. "F. R. Leavis: The 'Great Tradition' of the English Novel and the Jewish Part." *Nineteenth-Century Literature* 56, no. 2 (2001): 198–227.

Johnson, Joel T. "The Knowledge of What Might Have Been: Affective and Attributional Consequences of Near Outcomes." *Personality and Social Psychology Bulletin* 12, no. 1 (1986): 51–62.

Johnson, Marcia K., and Steven J. Sherman. "Constructing and Reconstructing the Past and the Future in the Present." In *Handbook of Motivation and Cognition: Foundations of Social Behavior*, edited by Edward T. Higgins and Richard M. Sorrentino, 2:482–526. New York: Guilford Press, 1990.

Johnston, Judith. "Sensate Detection in Wilkie Collins's *The Law and the Lady*." *Australasian Journal of Victorian Studies* 14, no. 2 (2009): 38–50.

Jones, Susan. "Modernism and the Marketplace: The Case of Conrad's *Chance*." *College Literature* 34, no. 3 (2007): 101–19.

Jordan, Julia. *Chance and the Modern British Novel: From Henry Green to Iris Murdoch*. London: Continuum, 2010.

Late Modernism and the Avant-Garde British Novel: Oblique Strategies. Oxford: Oxford University Press, 2020.

Joyce, James. *Ulysses*. Edited by Hans Walter Gabler, Wolfhard Steppe, and Claus Melchior. 1922. Reprint, New York: Vintage, 1993.

Kahneman, Daniel, and Dale T. Miller. "Norm Theory: Comparing Reality to Its Alternatives." *Psychological Review* 93, no. 2 (1986): 136–53.

Kahneman, Daniel, Paul Slovic, and Amos Tversky, eds. *Judgment under Uncertainty: Heuristics and Biases*. Cambridge: Cambridge University Press, 1982.

Kallich, Martin. *The Association of Ideas and Critical Theory in Eighteenth-Century England: A History of a Psychological Method in English Criticism*. The Hague: Mouton, 1970.

Kareem, Sarah Tindal. *Eighteenth-Century Fiction and the Reinvention of Wonder*. Oxford: Oxford University Press, 2014.

Kavanagh, Thomas M. *Dice, Cards, Wheels: A Different History of French Culture*. Philadelphia: University of Pennsylvania Press, 2005.

    Enlightenment and the Shadows of Chance: The Novel and the Culture of Gambling in Eighteenth-Century France. Baltimore: Johns Hopkins University Press, 1993.

    "Roulette and the *Ancien Régime* of Gambling." *Nottingham French Studies* 48, no. 1 (2009): 1–13.

Kaye, David H. "Statistical Significance and the Burden of Persuasion." *Law and Contemporary Problems* 46, no. 4 (1983): 13–23.

Keats, John. *Selected Letters*. Edited by Robert Gittings. Oxford: Oxford University Press, 2009.

Kent, Christopher. "The Average Victorian: Constructing and Contesting Reality." *Browning Institute Studies* 17 (1989): 41–52.

    "Probability, Reality and Sensation in the Novels of Wilkie Collins." *Dickens Studies Annual* 20 (1991): 259–80.

Kern, Stephen. *A Cultural History of Causality: Science, Murder Novels, and Systems of Thought*. Princeton, NJ: Princeton University Press, 2004.

    The Modernist Novel: A Critical Introduction. Cambridge: Cambridge University Press, 2011.

King, Jeannette. *Tragedy in the Victorian Novel: Theory and Practice in the Novels of George Eliot, Thomas Hardy, and Henry James*. Cambridge: Cambridge University Press, 1978.

King, Laura A., and Joshua A. Hicks. "Whatever Happened to 'What Might Have Been'?: Regrets, Happiness, and Maturity." *The American Psychologist* 62, no. 7 (2007): 625–36.

Klotz, Michael. "Manufacturing Fictional Individuals: Victorian Social Statistics, the Novel, and *Great Expectations*." *Novel* 46, no. 2 (2013): 214–33.

Knill, David C., and Alexandre Pouget. "The Bayesian Brain: The Role of Uncertainty in Neural Coding and Computation." *Trends in Neurosciences* 27, no. 12 (2004): 712–19.

Knoepflmacher, U. C. *Religious Humanism and the Victorian Novel: George Eliot, Walter Pater, and Samuel Butler*. Princeton, NJ: Princeton University Press, 1965.

Kolb, Margaret. "In Search of Lost Causes: Walter Scott and Adolphe Quetelet's Revolutions." *Configurations* 27, no. 1 (2019): 59–85.

    "Plot Circles: Hardy's Drunkards and Their Walks." *Victorian Studies* 56, no. 4 (2014): 595–623.

Koo, Minkyung, Sara B. Algoe, Timothy D. Wilson, and Daniel T. Gilbert. "It's a Wonderful Life: Mentally Subtracting Positive Events Improves People's Affective States, Contrary to Their Affective Forecasts." *Journal of Personality and Social Psychology* 95, no. 5 (2008): 1217–24.

Kramer, Dale. *Thomas Hardy: The Forms of Tragedy*. Detroit: Wayne State University Press, 1975.

Kray, Laura J., Adam D. Galinsky, and Keith D. Markman. "Counterfactual Structure and Learning from Experience in Negotiations." *Journal of Experimental Social Psychology* 45, no. 4 (2009): 979–82.

Kray, Laura J., Linda G. George, Katie A. Liljenquist, Adam D. Galinsky, Philip E. Tetlock, and Neal J. Roese. "From What *Might* Have Been to What *Must* Have Been: Counterfactual Thinking Creates Meaning." *Journal of Personality and Social Psychology* 98, no. 1 (2010): 106–18.

Krüger, Lorenz, Gerd Gigerenzer, and Mary Morgan, eds. *The Probabilistic Revolution, vol. 2: Ideas in the Sciences*. Cambridge, MA: MIT Press, 1987.

Krüger, Lorenz, Lorraine Daston, and Michael Heidelberger, eds. *The Probabilistic Revolution, vol. 1: Ideas in History*. Cambridge, MA: MIT Press, 1987.

Kukkonen, Karin. *Probability Designs: Literature and Predictive Processing*. Oxford: Oxford University Press, 2020.

Kurnick, David. *Empty Houses: Theatrical Failure and the Novel*. Princeton, NJ: Princeton University Press, 2012.

Lamb, Charles. *Elia and the Last Essays of Elia*. Edited by E. V. Lucas. London: Methuen, 1903.

Landman, Janet. "Regret and Elation Following Action and Inaction: Affective Responses to Positive versus Negative Outcomes." *Personality and Social Psychology Bulletin* 13, no. 4 (1987): 524–36.

Landow, George P. *Victorian Types, Victorian Shadows: Biblical Typology in Victorian Literature, Art, and Thought*. London: Routledge & Kegan Paul, 1980.

Lane, Christopher. *The Age of Doubt: Tracing the Roots of Our Religious Uncertainty*. New Haven, CT: Yale University Press, 2012.

Langbaum, Robert. "Hardy: Versions of Pastoral." *Victorian Literature and Culture* 20 (1992): 245–72.

Thomas Hardy in Our Time. Houndmills: Macmillan, 1995.

Laplace, Pierre-Simon. *Essai philosophique sur les probabilités*. 1814. 6th ed. Paris: Bachelier, 1840.

A Philosophical Essay on Probabilities. Translated by F. W. Truscott and F. L. Emory. New York: Wiley, 1902.

Larsen, Timothy. *Crisis of Doubt: Honest Faith in Nineteenth-Century England*. New York: Oxford University Press, 2006.

Laudan, Larry. *Truth, Error, and Criminal Law: An Essay in Legal Epistemology*. Cambridge: Cambridge University Press, 2006.

Law, Jules. "Transparency and Epistemology in George Eliot's *Daniel Deronda*." *Nineteenth-Century Literature* 62, no. 2 (2007): 250–77.

Lawrence, D. H. *Study of Thomas Hardy and Other Essays*. Edited by Bruce Steele. Cambridge: Cambridge University Press, 1985.

Leavis, F. R. *The Great Tradition: George Eliot, Henry James, Joseph Conrad*. London: Chatto & Windus, 1948.

Lee, Maurice S. *Uncertain Chances: Science, Skepticism, and Belief in Nineteenth-Century American Literature*. New York: Oxford University Press, 2012.

Lempert, Richard O. "Modeling Relevance." *Michigan Law Review* 75, nos. 5–6 (1977): 1021–57.

Levine, Caroline. "An Anatomy of Suspense: The Pleasurable, Critical, Ethical, Erotic Middle of *The Woman in White*." In *Narrative Middles: Navigating the Nineteenth-Century British Novel*, edited by Caroline Levine and Mario Ortiz-Robles. Columbus: Ohio State University Press, 2011.

The Serious Pleasures of Suspense: Victorian Realism and Narrative Doubt. Charlottesville: University of Virginia Press, 2003.

"Surprising Realism." In *A Companion to George Eliot*, edited by Amanda Anderson and Harry E. Shaw, 62–75. Malden, MA: Wiley-Blackwell, 2013.

Levine, George. "*Daniel Deronda*: A New Epistemology." In *Knowing the Past: Victorian Literature and Culture*, edited by Suzy Anger, 52–73. Ithaca, NY: Cornell University Press, 2011.

"Determinism and Responsibility in the Works of George Eliot." *PMLA* 77, no. 3 (1962): 268–79.

Dying to Know: Scientific Epistemology and Narrative in Victorian England. Chicago: University of Chicago Press, 2002.

Realism, Ethics and Secularism: Essays on Victorian Literature and Science. New York: Cambridge University Press, 2008.

The Realistic Imagination: English Fiction from Frankenstein to Lady Chatterley. Chicago: University of Chicago Press, 1981.

Levine, Herbert J. "The Marriage of Allegory and Realism in *Daniel Deronda*." *Genre* 15 (1982): 421–46.

Lewes, George Henry. "Dickens in Relation to Criticism." *Fortnightly Review* 11, no. 62 (1872): 141–54.

"Fechter in *Hamlet* and *Othello*." *Blackwood's Edinburgh Magazine* 90 (1861): 744–54.

"Hereditary Influence, Animal and Human." *Westminster Review* 66 (1856): 135–62.

The Physiology of Common Life. 2 vols. Edinburgh: William Blackwood, 1859.

The Principles of Success in Literature. Edited by Fred N. Scott. 1872. Reprint, Boston: Allyn and Bacon, 1894.

Problems of Life and Mind. Second Series: The Physical Basis of Mind. London: Trübner, 1877.

Problems of Life and Mind. Third Series. 2 vols. London: Trübner, 1879.

"Realism in Art: Recent German Fiction." *Westminster Review* 70 (1858): 488–518.

"Recent Novels: French and English." *Fraser's Magazine* 36 (1847): 689–95.

"Suicide in Life and Literature." *Westminster Review* 68 (1857): 52–78.

Lewis, David K. *Counterfactuals*. Cambridge, MA: Harvard University Press, 1973.

Lightman, Bernard V. *Victorian Popularizers of Science: Designing Nature for New Audiences*. Chicago: University of Chicago Press, 2007.

Lindberg, Matthew J., Keith D. Markman, and Hyeman Choi. "'It Was Meant to Be': Retrospective Meaning Construction through Mental Simulation." In *The Psychology of Meaning*, edited by Keith D. Markman, Travis Proulx, and Matthew J. Lindberg, 339–55. Washington, DC: American Psychological Association, 2013.

Lipton, Peter. "Alien Abduction: Inference to the Best Explanation and the Management of Testimony." *Episteme* 4, no. 3 (2007): 238–51.

Litvak, Joseph. *Caught in the Act: Theatricality in the Nineteenth-Century English Novel*. Berkeley: University of California Press, 1992.

Locke, John. *An Essay Concerning Human Understanding*. Edited by P. H. Nidditch. 1690. Reprint, Oxford: Clarendon Press, 1979.

Lodge, David. "Thomas Hardy and Cinematographic Form." *Novel* 7, no. 3 (1974): 246–54.

Longmuir, Anne. "The Scotch Verdict and Irregular Marriages: How Scottish Law Disrupts the Normative in *The Law and the Lady* and *Man and Wife*." In *Wilkie Collins: Interdisciplinary Essays*, edited by Andrew Mangham, 166–77. Newcastle upon Tyne: Cambridge Scholars, 2007.

Loofborouw, John. *Thackeray and the Form of Fiction*. Princeton, NJ: Princeton University Press, 1964.

Lothe, Jakob. *Conrad's Narrative Method*. Oxford: Clarendon Press, 1989.

Lougy, Robert E. "Vision and Satire: The Warped Looking Glass in *Vanity Fair*." *PMLA* 90, no. 2 (1975): 256–69.

Love, Heather. "Close but Not Deep: Literary Ethics and the Descriptive Turn." *New Literary History* 41, no. 2 (2010): 371–91.

Lubbock, J. W., and John Elliot Drinkwater Bethune. *On Probability*. London: Baldwin and Cradock, 1830.

Luhmann, Niklas. *Law as a Social System*. Edited by Fatima Kastner, Richard Nobles, David Schiff, and Rosamund Ziegert. Translated by Klaus A. Ziegert. Oxford: Oxford University Press, 2004.

Lukács, György. *Studies in European Realism: A Sociological Survey of the Writings of Balzac, Stendhal, Zola, Tolstoy, Gorki, and Others*, translated by Edith Bone. London: Hillway, 1950.

Lyons, John D. *The Phantom of Chance: From Fortune to Randomness in Seventeenth-Century French Literature*. Edinburgh: Edinburgh University Press, 2012.

Macaulay, Thomas Babington. "John Dryden." In *The Miscellaneous Writings of Lord Macaulay*, 1:183–231. London: Longman, Green, Longman, and Roberts, 1860.

MacEachen, Dougald B. "Wilkie Collins and British Law." *Nineteenth-Century Fiction* 5, no. 2 (1950): 121–39.

MacKenzie, Donald A. *Statistics in Britain, 1865–1930: The Social Construction of Scientific Knowledge*. Edinburgh: Edinburgh University Press, 1981.

Macpherson, Sandra. *Harm's Way: Tragic Responsibility and the Novel Form.* Baltimore: Johns Hopkins University Press, 2010.

Maher, Gerry. "The Verdict of the Jury." In *The Jury under Attack,* edited by Mark Findlay and Peter Duff, 40–55. London: Butterworths, 1988.

Maioli, Roger. *Empiricism and the Early Theory of the Novel: Fielding to Austen.* Cham: Palgrave Macmillan, 2016.

Mandel, David R., and Darrin R. Lehman. "Counterfactual Thinking and Ascriptions of Cause and Preventability." *Journal of Personality and Social Psychology* 71, no. 3 (1996): 450–63.

Mangum, Teresa. "Wilkie Collins, Detection, and Deformity." *Dickens Studies Annual* 26 (1998): 285–310.

Marcus, Sharon. *Between Women: Friendship, Desire, and Marriage in Victorian England.* Princeton, NJ: Princeton University Press, 2007.

Markman, Keith D., Igor Gavanski, Steven J. Sherman, and Matthew N. McMullen. "The Mental Simulation of Better and Worse Possible Worlds." *Journal of Experimental Social Psychology* 29, no. 1 (1993): 87–109.

Markman, Keith D., and Philip E. Tetlock. "Accountability and Close-Call Counterfactuals: The Loser Who Nearly Won and the Winner Who Nearly Lost." *Personality and Social Psychology Bulletin* 26, no. 10 (2000): 1213–24.

Markovits, Stefanie. *The Crisis of Action in Nineteenth-Century English Literature.* Columbus: Ohio State University Press, 2006.

Marks, Patricia. "'Mon Pauvre Prisonnier': Becky Sharp and the Triumph of Napoleon." *Studies in the Novel* 28, no. 1 (1996): 76–92.

Marshall, David. *The Figure of Theater: Shaftesbury, Defoe, Adam Smith, and George Eliot.* New York: Columbia University Press, 1986.

Martin, Daniel. "Wilkie Collins and Risk." In *A Companion to Sensation Fiction,* edited by Pamela K. Gilbert, 184–95. Malden, MA: Wiley-Blackwell, 2011.

Masson, David. *British Novelists and Their Styles.* Cambridge: Macmillan, 1859.

Matus, Jill L. *Shock, Memory and the Unconscious in Victorian Fiction.* New York: Cambridge University Press, 2009.

Maudsley, Henry. *Body and Mind: An Inquiry into Their Connection and Mutual Influence, Specially in Reference to Mental Disorders.* London: Macmillan, 1870.

Body and Will: Being an Essay Concerning Will in Its Metaphysical, Physiological & Pathological Aspects. London: Kegan Paul, Trench, 1883.

"Hamlet." *Westminster Review* 83 (1865): 65–94.

The Physiology of Mind. London: Macmillan, 1876.

Maynard, Jessica. "Telling the Whole Truth: Wilkie Collins and the Lady Detective." In *Victorian Identities: Social and Cultural Formations in Nineteenth-Century Literature,* edited by Ruth Robbins and Julian Wolfreys, 437–61. London: Macmillan, 1996.

McClennen, Edward F. *Rationality and Dynamic Choice: Foundational Explorations.* Cambridge: Cambridge University Press, 1990.

McCrea, Sean M. "Self-Handicapping, Excuse Making, and Counterfactual Thinking: Consequences for Self-Esteem and Future Motivation." *Journal of Personality and Social Psychology* 95, no. 2 (2008): 274–92.

McKeon, Michael. *The Origins of the English Novel, 1600–1740*. Baltimore: Johns Hopkins University Press, 1987.
  The Secret History of Domesticity: Public, Private, and the Division of Knowledge. Baltimore: Johns Hopkins University Press, 2005.
McKerrow, Raymie E. "Richard Whately and the Revival of Logic in Nineteenth-Century England." *Rhetorica* 5, no. 2 (1987): 163–85.
McKibbin, Ross. "Working-Class Gambling in Britain 1880–1939." *Past & Present*, no. 82 (1979): 147–78.
McMaster, Juliet. *Thackeray: The Major Novels*. Toronto: University of Toronto Press, 1971.
  "Thackeray's Things: Time's Local Habitation." In *The Victorian Experience: The Novelists*, edited by Richard A. Levine, 49–86. Athens: Ohio University Press, 1976.
McMullen, Matthew N., and Keith D. Markman. "Downward Counterfactuals and Motivation: The Wake-Up Call and the Pangloss Effect." *Personality and Social Psychology Bulletin* 26, no. 5 (2000): 575–84.
McWeeny, Gage. *The Comfort of Strangers: Social Life and Literary Form*. New York: Oxford University Press, 2016.
Menke, Richard. "Fiction as Vivisection: G. H. Lewes and George Eliot." *ELH* 67, no. 2 (2000): 617–53.
Menon, Patricia. *Austen, Eliot, Charlotte Brontë, and the Mentor-Lover*. Basingstoke: Palgrave Macmillan, 2003.
Meyer, Susan. "'Safely to Their Own Borders': Proto-Zionism, Feminism, and Nationalism in *Daniel Deronda*." *ELH* 60, no. 3 (1993): 733–58.
Meyler, Bernadette. "Wilkie Collins's Law Books: Law, Literature, and Factual Precedent." In *The Secrets of Law*, edited by Austin Sarat, Lawence Douglas, and Martha Merrill Umphrey, 1–31. Stanford, CA: Stanford University Press, 2012.
Mill, John Stuart. *A System of Logic, Ratiocinative and Inductive: Being a Connected View of the Principles of Evidence, and the Methods of Scientific Investigation*. Edited by John M. Robson. 2 vols. Toronto: University of Toronto Press, 1973.
Miller, Andrew H. "For All You Know." In *Stanley Cavell and Literary Studies: Consequences of Skepticism*, edited by Richard Eldridge and Bernard Rhie, 194–207. New York: Continuum, 2011.
  The Burdens of Perfection: On Ethics and Reading in Nineteenth-Century British Literature. Ithaca, NY: Cornell University Press, 2008.
  "'A Case of Metaphysics': Counterfactuals, Realism, *Great Expectations*." *ELH* 79, no. 3 (2012): 773–96.
  "Lives Unled in Realist Fiction." *Representations* 98, no. 1 (2007): 118–34.
  On Not Being Someone Else: Tales of Our Unled Lives. Cambridge, MA: Harvard University Press, 2020.
  Novels behind Glass: Commodity, Culture, and Victorian Narrative. Cambridge: Cambridge University Press, 1995.

Miller, Christopher R. *Surprise: The Poetics of the Unexpected from Milton to Austen*. Ithaca, NY: Cornell University Press, 2015.

Miller, D. A. *Narrative and Its Discontents: Problems of Closure in the Traditional Novel*. Princeton, NJ: Princeton University Press, 1981.

The Novel and the Police. Berkeley: University of California Press, 1988.

Miller, J. Hillis. *Thomas Hardy: Distance and Desire*. Cambridge, MA: Belknap Press of Harvard University Press, 1970.

Topographies. Stanford, CA: Stanford University Press, 1995.

Millgate, Jane. "History *versus* Fiction: Thackeray's Response to Macaulay." *Costerus* 2 (1974): 43–58.

Milton, J. R. "Induction before Hume." *The British Journal for the Philosophy of Science* 38, no. 1 (1987): 49–74.

Minto, William. *Logic: Inductive and Deductive*. London: John Murray, 1893.

Mintz, Alan. *George Eliot and the Novel of Vocation*. Cambridge, MA: Harvard University Press, 1978.

Molesworth, Jesse. *Chance and the Eighteenth-Century Novel: Realism, Probability, Magic*. Cambridge: Cambridge University Press, 2010.

Monk, Leland. *Standard Deviations: Chance and the Modern British Novel*. Stanford, CA: Stanford University Press, 1993.

Mordhorst, Mads. "From Counterfactual History to Counternarrative History." *Management and Organizational History* 3, no. 1 (2008): 5–26.

Moretti, Franco. *Distant Reading*. London: Verso, 2013.

Signs Taken for Wonders: On the Sociology of Literary Forms. London: Verso, 1997.

The Way of the World: The Bildungsroman in European Culture. London: Verso, 2000.

Morrell, Roy. "Hardy, Darwin and Nature." *The Thomas Hardy Journal* 2 (1986): 28–32.

Morris, Pam. *Realism*. London: Routledge, 2003.

Morson, Gary Saul. *Narrative and Freedom: The Shadows of Time*. New Haven, CT: Yale University Press, 1994.

Munting, Roger. *An Economic and Social History of Gambling in Britain and the USA*. Manchester: Manchester University Press, 1996.

Murphy, Sara. "Inadmissible Evidence: The Trial of Madeleine Smith and Collins's *The Law and the Lady*." *Victorian Literature and Culture* 44, no. 1 (2016): 163–88.

Nasco, Suzanne Altobello, and Kerry Marsh. "Gaining Control through Counterfactual Thinking." *Personality and Social Psychology Bulletin* 25, no. 5 (1999): 556–68.

Neil, Samuel. *The Art of Reasoning*. London: Walton and Maberly, 1853.

Nesson, Charles. "The Evidence or the Event? On Judicial Proof and the Acceptability of Verdicts." *Harvard Law Review* 98, no. 7 (1985): 1357–92.

Newsom, Robert. *A Likely Story: Probability and Play in Fiction*. New Brunswick, NJ: Rutgers University Press, 1988.

Norton, Sandy Morey. "The Ex-Collector of Boggley-Wollah: Colonialism in the Empire of *Vanity Fair*." *Narrative* 1, no. 2 (1993): 124–37.

Novak, Daniel. "A Model Jew: 'Literary Photographs' and the Jewish Body in *Daniel Deronda*." *Representations* 85, no. 1 (2004): 58–97.

Nowotny, Helga. *The Cunning of Uncertainty*. Cambridge: Polity, 2016.

Oberg, Barbara. "David Hartley and the Association of Ideas." *Journal of the History of Ideas* 37, no. 3 (1976): 441–54.

Ogilvie, John, ed. *The Imperial Dictionary, English, Technological, and Scientific*. 2 vols. London: Blackie and Son, 1851.

Ogilvie, John, and Charles Annandale, eds. *The Imperial Dictionary of the English Language: A Complete Encyclopedic Lexicon, Literary, Scientific, and Technological*. 4 vols. London: Blackie and Son, 1883.

O'Gorman, Francis, ed. *Victorian Literature and Finance*. Oxford: Oxford University Press, 2007.

Oliphant, Margaret. "Miss Austen and Miss Mitford." *Blackwood's Edinburgh Magazine* 107 (1870): 294–305.

"New Novels." *Blackwood's Edinburgh Magazine* 128 (1880): 378–404.

"The Old Saloon." *Blackwood's Edinburgh Magazine* 151 (1892): 455–74.

O'Neill, Onora. "Between Consenting Adults." *Philosophy & Public Affairs* 14, no. 3 (1985): 252–77.

Oram, Richard W. "'Catalogues of War': Thackeray's 'Essay on Pumpernickel.'" *Victorians Institute Journal* 15 (1987): 127–33.

"'Just a Little Turn of the Circle': Time, Memory, and Repetition in Thackeray's *Roundabout Papers*." *Studies in the Novel* 13, nos. 1–2 (1981): 156–67.

Ortiz-Robles, Mario. "Hardy's Wessex and the Natural History of Chance." *Novel* 49, no. 1 (2016): 82–94.

The Novel as Event. Ann Arbor: University of Michigan, 2010.

Paccaud-Huguet, Josiane. "Motion That Stands Still: The Conradian Flash of Insight." In *Joseph Conrad: Voice, Sequence, History, Genre*, edited by Jakob Lothe, Jeremy Hawthorn, and James Phelan, 118–37. Columbus: Ohio State University Press, 2008.

Pace, Timothy. "Who Killed Gwendolen Harleth? *Daniel Deronda* and Keats's 'Lamia.'" *The Journal of English and Germanic Philology* 87, no. 1 (1988): 35–48.

Paige, Nicholas D. *Before Fiction: The Ancien Régime of the Novel*. Philadelphia: University of Pennsylvania Press, 2011.

Pane, G. L. "The Unreal Path to a Real Place: Six Strategies of Representation in the Novels of Thomas Hardy." *Style* 51, no. 1 (2017): 52–75.

Paris, Bernard J. *Experiments in Life: George Eliot's Quest for Values*. Detroit: Wayne State University Press, 1965.

Pater, Walter. *Studies in the History of the Renaissance*. Edited by Matthew Beaumont. 1873. Reprint, Oxford: Oxford University Press, 2010.

Patey, Douglas Lane. *Probability and Literary Form: Philosophic Theory and Literary Practice in the Augustan Age*. Cambridge: Cambridge University Press, 1984.

Pattison, Mark. "History of Civilization in England." *Westminster Review* 68 (1857): 375–99.

Pavel, Thomas G. *Fictional Worlds.* Cambridge, MA: Harvard University Press, 1986.

Peacock, Thomas Love. *Miserrimus.* 2nd ed. London: Thomas Hookham, 1833.

Pearl, Sharrona. *About Faces: Physiognomy in Nineteenth-Century Britain.* Cambridge, MA: Harvard University Press, 2010.

Peters, John G. *Conrad and Impressionism.* Cambridge: Cambridge University Press, 2001.

Phillips, Matthew John. "Navigating Chance: Statistics, Empire, and Agency in R. L. Stevenson's *Treasure Island.*" *Nineteenth-Century Contexts* 39, no. 5 (2017): 399–412.

Pietruska, Jamie L. *Looking Forward: Prediction and Uncertainty in Modern America.* Chicago: University of Chicago Press, 2017.

Pinch, Adela. *Thinking about Other People in Nineteenth-Century British Writing.* Cambridge: Cambridge University Press, 2010.

Pinney, Thomas, ed. *Essays of George Eliot.* New York: Columbia University Press, 1963.

"More Leaves from George Eliot's Notebook." *Huntington Library Quarterly* 29, no. 4 (1966): 353–76.

Plato. *Phaedrus.* Translated by Alexander Nehamas and Paul Woodruff. Indianapolis: Hackett, 1995.

The Republic. Translated by C. D. C. Reeve. Indianapolis: Hackett, 2004.

Poisson, Siméon-Denis. *Recherches sur la probabilité des jugements en matière criminelle et en matière civile: précédées des règles générales du calcul des probabilités.* Paris: Bachelier, 1837.

Polson, John. *Monaco and Its Gaming Tables.* London: Elliot Stock, 1862.

Poole, Adrian. "'Hidden Affinities' in *Daniel Deronda.*" *Essays in Criticism* 33, no. 4 (1983): 294–311.

Shakespeare and the Victorians. London: Arden Shakespeare, 2004.

Poovey, Mary. *Genres of the Credit Economy: Mediating Value in Eighteenth- and Nineteenth-Century Britain.* Chicago: University of Chicago Press, 2008.

A History of the Modern Fact: Problems of Knowledge in the Sciences of Wealth and Society. Chicago: University of Chicago Press, 1998.

Porter, Theodore M. *The Rise of Statistical Thinking, 1820–1900.* Princeton, NJ: Princeton University Press, 1986.

"Statistics and the Career of Public Reason: Engagement and Detachment in a Quantified World." In *Statistics and the Public Sphere: Numbers and the People in Modern Britain, c. 1800–2000,* edited by Tom Crook and Glen O'Hara, 32–47. New York: Routledge, 2011.

Prendergast, Christopher. *Counterfactuals: Paths of the Might Have Been.* London: Bloomsbury, 2019.

Preyer, Robert. "Beyond the Liberal Imagination: Vision and Unreality in *Daniel Deronda.*" *Victorian Studies* 4, no. 1 (1960): 33–54.

Priestley, Joseph. *A Course of Lectures on Oratory and Criticism.* Edited by Vincent M. Bevilacqua and Richard Murphy. 1777. Reprint, Carbondale: Southern Illinois University Press, 1965.

Prince, Gerald. *A Dictionary of Narratology*. Lincoln: University of Nebraska Press, 2003.

Pringle, A. S. "The Verdict of 'Not Proven' in Scotland." *Juridical Review* 16, no. 4 (1904): 432–38.

Pritchett, V. S. *The Living Novel*. New York: Reynal & Hitchcock, 1947.

Proctor, Richard A. "Coincidences and Superstitions." *Cornhill Magazine* 26 (1872): 679–92.

    "Gambling Superstitions." *Cornhill Magazine* 25 (1872): 704–17.

    "Luck: Its Laws and Limits." *Longman's Magazine* 8 (1886): 256–69.

    "Poker Principles and Chance Laws." *Longman's Magazine* 2 (1883): 497–515.

Puckett, Kent. *Narrative Theory: A Critical Introduction*. Cambridge: Cambridge University Press, 2016.

Purdy, Richard Little, and Michael Millgate, eds. *The Collected Letters of Thomas Hardy*. Oxford: Clarendon Press, 1978.

Puskar, Jason Robert. *Accident Society: Fiction, Collectivity, and the Production of Chance*. Stanford, CA: Stanford University Press, 2012.

Qualls, Barry V. *The Secular Pilgrims of Victorian Fiction: The Novel as Book of Life*. Cambridge: Cambridge University Press, 1982.

Quetelet, Adolphe. *Sur l'homme et le développement de ses facultés, ou Essai de physique sociale*. 2 vols. Paris: Bachelier, 1835.

Quigley, Megan. *Modernist Fiction and Vagueness: Philosophy, Form, and Language*. Cambridge: Cambridge University Press, 2015.

Radick, Gregory. "Introduction: Why What If?" *Isis* 99, no. 3 (2008): 547–51.

Ragussis, Michael. *Figures of Conversion: "The Jewish Question" & English National Identity*. Durham, NC: Duke University Press, 1995.

Raven, James. "The Abolition of the English State Lotteries." *The Historical Journal* 34, no. 2 (1991): 371–89.

Rawlins, Jack P. *Thackeray's Novels: A Fiction That Is True*. Berkeley: University of California Press, 1974.

Rawls, John. *A Theory of Justice*. 1971. Rev. ed. Cambridge, MA: Belknap Press of Harvard University Press, 1999.

Ray, Gordon N. *Thackeray*. 2 vols. New York: McGraw-Hill, 1955.

Reade, Charles. *Readiana: Comments on Public Events*. London: Chatto & Windus, 1896.

Redwine, Bruce. "The Uses of Memento Mori in *Vanity Fair*." *Studies in English Literature* 17, no. 4 (1977): 657–72.

Reed, John R. "Law and Narrative Strategy in Wilkie Collins's *The Law and the Lady*." *Victorians Institute Journal* 36 (2008): 217–30.

Reid, Colbey Emmerson. "The Statistical Aesthetics of Henry James, or Jamesian Naturalism." *The Henry James Review* 30, no. 2 (2009): 101–14.

Reith, Gerda. *The Age of Chance: Gambling in Western Culture*. London: Routledge, 1999.

Richard, Jessica. *The Romance of Gambling in the Eighteenth-Century British Novel*. Houndmills: Palgrave Macmillan, 2011.

Richards, Joan L. "The Probable and the Possible in Early Victorian England." In *Victorian Science in Context*, edited by Bernard V. Lightman, 51–71. Chicago: University of Chicago Press, 1997.

Richardson, Angelique. "Hardy and Biology." In *Thomas Hardy: Texts and Contexts*, edited by Phillip Mallett, 156–79. London: Palgrave, 2002.

"Hardy and Science: A Chapter of Accidents." In *Palgrave Advances in Thomas Hardy Studies*, edited by Phillip Mallett, 156–80. Houndmills: Palgrave Macmillan, 2012.

"Heredity." In *Thomas Hardy in Context*, edited by Phillip Mallett, 328–38. Cambridge: Cambridge University Press, 2013.

Richardson, Brian. *Unlikely Stories: Causality and the Nature of Modern Narrative*. Newark: University of Delaware Press, 1997.

Ricoeur, Paul. *Freedom and Nature: The Voluntary and Involuntary*. Translated by Erazim V. Kohák. Evanston, IL: Northwestern University Press, 1966.

Riffaterre, Michael. *Fictional Truth*. Baltimore: Johns Hopkins University Press, 1990.

Riggs, Paul T. "Prosecutors, Juries, Judges and Punishment in Early Nineteenth-Century Scotland." *Journal of Scottish Historical Studies* 32, no. 2 (2012): 166–89.

Rintoul, Robert Stephen. "[Rev. of] *Vanity Fair*, by William Thackeray." *Spectator* 21 (1848): 709–10.

Roberts, Neil. *George Eliot: Her Beliefs and Her Art*. London: Elek, 1975.

Robinson, Roger. "Hardy and Darwin." In *Thomas Hardy: The Writer and His Background*, edited by Norman Page, 128–49. London: Bell & Hyman, 1980.

Rodal, Jocelyn. "Patterned Ambiguities: Virginia Woolf, Mathematical Variables, and Form." *Configurations* 26, no. 1 (2018): 73–101.

Rodensky, Lisa. *The Crime in Mind: Criminal Responsibility and the Victorian Novel*. New York: Oxford University Press, 2003.

Roese, Neal J. "Counterfactual Thinking." *Psychological Bulletin* 121, no. 1 (1997): 133–48.

"The Functional Basis of Counterfactual Thinking." *Journal of Personality and Social Psychology* 66, no. 5 (1994): 805–18.

"Twisted Pair: Counterfactual Thinking and the Hindsight Bias." In *Blackwell Handbook of Judgment and Decision Making*, edited by Derek J. Koehler and Nigel Harvey, 258–73. Malden, MA: Blackwell, 2004.

Roese, Neal J., and James M. Olson. "Counterfactuals, Causal Attributions, and the Hindsight Bias: A Conceptual Integration." *Journal of Experimental Social Psychology* 32, no. 3 (1996): 197–227.

"Self-Esteem and Counterfactual Thinking." *Journal of Personality and Social Psychology* 65, no. 1 (1993): 199–206.

"The Structure of Counterfactual Thought." *Personality and Social Psychology Bulletin* 19, no. 3 (1993): 312–19.

Rogers, Gayle. *Speculation: A Cultural History from Aristotle to AI*. New York: Columbia University Press, 2021.

Rohrbach, Emily. *Modernity's Mist: British Romanticism and the Poetics of Anticipation*. New York: Fordham University Press, 2016.

Romberg, Moritz. *A Manual of the Nervous Diseases of Man*. Edited by Edward H. Sieveking. 2 vols. London: Sydenham Society, 1853.

Rooney, Ellen. "Live Free or Describe: The Reading Effect and the Persistence of Form." *Differences* 21, no. 3 (2010): 112–39.

Rosdeitcher, Elizabeth. "Empires at Stake: Gambling and the Economic Unconscious in Thackeray." *Genre* 29, no. 4 (1996): 407–28.

Rose, Jacqueline. *Sexuality in the Field of Vision*. London: Verso, 2005.

Rosenberg, Charles E. "Contested Boundaries: Psychiatry, Disease, and Diagnosis." *Perspectives in Biology and Medicine* 49, no. 3 (2006): 407–24.

Rosenthal, Jesse. *Good Form: The Ethical Experience of the Victorian Novel*. Princeton, NJ: Princeton University Press, 2018.

Ross, Don. "The Economic and Evolutionary Basis of Selves." *Cognitive Systems Research* 7, nos. 2–3 (2006): 246–58.

"Economic Models of Addiction." In *What Is Addiction?*, edited by Don Ross, Harold Kincaid, David Spurrett, and Peter Collins, 131–58. Cambridge, MA: MIT Press, 2010.

Ross, Don, Carla Sharp, Rudy E. Vuchinich, and David Spurrett. *Midbrain Mutiny: The Picoeconomics and Neuroeconomics of Disordered Gambling: Economic Theory and Cognitive Science*. Cambridge, MA: MIT Press, 2008.

Ruskin, John. *The Works of John Ruskin*. Edited by E. T. Cook and Alexander Wedderburn. 39 vols. London: George Allen, 1903–12.

Rutland, William R. *Thomas Hardy: A Study of His Writings and Their Background*. Oxford: Blackwell, 1938.

Ruvolo, Ann Patrice, and Hazel Rose Markus. "Possible Selves and Performance: The Power of Self-Relevant Imagery." *Social Cognition* 10, no. 1 (1992): 95–124.

Ryan, Marie-Laure. *Possible Worlds, Artificial Intelligence, and Narrative Theory*. Bloomington: Indiana University Press, 1991.

Ryan, Vanessa. *Thinking without Thinking in the Victorian Novel*. Baltimore: Johns Hopkins University Press, 2012.

Rylance, Rick. *Victorian Psychology and British Culture, 1850–1880*. Oxford: Oxford University Press, 2000.

Said, Edward W. "Zionism from the Standpoint of Its Victims." *Social Text*, no. 1 (1979): 7–58.

Saint-Amour, Paul K. "Alternate-Reality Effects." *PMLA* 134, no. 5 (2019): 1136–42.

Salmon, Wesley C. "John Venn's Logic of Chance." In *Probabilistic Thinking, Thermodynamics, and the Interaction of the History and Philosophy of Science*, edited by Jaakko Hintikka, C. David Gruender, and Evandro Agazzi, 125–38. Dordrecht: D. Reidel, 1981.

Scarry, Elaine. *Dreaming by the Book*. Princeton, NJ: Princeton University Press, 2001.

"Enemy and Father: Comic Equilibrium in Number Fourteen of *Vanity Fair*." *Journal of Narrative Technique* 10, no. 3 (1980): 145–55.

Resisting Representation. New York: Oxford University Press, 1994.

Schad, John. "Reading the Long Way Round: Thackeray's *Vanity Fair*." *The Yearbook of English Studies* 26 (1996): 25–33.

Schoenbach, Lisi. *Pragmatic Modernism*. Oxford: Oxford University Press, 2012.

Schor, Hilary M. *Curious Subjects: Women and the Trials of Realism*. New York: Oxford University Press, 2013.

"The Make-Believe of a Middle: On (Not) Knowing Where You Are in *Daniel Deronda*." In *Narrative Middles: Navigating the Nineteenth-Century British Novel*, edited by Caroline Levine and Mario Ortiz-Robles, 47–74. Columbus: Ohio State University Press, 2011.

"Show-Trials: Character, Conviction and the Law in Victorian Fiction." *Cardozo Studies in Law and Literature* 11, no. 2 (1999): 179–95.

Schramm, Jan-Melissa. *Testimony and Advocacy in Victorian Law, Literature, and Theology*. Cambridge: Cambridge University Press, 2000.

"Towards a Poetics of Wrongful Accusation." In *Fictions of Knowledge: Fact, Evidence, Doubt*, edited by Yota Batsaki, Subha Mukherji, and Jan-Melissa Schramm, 193–212. New York: Palgrave Macmillan, 2011.

Schum, David A. *The Evidential Foundations of Probabilistic Reasoning*. Evanston, IL: Northwestern University Press, 2001.

Schwarz, Daniel R. *Conrad: The Later Fiction*. London: Macmillan, 1982.

Scott, Walter. *The Journal of Sir Walter Scott: From the Original Manuscript at Abbotsford*. 2 vols. Edinburgh: David Douglas, 1890.

Sedgwick, Eve Kosofsky. *Epistemology of the Closet*. Berkeley: University of California Press, 1990.

The Weather in Proust. Edited by Jonathan Goldberg. Durham, NC: Duke University Press, 2011.

Semmel, Bernard. *George Eliot and the Politics of National Inheritance*. New York: Oxford University Press, 1994.

Seneta, Eugene, Karen Hunger Parshall, and François Jongmans. "Nineteenth-Century Developments in Geometric Probability: J. J. Sylvester, M. W. Crofton, J.-É. Barbier, and J. Bertrand." *Archive for History of Exact Sciences* 55, no. 6 (2001): 501–24.

Serpell, C. Namwali. *Seven Modes of Uncertainty*. Cambridge, MA: Harvard University Press, 2014.

Shaffer, E. S. "George Eliot and Goethe: 'Hearing the Grass Grow.'" *Publications of the English Goethe Society* 66, no. 1 (2016): 3–22.

Shakespeare, William. *Hamlet*. Edited by Harold Jenkins. London: Methuen, 1982.

Macbeth. 3rd ed. Edited by Sandra Clark and Pamela Mason. London: Arden Shakespeare, 2015.

Shapiro, Barbara J. "Beyond Reasonable Doubt." In *Fictions of Knowledge: Fact, Evidence, Doubt*, edited by Yota Batsaki, Subha Mukherji, and Jan-Melissa Schramm, 19–39. New York: Palgrave Macmillan, 2011.

"Beyond Reasonable Doubt" and "Probable Cause": Historical Perspectives on the Anglo-American Law of Evidence. Berkeley: University of California Press, 1991.

"Circumstantial Evidence: Of Law, Literature, and Culture." *Yale Journal of Law & the Humanities* 5, no. 1 (1993): 219–23.

Probability and Certainty in Seventeenth-Century England: A Study of the Relationships between Natural Science, Religion, History, Law, and Literature. Princeton, NJ: Princeton University Press, 1983.

Shaw, Harry E. *Narrating Reality: Austen, Scott, Eliot.* Ithaca, NY: Cornell University Press, 1999.

Shaw, W. David. *Victorians and Mystery: Crises of Representation.* Ithaca, NY: Cornell University Press, 1990.

Shenefelt, Michael, and Heidi White. *If A, Then B: How the World Discovered Logic.* New York: Columbia University Press, 2013.

Shillingsburg, Peter L. *William Makepeace Thackeray: A Literary Life.* Basingstoke: Palgrave, 2001.

Showalter, Elaine. *The Female Malady: Women, Madness, and English Culture, 1830–1980.* New York: Pantheon, 1985.

Hystories: Hysterical Epidemics and Modern Culture. New York: Columbia University Press, 1997.

Shulman, James Lawrence. *The Pale Cast of Thought: Hesitation and Decision in the Renaissance Epic.* Newark: University of Delaware Press, 1998.

Shuttleworth, Sally. *George Eliot and Nineteenth-Century Science: The Make-Believe of a Beginning.* Cambridge: Cambridge University Press, 1984.

Skinner, Quentin. *Hobbes and Republican Liberty.* Cambridge: Cambridge University Press, 2008.

Small, Helen. "Chances Are: Henry Buckle, Thomas Hardy, and the Individual at Risk." In *Literature, Science, Psychoanalysis, 1830–1970,* edited by Helen Small and Trudi Tate, 64–85. Oxford: Oxford University Press, 2003.

Smith, Adam. *Lectures on Rhetoric and Belles-Lettres.* Edited by John M. Lothian. Carbondale: Southern Illinois University Press, 1971.

The Theory of Moral Sentiments. Edited by D. D. Raphael and A. L. Macfie. 1759. Reprint, Indianapolis: Liberty Fund, 1982.

Smith, Jonathan. *Fact and Feeling: Baconian Science and the Nineteenth-Century Literary Imagination.* Madison: University of Wisconsin Press, 1994.

Smith, Roger. "The Background of Physiological Psychology in Natural Philosophy." *History of Science* 11, no. 2 (1973): 75–123.

"The Physiology of the Will: Mind, Body, and Psychology in the Periodical Literature, 1855–1875." In *Science Serialized: Representations of the Sciences in Nineteenth-Century Periodicals,* edited by Geoffrey Cantor and Sally Shuttleworth, 81–110. Cambridge, MA: MIT Press, 2004.

Snyder, Laura J. *Reforming Philosophy: A Victorian Debate on Science and Society.* Chicago: University of Chicago Press, 2006.

Soja, Edward W. *Postmodern Geographies: The Reassertion of Space in Critical Social Theory.* London: Verso, 1989.

Spellman, Barbara A., and David R. Mandel. "When Possibility Informs Reality: Counterfactual Thinking as a Cue to Causality." *Current Directions in Psychological Science* 8, no. 4 (1999): 120–23.

Spencer, Herbert. *Philosophy of Style.* 1852. Reprint, New York: D. Appleton and Co., 1872.

Steele, William. *A Summary of the Powers and Duties of Juries in Criminal Trials in Scotland.* Edinburgh: Thomas Clarke, 1833.

Steinlight, Emily. *Populating the Novel: Literary Form and the Politics of Surplus Life.* Ithaca, NY: Cornell University Press, 2018.

Steinmetz, Andrew. *A Manual of Weathercasts: Comprising Storm Prognostics on Land and Sea.* London: George Routledge and Sons, 1866.

Stephen, James Fitzjames. "Buckle's History of Civilization in England." *Edinburgh Review* 107, no. 218 (1858): 465–512.

    "The License of Modern Novelists." *Edinburgh Review* 106, no. 215 (1857): 124–56.

    "The Relation of Novels to Life." In *Cambridge Essays*, 148–92. London: John W. Parker, 1855.

Stephen, Leslie. "An Attempted Philosophy of History." *Fortnightly Review* 27, no. 161 (1880): 672–95.

Sternberg, Meir. "Telling in Time (II): Chronology, Teleology, Narrativity." *Poetics Today* 13, no. 3 (1992): 463–541.

Stewart, Garrett. *Dear Reader: The Conscripted Audience in Nineteenth-Century British Fiction.* Baltimore: Johns Hopkins University Press, 1996.

    Death Sentences: Styles of Dying in British Fiction. Cambridge, MA: Harvard University Press, 1984.

    "Signing Off: Dickens and Thackeray, Woolf and Beckett." In *Philosophical Approaches to Literature: New Essays on Nineteenth- and Twentieth-Century Texts*, edited by William E. Cain, 117–39. Lewisburg, PA: Bucknell University Press, 1984.

Stigler, Stephen M. *The History of Statistics: The Measurement of Uncertainty before 1900.* Cambridge, MA: Belknap Press of Harvard University Press, 1986.

    "Who Discovered Bayes's Theorem?" *The American Statistician* 37, no. 4 (1983): 290–96.

Stocking, George W. *Victorian Anthropology.* New York: Free Press, 1991.

Stokes, John. "Rachel's 'Terrible Beauty': An Actress among the Novelists." *ELH* 51, no. 4 (1984): 771–93.

Stone, Carole. "George Eliot's *Daniel Deronda*: 'The Case-History of Gwendolen H.'" *Nineteenth-Century Studies* 7, no. 1 (1993): 57–67.

Stone, Wilfred. "The Play of Chance and Ego in *Daniel Deronda*." *Nineteenth-Century Literature* 53, no. 1 (1998): 25–55.

Sudrann, Jean. "'The Philosopher's Property': Thackeray and the Use of Time." *Victorian Studies* 10, no. 4 (1967): 359–88.

Suk, Julie. "The Moral and Legal Consequences of Wife-Selling in *The Mayor of Casterbridge*." In *Subversion and Sympathy: Gender, Law, and the British Novel*, edited by Martha C. Nussbaum and Alison L. LaCroix, 26–47. New York: Oxford University Press, 2013.

Sutherland, J. A. "The Expanding Narrative of *Vanity Fair.*" *Journal of Narrative Technique* 3, no. 3 (1973): 149–69.

Thackeray at Work. London: Athlone Press, 1974.

"Wilkie Collins and the Origins of the Sensation Novel." *Dickens Studies Annual* 20 (1991): 243–53.

Swann, Brian. "George Eliot's Ecumenical Jew, or The Novel as Outdoor Temple." *Novel* 8, no. 1 (1974): 39–50.

Tabb, Kathryn. "Locke on Enthusiasm and the Association of Ideas." In *Oxford Studies in Early Modern Philosophy*, vol. 9, edited by Donald Rutherford, 75–104. Oxford: Oxford University Press, 2019.

Tanner, Tony. *Adultery in the Novel: Contract and Transgression.* Baltimore: Johns Hopkins University Press, 1979.

Taube, Myron. "Thackeray and the Reminiscential Vision." *Nineteenth-Century Fiction* 18, no. 3 (1963): 247–59.

Taylor, Jenny Bourne. *In the Secret Theatre of Home: Wilkie Collins, Sensation Narrative, and Nineteenth-Century Psychology.* London: Routledge, 1988.

"The Later Novels." In *The Cambridge Companion to Wilkie Collins*, edited by Jenny Bourne Taylor, 79–96. Cambridge: Cambridge University Press, 2007.

Taylor, Shelley E., and Sherry K. Schneider. "Coping and the Simulation of Events." *Social Cognition* 7, no. 2 (1989): 174–94.

Teigen, Karl Halvor. "The Proximity Heuristic in Judgments of Accident Probabilities." *British Journal of Psychology* 96, no. 4 (2010): 423–40.

"When the Unreal Is More Likely than the Real: Post Hoc Probability Judgements and Counterfactual Closeness." *Thinking & Reasoning* 4, no. 2 (1998): 147–77.

Tennyson, Alfred. *Alfred Tennyson: The Major Works.* Edited by Adam Roberts. New York: Oxford University Press, 2009.

Tetlock, Philip E., and R. N. Lebow. "Poking Counterfactual Holes in Covering Laws: Cognitive Styles and Historical Reasoning." *American Political Science Review* 95, no. 4 (2001): 829–43.

Thackeray, William Makepeace. *The Adventures of Philip: On His Way through the World Shewing Who Robbed Him, Who Helped Him, and Who Passed Him By.* Edited by Judith Law Fisher. 1861–62. Reprint, Ann Arbor: University of Michigan Press, 2010.

Contributions to the Morning Chronicle, edited by Gordon N. Ray. Urbana: University of Illinois Press, 1955.

"The Four Georges. I. – George the First." *Cornhill Magazine* 2 (1860): 1–20.

"The Four Georges. IV. – George the Fourth." *Cornhill Magazine* 2 (1860): 385–406.

The History of Henry Esmond. Edited by Edgar F. Harden. 1852. Reprint, New York: Garland, 1989.

The History of Pendennis. Edited by Peter L. Shillingsburg and Nicholas Pickwoad. 1848–50. Reprint, New York: Garland, 1991.

The Letters and Private Papers of William Makepeace Thackeray. Edited by Gordon N. Ray. 4 vols. Cambridge, MA: Harvard University Press, 1945.

The Newcomes: Memoirs of a Most Respectable Family. Edited by Peter L. Shillingsburg and Rowland McMaster. 1854–55. Reprint, Ann Arbor: University of Michigan Press, 1996.

The Oxford Thackeray. Edited by George Saintsbury. 17 vols. London: H. Frowde, 1908.

"On Some Late Great Victories." *Cornhill Magazine* 1 (1860): 755–60.

Vanity Fair. Edited by Peter L. Shillingsburg. 1848. Reprint, New York: W. W. Norton, 1994.

Thale, Jerome. *The Novels of George Eliot.* New York: Columbia University Press, 1959.

Thiher, Allen. *Fiction Refracts Science: Modernist Writers from Proust to Borges.* Columbia: University of Missouri Press, 2005.

Thomas, David Wayne. *Cultivating Victorians: Liberal Culture and the Aesthetic.* Philadelphia: University of Pennsylvania Press, 2004.

Thurschwell, Pamela. "George Eliot's Prophecies: Coercive Second Sight and Everyday Thought Reading." In *The Victorian Supernatural,* edited by Nicola Brown, Carolyn Burdett, and Pamela Thurschwell, 87–105. Cambridge: Cambridge University Press, 2004.

Tillers, Peter, and Eric D. Green, eds. *Probability and Inference in the Law of Evidence: The Uses and Limits of Bayesianism.* Dordrecht: Kluwer, 1988.

Tillotson, Geoffrey, and Donald Hawes, eds. *William Thackeray: The Critical Heritage.* London: Routledge & Kegan Paul, 1968.

Tobin, Vera. *Elements of Surprise: Our Mental Limits and the Satisfactions of Plot.* Cambridge, MA: Harvard University Press, 2018.

Todorov, Tzvetan. *Introduction to Poetics.* Translated by Richard Howard. Minneapolis: University of Minnesota Press, 1981.

The Poetics of Prose. Translated by Richard Howard. Ithaca, NY: Cornell University Press, 1977.

Toker, Leona. *Towards the Ethics of Form in Fiction: Narratives of Cultural Remission.* Columbus: Ohio State University Press, 2010.

Tomashevsky, Boris. "Thematics." In *Russian Formalist Criticism: Four Essays,* edited by Lee T. Lemon and Marion J. Reis, 61–95. Lincoln: University of Nebraska Press, 1965.

Tondre, Michael. *The Physics of Possibility: Victorian Fiction, Science, and Gender.* Charlottesville: University of Virginia Press, 2018.

Traver, Teresa Huffman. "The Law and the Nation: Wilkie Collins and Scottish Identity." *Victorians Institute Journal* 37 (2009): 67–92.

Trevelyan, G. M. "If Napoleon Had Won the Battle of Waterloo." In *If It Had Happened Otherwise,* edited by J. C. Squire, 299–312. London: Sidgwick & Jackson, 1972.

Tribe, Laurence. "Trial by Mathematics: Precision and Ritual in the Legal Process." *Harvard Law Review* 84, no. 6 (1971): 1329–93.

Trollope, Anthony. *An Autobiography and Other Writings.* Edited by Nicholas Shrimpton. 1883. Reprint, New York: Oxford University Press, 2014.

Barchester Towers. Edited by Michael Sadleir and Frederick Page. 1857. Reprint, Oxford: Oxford University Press, 2008.

Tromp, Marlene. "Gwendolen's Madness." *Victorian Literature and Culture* 28, no. 2 (2000): 451–67.

Trotter, David. "The Invention of Agoraphobia." *Victorian Literature and Culture* 32, no. 2 (2004): 463–74.

Tubbs, Robert. *Mathematics in Twentieth-Century Literature and Art: Content, Form, Meaning*. Baltimore: Johns Hopkins University Press, 2014.

Tucker, Irene. *A Probable State: The Novel, the Contract, and the Jews*. Chicago: University of Chicago Press, 2000.

Tykocinski, Orit E., and Thane S. Pittman. "The Consequences of Doing Nothing: Inaction Inertia as Avoidance of Anticipated Counterfactual Regret." *Journal of Personality and Social Psychology* 75, no. 3 (1998): 607–16.

Tylor, Edward Burnett. *Primitive Culture: Researches into the Development of Mythology, Philosophy, Religion, Art, and Custom*. London: John Murray, 1871.

Tytler, Graeme. "'Know How to Decipher a Countenance': Physiognomy in Thomas Hardy's Fiction." *The Thomas Hardy Yearbook* 27 (1998): 43–60.

Van Evra, James. "Richard Whately and the Rise of Modern Logic." *History and Philosophy of Logic* 5, no. 1 (1984): 1–18.

Vargish, Thomas. *The Providential Aesthetic in Victorian Fiction*. Charlottesville: University Press of Virginia, 1985.

Venn, John. *The Logic of Chance: An Essay on the Foundations and Province of the Theory of Probability*. 1866. 3rd ed. London: Macmillan, 1888.

"Science of History." *Fraser's Magazine* 65 (1862): 651–60.

On Some of the Characteristics of Belief, Scientific and Religious: Being the Hulsean Lectures for 1869. London: Macmillan, 1870.

"Statistical Averages and Human Actions." *Temple Bar* 15 (1865): 495–504.

Verburgt, Lukas M. "John Venn's Hypothetical Infinite Frequentism and Logic." *History and Philosophy of Logic* 35, no. 3 (2014): 248–71.

"The Objective and the Subjective in Mid-Nineteenth-Century British Probability Theory." *Historia Mathematica* 42, no. 4 (2015): 468–87.

Vigar, Penelope. *The Novels of Thomas Hardy: Illusion and Reality*. London: Athlone Press, 1974.

Vogl, Joseph. *On Tarrying*. Translated by Helmut Müller-Sievers. Chicago: Seagull, 2011.

Volpicelli, Robert. "Modernist Low Vision: Visual Impairment and Weak Narrative in Conrad and Joyce." *Novel* 51, no. 1 (2018): 60–78.

Voskuil, Lynn M. *Acting Naturally: Victorian Theatricality and Authenticity*. Charlottesville: University of Virginia Press, 2004.

Vrettos, Athena. *Somatic Fictions: Imagining Illness in Victorian Culture*. Stanford, CA: Stanford University Press, 1995.

Wagner, Jodi. "Gambling as Simulation in *Daniel Deronda*." *George Eliot–George Henry Lewes Studies*, nos. 58–59 (2010): 95–110.

Wagner, Tamara S. *Financial Speculation in Victorian Fiction: Plotting Money and the Novel Genre, 1815–1901*. Columbus: Ohio State University Press, 2010.

Waldman, Theodore. "Origins of the Legal Doctrine of Reasonable Doubt." *Journal of the History of Ideas* 20, no. 3 (1959): 299–316.

Walker, David M. *A Legal History of Scotland: The Nineteenth Century*. Edinburgh: Butterworths, 2001.

Wall, Byron E. "John Venn, James Ward, and the Chair of Mental Philosophy and Logic at the University of Cambridge." *Journal of the History of Ideas* 68, no. 1 (2007): 131–55.

"John Venn's Opposition to Probability as Degree of Belief." *Studies in History and Philosophy of Science* 37, no. 4 (2006): 550–61.

Walls, Joan. "The Philosophy of David Hartley and the Root Metaphor of Mechanism: A Study in the History of Psychology." *Journal of Mind and Behavior* 3 (1982): 259–74.

Ward, Megan. "*The Woodlanders* and the Cultivation of Realism." *Studies in English Literature* 51, no. 4 (2011): 865–82.

Warner, Michael. "Uncritical Reading." In *Polemic: Critical or Uncritical*, edited by Jane Gallop, 13–38. New York: Routledge, 2004.

Warren, Howard C. *A History of the Association Psychology*. New York: Scribner, 1921.

Watt, Ian. *Conrad in the Nineteenth Century*. Berkeley: University of California Press, 1979.

Essays on Conrad. Cambridge: Cambridge University Press, 2000.

The Rise of the Novel: Studies in Defoe, Richardson and Fielding. 2nd ed. Berkeley: University of California Press, 2001.

Watts, Isaac. *Logic; or, The Right Use of Reason in the Enquiry after Truth*. 1725. Reprint, London: C. and J. Rivington, 1824.

Webster, Harvey Curtis. *On a Darkling Plain: The Art and Thought of Thomas Hardy*. Chicago: University of Chicago Press, 1947.

Wellman, Carl. *An Approach to Rights: Studies in the Philosophy of Law and Morals*. Dordrecht: Kluwer, 1997.

Wells, Gary L., and Igor Gavanski. "Mental Simulation of Causality." *Journal of Personality and Social Psychology* 56, no. 2 (1989): 161–69.

Welsh, Alexander. *George Eliot and Blackmail*. Cambridge, MA: Harvard University Press, 1985.

Strong Representations: Narrative and Circumstantial Evidence in England. Baltimore: Johns Hopkins University Press, 1992.

Wess, Robert. "The Probable and the Marvelous in *Tom Jones*." *Modern Philology* 68, no. 1 (1970): 32–45.

Whately, Richard. *Elements of Logic*. 1826. 3rd ed. London: B. Fellowes, 1829.

Elements of Rhetoric: Comprising an Analysis of the Laws of Moral Evidence and of Persuasion, with Rules for Argumentative Composition and Elocution. Edited by Douglas Ehninger. 1828. 7th ed., 1846. Reprint, Carbondale: Southern Illinois University Press, 1963.

"Modern Novels [Rev. of *Northanger Abbey* and *Persuasion*, by Jane Austen]." *The Quarterly Review* 24, no. 48 (1821): 352–76.

Whewell, William. *Mechanical Euclid*. London: John W. Parker, 1837.

Thoughts on the Study of Mathematics as Part of a Liberal Education. Cambridge: J. and J. J. Deighton, 1835.

White, Katherine, and Darrin R. Lehman. "Looking on the Bright Side: Downward Counterfactual Thinking in Response to Negative Life Events." *Personality and Social Psychology Bulletin* 31, no. 10 (2005): 1413–24.

Whitman, James Q. *The Origins of Reasonable Doubt: Theological Roots of the Criminal Trial*. New Haven, CT: Yale University Press, 2008.

Whitworth, Michael. *Einstein's Wake: Relativity, Metaphor, and Modernist Literature*. Oxford: Oxford University Press, 2001.

"The Physical Sciences." In *A Companion to Modernist Literature and Culture*, edited by David Bradshaw and Kevin J. H. Dettmar, 39–49. Malden, MA: Blackwell, 2006.

Wickens, G. Glen. "Literature and Science: Hardy's Response to Mill, Huxley and Darwin." *Mosaic* 14, no. 3 (1981): 63–79.

Wickman, Matthew. "Robert Burns and Big Data; or, Pests of Quantity and Visualization." *Modern Language Quarterly* 75, no. 1 (2014): 1–28.

Widdowson, Peter. *Hardy in History: A Study in Literary Sociology*. London: Routledge, 1989.

Wigmore, John H. "Required Numbers of Witnesses: A Brief History of the Numerical System in England." *Harvard Law Review* 15, no. 2 (1901): 83–108.

Wilkinson, Ann Y. "The Tomeavesian Way of Knowing the World: Technique and Meaning in *Vanity Fair*." *ELH* 32, no. 3 (1965): 370–87.

Williams, Daniel. "Rumor, Reputation, and Sensation in *Tess of the d'Urbervilles*." *Novel* 46, no. 1 (2013): 93–115.

"Slow Fire: Serial Thinking and Hardy's Genres of Induction." *Genre* 50, no. 1 (2017): 19–38.

Williams, Kathleen, ed. *Jonathan Swift: The Critical Heritage*. London: Routledge, 1970.

Williams, Raymond. *The English Novel: From Dickens to Lawrence*. New York: Oxford University Press, 1973.

Marxism and Literature. Oxford: Oxford University Press, 1977.

Willock, Ian Douglas. *The Origins and Development of the Jury in Scotland*. Edinburgh: Stair Society, 1966.

Wilson, Timothy D., and Daniel T. Gilbert. "Affective Forecasting: Knowing What to Want." *Current Directions in Psychological Science* 14, no. 3 (2005): 131–34.

Witemeyer, Hugh. *George Eliot and the Visual Arts*. New Haven, CT: Yale University Press, 1979.

Wolfreys, Julian. "The Haunted Structures of *The Mayor of Casterbridge*." In *A Companion to Thomas Hardy*, edited by Keith Wilson, 299–312. Malden, MA: Wiley-Blackwell, 2009.

Wollaeger, Mark. *Joseph Conrad and the Fictions of Skepticism.* Stanford, CA: Stanford University Press, 1990.

Woloch, Alex. "*Daniel Deronda*: Late Form, or after *Middlemarch.*" In *A Companion to George Eliot*, edited by Amanda Anderson and Harry E. Shaw, 166–77. Malden, MA: Wiley-Blackwell, 2013.

Womble, David A. P. "*Phineas Finn*, the Statistics of Character, and the Sensorium of Liberal Personhood." *Novel* 51, no. 1 (2018): 17–35.

Wood, Jane. *Passion and Pathology in Victorian Fiction: Body, Mind, and Neurology.* Oxford: Oxford University Press, 2001.

Woolf, Virginia. *The Essays of Virginia Woolf, vol. 3: 1919–1924.* Edited by Andrew MacNeillie. San Diego: Harcourt Brace Jovanovich, 1988.

Wordsworth, William. *The Thirteen-Book Prelude.* Edited by Mark L. Reed. Ithaca, NY: Cornell University Press, 1991.

Wright, Daniel. *Bad Logic: Reasoning about Desire in the Victorian Novel.* Baltimore: Johns Hopkins University Press, 2018.

Wright, John P. "Association, Madness, and the Measures of Probability in Locke and Hume." In *Psychology and Literature in the Eighteenth Century*, edited by Christopher Fox, 103–27. New York: AMS Press, 1987.

Yang, Tianming, and Michael N. Shadlen. "Probabilistic Reasoning by Neurons." *Nature* 447, no. 7148 (2007): 1075–80.

Yeazell, Ruth Bernard. *Art of the Everyday: Dutch Painting and the Realist Novel.* Princeton, NJ: Princeton University Press, 2008.

Young, Robert M. *Mind, Brain, and Adaptation in the Nineteenth Century: Cerebral Localization and Its Biological Context from Gall to Ferrier.* New York: Oxford University Press, 1990.

Zabell, Sandy L. "The Probabilistic Analysis of Testimony." *Journal of Statistical Planning and Inference* 20, no. 3 (1988): 327–54.

"The Subjective and the Objective." In *Philosophy of Statistics*, edited by Prasanta S. Bandyopadhyay and Malcolm R. Forster, 1149–74. Oxford: Elsevier, 2011.

Zemka, Sue. *Time and the Moment in Victorian Literature and Society.* Cambridge: Cambridge University Press, 2012.

Ziolkowski, Theodore. *Hesitant Heroes: Private Inhibition, Cultural Crisis.* Ithaca, NY: Cornell University Press, 2004.

Zuylen, Marina van. *Monomania: The Flight from Everyday Life in Literature and Art.* Ithaca, NY: Cornell University Press, 2018.

Index

Note: *italics* = figure

accident, 31, 100, 101, 109, 119, 178, 199
accidental discovery, 80, 87, 89, 90, 98
action, 40, 53, 66
actuarial justice (Feeley and Simon), 13, 79
Adam, 1, 2
additive logic, 89, 97
Aeneas, 46
Aeschylus: *Oresteia*, 46, 49
affective forecasting (Wilson and Gilbert), 119
Age of Reason, 204
agency, 45, 46, 47, 48, 53, 59, 61
aggregates, 43, 45, 196, 197, 198, 201
    versus particulars, 4
agoraphobia, 63, 65
Ahmed, Sara, 104
Ainslie, George, 50, 51, 52
akrasia, 51, 65, 66
Albert, Prince, 19
Alison, Archibald, 85
    Practice of Criminal Law of Scotland (1833),
        83
allegory, 35, 61, 173
alternation as diagnosis, 64
analogy, 26, 61, 66, 137, 168, 210
Anderson, Amanda, 66, 67
Anderson, Katharine, 187
angel, 124
annuity schemes, 22
Anscombe, Elizabeth, 45
anthropometry, 104
Aquinas, St. Thomas, 118
Arbuthnot, John: "Essay on Mathematical
        Learning" (1701), 20
Archer, William, 198
archery, 42, 44
Aristotle, 29, 33, 35, 50, 195
    Poetics, 29
Armstrong, Isobel, 12
Arnauld, Antoine, 8

Arnold, Matthew, 187
    "Literature and Science," 18
arsenic, 96, 98
art, 199
Art of Uncertainty
    book argument, 2, 3
    chapter by chapter, 12–15
    coda, 202–13
    engagement with discourses surrounding
        probability, 36
    intermediate scale of individual subject, 10
    probable realisms, 152–201
    provisional judgments, 78–105
    two parts, 12
Asmodeus, 140, 146
associationism, 23–26
    models of mind, 4
    residual importance, 24
Austen, Jane, 32, 34, 216
automatic agency (Maudsley), 49
Auyoung, Elaine, x, 18

Babbage, Charles, 19, 104
    *Comparative View of Institutions for Assurance
        of Lives* (1826), 21
Bacon, Francis, 118
Baier, Annette, 186
Bain, Alexander, 4, 47, 203
    physiological psychology, 24
Bain, Alexander (works)
    Emotions and Will (1859), 47
    English Composition and Rhetoric (1866), 26
    English Grammar (1863), 26
    Senses and Intellect (1855), 47
Balzac, Honoré de, 30, 31
Barthes, Roland, 30, 31, 32
Bartlett poisoning case, 86
Bayes, Thomas, 8
Bayesian inference, 10

CAMBRIDGE STUDIES IN NINETEENTH-CENTURY
LITERATURE AND CULTURE

GENERAL EDITORS
Kate Flint, *University of Southern California*
Clare Pettitt, *King's College London*

Titles published

Milton Keynes UK
Ingram Content Group UK Ltd.
UKHW011452110324
439009UK00011B/26